THE FORMATION OF MUSCOVY 1304–1613

LONGMAN HISTORY OF RUSSIA

General Editor: Harold Shukman

Kievan Russia 850–1240
Dimitri Obolensky

*The Crisis of Medieval Russia 1200–1304
John Fennell

*The Formation of Muscovy 1304–1613
Robert O. Crummey

*The Making of Russian Absolutism 1613–1801
Paul Dukes

Russia in the Age of Reaction and Reform 1801–1881
David Saunders

*Russia in the Age of Modernisation and Revolution 1881–1917
Hans Rogger

The Russian Revolution 1917
Steve Smith

*The Soviet Union since 1917
Martin McCauley

*already published

LONGMAN HISTORY OF RUSSIA

The Formation of Muscovy 1304 – 1613

ROBERT O. CRUMMEY

LONGMAN
London and New York

Longman Group UK Limited
Longman House, Burnt Mill, Harlow
Essex CM20 2JE, England
Associated companies throughout the world

*Published in the United States of America
by Longman Inc., New York*

© Longman Group UK Limited 1987

First published 1987

British Library Cataloguing in Publication Data

Crummey, Robert O.
 The formation of Muscovy 1304-1613. —
 (Longman history of Russia)
 1. Soviet Union — History — 1237-1480
 2. Soviet Union — History — Period of consolidation, 1462-1605
 I. Title
 947'.03   DK71

ISBN 0-582-49152-5 CSD
ISBN 0-582-49153-3 PPR

Library of Congress Cataloging-in-Publication Data

Crummey, Robert O.
 The formation of Muscovy, 1304-1613.

 (Longman history of Russia)
 Bibliography: p.
 Includes index.
 1. Soviet Union — History — 1237-1480.
 2. Soviet Union — History — Period of consolidation, 1462-1605.
 3. Soviet Union — History — Epoch of confusion, 1505-1613.
 I. Title.
 II. Series.
 DK100.C78   1987   947   86-16033

ISBN 0-582-49152-5 CSD
ISBN 0-582-49153-3 PPR

Produced by Longman Singapore Publishers (Pte) Ltd.
Printed in Singapore.

Contents

List of maps

(N.B. These maps are based on a wide variety of sources. Sketches for most of the maps were taken from *Atlas istorii SSSR*, Chast I, eds K. V. Bazilevich, I. A. Golubstov, M. A. Zinovev. Moscow, 1950.).

Note on transliteration, dates and sources

In transliterating Russian names and terms, I have followed the Library of Congress system, except for soft and hard signs and the diaeresis on ë which I have omitted. Since this book is intended for the general reader as well as the specialist, I have tried to reduce the culture shock students suffer when dealing with large numbers of Russian names and terms. For this reason, I have given familiar names of people and places in the form best known to English and American readers (e.g. Moscow for the city, Alexander Nevskii, St Sergius, Joseph of Volokolamsk) and used English spelling for first names when the Russian is very similar (e.g. Michael, Daniel, Alexis, Peter). To do so, inevitably leads to some inconsistencies. Two are deliberate. When a first name appears with a patronymic or surname, I normally use the Russian form for both (e.g. Michael, but Mikhail Olelkovich; Daniel, but Daniil Adashev). In women's first names the second 'i' in the ending is omitted (e.g. Maria, not Mariia). The names of non-Russian places and people appear in the version most familiar to English-speaking readers (e.g. Tamerlane, Cyprian, Photius, John III).

Between 1304 and 1613, Russian historical sources date events according to the Byzantine ecclesiastical calendar based on the assumption that Christ was born 5,508 years after the Creation. The year began on 1 September. Therefore the first eight months of 1304 belong to the year 6812 and the last four to 6813. Conversely, if a chronicle gives the years in which an event took place but does not specify the month, it is unclear in which of two years, according to modern calendars, it occurred. Thus 7060 could be either 1551 or 1552 or, for short, 1551/2. All writers on early Russian history follow these principles in translating dates into modern terms.

Although they would like to know far more than they do, historians of Muscovite Russia have an extensive body of sources from which to work. For political events, the most important are the chronicles most of which have been published in the Complete Collection of Russian Chronicles (*Polnoe sobranie russkikh letopisei*). A number of the grand princes' wills and treaties with their kinsmen have also come down to us. Concerning Muscovy's international relations, we have extensive fragments of diplomatic correspondence and accounts of the exchanges of ambassadors from the fifteenth century on. Information about the Muscovite economy and social relations is considerably sparser, especially before the late fifteenth century: some fragmentary land cadastres survive and the archives of the great Eastern Orthodox monasteries contain documents on estate management and peasant life. Historians derive many of their impressions of Muscovite institutions and customs from the accounts of foreign diplomats and travellers who visited Russia, especially in the sixteenth century. Moreover, we learn a great deal about official Muscovite thinking and widely accepted ideals, values and standards of beauty from polemical writings and works of literature and art. Finally, any historian of Muscovite Russia owes a great debt to earlier scholars whose work of reconstruction and analysis has helped greatly in making these sources intelligible.

Abbreviations

AAE   *Akty, sobrannye v bibliotekakh i arkhivakh Rossiiskoi imperii Arkheograficheskoiu ekspeditsieiu.* 4 vols. St Petersburg, 1836.

DDG   *Dukhovnye i dogovornye gramoty velikikh i udelnykh kniazei XIV–XV vekov*, eds. S. V. Bakhrushin and L. V. Cherepnin. Moscow–Leningrad, 1950.

FzOG   *Forschungen zur osteuropäischen Geschichte.*

GVNiP   *Gramoty Velikogo Novgoroda i Pskova*, ed. S. N. Valk. Moscow–Leningrad, 1949.

JfGO   *Jahrbücher für Geschichte Osteuropas.*

PRP   *Pamiatniki russkogo prava*, 8 vols. Moscow, 1952–63.

PSRL   *Polnoe sobranie russkikh letopisei.*

Structure   *The Structure of Russian History*, ed. Michael Cherniavsky. New York, 1970.

TODRL   *Trudy Otdela drevnerusskoi literatury.*

TR   Priselkov, M. D., *Troitskaia Letopis. Rekonstruktsiia teksta.* Moscow–Leningrad, 1950.

Notes on plates

(between pages 192 and 193)

Plate 1 *Ustiug Annunciation.* Novgorodian (?). Late 1100s.

This icon illustrates the sophistication of painters in Russia before the Mongol invasion. It portrays the Archangel Gabriel announcing to the Virgin Mary that she will bear the Christ, shown in embryonic form on her breast. Note that, from the top of the panel, God, the 'Ancient of Days', looks down on the scene. The unknown artist created a harmonious composition, united by the curving lines of the figures and the Archangel's gesturing hand. He painted the central figures with great skill: their faces are strong, yet delicate, and the drawing of their garments and the Archangel's wings is fine. The icon's colours are rich, varied and subtle.

Plate 2 The Cathedral of the Dormition, Vladimir. 1185–1189.

The national cathedral of north-east Russia in pre-Mongol times and model for the cathedral of the same name, built in 1475–1478 in Moscow under the patronage of Grand Prince Ivan III. Set on a bluff above the Kliazma river, this imposing church has a dominant cupola in the centre and smaller ones on the four corners of the structure. Delicate carving on the façade, the apses, and the supporting drums of the cupolas give lightness and grace to the exterior of the massive building.

Plate 3 The Church of the Veil on the Nerl, Bogoliubovo (near Vladimir). 1165.

This small votive church is probably the loveliest work of architecture constructed in north-east Russia before the Mongol invasion. Although frequently restored over the centuries, it retains its harmonious proportions and remarkable verticality which, unlike many Russian churches, leads the viewer's eye upward toward heaven. The plan is simple – three aisles and apses surmounted by a single cupola. Like the Dormition Cathedral in Vladimir, the church was constructed of soft white stone that could be decorated with delicate carving. The 'typically Russian' onion-shaped cupola is the work of nineteenth-century restorers.

Plate 4 Our Saviour on Ilina Street, Novgorod. 1374.

A fine example of Novgorod architecture of the fourteenth century, this solid church of stucco-covered brick has a simple design. It is, in essence, a square with a single cupola. The exterior walls reflect its division into three aisles. The roof is gabled on all four sides. Abstract decorations in the brickwork of the façades and the drum of the cupola lighten the church's effect on the viewer.

Plate 5 Theophanes the Greek, *Old Testament Trinity*. Fresco in the Church of Our Saviour on Ilina Street. 1378.

The *Old Testament Trinity* depicts the three angels who visited Abraham and Sarah. In Eastern Orthodox iconography, they symbolize the Holy Trinity. Theophanes the Greek's painting combines skilful composition and drawing with great expressive power. The triangular arrangement of the figures, their staffs, and the sweep of the central angel's wings, give the scene rhythm and harmony. With a few brush strokes in a minimum of colours – white, and brown tones – Theophanes conveys to the viewer the angels' majesty and serenity.

Plate 6 *Elijah*. Novgorodian. Early fifteenth century.

The icons of Novgorod are celebrated for their use of blocks of brilliant colour, their simple composition, and their fine drawing, emphasized by dark outlines around the figures. This *Elijah* is an excellent example. Set against a bright red background, the dark brown of his cloak, and the off-white of the halo, the stern face of the prophet stares out at the viewer. The artist stressed the severity of the image by sharply outlining his head and face, particularly his eyes.

Plate 7 Andrei Rublev, *Saviour*. c. 1410.

The *Saviour* is a variant of the theme, *Christ, the All-Powerful*, in which Christ represents the omnipotence and righteous judgment of God. Rublev treated the theme with unsurpassed subtlety and power. Through his penetrating eyes which dominate the icon, Christ looks out at the viewer. The face reflects the awe-inspiring majesty of God, but it is also an intensely human face, full of compassion as well as determination. In effect, Rublev's painting is a pictorial statement of the doctrine of the Incarnation, the conviction that Christ was both God and man.

Plate 8 The Kremlin, Moscow.

The Moscow Kremlin took on its present appearance in the reign of Ivan III. The Italian masters, Marco and Piero Antonio Solari, reconstructed the brick fortification walls and towers between 1485 and 1495. Within the Kremlin, we can see, from left to right, the cupolas of the Cathedral of the Annunciation, the Cathedral of the Archangel Michael, the Cathedral of the Dormition, and the so-called Bell Tower of Ivan the Great, completed in 1600.

Plate 9 Andrei Rublev, *Trinity. c.* 1411.

In spite of the similarity in the arrangement of the figures, Rublev's famous icon of the *Old Testament Trinity* is more spacious, more delicate, and less intense in its emotional impact than Theophanes's fresco. Rublev's *Trinity* admirably illustrates the qualities that made him the finest painter of medieval Russia. The bodies of the three angels, which form a circle in the centre of the picture, are gracefully curved and their features are delicate. The circle, in turn, draws attention to the cup on the table symbolizing God's self-sacrificing love. The angels' staffs lead the eye outward to the objects – the stylized house, tree and mountain – in the background. Rublev's use of colour is particularly striking: even a black-and-white reproduction hints at it by showing the contrast between the dark robes of the central angel and the light, diaphanous effect of the garments of the other two.

Plate 10 Dionysius, *Crucifixion.* 1500.

In this icon, Dionysius painted Christ on a high cross with the Virgin on his right and St John and the centurion on his left. The skull of Adam can be seen under the hill on which the cross stands. Dionysius's manner is more direct and sensual than Rublev's. His work displays a fine sense of line and proportion. The curve of Christ's body on the cross dominates the composition and the intense colours of the robes of the secondary figures underline the central importance of the pale and fragile body of the Saviour.

Plate 11 The Cathedral of the Dormition, Moscow. 1475–1478.

When Ivan III had the Cathedral of the Dormition rebuilt, he instructed the architect, the Italian known as Aristotle Fioravanti, to model his design on the Vladimir cathedral of the same name. Fioravanti followed his orders, and did so imaginatively. His creation has excellent proportions but appears smaller and closer to the ground than its prototype. Like its precursor, the Moscow cathedral has five cupolas, but Fioravanti grouped them closer together and made them more nearly equal in size than the Vladimir builders had done. He decorated the façades with rectangular support columns, and decorative columns and frescos. Note, in particular, the fresco of the Virgin, patroness of Moscow, above the main doorway leading in from the great Kremlin Square.

Plate 12 *St George and the Dragon.* Novgorodian. Sixteenth century.

This icon provides further evidence of the Novgorodian painters' fondness for simple composition and bright colours. The curve formed by St George's body and the horse's hindquarters dominates the picture and the saint's spear further unifies it. Unlike many icons, this one gives the impression of violent motion: both the rider and horse lean backward toward the dragon's head and St George's cloak flows behind him. The hand of God in blessing can be seen in the upper right corner. The fiery red of St George's cloak, reflected in more subtle tones elsewhere on the panel, stands out sharply against the gold background.

Plate 13 The Church of the Ascension, Kolomenskoe (near Moscow). 1532.

Located at a favourite summer residence of the imperial family on the outskirts of Moscow, this church is a fine example of the adaptation to brick construction of motifs from the folk tradition of wooden architecture. Its form perfectly reflects its name, for its vertical lines draw the eye of the viewer upward. It is an octagonal structure, topped with a steep 'tent-shaped' roof. Symmetrical stairs and porches lead into the very small, high sanctuary. Lines of small white stones lighten the appearance of the tent and rectangular columns and *kokoshniki* (headdress-like gables) break the surface of the vertical outer walls of the octagon.

Plate 14 The Cathedral of the Archangel Michael, Moscow. 1505–1508.

Like the nearby Dormition Cathedral, this church, which served as the burial place of the ruling family, combined native and Italian elements. Its architect, Aleviso Novi, adapted the now traditional arrangement with three aisles and a cluster of five cupolas. The Italian touch appears in the shell-shaped decorations in the gables and the delicate decorative columns on the facades.

Plates 15 and 16 *The Church Militant.* 1552–1553.

This icon, sometimes also called *The Blessed Army*, celebrates Muscovy's conquest of Kazan in 1552. It depicts the Archangel Michael and Ivan IV riding back in triumph toward the holy city (Moscow) at the head of the armies of Christian saints and warriors. Before them appears the Virgin, Mother of God, protectress of the city. The large figure among the troops holding the cross is Vladimir Monomakh, Grand Prince of Kiev in the early 1100s. Behind the victorious troops burns Kazan. The icon's political message is unusual. The work is characteristic of a new fashion in painting, however, in its composition, crowded with many figures, and its innovative subject matter.

Plate 17 The Cathedral of St Basil, Moscow. 1555–1561.

Ivan IV had this extraordinary church constructed to celebrate the conquest of Kazan. The building actually consists of nine separate sanctuaries. In the centre is a high tent-shaped structure which resembles the Kolomenskoe church. Around it are eight chapels, each with its own onion-shaped cupola. To create the impression of inspired excess, the architects made lavish use of many popular decorative devices – porches, stairways, *kokoshniki*, faceted brickwork and brightly coloured tiles.

Preface

This book is a short history of Muscovite Russia from 1304 to 1613. It is a work of historical synthesis, designed, above all, for students and the educated general reader. At the same time, I hope to offer specialists in Russian history something of value by incorporating the findings of the best recent monographic studies on the period and providing summaries of the most fruitful debates on its interpretation.

In writing *The Formation of Muscovy*, I have attempted to fill an important gap in the literature on Russian history. At present, there is only one general study of Muscovite Russian history in English – A. E. Presniakov's *The Tsardom of Muscovy*. Presniakov's work needs no justification. On the eve of the revolution, the author established himself as one of the greatest scholars of Muscovite history: the discerning reader will quickly notice his imprint on my own thinking. At the same time, his excellent little book differs radically from this one. Presniakov originally wrote for Russian readers who already knew the stories and the personalities of the period. St Sergius, Dmitrii Donskoi and Ivan the Terrible belonged to their cultural heritage. His book, therefore, presents the main features of Muscovite history in extremely compressed, abstract form and, in addition, unlike the present work, concentrates on the sixteenth and seventeenth centuries.

The Formation of Muscovy, like Presniakov's book, is the creation of one author in a particular place and time, California in 1985. It undoubtedly reflects my personal eccentricities and the peculiarities of the world in which I live. From such a vantage point, Russians of medieval times often seem very distant and unapproachable.

My timing may be faulty as well. As one of my colleagues enjoys asking, 'Is it time to sum up?' To this eternal question, I offer the eternal answer. In the ever-flowing stream of historical study, it is never the perfect time to summarize the state of the art. At the same time, waiting for the right moment for synthesis means never making the attempt. In 1985, many important problems of Muscovite history remain unresolved. Yet writing when I do, I can reap the fruits of a renaissance of medieval Russian studies both in the Soviet Union and the world beyond. As a historian of Muscovy, I cannot stand, let alone walk, without the accomplishments of the great Soviet medievalists who reached the peak of their creativity in the 1950s and 1960s. In more recent times, my Western colleagues have made impressive strides in the study of Muscovite institutions, society and culture. Many of their most interesting publications, particularly those on literature and polemical writings in the fifteenth and sixteenth centuries, dramatically challenge received wisdom. At present, the jury of historical consensus is still deliberating the fate of their hypotheses. Without their collective assistance, I could do no more than repeat the ideas of the great Russian historians of pre-revolutionary times.

As I write, the study of history moves on. Some of the 'facts' which I confidently present to the reader will soon be unmasked as fiction. Some of my generalizations undoubtedly will not stand the test of time. I hope, however, that readers in years to come will find in this book helpful analysis and stimulating impressions and textures of a world remote and, in some ways, very different from our own. If I give my readers only a small fraction of the historical nourishment which I have received from my predecessors in Muscovite history, I will be content.

I owe many people a debt of gratitude. My work rests on the findings of innumerable predecessors and colleagues, only some of whom are acknowledged in the bibliography. John Fennell and Gustave Alef have given invaluable advice on the manuscript and saved me from many errors. They are in no way responsible for my failings as an author. Harry Shukman has been an encouraging and helpful editor. Jack E. Kollmann, Jr, a gifted historian and artist, helped greatly in the selection and preparation of the illustrations: a number of them are his own photographs. Closer to home, I have enjoyed the camaraderie of my colleagues in the Department of History of the University of California, Davis, and the patient support of my family – Nancy and the boys – who put up with me through thick and thin. Without the help of all of these people, I could not have written this book.

ROBERT O. CRUMMEY
Davis, California
20 December, 1985

TO THE BOYS –

Reed, John, Julian and Dan

CHAPTER ONE

Land and people

This book tells the story of the rise of the late medieval Russian monarchy with Moscow as its capital. It describes the ways in which the princes of Moscow mobilized the natural and human resources of their domains in order to establish their control over north-east Russia and ultimately to claim sovereignty over all Eastern Orthodox Christians of East Slavic language and culture.

Readers of East European ancestry already realize that I am using words which are confusing and charged with emotion. By 'Russian', I mean the ancestors of our contemporaries of Great Russian nationality and the territories in which they lived.

In telling our tale, our first task is to describe the resources available to any would-be leader of the Russian lands. In 1304, the prospects for the future political consolidation and economic and social development of north-east Russia looked poor. For one thing, the entire core of the future monarchy suffered from serious natural disabilities.

The Muscovite state arose in far harsher geographical surroundings than the national monarchies of western Europe. The city of Moscow is located at a latitude of 55° 45′, far to the north of London and the cities of the United States and Canada, excluding Alaska. In the English-speaking world, Edinburgh and Glasgow are the only very large cities that lie so far north. Moreover, we must remember, Moscow is situated near the southern border of the late medieval monarchy that bore its name.

In keeping with its location, the Moscow region has a continental climate. The mean temperature in January is −10.3°C (13.5°F) and, in July 17.8°C (64°F). In the United States, similar conditions can be found in northern Minnesota and the Dakotas: nowhere in Britain are winters so harsh. On the average, in Moscow fewer than 150 days a year are free of frost.[1]

All of northern and central Russia is an extension of the north European plain. The landscape is essentially flat; a traveller scarcely notices the upland watersheds north and west of Moscow. At the same time, the countryside around the city is far from monotonous. The terrain is slightly rolling and many rivers, streams and ravines cut through the land.

A mixture of deciduous and evergreen forest makes up the natural vegetation of the Russian heartland. In this zone, the grey forest soil can be farmed although it is not especially fertile. Within the territory of the future Muscovite state, however, one area stands out as a fortunate exception – the Vladimir Opole, a pocket of rich loess-like soil covering more than 4,000 square kilometres. In this region to the east of Moscow emerged the first great political and cultural centre of north-east Russia.[2]

While the natural blessings of Moscow pale before those of Paris, they are far more promising than the conditions in most other areas of northern Russia. North of the mixed forest zone lies the evergreen forest, the *taiga*. In this vast area, which, in 1300, served as the hinterland of the city-empire of Novgorod, the climate is even harsher than in Moscow, the growing season is very short and subject to untimely frosts and the soil is acidic and infertile. Throughout history, agriculture has taken second place: the inhabitants of the *taiga* have lived primarily by exploiting the resources of the forest and its lakes and rivers.

In the historical circumstances of the year 1304, then, the mixed forest zone, the core area of the future Muscovite state, provided the best available conditions for Russian peasant farmers. Admittedly the grasslands to the south were more fertile, but they were controlled by nomad warriors and herdsmen. The mixed forest gave its population shelter from nomadic raids and could be farmed.

As earlier historians delighted in pointing out, the mixed forest zone of north-east Russia has other advantages as well. Rivers criss-cross the Russian plain and, throughout history, have given the inhabitants of the area an easy way to travel and transport goods. Moreover, in pre-modern times, the harshness of the climate served a useful purpose: travel across the plain was easiest in winter when water and land were frozen. By contrast, in the spring melting snow and heavy rain produced the *rasputitsa* (roadlessness) when movement across the country was virtually impossible.[3]

For centuries, this harsh land sustained a sparse population. According to the most recent estimate, in 1550 Tsar Ivan IV of Moscow ruled between 6 and 6.5 million subjects. The population of his domain was not evenly distributed. In the relatively fertile lands around Moscow and the rich Vladimir region to the east, the population density was probably about 10 people per square kilometre.[4]. At the other end of the scale, the vast Novgorod lands – all of the far northern and north-western territories of Ivan's realm – had, in the late fifteenth century, slightly more than half a million inhabitants or less than 2 per square kilometre.[5] The average population density for all of Ivan IV's domains was about 4 people per square kilometre – a figure only one-fifth or one-tenth of the average for the more highly developed regions of Western Europe in the same period.[6]

How the population of the Russian lands changed over time is a complex and controversial subject.[7] Any estimates of the population of the Russian lands before the fifteenth century are, at best, educated guesses. Thus it is very difficult even to assess the impact of crises like the Mongol invasion of

1237–40. In all probability, the invaders caused heavy loss of life in those cities which they besieged and captured. Moreover, Mongol military operations later in the century devastated the exposed eastern most regions of the Russian lands, particularly around the capital, Vladimir.[8] The overall impact of their conquest, however, may not have been as devastating as earlier generations believed.[9] In addition, historians agree, the Russian lands soon recovered from the blow: signs of renewed economic and institutional vigour in the early 1300s suggest that the population was again on the rise.

The Black Death changed all that. Striking Russia from the west in 1352, plague devastated the main centres of population, claiming thousands of victims, ranging from the reigning prince of Moscow and the head of the Orthodox Church in Russia to the humblest of men and women. While the surviving Russian sources do not permit even rough statistical estimates of the casualties, the damage in the affected areas may well have equalled the devastation in western Europe where roughly a third of the population perished. Moreover, after its initial onslaught, the Black Death continued to plague the Russian lands for more than a century. Well into the 1400s, regular, severe recurrences of the disease carried off many victims.[10] Which categories of people died remains a controversial subject. Without doubt, the small urban population suffered severe losses. Scholars disagree, however, on the extent to which the disease attacked the scattered rural population.[11]

From the middle of the fifteenth century until the last decades of the sixteenth, the population of the Russian lands rose steadily.[12] Political conditions provide one of many explanations for the change. For, in precisely the same period, the rulers of Moscow took control of vast territories in the Russian lands and beyond and built a simple, but effective army and administration. With the emergence of a strong monarchy, the population of the core areas of north-east Russia was safer from the ravages of invasion and civil war than ever before.

In the late 1500s and early 1600s, however, a combination of crop failure and famine, disease, military casualties, soaring taxes and domestic unrest led to a severe drop in the population of the central regions of the Muscovite monarchy and, in particular, the Novgorod lands. Some of the losses unquestionably resulted from the flight of peasants who could no longer bear the conditions of life in their old homesteads.[13] For this reason, the precise nature of the demographic crisis of the late sixteenth century remains unclear.[14] Did it lead to an absolute reduction in the population of the Russian lands or was it instead a painful and disruptive process of shifting much of the population from the old areas of settlement to the newly conquered frontier territories to the east and south? The problem remains to be solved.

Until modern times, the forest dominated the landscape of north-east Russia. Before the sixteenth century, most Russian peasants lived in isolated settlements of between one and four households. In most cases, 'axe did not meet with axe': in other words, one hamlet's fields and meadows had no common borders with its neighbours'. The surrounding forest provided food, fuel, building material and other resources which the peasants used to sustain their simple, self-contained life.[15]

Farming provided the peasants with their staple food. In their fields and clearings, they grew two main crops – rye and oats. They made their bread and some other dishes from rye flour while oats fed both men and animals. There were good reasons for their choices. Most of the east Russian lands lay too far north for the cultivation of wheat. Barley was an important crop only in the more remote and primitive northern regions since, in more favourable conditions, rye gave better yields.[16] Unlike their western European counterparts, Russian peasants made little use of pulses, such as peas.[17]

Since peasants in Muscovite times had virtually unlimited quantities of land at their disposal, they used extensive methods of cultivation. As late as the sixteenth century, the simple slash-and-burn technique remained widespread.[18] Choosing a promising patch of forest, the peasants cut down the trees, then created a clearing by burning the logs and underbrush. The resulting ash fertilized the soil and, for a time, the new field would give high yields. When the soil began to show signs of exhaustion, the peasants abandoned the clearing and began the process all over again at a new location.

As time passed, the peasants of the more fertile areas of the emerging Muscovite state tended to establish permanent fields which they sowed with grain or left fallow. This development, in turn, led, by the late fifteenth century at the latest, to the rotation of crops – a winter grain, usually rye, a summer grain, most often oats, and fallow. At first irregular, the rotation of crops gradually became somewhat more systematic. At the same time, contemporary documents present a wide variety of patterns of land use, including regular crop rotation followed by long periods of fallow. Moreover, particularly on the estates of the monasteries, the peasants began to cultivate large enclosed fields communally, subdividing them into strips on which individual households could cultivate their share of the common crops.[19] Even after these innovations, it is unclear whether we can legitimately speak of the use of the 'three-field system' in sixteenth-century Russian agriculture.[20]

For one thing, techniques of cultivation remained rudimentary and economical. Most peasants used simple implements – a *sokha* for ploughing, scythes for cutting hay, and axes. The sokha, a scratch plough – something of a cross between a harrow and a plough – usually had two tines with metal tips. The device was ideally suited to a forest environment where soils are thin. Since the sokha was comparatively light, it could easily be manoeuvred around rocks and stumps. It was also cheap, being easy to make and repair and requiring only one horse to pull it.[21] On the negative side, the sokha could not cut through very dense soil or thick turf and could not turn the earth over like a modern plough.

In spite of owning cattle and other livestock, moreover, Russian peasants made very limited use of manure as fertilizer. Only on the best-organized large estates – those of the ruling dynasty and the monasteries – were they regularly obliged to do so.[22] In other situations the difficulty of transporting manure to scattered and distant fields apparently inhibited the peasants from using it. Yet, without it, more intensive farming was impossible.

As long as the Russian peasants had as much land as they could work using traditional methods, however, they had little reason to make further innovations. Their grain crops yielded a comparatively low return – an average of three or four times the amount of seed sown for rye and a ratio of about three to one for oats.[23] Yet these figures are not significantly lower than the averages for western Europe in the same period.[24]

The productivity of agriculture varied greatly from one region to another. In the fertile Vladimir Opole, grain yields tended to be higher than the average for the Russian lands. At the other end of the scale, peasants of the northern forest areas might reap as little as one and a half times or twice the amount of grain that they sowed.[25] Like their counterparts to the west, Russian peasants, under the best of circumstances, probably produced enough surplus grain to survive one poor harvest. Two or more lean years would bring disaster. In the far north a single bad harvest meant the threat of starvation.

In addition to growing grain, Russian peasants mustered all of the other resources which their environment provided. Meadows and the forest fed their domestic animals. According to one educated guess, the average peasant household in medieval Russia owned one work-horse, one or two cows, a few sheep or goats, a small flock of domestic fowl and one or two pigs.[26] By the standards of our own day, all of these animals were very small.[27] All had their place in the domestic economy. The horse served as the primary draft animal, while the cows provided milk products and meat. Dairying played a particularly large part in the economy of regions, like the far north, in which the climate and soil made the cultivation of grain especially difficult.[28]

In a northerly climate, raising livestock is no easy task. In the short summer season, the animals can graze in the meadows and nearby forest. For at least 200 days a year, however, they have to be kept in stalls. To feed them through the long winter, the peasants of earlier times had to cut and cure prodigious quantities of hay – about 0.3 of a tonne per cow.[29] Thus, access to extensive meadowlands was indispensable.

The peasants likewise depended on the resources of the forest. They lived in wood huts heated by wood fires and worked with wooden tools and implements. The forest also provided many important elements in their diet – mushrooms, honey, berries and wild game.[30] Bark served many purposes, among them, as a substitute for paper. In an emergency, moreover, it could be ground up and fed to people and animals as a poor substitute for grain.

The lakes and rivers that dot the Russian landscape provided many varieties of fish for the tables of rich and poor alike. The catch was an extremely important source of animal protein, not least because the Eastern Orthodox Church requires long and rigorous periods of fasting. Understandably, fishing rights were highly prized and the subject of frequent disputes.

In good times, then, the Russian peasant had a simple and monotonous, but adequate diet. It consisted mainly of rye bread, dairy products and vegetables, primarily cabbage, supplemented by fish and, more rarely, meat. An adequate supply of grain was crucial: it is estimated that an adult needed about 0.5 kilogram of rye a day in order to live and work.[31] The delicacies gathered in the forest gave welcome variety to this otherwise predictable menu.

Thus, as long as the peasants had enough land to suit their methods of cultivation and had regular access to forest, meadow and stream, they could usually maintain a satisfactory standard of living. They needed little that they could not produce themselves: salt and metal blades for tools were the obvious exceptions. If they were deprived of one or more of these resources, however, their position could quickly become desperate.

As the Muscovite monarchy emerged, the peasants – the vast majority of its population – lived in a world of simple social and political relationships. The smallest organizational unit was the family household. In contrast to later periods of Russian history, the peasant family, up to the sixteenth century, consisted of a couple and their growing children. It was an economic unit, formed by marriage, usually when the partners were very young. As such, however, it might include one or more outsiders, taken in to help with the work. Once the couple's children reached maturity, however, they usually married and set up their own separate households. In this way, human settlement gradually moved across the land.[32]

Outside of their own family, the peasants owed primary allegiance to the commune. While we have very little information on the structure and functioning of peasant communes before the sixteenth century, historians usually assume that, by that time, the institution already had a long history and deep roots. Through the commune, the peasants of several hamlets, a village or a district chose elders who were responsible for representing them in dealings with the outside world and settling the most important issues in their common life. As scattered sources from the sixteenth century and the much fuller records of later periods suggest, representatives of the commune's households met periodically to resolve disputes among members, divide up shared resources such as fields cultivated in common, and decide what share of the community's obligations each household had to bear.[33]

In the fifteenth and sixteenth centuries, the ambitious but rudimentary royal administration in Moscow saw the commune as a useful instrument in governing the realm. Legal enactments and administrative ordinances recognized its traditional functions and defined them to suit the needs of the prince's officials. For example, the government made the commune's members collectively responsible for payment of taxes: if one household did not pay its share, the other villagers had to make up the arrears. In such ways, the royal government exploited the peasant tradition of mutual responsibility and solidarity and, in so doing, shaped the commune according to its own needs.

The changes in the commune's role accompanied even broader changes in the lives of the Russian peasants in the sixteenth century. Beginning in the late 1400s, outside forces began to intrude on the peasants' isolated world.

First, rising population meant that, in the most densely settled regions, the peasants' fields increasingly became contiguous. For the first time, it became important to establish property lines and define rights of ownership of the land.

Secondly, over the centuries, more and more peasant land fell into the hands of the nobles and the monasteries. While the peasants continued to farm the land as always, becoming part of a manor meant paying dues to the lord in produce, labour and money. In one contract with the monastery on whose manor they lived, the peasants undertook to perform a wide variety of services, including cultivating the monks' fields, mowing their hay, repairing their fences, building their weirs, weaving their fishing-nets and baking their bread.[34] Under other arrangements, peasants gave their lords specified amounts of rye and oats, butter, cheese, flax and a small amount of money.[35] By the end of the fifteenth century, such cash payments often formed part of the peasants' dues. At that time, their obligations were significant, but not crippling: using figures from the Staraia Russa area of the Novgorod lands, a recent study indicates that the peasants' payments to their lords amounted to about 28 per cent of their grain crop, which, as we have noted, was only one of several likely sources of income. Over the course of the sixteenth century, these obligations appear to have risen, although the pattern of change in the Novgorod lands was complex and, in some districts, the real value of peasant dues may actually have declined. In difficult times, moreover, the peasants were obliged to borrow grain from their lords at about 7 per cent interest.[36] The latter had every reason to help the peasants out, for, if they ceased to farm, the lord, who needed their produce and labour, would also suffer.

In broader terms, the peasant, while clearly the weaker party, had considerable leverage in his dealings with his lord. His strongest weapon was the possibility of moving away from the lord's manor: for, in a country with a chronic shortage of labour, owners of estates had to compete for workers. From the middle of the fifteenth century until the very end of the sixteenth, Muscovite law specified a particular time – the two weeks surrounding St George's Day in November – when any peasant who had met his obligations and paid his debts could legally leave his lord's land. In practice, peasants probably moved whenever they chose.[37]

Finally, – and most importantly – by the end of the fifteenth century, the Muscovite monarchy already made a wide variety of demands on the peasants. They had to pay taxes and fees, nominally in money, and provide specified goods and services, such as working on the prince's lands and construction projects, and supplying his officials and troops. As the royal administration and army grew, so did the peasants' obligations. In particular, in the second half of the sixteenth century, the military and political adventures of Ivan IV laid unprecedentedly heavy burdens on the peasants, many of whom could not or would not bear them.[38] Over the course of the century, in the Novgorod lands, the peasants' tax bill per unit of cultivated land rose from 12 Moscow *dengi* per year, at the very most, to 97, adjusted to allow for the steady devaluation of the coinage! In real purchasing power, taxes reached their zenith in the 1560s: thereafter, although their nominal value continued to rise, soaring grain prices meant that, in reality, they took away a smaller proportion of the peasants' crops.[39]

Rising obligations to the outside world meant that some or all of the peasant's surplus production – and perhaps some of the resources needed for his own sustenance – now went to others. Moreover, the need to meet them forced him into at least limited contact with the market. Even so, the peasant's greatest asset remained his ability to support himself with the resources of his own tenement. Without it, surviving the natural and man-made catastrophes of the late sixteenth century would have been impossible.[40]

All the same, the calamities of the late 1500s and early 1600s changed the peasants' lives in a number of ways. Under their blows, many abandoned their homes to seek shelter on landlords' estates or flee to the frontiers of the realm. Their flight left their former neighbours in a very difficult situation, for, given the practice of collective responsibility, those who remained at home had to pay taxes for the fugitives as well as for themselves. Among those who stayed, moreover, families tended to work smaller allotments than before and a number abandoned the three-field rotation of crops.[41]

By the middle of the seventeenth century, even more profound consequences of the crisis had become clear. First of all, the pattern of peasant settlement had changed dramatically. Many sixteenth-century hamlets had disappeared from the map to be replaced by fewer, much larger villages whose inhabitants worked bigger fields than before.[42] Secondly, under pressure of its own need for reliable tax revenues and the landlords' demands for a predictable supply of labour, the Muscovite government took decisive steps to end all movement of the peasant population, legal or illegal. At the culmination of a long legislative process, the Law Code of 1649 bound the peasants for ever to the locations where they lived and stipulated that, if they ran away, their lords had a limitless right to bring them back. The peasants' world had changed for ever.

Leaving aside ecclesiastics, the other main group in Muscovite society was the nobility. Bound to the peasantry by their shared dependence on the land and its fruits, the nobles had one primary function. They were warriors. Trained from childhood to ride and to fight, noblemen made up the retinues of the ruling princes of the Russian lands and the armies and raiding parties that dominated a world of continuous, savage warfare.

By origin and in composition, the nobility – if we can legitimately use the word – was a diverse and amorphous group. Muscovite society had no clear way of defining who was a noble. Just as in later centuries, Russian nobles ranged from members of the great clans which gathered at the court of the ruling dynasty down to rank-and-file fighting men whose occupation alone distinguished them from peasants. Moreover, even if we disregard their fanciful claims to distinguished foreign ancestry, they undoubtedly came from

8

many different backgrounds. Some were princes, members of cadet branches of the royal houses of north-east Russia and Lithuania – the Riurikovichi and Gediminovichi. Regardless of their social standing or personal fate, their title passed to all of their male descendants. Other noble clans had no title, but, through generations of military and administrative service, had established their right to serve the prince of the land in positions of responsibility.

At the beginning of the fourteenth century, north-east Russia was fragmented into many independent principalities, some large and some small, each ruled by one of the branches of the line of Riurik. Every ruling prince had his own force of military retainers who, in turn, might well have their own retinues of fighting men.

All of these princes and warriors had a suzerain, the grand prince of Vladimir, to whom they technically owed their loyalty and obedience. In a major emergency, it was the grand prince's duty to summon the local princes and their men-at-arms to defend the Russian land. In practice, however, any prince was free to choose whether he and his men would take part in a given campaign. His warriors had similar freedom of action. In law and in practice, they had the right to leave his entourage at any time and enter the service of another master.

As the princes of Moscow gradually united the east Russian lands under their sceptre, the position and rights of noble warriors changed dramatically. When Moscow annexed the other principalities of Russia, its rulers took the nobles of the area into their service. They permitted some of them to come to Moscow to be part of their court and bodyguard: others they enlisted to serve from their ancestral homelands.

By the late fifteenth century, the grand princes of Moscow had hammered home a clear and simple message: as the leaders of the nation, they expected to be obeyed. Warriors were to appear for muster when summoned. Whatever the traditional legal formulae, moreover, the so-called 'right of departure' became a dead letter. Rulers such as Ivan III treated attempts to leave their service as acts of treason punishable by a variety of sanctions, even death.[43] Moreover, even though most nobles owned their lands in absolute tenure (*votchina*), the grand princes had no compunctions about confiscating them for acts of disloyalty. The connection between the right to own land and loyal service to the monarch became even clearer when Ivan III established the *pomeste* system of conditional service tenure estates in Novgorod at the end of the century.[44]

By Ivan's time, then, the basic structure of the warrior nobility was already clear. At the top stood the boyars, the small group of men and their clans who commanded the ruler's armies and acted as his advisers and courtiers.[45] Below them was an equally small, but less prestigious group of families whose members served their royal master as governors of the provinces of his realm and in many other capacities, including, of course, in battle.[46] A rung still lower on the ladder were the lesser members of the grand prince's entourage who guarded his security and formed the core of his army on campaign.

Finally, the majority of the military servitors lived on their estates in the provinces and, when summoned, appeared for muster with the rest of the nobles from their area.

In the same period, the Muscovite army grew into a highly effective fighting force. In Russia, centuries of experience battling the mounted warriors of the steppe exaggerated the general medieval tendency to make warfare the business of noble cavalrymen. Like the Mongols and Tatars against whom they fought, Russian warriors strove for speed and mobility above all else. They wore relatively light chain mail and, as weapons, used mainly bows and arrows and swords. As Western European observers noted, they fought like mounted raiders, suddenly charging down on the enemy in apparent disarray and, if they met strong resistance, retreating just as quickly, firing as they went.[47]

The disorder was more apparent than real, however. In the late fifteenth and sixteenth centuries, the grand princes of Moscow could fight sustained wars with well-organized armies made up of many thousands of men. In the most elaborate campaigns, the cavalry, which constituted the overwhelming majority of the entire force, was divided into five large subdivisions – the main corps, the advance and rearguards and the left and right wings. In addition, the army had auxiliary units to give it greater versatility and firepower. Already in the fifteenth century, artillery played a significant part in Russian military operations. Then, in the sixteenth, the royal government created units of arquebusiers and musketeers to fight mainly on foot, firing precursors of the modern rifle. However exotic it might appear to Western eyes, the Muscovite army had became formidable.

Muscovite cavalrymen paid dearly for the privilege of defending their country. Military service was a lifelong and virtually full-time occupation fraught with hazards. Usually a young man registered for service at the age of fifteen.[48] From then on, the government required him to appear for muster early each spring and remain in arms until late fall. In addition, over the winter, the Muscovite government often maintained a skeleton force on the southern frontier facing the Crimean Tatars. A cavalryman could retire from service only if the officials who reviewed the troops certified him as too old or infirm for further service, a status they were most reluctant to grant. If the careers of the most prominent generals of the late sixteenth century are any indication, military servitors led an extremely strenuous life, on campaign continually, moving back and forth across the country from one battle zone to another. Leaves to rest and put one's personal affairs in order were rare indeed.[49]

The cavalryman's lot was not a pleasant one. As always, soldiers frequently risked death in battle. While we have virtually no records of the casualties which medieval Russian armies suffered, the high number of noblemen recorded as childless in family genealogies suggests that many of them died young in war. Even for those who lived to a ripe old age, military service was no picnic. For at least eight or nine months a year they lived on dried meat and hard tack, alternately sweltering and shivering from cold and rain.

Military service had an economic dimension as well. Each cavalryman had to provide his own horses and weapons and was expected to bring along his own supply of food. That meant that he needed an estate – land with peasants to work it – in order to provide his supplies as well as to feed his family. The right to own a manor had its price, however. By the mid-sixteenth century, the rulers of Muscovy had made clear that they expected every able-bodied man who held an estate – whether on allodial (votchina) or conditional (pomeste) tenure – to serve them in some capacity, usually in the army. Moreover, if nobles owned more than a minimal amount of land, they were responsible for bringing with them a number of other warriors corresponding to the size of their estates.

These governmental regulations built upon social reality. Like the independent princes before them, the more powerful nobles of the fifteenth and sixteenth centuries maintained small bodies of armed retainers who followed them into battle and attended them on great state occasions. Often members of nobles' retinues were slaves. The most recent study suggests that, in the late sixteenth century, such slaves may have constituted as much as one-third of the entire Muscovite army.[50]

In mobilizing the resources of a poor society, the Muscovite government chose to pay its military servitors with grants of land. For many of the lesser nobles, these estates were their only source of livelihood, providing them with food and other agricultural and forest products. A royal grant was by no means the only way to acquire land: a Russian noble could also inherit it, buy it or obtain it as a dowry.[51] For all nobles, however, great or petty, ownership of populated land, however they acquired it, was the key to economic survival.

Retaining title to an estate from one generation to the next was not easy. Technically, all conditional tenure estates reverted to the crown on the death or disqualification of each owner. If a man had served well and left a son of military age when he died, the government would probably grant his lands to his heir. Allodial (votchina) estates presented a different problem. Following a widespread custom in central and eastern Europe, Russian nobles divided their lands among all of their sons and made provision for their widows and daughters as well. Thus, over several generations, a clan's ancestral estate might be subdivided into holdings too small to support the men who inherited them. Unless its members found ways to gain control of additional tracts of land – either through royal grants as a reward for service or by purchase with money earned in the prince's employ – the clan slowly slipped into poverty and obscurity.[52] Economic pressures, then, reinforced the rulers' demand that the nobles of the Russian lands fight in their armies and help them administer their domains.

Given the circumstances in which they lived, Russian nobles understandably found it difficult to manage their estates. For the most part, they made little attempt to do so, contenting themselves with collecting provisions and dues in money from the peasants who worked the land. The problems of estate management varied from one noble to the next. The wealthy few often owned several estates scattered across the country. They therefore relied on stewards to collect their dues. When the requirements of service permitted, the poorer nobles lived on their manors and farmed part of them with the help of household servants or slaves. Beyond this, we have very little information about the practices of medieval Russian landlords. There is, however, one measure of their involvement in exploiting the potential of their lands – the size of the demesne, the portion of the estate which the lord set aside for his own use. In the Novgorod lands at the end of the fifteenth century, the percentage of demesne on conditional tenure estates was small – less than 10 per cent. The proportion of demesne on the average estate rose in the sixteenth century to about one-quarter of the arable, still a modest area about the size of a peasant family's holding. Moreover, in cases in which small landlords took over the direct management of most or all of their land, they did so for lack of alternatives: in the crisis of the late sixteenth century, many of them found themselves without peasants to work the land on their behalf. For the most part, then, secular landlords, great and small alike, treated their estates as sources of income to be exploited with as little effort and ingenuity as possible.[53]

When at home in the country, rank-and-file nobles were probably almost indistinguishable from peasants. Evidence from later periods suggests, for example, that their houses were glorified log cabins. In them, they lived simply, eating the same food as their tenants. Moreover, the lord may well have been illiterate like his peasants.

Members of the aristocratic clans of the royal court lived in a completely different world. By the end of the fifteenth century, a group of powerful families – both princely and non-titled – had gathered around the throne of the princes of Moscow. Over the generations, their members served as the princes' generals, administrators and advisers. In return, they received offices which allowed them to collect produce and revenue from the population (kormlenie), recognition of their high rank and, occasionally, grants of crown or confiscated land.[54] In a society without patents of nobility or an elaborate hierarchy of honorific titles, the greatest distinction to which a layman could aspire was the rank of boyar, signifying membership in the ruler's informal council of advisers, the Boyar Duma.[55]

Like any élite, the Muscovite court aristocracy changed continually. At the same time, the word 'aristocracy' seems appropriate to describe the group, for a remarkable number of clans held their places of power beside the throne for generations. By the end of the fourteenth century, several of the great non-titled clans of later periods had already established themselves as the grand princes' leading advisers.[56] In the next two centuries, the ranks of non-titled boyars continued to grow; new men whose talent and loyalty made them invaluable to the ruler joined the evolving core of distinguished families at court. By contrast, the formerly independent princes of north-east Russia entered Moscow's service relatively late. Many powerful princely clans jumped on the Muscovite bandwagon in the latter half of the fifteenth and first decades of the sixteenth centuries once its princes had clearly established their dominance over north-east Russia. Ivan III and his successors welcomed the princes into their service, but watched them carefully and kept them from positions of real power until they had proved their trustworthiness.[57] Clans, of course, could fall from grace as easily as they rose to power. In each generation, a few once-prominent families fell into disgrace, slipped into obscurity or died out altogether.

As more and more aristocratic clans entered Moscow's service, their arrival posed a problem for their royal masters and for themselves. As hereditary warriors and traditional leaders, both the newcomers and the long-established royal servitors had an acute awareness of their position in society and were very sensitive to slights to their honour. How, then, could the newcomers fit harmoniously into the social life of the court and the hierarchy of service ranks?

In answer, an elaborate system of precedence ranking (*mestnichestvo*) appeared and grew until its full flowering in the late sixteenth and early seventeenth centuries. Historians argue about almost every feature of the system – precisely when it arose, how it affected the functioning of the royal government and army and what it meant to individual aristocrats and their clans. Even so, there is now a rough consensus regarding its most important features.

Once the system took shape at the turn of the fifteenth and sixteenth centuries, each prominent noble courtier occupied a particular rung on an invisible ladder of precedence. The individual derived his ranking from the positions that he and his relatives had held in royal service and from the genealogical distinction of his clan. In doubtful cases, rank in service – particularly the most recent instances – was decisive. No one could be expected to sit at the prince's table or serve in the royal army in a position less honourable than that occupied by a less distinguished rival. For to do so would not only bring humiliation, but would also establish a dangerous precedent for the future.

Thus when an aristocratic servitor believed that he had been assigned a position beneath a less worthy rival, he had the right to protest the assignment to the ruler and the Boyar Duma. If necessary, he and his rival would be obliged to provide documents supporting their claims about their past service positions and the relative merits of their families.

Mestnichestvo had an ambiguous effect on the fighting capacity of the army and the decorum of court life. On the one hand, the protests that the system engendered were very disruptive. When commanders of army units refused to cooperate or even to communicate with one another for reasons of precedence, the consequences could be devastating. Yet, for the men in question, such behaviour made sense. In suits over precedence, the most telling evidence was the record of the most recent service assignments of the parties involved. For this reason, if a man accepted a posting lower than he deserved, he would set a fatal precedent for himself and his entire clan. Rather than do so, he would protest – immediately and vehemently – regardless of the cost.

On the other hand, the ruler could turn the system to his own advantage. First of all, the frequent and acrimonious disputes among aristocratic clans helped to prevent them from forming a solid phalanx against the crown. Moreover, since they were the final judges of precedence disputes, the prince and his closest advisers could make decisions protecting or advancing the men and families whom they favoured.[58]

Once they entered Muscovite service, Russian aristocrats found their lives transformed. Although a number of prominent clans retained extensive landholdings in their region of origin, they moved to the capital, Moscow, in both a physical and a spiritual sense.[59] Their entire lives increasingly centred on service to the ruler and the rewards and honours that it would bring. They therefore found it necessary to remain at court in the hope that personal contact with the prince and his entourage would lead to future preferment.

While they crowded around the throne, Russian aristocrats gradually lost touch with their home areas. Over time, they transformed their ancestral estates into mere sources of revenue and supplies to support them in Moscow or they lost them altogether. Their royal masters did everything in their power to encourage this tendency. It was a matter of policy, for example, not to send an aristocrat back to his native region on royal business.[60]

The boyars built their power on a foundation of personal relationships. Direct contact with the ruler – or, if he was incompetent, those who ruled in his name – was of crucial importance. Until the sixteenth century, the court remained small enough to allow the grand prince to get to know all of his courtiers and bodyguards. Moreover, the powerful boyar clans buttressed their position by making complex alliances with one another cemented, above all, by astutely arranged marriages. Usually, the most influential clans were those which had matrimonial ties to the ruling dynasty itself. These royal in-laws, in turn, became highly desirable marriage partners and the centres of entire constellations of matrimonial and political relationships.[61] Finally, although we have virtually no evidence for so early a period, it is likely that, like their heirs in later generations, the boyars of the Muscovite period acted as patrons of less powerful and well-connected men.[62]

All of these personal ties served, among other things, as a form of insurance. As we know, however, a good insurance policy is no guarantee against catastrophe. The boyars' position had glaring weaknesses as well as strengths. Their dependence on the ruler or his surrogates and upon the shifting tides of court politics left them vulnerable to attack. If individuals or clans fell under suspicion of disloyalty or simply became too powerful, they could be disgraced and exiled, have their property confiscated and even go to the scaffold at a moment's notice. The purges of Ivan IV's reign in the late sixteenth century revealed the boyars' Achilles' heel most dramatically. Even in more harmonious times, however, they faced the threat of sudden calamity.[63]

Running these risks brought the members of the great boyar clans many rewards. In addition to the prospects of wealth and power, life at court brought them to Moscow, the most awe-inspiring of Russian cities, and made them participants in an increasingly elaborate web of court ceremonies and ecclesiastical rituals.[64]

From simple beginnings, the magnates and their families gradually developed an extravagant style of life to fit their social standing and ceremonial role. By the sixteenth century, they lived in conditions completely different from those of their country cousins, to say nothing of the peasants. For formal occasions at least, men and women dressed in caftans and robes of brocade or other rich textiles. Elaborate jewellery formed an essential part of their attire. In the city, boyars lived in comfortable houses, sometimes built of brick, attended by large numbers of servants, retainers and dependents. If the menus of court banquets are any indication, they enjoyed a richer diet, particularly in meat and fowl, than ordinary Muscovites. Alcohol – above all wines and mead – lubricated court life.[65] Russians began to distil vodka in the sixteenth century, but, at first, the drink was apparently not much used at official royal functions.[66] Even so, the drunken banquets of the Muscovite court were the scandal of Europe and the despair of foreign ambassadors. While they stayed in Moscow, the great aristocrats of the court enjoyed all of the material comfort and glamour that their society could provide. No wonder the provincial cavalrymen who lived far simpler and more austere lives dreamed of promotion to the ranks of the tsars' courtiers!

Women occupied an ambiguous position in Muscovite court society. On the surface, they were powerless. After all, warfare and administration were male monopolies. Men likewise dominated social life: the celebrated court banquets were stag affairs. Royal and boyar women, unlike their less privileged sisters, lived in seclusion in their own section of the family residence, known as the *terem*. Historians have offered various hypotheses concerning the origin of this custom: the name suggests the influence of neighbouring Moslem societies. At the same time, upper-class Muscovite women may have lived in seclusion precisely because of their importance; for it was they who, through marriage, held together the elaborate network of alliances among boyar clans. This role gave them far more influence than historians have recognized until very recently.[67] As married women, they served as human bridges between clans. As widows, they had an important voice in managing and disposing of the family property.[68] Finally, at court, prominent boyar women attended the ladies of the royal family and served as the children's nannies. The most forceful and energetic of them probably wielded far greater influence than the sources give them credit for.

Throughout medieval times, the overwhelming majority of Muscovites, from boyars to peasants, depended on the land for their living. To be sure, the rural economy was not entirely autarkic, as Soviet historians delight in pointing out.[69] Neither peasants nor their lords could survive without at least limited contacts with the market. For one thing, even the poorest cottar had to have salt. A number of monasteries, some lay landlords and the peasants of some districts produced that indispensable staple for sale.[70]

Moreover, peasants had to meet obligations to their landlords and the government. To do so, they often had to sell something – one of their animals, some other food such as cheese or fish, or simple pieces of handwork like carved wooden spoons – for cash or goods which they lacked. Such contacts with the market, however, were probably infrequent and peripheral to the peasants' essentially isolated and autonomous life. From beginning to end the economy of the Muscovite state was overwhelmingly agrarian and its people – nobles and peasants alike – largely self-sufficient.

Finding patterns of change and development in such sameness is no easy task. Some Soviet scholars claim to see a steadily rising curve of economic activity in the fourteenth and fifteenth centuries which, in turn, provided the socio-economic foundation for the political unification of north-east Russia.[71] This simple scheme presents at least two problems. First of all, unilinear economic development is difficult to find in human history. Pre-industrial societies went through alternating periods of prosperity and hardship, often depending on changing weather and the presence or absence of epidemic disease. Secondly, historians have very little written testimony on the state of the economy before the middle of the fifteenth century, and archaeological evidence, while very valuable, does not address many important issues. Far more likely is a zigzag sequence of economic development similar and roughly parallel to the patterns of rise and fall of the population of the Russian lands.

In our present state of ignorance, we can discuss only two more features of the Muscovite economy with any degree of assurance. First, international trade was of vital importance and remained remarkably stable in an age of rapid political change. For centuries, the Russian lands exported the products of the forest, especially furs. In return, they imported a variety of luxury and speciality goods primarily for the consumption of the most powerful members of society. In other words, Russian merchants and their trading partners dealt in goods which, although transported in small quantities, brought reliable profits. Like merchants throughout the medieval world, they ran great risks – disastrous weather, pirates and highwaymen, and political complications – for great gain.

In medieval times, Russia's foreign trade flowed through two channels – southward on the great rivers through the steppe to the Near East and westward through Novgorod and the Baltic Sea to Western Europe. Well established in Kievan times, the Eastern trade received new vigour from the Mongol conquest of the mid-1200s. After they had pacified the Russian lands, the Mongols worked to keep the main trade routes secure whereas, before their arrival, nomadic raiders had disrupted them seriously. The conquest also changed the patterns of the Eastern trade. The regional Mongol capital, Sarai, near the mouth of the Volga, became its hub. Russian trappers and traders gathered furs and shipped them down the river to Bulgar, the capital of the Turkic principality of the same name, on the middle Volga near the confluence of the Kama. Russian traders most often sold their goods there:

the merchants of Bulgar, who strove for a monopoly over the Volga trade route, then shipped them on to Sarai.[72]

Russia's most important exports to the countries of the Near and Middle East were the finest furs, such as sable and ermine, prized by the upper classes in Asia and Europe alike. In addition, the Russian lands exported other forest products such as wax and honey and limited quantities of linen and timber. Moreover, Russian merchants resold some woollen cloth imported from Western Europe.[73] In later times, they added hawks and falcons, leather, and walrus tusks to their list of wares.

For their part, year after year, Asian merchants shipped the same array of goods to Russia – luxurious silk and cotton textiles like brocade and taffeta, carpets, spices, soap and incense, and pearls and precious stones. As we have seen, the most powerful nobles of the grand princes' court required such goods to maintain an opulent style of life and present a suitably distinguished image to rival courtiers and to their social inferiors. Over the course of time, as the collections of the Armoury in the Moscow Kremlin eloquently testify, the boyars also acquired a taste for Damascus swords and decorative armour from the Near East. The leaders of the Eastern Orthodox Church were even more reliable consumers of imports from the East. The Orthodox liturgy is unimaginable without incense. Other goods from the nearby Moslem lands were also consecrated to the glory of the Christian God – textiles and jewels for vestments, liturgical vessels and icon covers.

In the fifteenth century, the configuration of Russia's Eastern trade changed in several ways in response to new political conditions. As the Mongol Empire broke apart, its fragments took on a political and economic life of their own. Using the Don river, Moscow merchants began to trade directly with the Crimea and with the Genoese who maintained a 'factory' in Kaffa. Within the commercial community of Moscow, there emerged a distinct group known as the 'Kaffa-merchants (*gosti-surozhane*)' – probably made up of native Russians – who specialized in the Crimean trade. Merchants of various nationalities, including Armenians and Genoese, also came to Moscow from the Crimea with their wares.[74] Moreover, Kazan, on the middle Volga, replaced Bulgar as the pivot of trade on the river. Its annual fair attracted merchants of many origins, Russians included.[75]

By the fifteenth century, another of the Mongols' successors – the nomadic Nogai Horde – played a different, but even more crucial role in the economy of the Muscovite monarchy. The Nogais fed its army's insatiable need for horses. In the grasslands east of the Volga, they raised thousands of the animals: in the sixteenth century, they drove about 20,000 horses a year to Moscow's markets.[76]

Medieval Russia's trade with Western Europe followed equally consistent patterns. In this case, a Russian city, Novgorod, occupied the central position on the routes. Its location on the Volkhov river gave its people easy access by river and lake to the Baltic Sea, the upper Volga basin – the heartland of the Muscovite state – and the vast forest tracts of the Russian north. From early times, Novgorod acted as intermediary between other parts of the

Russian lands and north-western Europe. Once again, furs were the main export commodity. The ruling oligarchy of Novgorod claimed jurisdiction over vast territories in the Russian north and sent in agents to collect tribute in furs. Moreover, like their later counterparts in North America, trappers plied their trade, moving further and further afield in search of the best pelts once they had exhausted more accessible areas.

The fur trade was a fiercely competitive and violent business. Novgorod's agents fought to control the supply of the best furs which, by the fourteenth century, came from the most remote corner of European Russia, far to the north and east of the upper Volga. There they encountered direct competition from other Russians and Asian merchants who wanted pelts for the Eastern trade. One Novgorodian response, in the late fourteenth century, was a campaign of raids by armed bands of robber-merchants. These freebooters of the forest, called the *ushkuiniki*, sacked a number of northern Russian towns in order to reassert Novgorod's control over the trade passing through them.[77]

Once the furs had been collected in Novgorod, merchants exchanged them for a variety of goods. Another product of the forest – wax – was also in great demand. In return, Novgorodian merchants bought woollen cloth manufactured in the industrial towns of Flanders. Other imports included salt, metal products, beer and wine, and herring. Of particular significance was the import of precious metals – silver and, to a lesser extent, gold; for, as far as we know, in medieval times the Russian lands had no mines of their own.[78]

The business practices of Novgorod's traders changed over the centuries. In earliest times, merchants from the city travelled across the Baltic to Sweden and northern Germany and established a base on the island of Gotland. By the same token, German and Swedish merchants came and settled in Novgorod. The situation gradually changed, however, with the emergence, in the mid-1200s, of the Hanseatic League, the commercial alliance of north German trading cities centred on Lübeck. To dominate trade in the Baltic, the Hansa established a chain of factories stretching from London and Bergen in the west to Novgorod in the east. In the latter, their merchants lived in their own quarter of the city, governed by its own laws, and shipped all Russian exports westward through the Baltic in their sturdy freighters. Their Russian counterparts restricted themselves to collecting the furs and other goods in the hinterland and bringing them to Novgorod for sale.[79]

In the fifteenth century, the commercial stranglehold of the Hanseatic League began to weaken. To an increasing extent, Russian goods passed through the German cities on the eastern Baltic coast such as Reval (Tallinn), a member of the Hansa, and Narva, which was not. Moreover, in Russia, just as elsewhere, the Hansa found themselves in direct conflict with the rising national monarchies of Europe. In 1494, Ivan III of Moscow ordered the Hansa to close their Novgorod base. His action was part of a campaign to open the greatest possible number of outlets for Russia's foreign trade, including his own new Baltic fortress, Ivangorod. The effort achieved its objectives: even though the Hansa briefly reopened their Novgorod office in 1514, they never re-established their former monopoly. In the sixteenth century, Russia's Baltic trade continued, but under considerably more flexible conditions than before.[80]

Even at its zenith, Novgorod never had complete control of Russia's trade with Western and Central Europe. The area's staple exports also passed through Pskov and Smolensk either by river to Baltic ports such as Riga or overland to the cities of Poland and Lithuania. The merchants who plied these routes bought and sold essentially the same commodities as their counterparts in Novgorod. The overland route through Poland also served as a conduit for trade with the Crimea.[81]

Changing political and economic conditions made it increasingly difficult for any city or alliance to monopolize international trade. By the sixteenth century, in addition to clashes with the kings and queens of Europe, the Hansa had to deal with the ambition of rival traders, particularly from the cities and towns of the Netherlands. Working as individuals and families, Dutch merchants and shippers began to transport goods back and forth between Western and Eastern Europe through the Baltic. Over the course of the 1500s, they displaced the Hansa and achieved dominance over the Baltic trade. The Dutch deserved their victory; they made fewer demands on their trading partners and gave better service than their rivals.

In 1554, Muscovy suddenly acquired another new trading partner, England. How this came about is a familiar story. A group of London merchants decided to stake its claim to a share in Europe's trade with the Orient. Since their Spanish and Portuguese rivals already monopolized the familiar routes to Asia, they financed an expedition which sailed off, in 1553, to find a passage along the northern coasts of Europe and Asia to China. In one sense the outcome was tragic: autumn storms forced two of the three ships ashore on the barren Arctic coast where all of their crewmen perished. The third ship under the command of Richard Chancellor took refuge in the White Sea.

When he discovered that he had, by chance, landed in the domains of the tsar of Muscovy, Chancellor made the best of his opportunity. For his part, Ivan IV welcomed new commercial and diplomatic contacts, particularly those not dependent on the shifting political currents in the Baltic. The tsar issued a charter granting English merchants freedom to trade in his domains. Thus began nearly a century of lively interchange between the two countries.

The English sponsors of the venture, incorporated as the Russia Company, quickly established trading bases in Moscow and Kholmogory, located where the northern Dvina empties into the White Sea. From there, the company's agents travelled through the country, buying goods from local merchants and from the Muscovite government. The list of wares which they traded has a distinctly military flavour. While English merchants bought such traditional Russian staples as furs, wax and hides, they were primarily interested in naval stores – rope and tar – for their country's fleet. In return, at the tsar's insistence, they provided metal products and saltpetre and sulphur for munitions as well as their principal ware – cloth.[82]

While initially cordial, the relations between Muscovy and England were never easy. Like the Hansa before it, the Russia Company desired a monopoly over Russia's export trade and demanded, in addition, the right to carry on commerce within the country and, through it, with Persia (Iran). Understandably, the defenders of Muscovite interests – the tsar's government and the native merchants – took a very different view of the situation. From Ivan IV's perspective, the English had their uses as reliable trading partners and as potential military and diplomatic allies against common enemies, especially the Roman Catholic powers of Central Europe led by the Habsburgs. During the Livonian War against a coalition of enemies to the west, Ivan's government had little choice but give in to most English demands. Under the prodding of Russian merchants, however, the tsar refused to allow the Russia Company's agents to participate in domestic commerce. Moreover, once Muscovy had extricated herself from the war, her government took a much tougher line, rescinding some privileges such as the right to trade with Persia across Russian territory and courting Dutch commercial interests which were eager to join in the northern trade.[83] By 1600, the days of the English ascendancy in Muscovite foreign trade through the White Sea were numbered.

As this story suggests, the tsar's government played a very significant role in the economic and commercial life of the realm. This situation was, of course, by no means unique to Russia. Like other monarchs of the time, Queen Elizabeth consistently supported the demands of the Russia Company and made their policy hers. Ivan IV, however, went much further than she in regulating the economic activities of his subjects. In jaundiced tones, Giles Fletcher observed that, among other measures to fill the royal coffers, the tsars had made vodka their monopoly and would, from time to time, monopolize the sale of domestic commodities such as wax and of foreign imports.[84]

The accuracy of Fletcher's comments and the inferences which he drew from them remain a bone of contention.[85] To what extent did the Muscovite government control the economy? The answer must be sought in two areas – royal monopolies and tax farming, techniques used in other countries as well. By the late sixteenth century, the Muscovite monarchy officially controlled the sale of vodka and caviare. Moreover, in moments of fiscal stringency, as Fletcher charged, its agents confiscated or bought up a wide variety of goods and resold them on their own terms. The crown engaged in this practice only intermittently, however, and, in volume and value, the goods involved constituted only a small part of the country's commerce. The government also recruited merchants to collect indirect taxes, by far its largest source of revenue. Here, too, the available evidence is scattered and ambiguous. Work as tax-farmers undoubtedly burdened the merchants who did it and distracted them from their own businesses. At the same time, tax-farming usually provides opportunities for quick and sure profits. Was this true in Muscovy, however, and did the local merchants see the situation in this light?

Apparently they did not: in the early seventeenth century, the wealthiest merchants avoided duty as tax-collectors.[86]

Did the economic policies of the Muscovite government in the late sixteenth and seventeenth centuries warp the country's development by crushing private initiative? In the present state of our understanding, we can offer only the following suggestions. Governmental policy undoubtedly interfered with the free play of the market and placed greater burdens on Russian merchants than their Western European rivals had to bear. At the same time, the merchants tenaciously defended their own interests and, when seriously threatened by unfair foreign competition, convinced the tsar to adjust his policies in their favour. In short, the government had great influence on the economy, but it was not all-powerful, nor were Russian merchants as supine as has sometimes been supposed.

In addition to the importance of foreign trade, scholars are also in general agreement on a second feature of Muscovite economic development, namely that, in the late fifteenth century and the first half of the sixteenth, the country's economy went through a period of rapid growth. In a stimulating and partisan book, D. P. Makovskii argued that, in this period, the Muscovite economy developed very rapidly. The signs, he suggested, were everywhere. The government undertook major building projects, such as the enormous fortress at Smolensk. So did the church. More and more, a money economy shaped men's lives. Landlords, he claimed, increasingly collected their rents in money and, responding to the rapid growth of the urban population, lords and peasants alike began to produce for the market. The hiring of wage labourers became common. In the process, successful producers and traders accumulated significant amounts of capital. In short, Makovskii claimed that, by the middle of the sixteenth century, Muscovy had moved well along the same path of economic and social development as the countries of Western Europe. All this changed, however, in the last decades of the century. Ivan IV's reign of terror (the *oprichnina*) and the accompanying policy of expanding the politically expedient, but economically disastrous pomeste system of conditional noble landholding deflected Russia from its natural course of development. The government's fatal intervention turned Muscovy towards a backward command economy and serfdom.[87]

Other scholars present more limited and nuanced pictures of the same broad trends. In particular, in his work on society and government in the northernmost parts of the country in the sixteenth century, N. E. Nosov carefully chronicled the rise of dynasties of wealthy peasants who made fortunes by investing in the manufacture and trading of salt. These families soon distanced themselves from their less resourceful neighbours and, through their success in business, assumed the leadership of local society.[88]

While many of Makovskii's theses arouse violent controversy, we may safely conclude that, in the early and middle decades of the sixteenth century, Muscovy enjoyed a time of economic expansion and prosperity. The impressive building projects of the period and a lively foreign trade testify to this. At the same time, it is important to remember that the territories which made up the Muscovite state were by no means uniform. As Nosov convincingly showed, the far north thrived – a development further stimulated by the opening of trade with England via the northern Dvina and the White Sea. The extent to which the same can be said of other regions of the country, however, is another matter. Moreover, we must keep in mind that the Muscovite economy as a whole remained overwhelmingly rural and that most of the tsar's subjects had very limited, if any, contact with the market. As Makovskii himself admits, the government and the large landlords, above all, the monasteries, were the most active builders and traders.

Finally, as we shall see, the Muscovite economy underwent a series of severe crises at the end of the sixteenth century, beginning late in the reign of Ivan IV. The 'terrible' tsar must bear some responsibility for the rising tide of misery: his government raised taxes and other demands on the population, and his notorious purges seriously disrupted life in the regions which they attacked. His regime, however, cannot be blamed for the disastrous weather conditions and epidemic disease which contributed to the collapse of the economy.

One obvious measure of the vigour of medieval Russia's economy is the size and structure of her cities and towns, the central focal points of international trade and primary beneficiaries of the sixteenth-century boom. In all likelihood, the urban population of the Russian lands was small: long afterwards, in the late eighteenth century, it did not exceed 3 or 4 per cent of the total population.[89] Moreover, for so vast an area, the number of cities and towns was not large. Admittedly, defining the concepts 'town' or 'city' in a medieval Russian context presents difficulties. If, however, we accept A. M. Sakharov's sensible judgement that, to be a town, a place has to have both administrative functions and some artisan population, we must also agree with his conclusion that, from the Mongol conquest to the end of the fifteenth century, the Russian lands had only about twenty-nine legitimate urban centres.[90] Had he continued his study into the sixteenth century, he would probably have found more.[91]

Medieval Russian towns performed a wide variety of functions. Early in their history, some served as the capitals of independent principalities. Then, as the rulers of Moscow extended their control over north-east Russia, these cities and others were transformed into regional centres of the royal administration. A considerable number of 'towns', however, particularly those close to the frontiers, were little more than military outposts.

Many Russian townsmen made their living as artisans. In their shops, they worked with metal, wood and leather, turned pots and wove cloth, producing a wide variety of goods, mostly practical items for everyday use – locks and keys, buckets, boots, combs and candles – all of which they manufactured for local consumption. In a world at war, some specialized in making chain mail, others cast cannon or hand-guns, while still others took part in the construction of the massive fortifications that dotted the Russian landscape. Some craftsmen filled the orders of patrons: founders cast bells and jewellers made icon and book covers for the church. Russian artisans had little contact with wider markets: their wares rarely figure in the country's exports and the staples of long-range internal trade were regional specialities from the countryside such as salt and fish.[92]

No Russian town bore much resemblance to the modern tourist's mental image of a medieval city, derived from places such as Siena or Rothenburg. To sixteenth-century Western Europeans as well, Moscow and other urban centres looked strange; as Richard Chancellor, the first official English visitor, put it, they were '. . . for beauty and fairness nothing comparable to ours . . .' because they were '. . . built out of order and with no handsomeness . . .'[93] The largest of them, Moscow and Novgorod, rivalled most contemporary European cities in population. What most impressed foreign travellers about them, however, was the enormous area which they covered. For, unlike European city dwellers, Russian townspeople often built their houses on large lots which also had space for outbuildings and sheds. In their yards, they gardened and raised livestock, in this way producing much of their own food.[94] Clearly, then, one reason why the peasants produced little for the market was the very limited demand for their surplus.

Other features of Russian urban life also surprised contemporary Western Europeans. With the exception of fortifications, the most important churches and a few boyars' palaces, all buildings were of wood. The typical small town had the following appearance. Probably located on the higher of the two banks of a river, it consisted of one or two plastered brick or stone churches and a jumble of log houses and sheds set in large yards. There was probably at least one large central market area where traders set up temporary booths. For protection, the town was surrounded by a log stockade with lookout towers and a few gates at which the authorities could control people's movement in and out. In larger communities, some artisans lived outside of the main fortifications. In particular, men whose crafts required a regular supply of water or worked with fire lived and plied their trade beside the river.

In certain respects, medieval Russian towns must have seemed dirty and disorderly even to men accustomed to the unsanitary conditions of contemporary European cities. Pigs and chickens wandered to and fro and manure and trash piled up, much to the delight of later archeologists. In spring and autumn, the towns, which had no cobblestone paving, became seas of mud like the countryside. In the larger Russian cities, however, the inhabitants came up with an ingenious solution – layers of logs laid across the main streets in place of paving stones. If one layer sank into the mud, another could quickly be built over it. In Novgorod, archaeologists have uncovered as many as twenty-five levels of log 'paving'.[95]

Historians' descriptions of the social structure of medieval Russian towns contain few surprises. Leaving aside the royal governor, his staff and household and the garrison, an oligarchy of merchants or former merchants stood at the top of society. Those united by a particular speciality – the Moscow merchants who traded with the Crimea, for example – sometimes formed their own corporations. In the capital, the structure of the merchant community evolved to the point, in the 1580s, at which, with the government's encouragement, a whole hierarchy of corporate bodies took shape. In descending order of prestige, these were the merchants (*gosti*), the *gost* hundred, and the woolen drapers' hundred (*sukonnaia sotnia*).[96]

Below them on the hierarchy were the artisans who apparently constituted the bulk of the urban population. Within their ranks there was undoubtedly great diversity of income and prestige. While men who practised the same craft probably felt a sense of mutual solidarity, medieval Russian artisans apparently did not organize themselves into guilds.

Many townsmen and women, especially in large cities like Moscow, did not fit any of these categories. The most powerful nobles and the wealthiest merchants had large numbers of retainers and domestic servants, most of whom were legally slaves. The clergy also formed a significant part of the urban population: early Russian towns had many churches and the largest of them supported several priests, deacons and other employees. Monasteries and convents were often located within or on the edge of urban centres. The church's role did not end there, however: ecclesiastical corporations owned a great deal of additional property on which its dependants carried on trade and artisan work. Yet, in keeping with the medieval notion that servants of God should enjoy a legal status completely distinct from that of the laity, these church people were exempt from many of the burdens of taxation which afflicted their competitors who did not share their legal privileges.

To complete the picture, let us look briefly at the two metropolitan centres of the Russian lands which dwarfed all others – Novgorod and Moscow. During the period under consideration, the two cities changed places: in 1300, Novgorod was by far the larger, but, by 1600, Moscow thoroughly overshadowed it. At the height of its development, Novgorod had a population of about 30,000 – a figure comparable to the size of all but the very largest centres anywhere in Europe.[97] The city is located on the flat and marshy banks of the Volkhov just above the point at which it flows out of Lake Ilmen. It apparently began as three separate villages spread along both banks of the river. In time they coalesced and the central citadel, the Detinets or Kremlin, was built on the highest point of the left bank. At the height of the city's development, the Kremlin functioned as its ecclesiastical and symbolic centre: behind its thick brick walls stood the Cathedral of St. Sophia, the official residence of the archbishop, and the bell tower which symbolized the republic's independence. The centres of the secular administration and business were located across the river, on the Trade Side. Two important enclaves – the court of the prince or his governor and the foreign merchants' quarter – were also situated there. A single wooden bridge connected Novgorod's two halves.

Outside of its central nuclei, Novgorod sprawled across an extensive area on both banks. The suburban districts, some of which have been the subject of imaginative archaeological research, provide us with our image of the medieval Russian town – log-covered streets meandering between log houses and outbuildings set on large lots. As the modern tourist can see, small parish churches of plastered brick dotted the city. In spite of its location near international borders, Novgorod was not heavily fortified: indeed, only in the late fourteenth century, were earthworks built around the whole city. On the approaches to the city loomed large monasteries—St George's, for example, guarded the point, south of the city, where Lake Ilmen empties into the Volkhov.[98]

In spite of some similarities, Moscow ultimately presents a quite different picture. First mentioned in 1147, Moscow grew outward from its core, a small wooden fort on a hill on the left bank of the Moskva river. From the beginning, as Wolfgang Knackstedt has recently emphasized, the city functioned primarily as an administrative centre for its princes and for the leaders of the Eastern Orthodox Church in Russia. Many of the earliest settlements around the central stockade existed to provide supplies for the courts of the prince and the metropolitan; others belonged to the warriors who served the ruler.

From the beginning, the Kremlin formed the core of the city. The prince and the metropolitan both resided within its walls. Several cathedrals and other churches occupied prominent positions in the complex. Over the course of time, the most prominent boyar clans received the right to build residences within the citadel – a particularly graphic sign of royal favour. In the first centuries of its existence, the Moscow Kremlin went through an almost continuous process of construction and renovation. In the late fourteenth century, glistening white stone walls replaced the log stockade, and stone and brick churches took the place of wooden ones.

The rising capital of north-east Russia quickly overflowed the boundaries of the Kremlin. The area immediately to the east, later known as the Kitai-Gorod, became the home of boyars, merchants and artisans. It became a major commercial centre: the city's most important market, Red Square, was once an open plot of ground beside the Kremlin wall, alternately dusty or muddy depending on the season, on which many traders and artisans peddled their wares. Moreover, scattered settlements appeared in all directions around the fringes of the central city. As the population of the centre became more dense, men whose business required a good deal of space – horse-traders, for example – moved their operations to these growing outlying areas. As in Novgorod, a number of monasteries and convents, some heavily fortified, stood on the approaches to the city.

Life in Moscow was a risky proposition. The entire city, built mostly of wood, had frequent and often catastrophic fires. Moreover, most of the city, like Novgorod, lay open to attack: in particular, the outer suburbs were not fortified until late in the sixteenth century.[99]

By that time, Moscow had become, by any standards, a major urban centre. While the frequently quoted statement that the city had 100,000 inhabitants is probably an exaggeration, it undoubtedly had a considerably larger population than any potential rival. Thanks to the building projects of its rulers, by 1600 the Kremlin looked much as it does today. Immediately to the east, the Kitai-Gorod had taken on many characteristics of a central city district, among them a relatively dense population, several administrative offices and a number of stone houses. In 1535, the government built a stone wall around it. The outer districts of the city – the so-called White and Earthen Cities – had a far less concentrated population and the semi-rural mixture of houses and gardens which we have seen elsewhere. Conditions of life in the district south of the Moskva were particularly difficult; for one thing, it was notorious for its mud.[100]

Moscow flourished, above all, as the capital of the late medieval monarchy that bore its name. Its rulers gathered the limited natural and human resources which we have catalogued and moulded them into a strong nation-state. How they did so is the theme of the following chapters.

REFERENCES AND NOTES

1. Lydolph, *Geography*, p. 4.
2. Goehrke, 'Die geographischen Gegebenheiten', p. 30.
3. Ibid., pp. 25–6.
4. Goehrke, 'Zur Problem von Bevölkerungsziffer', pp. 75-6, 83.
5. Shapiro *et al.*, *Agrarnaia istoriia. Vtoraia polovina XV v.*, pp. 321–2.
6. Goehrke, 'Zur Problem von Bevölkerungsziffer', p. 85; see also Slicher van Bath, *Agrarian History*, pp. 81–2.
7. For a good survey, see Goehrke, *Wüstungen*, pp. 63–78.
8. Halperin, *Russia and the Golden Horde*, pp. 75–80.
9. Fennell, *The Crisis of Medieval Russia*, pp. 86–90.
10. Alef, 'The crisis of the Muscovite aristocracy', pp. 37–8.
11. Compare Langer, 'The Black Death' with Smith, *Peasant Farming*, pp. 120–1.
12. Kopanev, 'Naselenie'.
13. Shapiro *et al.*, *Agrarnaia istoriia XVI veka*, pp. 294-9.
14. On this issue, compare Goehrke, *Wüstungen*, p. 163 with his 'Zur Problem von Bevölkerungsziffer'.
15. Smith, *Peasant Farming*, pp. 114, 122, 222–3.
16. Shapiro, *Problemy*, pp. 30–6.
17. Smith, *Peasant Farming*, p. 88; Slicher van Bath, *Agrarian History*, pp. 171–2.
18. Kochin, *Selskoe khoziaistvo*, pp. 129–43. For illustrations, see Smith, *Peasant Farming*, plates 4 and 5.
19. Smith, *Peasant Farming*, pp. 27–9.
20. Ibid., pp. 29–32; Confino, *Systèmes agraires*, pp. 29-37.
21. Shapiro, *Problemy*, pp, 26–30. For illustrations, see Smith, *Peasant Farming*, plates 1–3 and Kochin, *Selskoe khoziaistvo*, plates 1 and 2.
22. Shapiro, *Problemy*, pp. 57–61.
23. Ibid., pp. 65–7; Smith, *Peasant Farming*, pp. 86–7.
24. Slicher van Bath, *Agrarian History*, p. 172.
25. Rozhkov, *Selskoe khoziaistvo*, pp. 55–7.
26. Gorskii, *Ocherki*, pp. 69–70.
27. Smith, *Peasant Farming*, pp. 44–5.
28. Shapiro, *Problemy*, pp. 67–9.

29. Smith, *Peasant Farming*, p. 91.
30. Ibid., pp. 47–79; Smith and Christian, *Bread and Salt*, pp. 5–26.
31. Smith, *Peasant Farming*, p. 91.
32. Ibid., pp. 80–3.
33. Kopanev, *Krestianstvo*, pp. 220–3.
34. Smith, *Enserfment*, pp. 40–1.
35. Blum, *Lord and Peasant*, pp. 102–3.
36. Shapiro *et al.*, *Agrarnaia istoriia. Vtoraia polovina XV v.*, pp. 147–9; *Agrarnaia istoriia XVI veka*, pp. 286–9.
37. Hellie, *Enserfment*, pp. 81–7.
38. Gorskii, *Ocherki*, pp. 230–2.
39. Shapiro *et al.*, *Agrarnaia istoriia XVI veka*, p. 27.
40. Smith, *Peasant Farming*, pp. 223–6.
41. Shapiro *et al.*, *Agrarnaia istoriia XVI veka*, pp. 267–9.
42. Goehrke, *Wüstungen*, pp. 236–51, 260.
43. Alef, 'Erlöschen', pp. 70–4.
44. Individual instances of conditional landholding occurred as early as 1328 (Blum, *Lord and Peasant*, pp. 84–5; Rozhdestvenskii, *Sluzhiloe zemlevladenie*, pp. 41–4). I agree, however, with S. B. Veselovskii that the pomeste system – the royal government's systematic use of conditional land grants to support its warriors – began only at the very end of the 1400s (Veselovskii, *Feodalnoe zemlevladenie*, pp. 281–4).
45. Historians and philologists have proposed two possible derivations for the word 'boyar', suggesting that it may originally have meant either 'a warrior' or 'someone who has responsibility for something' (i.e. an official or administrator).
46. See Alef, 'Reflections'.
47. *Rude & Barbarous Kingdom*, pp. 176–86.
48. Rozhdestvenskii, *Sluzhiloe zemlevladenie*, pp. 297–8.
49. Crummey, 'Crown and Boiars', pp. 566–8.
50. Hellie, *Slavery*, pp. 467–9.
51. Alekseev, *Agrarnaia i sotsialnaia istoriia*, pp. 42–67.
52. Veselovskii, *Feodalnoe zemlevladenie*, pp. 165–202.
53. Ibid., pp. 309–13; Shapiro *et al.*, *Agrarnaia istoriia. Vtoraia polovina XV v.*, pp. 350–4; *Agrarnaia istoriia XVI veka*, pp. 280–5.
54. Alekseev, *Agrarnaia i sotsialnaia istoriia*, p. 64.
55. The word 'boyar' was, and is, sometimes used in a more general sense to mean 'magnate' or 'great noble'.
56. See Veselovskii, *Issledovaniia po istorii klassa sluzhilykh zemlevladeltsev*.
57. See Alef, 'Reflections' and 'Crisis'.
58. Shmidt, *Stanovlenie*, pp. 262–307; Kleimola, 'Status'; Crummey, 'Reflections'.
59. Rozhdestvenskii, *Sluzhiloe zemlevladenie*, pp. 148–223.
60. *Rude & Barbarous Kingdom*, p. 150; see also Alef, 'Reflections', pp. 83–91.
61. See Shields Kollmann, 'Kinship' and 'Boyar clan'.
62. See Crummey, *Aristocrats*, pp. 103–6.
63. Kleimola, 'Changing face'; see also Alef, 'Aristocratic politics,' pp. 80–1.
64. On court ceremonies, see Zabelin, *Domashnii byt*, pp. 367–435; see also Alef, 'Adoption' and Crummey, 'Court spectacles'.
65. *Ocherki russkoi kultury*, vol. 1, pp. 304–5.
66. Smith and Christian, *Bread and Salt*, pp. 100–5.
67. Shields Kollmann, 'Seclusion'.

68. Goehrke, 'Witwe'.
69. Sakharov, *Obrazovanie*, pp. 26–43; Cherepnin, *Obrazovanie*, pp. 149–452.
70. For a thorough discussion of salt production, see Smith and Christian, *Bread and Salt*, pp. 27–73.
71. See Cherepnin, *Obrazovanie*.
72. Martin, 'Land'.
73. Ibid., p. 415.
74. Cherepnin, *Obrazovanie*, pp. 398–401; see also Syroechkovskii, *Gosti-surozhane*.
75. Keenan, 'Muscovy and Kazan, 1445–1552', pp. 104–7.
76. Ibid., pp. 114–15.
77. See Martin, 'Uškujniki'.
78. Khoroshkevich, *Torgovlia*; see also Roublev, 'Tribute', pp. 58–9.
79. For a summary, see Birnbaum, *Lord Novgorod: Essays*, pp. 49–52.
80. Kazakova, *Russko-livonskie otnosheniia*, pp. 116–20, 261–337; Esper, 'Russia'.
81. Cherepnin, *Obrazovanie*, pp. 402–7.
82. Willan, *Early History*.
83. See Baron, 'Ivan' and 'Muscovy Company'.
84. *Rude & Barbarous Kingdom*, pp. 167–8; Baron, 'Ivan', pp. 576–83.
85. For a variety of opinions, see Lyashchenko, *History*, pp. 225–6; Bushkovitch, *Merchants*; and Baron, 'Ivan'.
86. Bushkovitch, *Merchants*, pp. 151–8, 166–7.
87. Makovskii, *Razvitie*. For a good summary of Makovskii's ideas, see Hellie, 'Foundations'.
88. Nosov, *Stanovlenie*, pp. 240–84.
89. Baron, 'Town', p. 118.
90. Sakharov, *Goroda*, p. 128. For a different view of medieval Russia's urban development, see Cherepnin, *Obrazovanie*, pp. 329–35.
91. See Tikhomirov, *Rossiia*.
92. *Ocherki russkoi kultury*, vol. 1, pp. 156–221; Sakharov, *Goroda*, pp. 130–59.
93. *Rude & Barbarous Kingdom*, p. 23.
94. See Thompson, *Novgorod*, Ch. 4.
95. *Ocherki russkoi kultury*, vol. 1, pp. 248–53.
96. Baron, 'Ivan', p. 584; Bushkovitch, *Merchants*, pp. 13–16.
97. Goehrke, 'Einwohnerzahl', pp. 44–5.
98. Tikhomirov, *Rossiia*, pp. 299–300. For a summary with helpful maps, Birnbaum, *Lord Novgorod: Essays*, pp. 55–69.
99. Knackstedt, *Moskau*.
100. Tikhomirov, *Rossiia*, pp. 66–84.

CHAPTER TWO

Moscow and its rivals, 1304–1380

In the fourteenth and fifteenth centuries, the princes of Moscow gathered the resources of the harsh lands of north-east Russia and used them to create a strong monarchy. The process by which they did so, however, was not as simple as some surveys of Russian history have suggested. There was nothing inevitable about Moscow's rise to pre-eminence. In the years between 1304 and 1380, the principality of Moscow was only one of a number of rival centres of power within the Russian lands. In the fourteenth century, the balance of these competing forces shifted continually. Only in the mid-1400s, did the scales tilt decisively to Moscow's side.

Moreover, in 1304, a single fact dominated the political life of north-east Russia: the area was a remote province of the Mongol Empire. The Mongols were the most powerful of the nomadic peoples who, from time immemorial, had used the ease of movement across the Eurasian plain to invade the grasslands of European Russia from inner Asia. Under the charismatic leadership of Chingis Khan, the warring tribes of Mongolia united and, within a single lifetime, created an empire which conquered the complex sedentary civilizations of China, Central Asia and Persia.

The Russians' first contact with the Mongols was mysterious and disturbing. The momentum of the conquest of Persia brought a Mongol raiding party into the steppes north of the Black Sea. There, on 31 May 1223, on the Kalka river, they soundly defeated some of the princes of southern Russia who attempted to stop their advance.

Worse was to come. In 1237, Batu, Chingis Khan's grandson, undertook a systematic campaign to extend the territory of the western part of his grandfather's empire. His troops conquered the Bulgar state on the Volga and, in the winter of 1237–38, turned on the Russian principalities. Mongol forces first captured and sacked Riazan, then, following the river valleys, destroyed the small town of Moscow on their way to their main goal, Vladimir, the capital city of north-east Russia. After several days of bitter resistance, Vladimir fell and suffered the devastation that the Mongols meted out to all who resisted them.[1] The southern Russian lands did not have long to wait. Batu's forces devastated Kiev late in 1240 and continued their advance through the south-west Russian principalities – Galicia and Volynia – into Poland and Hungary. By the end of the following year, Mongol detachments approached Vienna and all Europe seemed at their mercy. At that point, domestic problems within the empire suddenly put an end to their westward advance. Thereafter, the Mongols concentrated on consolidating their rule over the enormous territories which they had overrun.

The Russian accounts of the conquest eloquently convey its devastating impact, both material and psychological. The Mongol invaders killed or imprisoned thousands of Russians and looted cities and towns. The poems lamenting the catastrophe express a mood of profound grief and paralysing helplessness at the savagery and overwhelming might of the conquerers. The long-range demographic, economic and social consequences of the conquest are very difficult to assess, however. Clearly it was no brief but passing calamity, soon to be forgotten, for remnants of the invading army – in later times called Tatars – settled in the steppes of south-eastern Europe to rule or to raid the Russian lands.

The conquest presented the princes of Russia with a cruel political dilemma – whether to continue to resist the Mongols or to accept their suzerainty as inevitable and make the best of the situation. Two southern princes – Daniel of Galich and Michael of Chernigov – made dramatic, but ultimately futile, gestures of resistance. In the north, Alexander Nevskii chose the opposite path, collaboration with the conquerors.[2]

In the first decades after the conquest, the rulers of the Golden Horde, the westernmost subdivision of the Mongol Empire, created a simple, but effective, system of administration for the Russian lands. They made a few clear demands on their new subjects – unequivocal recognition of their overlordship, payment of taxes and, when required, provision of recruits. As an aid in governing, they kept census records of the population of many parts of the empire: the first Mongol census of the Russian lands mentioned in the sources took place in 1257. At the same time, the khans did not try to replace the ruling élite of Russian society. As a condition of keeping their thrones, however, the princes of Russia were required to swear loyalty to their Mongol suzerains and receive the khans' patent of approval, at first, on some occasions, at the Mongolian capital of Karakorum and later at the Horde's capital, Sarai, on the lower Volga.

For roughly the first century of their rule, the khans appointed their own officials, usually called *baskaki*, to take responsibility for their Russian domains. The sparse sources at our disposal do not spell out the details of the Mongol officials' duties with any clarity. Most probably, the baskaki had responsibility for enforcing obedience to the Horde and maintaining law and order. In addition, the khans of the Golden Horde periodically sent officials, probably tax farmers, into the main centres of Russia to collect their revenues.[3] On several occasions – in Novgorod in 1257 and in the towns of Suzdalia in 1262, for example – their appearance aroused the local population to revolt against their Mongol overlords.[4]

Paradoxically, the conquest strengthened some of the fundamental institutions of Russian society. When they invaded the Russian lands, the Mongols encountered a fragmented community, divided into a number of principalities ruled by members of a single dynasty – the house of Riurik. Despite being, in theory, kinsmen, the Russian princes engaged in frequent feuds, civil wars and vendettas against each other. Over the years, moreover, the rulers of the most important regional centres far from Kiev – particularly Galicia in the south-west and Suzdalia in the north-east – increasingly turned their attention away from the old capital and concentrated on strengthening the local foundations of their power. Even in a time of national disaster, however, the grand prince remained, at least theoretically, the first among the princes and symbolic leader of the community. Once established as overlords, the khans of the Golden Horde found it advantageous to support the ruling princes of Russia, as long as they remained loyal, and to act as arbiters when internecine disputes among them flared out of control. In particular, the Mongol rulers supported the claims of the grand princes, whose capital was now Vladimir, to primacy among Russia's rulers.[5] Moreover, as time passed, the Mongols increasingly left the maintenance of law and order and the collection of taxes within Russia to the local rulers themselves.

The hierarchy of the Eastern Orthodox Church in Russia likewise enjoyed the Mongols' protection. When they founded their empire, the Mongols adhered to their own animist traditions and treated the religions of the conquered peoples with respect. Thus, in the patent of 1261 and later grants, the khans of the Golden Horde exempted the church and its dependants from taxation and military service and guaranteed it undisturbed possession of its lands. In return, the leaders of the Russian Church recognized Mongol overlordship by agreeing to offer prayers for the Khans.[6]

As a result, in 1304, sixty-odd years after their devastating onslaught, the Mongols played an ambivalent role in the lives of the rulers and people of north-east Russia. Without doubt, the initial conquest was extremely destructive and small, more localized raids from the steppe remained an unpleasant fact of Russian life, particularly in times of political discord within the Golden Horde itself. In 1298, for example, Moscow and many other towns suffered devastation once again.[7] At the same time, the Mongols, in effect, lent support to two institutions that served as rallying points and sources of cohesion within the Russian community – the office of grand prince and the Eastern Orthodox Church.

In the fourteenth century, the princes of the Russian lands had to deal with yet another new force on the international scene – Lithuania. The Grand Duchy had appeared on the map of Europe in the mid-1200s in response to the advance of the German crusading orders of knights. Mindovg (Mindaugas), its first important ruler, united the Lithuanian tribes and extended his rule into the Slavic territory of Polotsk. From the beginning, Lithuania hung between East and West – between the Roman Catholic and Eastern Orthodox worlds, the German knights and the Golden Horde.

After an interregnum, Gedimin (Gediminas, 1316–41) resumed the work of construction. He extended his control over the territory of present-day Belorussia, lands with an East Slavic, Eastern Orthodox population that had once been part of the Kievan realm. Acquisition of this area had several consequences. Since the Mongols had once controlled it, the rulers of the Golden Horde looked at the rising power of Lithuania with a suspicious eye. Moreover, as the ruler of a large Slavic population, Gedimin inevitably became a powerful force in the political life of the principalities of north-east Russia. For example, he made matrimonial alliances with several of their rulers. Finally, although Gedimin was a pagan, he exercised strong influence in the affairs of the Eastern Orthodox Church because so many of his subjects were members. From the early 1300s, then, the Grand Duchy was a force to be reckoned with in the political and ecclesiastical affairs of the Russian lands.

A visitor to north-east Russia in 1304 could scarcely have imagined that, within two centuries, this remote corner of the Mongol empire would be transformed into a powerful nation-state. Still less could he have foreseen that Moscow would be its capital. The grand prince and the head of the Russian Orthodox Church, a refugee from ruined Kiev, both resided in Vladimir.

The city of Novgorod, far to the west, was the largest and most prosperous city in the Russian lands. Good fortune had saved it, in 1223, from the worst ravages of the Mongol invasion. In the long run, however, its leaders reluctantly recognized the sovereignty of the khan and saw that the people paid taxes to him.

Thus spared from destruction, Novgorod continued to thrive under Mongol rule. In the early fourteenth century, it had a population of about 22,000 – by far the largest in Russia.[8] Since the city was Russia's most important centre of trade and artisan production, the rulers of the Golden Horde were content to leave it in peace and prosperity as long as tax revenues flowed into their coffers. The city's wealth also attracted the greedy eyes of the princes of north-east Russia, eager to gain decisive influence over the city-republic and its resources.

The political structure of Novgorod had marked similarities to that of other city-states in medieval Europe. Oligarchical tendencies vied with democratic traditions and, ultimately, the former predominated. Historians of Russia have given the city's institutions intense scrutiny because they present a dramatic contrast to the powerful monarchy built by the princes of Moscow. Until recently, scholars tended to stress the democratic nature of the Novgorod polity, pointing to the important role of the *veche* or popular assembly in which all men might take part.[9] Contemporary Soviet writers – V. L. Ianin above all – paint a very different picture. An oligarchy of wealthy 'boyar' families, they argue, completely dominated the city's political life.

After Ianin's seminal study of the political leaders of Novgorod, historians have reached a consensus on the main lines of the city's political development. The nominal head of the secular administration was the prince, chosen, beginning early in the twelfth century, by the people of Novgorod themselves.

From earliest times, the prince served primarily as the city's military commander – its hired mercenary, as it were.

The veche elected the prince and expressed the will of the populace at large. This assembly had few of the features of a modern representative body: in Novgorod and other cities of medieval Russia, it met at irregular intervals and had no clearly defined structure or jurisdiction. Moreover, the city was divided into districts, each of which had its own assembly. Further, to complicate matters, a group of citizens with a grievance might well declare themselves a veche on the spur of the moment in order to legitimize some action that they intended to take. In spite of the veche's instability, it gave the assembled citizens of the whole city a decisive voice in time of war or domestic political crisis. The veche tradition, moreover, convinced Novgorod's people that they had the right to be consulted on issues of crucial importance in their lives.

In practice, elected officials, especially the *posadniki* or lords mayor, had decisive influence in Novgorod's day-to-day political life. As Ianin has shown, the posadniki came from a relatively small group of wealthy families. In the republic's early years, the prince and the mayors shared power. Over the course of time, however, the prince's prerogatives within the city's life were more and more narrowly restricted. In addition to his religious functions, the archbishop of Novgorod increasingly played the role of head of state, especially when factional feuds within the oligarchy neutralized the posadniki. A second official, the *tysiatskii*, also shared power with the prince and mayor. Originally a subordinate of the prince, the tysiatskii was elected, beginning at the end of the twelfth century, and served as commander of the citizen militia and judge of the commercial court. Gradually, Ianin argues, the ruling oligarchy took control of this office as well.

Just before 1300, a series of reforms consolidated the oligarchy's hold on Novgorod. The prince's powers within the local administration were further curtailed and those of the bishop rose correspondingly. In order to make the oligarchy's rule more stable and effective, its members formed the Council of Lords, an executive body of the republic, in which 'boyar' families of each of the city's districts were represented, usually by former posadniki. In addition, mayors began to hold office for only one year at a time.[10] When this reform did not put an end to destructive feuding within the oligarchy, the structure of government underwent further changes in the fourteenth and fifteenth centuries. Each district had its own posadnik, and increasingly these men functioned together as joint heads of state. Eventually, in 1423, the number of posadniki rose to twenty-four with the result that each prominent family had, in effect, its own representative at the helm of the republic at all times.[11]

The attempt to achieve stability failed. Until the last days of Novgorod's independence, factional feuds within the élite continued. Moreover, the masses of Novgorodians continued to claim the right to a political voice. To the end, stormy public assemblies and popular revolts punctuated the life of the republic.

Two other problems plagued the republic and ultimately doomed it to extinction. First and foremost, Novgorod lacked an effective army of its own. The city militia, the citizens in arms, were no match for mounted noble warriors who spent a lifetime on campaign. Thus, for its defence, the republic depended, in an emergency, on its nominal prince and the troops which he might bring with him. When the final confrontation came, late in the fifteenth century, Novgorod was helpless to fight the prince of Moscow and his army. Second, with rare exceptions, the lands of Novgorod's northern empire were unsuitable for agriculture. In lean years, the city could not feed itself from the surrounding countryside, and its people depended on grain imported from the more fertile areas of north-east Russia, the heartland of the Muscovite monarchy whose rulers could cut off the supply if they chose. Thus, in 1300, Novgorod was the largest and most vigorous city in Russia. Two centuries later, however, it was a conquered province of the Muscovite state.

In 1304, no one could have foreseen such an outcome. The principality of Moscow had first emerged as a significant political force in north-east Russia only recently, at the very end of the thirteenth century. Before long, however, its ambitious rulers were locked in a bitter struggle with the princes of Tver, another rapidly rising power, for leadership within the Russian lands.

In the first, and most dramatic phase of their conflict, the rulers of Moscow and Tver fought one another for the office of grand prince of Vladimir and recognition as primary protectors of the Eastern Orthodox Church. Why were these shadowy objectives worth dying for? Possession of the title of grand prince, after all, did not necessarily make a man an effective leader of the Russian community.

To understand the attractiveness of these objectives, we must keep in mind the ways in which political power could be exercised in fourteenth-century Russia. A prince and the warriors in his retinue ruled a scattered population of peasants by the simplest of means. Administration meant little more than enforcing obedience to the prince's will and collecting his taxes, sometimes by brute force. Other than the swords of his retinue, a prince had only the aura of his office to make men do his will. More than any other ruler, the grand prince of Vladimir had the right to command men's loyalties, for, by tradition, he was the supreme leader of the Russian lands. Even though, in 1304, the title did not give its holder any soldiers or revenues which he did not have already, men killed and died in order to possess it.

In such a world, the favour of the church's leaders could be an advantage of great significance. The Eastern Orthodox Church alone had an organizational structure that transcended the political divisions within the Russian lands and extensive diplomatic and cultural contacts outside of Russia in the rest of the 'Byzantine commonwealth'. It was, moreover, the primary source of the community's beliefs and moral aspirations, the source of censure or consolation.

In the struggle for leadership, the princes of the north-east fought for more tangible things as well – territory and money. In the early fourteenth century, the rulers of Moscow and Tver both founded their power on control of consolidated blocks of land which they took any opportunity to expand. Between 1301 and 1304, Daniel and Iurii of Moscow extended their control over the entire valley of the Moskva from Mozhaisk to Kolomna and annexed Pereiaslavl, thus increasing the size of their principality threefold.[12] Both rivals also aspired to increase their incomes, particularly by profiting from the collection of taxes for the Mongols. Control of Novgorod, the wealthiest of Russian cities, was the key to improving one's financial fortunes.

More than anything else, achieving leadership within the Russian lands depended on the favour of the khans of the Golden Horde. Without their patent, no grand prince or local prince could hold office. Moreover, calling in their armies could guarantee him victory over his rivals.

Did Moscow have any intrinsic advantages in the struggle with Tver for the leadership of north-east Russia? For more than 100 years historians have provided a long list of reasons why Moscow was destined to emerge victorious. In particular, many have argued that the city's geographical location was especially favourable. As a glance at a map makes clear, Moscow is located in the middle of a network of rivers. The Kremlin, its citadel, rises above the Moskva which flows into the Oka and on into the Volga. Many other rivers connected by short portages link the city with the upper Volga valley to the north-west, the Oka valley to the south and the Vladimir region to the east. Without question, Moscow was well situated to be a centre of trade and communications. It is much less clear to what extent men actually made use of these potential trade routes. Carsten Goehrke, for one, has suggested that trade routes ran through Moscow only after the city had achieved political hegemony for reasons unconnected with geography.[13]

In addition, many scholars have argued that, in a time of continuous military danger, Moscow's location offered a relatively secure haven. It lies in the zone of mixed forest, well north of the steppe, the centre of Mongol power. Dense forests and swamps protect it to the east and west. Moreover, the Mongol invasion and later raids caused far greater devastation in the Vladimir–Suzdal area than in the western parts of north-east Russia, including Moscow and Tver.[14] As a consequence, generations of scholars have suggested, the area around Moscow drew refugees from the two former centres of Russian political life – Kiev in the south and Vladimir. Once again, however, we have entered the realm of speculation since we have very little hard evidence about the distribution and movement of Russia's population before the sixteenth century.

Undoubtedly Moscow had a promising location, but so did its rival, Tver. The latter, now called Kalinin, occupies a commanding position on the upper Volga river on the route that connected Novgorod with north-east Russia and the Golden Horde. Tver lacked Moscow's natural defences, but was situated considerably further away from Russia's southern and eastern frontiers. It was therefore a particularly attractive goal for refugees from less secure regions.[15] On balance, then, both cities had favourable geographical settings.

Why, then, was it the princes of Moscow who became the leaders of Russia? There is no simple answer. To attack the question, we must examine the confused ebb and flow of Russian politics in the fourteenth and fifteenth centuries, paying particular attention to the Moscow princes' relations with the rulers of the Golden Horde, the leaders of the Eastern Orthodox Church, the rulers of other Russian principalities and their own subjects.

We must also take into consideration the political style and personal qualities of the princes of Moscow. In a world without highly developed institutions, political leaders exercised power through personal relationships. In Russia, the power and prestige of the grand princes varied with the men who bore the title.

In his course of lectures, V. O. Kliuchevskii, the great historian of the late nineteenth century, argued that Moscow rose to pre-eminence within Russia, in part, because its princes had a low standing within the Riurikovich dynasty. In one respect, the princes of Tver, also comparative upstarts, stood still lower on the family tree. Far more important in the eyes of contemporaries, however, was the fact that the founder of the Moscow line of the dynasty, Daniel, died in 1303 before inheriting the office of grand prince, thus, by tradition, disqualifying his descendants from the succession for ever. His heirs, therefore, had no stake in the traditional order of succession to the grand princely throne. They were therefore willing to try radical new methods to increase their power and defeat their rivals.[16]

The most striking evidence of the Moscow princes' political dexterity was their remarkable ability to manipulate the rulers of the Golden Horde. Time and again, as we shall see, they somehow convinced the khans and their advisers to invest them with the title of grand prince and support them against the other princes of Russia.

The early princes of Moscow are shadowy men. Kliuchevskii, a lecturer renowned for his verbal portraits of historical figures, remarked, 'All princes of Moscow up to Ivan III were as similar as two drops of water so that the observer sometimes has trouble deciding which of them was Ivan and which Vasilii'.[17] He then went on to describe them collectively as cautious, calculating, petty men with no soaring visions and no morally edifying qualities. There is some truth to his observations. The sources give us very little direct evidence of the personal features or ideals of Moscow's rulers. Moreover, their actions – and those of their rivals – suggest that they were all, to some extent, greedy and ruthless men. A world of incessant warfare and political intrigue required such unpleasant qualities for survival.

Ultimately, however, Kliuchevskii was mistaken. The actions of Moscow's most important rulers reveal men of very different personalities and individual political styles. Ivan I, 'the Moneybag', for example, had almost nothing in common with Dmitrii Donskoi. Moreover, although perhaps uninspiring as individuals, Moscow's rulers, as a family, achieved a remarkable feat: over the course of two centuries they made themselves lords of north-east Russia and their capital the centre of a strong nation-state.

The struggle between the two upstart rivals, Moscow and Tver, began in

36

1304 on the death of Grand Prince Andrew. Michael of Tver and Iurii of Moscow both claimed his throne. At first, Michael (1304–18) appeared to hold all of the cards. Within the Russian lands, the great nobles of the grand prince's court and the leaders of the church supported his candidacy.[18] More important still, the khan granted him the patent to the throne.

From the beginning of his reign, however, Michael antagonized influential forces within Russia. For reasons that are not clear, the leaders of Novgorod, whose economic resources and political support he needed, consistently objected to his leadership. The city reluctantly recognized his suzerainty only in 1307 and later rebelled against him on several occasions. Each time, Michael had no choice but to use his troops from Tver to subdue it and once, when military intervention failed, he had to cut off the city's supply of grain from the east in order to starve its people into submission.

Iurii of Moscow likewise never acquiesced in his victory. Early in Michael's reign, he prevented the grand prince from taking Pereiaslavl which was traditionally a possession of the reigning grand prince. Moreover, Iurii eagerly fished in Novgorod's troubled waters. He encouraged the city's resistance to Michael, on one occasion sending agents to help its leaders organize their defences. For their part, the Novgorodians encouraged Iurii to intervene as a useful counterweight to the grand prince's pretensions.

Michael made a particularly serious blunder when he alienated Metropolitan Peter, the new head of the Russian Orthodox Church. When the office of metropolitan became vacant in 1305, the patriarch of Constantinople rejected Michael's hand-picked candidate and instead selected Peter, the abbot of a monastery in Galich in south-west Russia. From the patriarch's point of view, the appointment made very good sense, for in addition to Peter's strong personal qualifications, the choice headed off an attempt by the ruler of Galicia to set up a separate ecclesiastical hierarchy. Under Peter's leadership, the Eastern Orthodox Church would remain united throughout the Russian lands.[19]

Frustrated by the choice of Peter, Michael and the leaders of the church in Tver foolishly did everything in their power to express their resentment. At the climax of a succession of indignities, the new metropolitan even had to defend himself before an ecclesiastical council that met in Pereiaslavl in 1310 or 1311. The precise nature of the charges against Peter is not clear: it may well have been simony, a label that covered a wide variety of administrative sins.

In the end, Peter retained his throne and, after his embittering experiences, the metropolitan was no friend of the house of Tver. In his fight for survival, he received support, not only from the patriarch, but also, in all probability, from Iurii of Moscow. As head of the church, Peter played an independent role in Russian political life, on occasion directly thwarting Michael's policies. The stage was set for an alliance with the house of Moscow.

Finally, and fatally, Michael lost the confidence of the khan, the key to power in Russia. In 1312, Uzbek, the first Moslem ruler of the Horde, ascended the throne. At first, the new khan recognized the prince of Tver as grand prince. Within a few years, however, Uzbek threw his support to Iurii after the prince of Moscow paid an extended visit to his court in Sarai. In 1317, Iurii returned to north-east Russia in triumph with Uzbek's patent as grand prince of Vladimir, a new wife – Konchaka, the khan's sister – two Mongol officials, and a Tatar army. Shocked by this sudden turn of fortune, Michael agreed to give up the grand princely title, presumably as a temporary measure. When Iurii attempted to press his advantage by attacking Tver in alliance with Novgorod, however, Michael was equal to the challenge. His army crushingly defeated his enemies.

Ironically, victory in the field caused more problems than it solved. First of all, recognizing that no Russian prince was strong enough to resist the Horde for any length of time, he agreed not to reclaim the title of grand prince without the khan's approval. In a treaty that Michael concluded with Novgorod at about this time, he referred to himself merely as 'prince' and to Iurii as 'Grand Prince'.[20] Secondly, in the battle, Michael's army took a number of prominent prisoners, including Iurii's wife, Konchaka. To the victor's great embarrassment, she died mysteriously while in captivity. Michael's enemies suspected poison. Finally, from the khan's perspective, the victory proved that Michael was dangerous because he commanded the most powerful military force within north-east Russia.[21]

Ultimately the fate of the contending Russian princes lay in the hands of Khan Uzbek. In 1318, Iurii and Michael went to Sarai for judgement. By the time Michael reached the khan's court, his enemies had prepared a case against him. Although he protested his innocence, he was condemned to death for withholding tribute payments, resisting the khan's authority and murdering his sister. The chronicles of Tver movingly described his execution as martyrdom.[22]

Against all odds, Iurii of Moscow had emerged victorious. Although losing on all other fronts, he had won the support of the Golden Horde. How he did so is not clear. His contemporaries and later writers suspected that he bribed the khan's officials lavishly. Perhaps, more than his rival, he had the social graces and diplomatic skill needed to win admiration and support at the court of a Tatar khan. Surely Iurii succeeded in convincing Khan Uzbek that he would be a particularly loyal agent within the Russian principalities. From Uzbek's point of view, moreover, the prince of Moscow was the ideal instrument in pursuing a strategy of 'divide and rule' precisely because he was weaker and more dependent than the ruler of Tver.

Iurii's brief reign (1318–22) was a time of great confusion. As grand prince, Iurii attempted to increase his power by taking responsibility for the collection and delivery of the tribute payments to the Horde from all of the principalities of north-east Russia. In 1321, this policy brought him into conflict with Dmitrii, Michael's successor on the throne of Tver. Dmitrii opposed Iurii's pretensions and defended his right, as prince of Tver, to maintain direct relations with the khan.[23] Raising an army from his own domains and the territories to the east, Iurii advanced on Tver and forced Dmitrii to promise not to claim the grand princely throne and to hand over his people's share of the Mongol tribute.

Just when Iurii seemed secure, he made a fatal mistake. Instead of proceeding to Sarai with the khan's tax receipts, he went to Novgorod where he led the defence of the republic in a war with Sweden. By doing so, he forfeited the khan's trust. His rival, Dmitrii went to Sarai, probably with details of Iurii's misconduct, and emerged with the patent to the grand princely throne. Iurii quickly realized the danger of his position. In response to a summons from the khan, he set out for the Horde with his treasury, but, Dmitrii's younger brother, Alexander, thwarted his mission by ambushing his party and stealing the money.

Finally, in 1325, Iurii went to Sarai to face the consequences of his insubordination. Retribution came from an unexpected quarter; taking the law into his own hands, Dmitrii murdered him in revenge for his father's execution. That rash act also destroyed Dmitrii. After a delay of nearly a year, Khan Uzbek ordered his execution.

The thrones of Moscow and Tver passed to the deceased rulers' younger brothers, Ivan and Alexander. In spite of Ivan's persistent attempts to curry favour with the khan, Alexander initially won recognition as grand prince. Why Uzbek gave Alexander the throne is hard to determine. Probably Iurii's betrayal of the Horde's interests still rankled.

Disaster soon befell Tver. In 1327, Khan Uzbek sent his cousin Chol-Khan to occupy the city with a Tatar force. According to Russian chroniclers, Chol-Khan intended to make himself ruler of the principality and to destroy the Christian faith. Whatever their intentions, he and his men settled into Prince Alexander's residence and began to mistreat the local population in order to provoke a revolt. When they complained to him, Alexander advised his subjects not to offer resistance. Eventually, however, Chol-Khan and his men persecuted the Tverians beyond endurance. A spontaneous revolt broke out and the citizens lynched any Tatars they could find.

Vengeance followed swiftly. With the khan's blessing, Ivan of Moscow led a punitive expedition which sacked the city and a number of lesser towns and forced Alexander to flee into exile in Pskov.[24] From there, the prince of Tver fought valiantly to regain his lost throne. After years of effort, he finally succeeded, in 1338, in winning the khan's patent to rule his homeland. Only a year later, however, Alexander was abruptly summoned to the Horde and executed.[25] Moscow's triumph was complete.

The Tver revolt of 1327 and its aftermath dramatically changed the alignment of political and military forces within north-east Russia. At a single stroke, Tver was ruined and its princes lost their claim to the office of grand prince of Vladimir. The khan, the real ruler of north-east Russia, threw his support to the princes of Moscow, seeing them as the Horde's most reliable agents in the Russian lands.

Ivan I, the 'Moneybag', of Moscow (1331–40) made the best of his opportunities. Muscovite sources of later times give him credit for remarkable achievements. In the words of the Trinity Chronicle.

When Grand Prince Ivan Danilovich sat on the grand princely throne of all Russia, there was great peace for forty years; the pagans ceased to fight against the Russian land and kill Christians; the Christians found rest and relief from great oppression, the many burdens and from Tatar violence, and there was great peace in all the land.[26]

Fourteenth-century reality was not so tranquil. Nevertheless, using very limited resources, Ivan strengthened Moscow's claim to pre-eminence among the principalities of the north-east.

To generations of historians, Ivan I has been the epitome of the early rulers of Moscow. His actions reveal him as a crafty and ruthless opportunist, an ambitious and grasping landowner and tax-collector. In his career, we see little of the visionary and absolutely no signs of a chivalrous crusader. He pursued limited goals by devious means. Yet his unattractive personal qualities equipped him well for the political struggles of his day.

The greatest of Ivan's victories came even before he became grand prince. In 1325, after years of cooperation with the house of Moscow, Metropolitan Peter moved his residence to Ivan's capital and prepared a tomb for himself in the new stone Church of the Dormition. Peter's acts had lasting significance. From that time on, Moscow was the residence of the head of the Russian Orthodox hierarchy and its princes played the role of primary protectors of the church. Moreover, in 1339, Peter's successor, Theognostus, canonized him. Moscow became a pilgrimage centre and even Peter's patron, the unscrupulous Ivan I, acquired an aura of sanctity in the eyes of later generations!

The metropolitans' alliance with Moscow offered benefits to both sides. The leaders of the Russian Church struggled repeatedly to preserve the unity of the hierarchy in the face of the attempts of the rulers of Lithuania to set up a separate metropolitanate in their own domains. The princes of Moscow had every reason to support them. For their part, the metropolitans usually backed Moscow's claims to unify and lead their Russian flock, reasoning 'that Moscow's policy of appeasing the Mongols and winning the khan's support by being loyal to him coincided much better with the interests of the Church and the Byzantine Commonwealth' than the alternatives.[27] For example, Theognostus was a Greek by nationality and not Ivan's nominee for the metropolitan throne. Once in office, however, he supported Ivan's political efforts. In 1328, he excommunicated Alexander of Tver and the people of Pskov who had given him asylum.

During his reign, Ivan I also established that the princes of Moscow had first claim on the grand princely throne. With the benefit of hindsight, we can see that, after him, his heirs retained the title and office almost without interruption. At the same time, Ivan did not receive the prize without a struggle. After the defeat of Tver, the khan apparently decided to keep the grand prince weak by setting up, in its place, another rival to Moscow. He accordingly divided the office between two claimants, Ivan I and Alexander of Suzdal, a serious contender for the office since he ruled a relatively large principality and was a direct descendant of an earlier grand prince. The prince of Moscow won recognition as ruler of Novgorod and some of the other territories that traditionally accompanied the title. Only when Alexander died in 1331, however, did Ivan become sole grand prince.

Winning the throne was only the first step to power. As Presniakov observed, the central fact of Russian political life in the early fourteenth century was the grand princes' struggle to exert real leadership and exercise effective authority with resources that were inadequate for the task.[28] Ivan struggled hard to make his authority felt throughout north-east Russia, but, in the end, achieved only limited success. For example, taking advantage of the rising power of Lithuania to the west, the leaders of Novgorod and Pskov ignored the grand prince's wishes on many occasions. Closer to home, Ivan was more successful. When he and the khan attempted to capture Smolensk in 1339, he was able to gather troops from most principalities of north-east Russia; only two local princes – the rulers of Iaroslavl and Beloozero – seem to have opposed him. Moreover, he convinced a number of leading nobles of other principalities, especially Tver, to transfer their allegiance to him.[29]

Ivan's throne ultimately rested on the support of the khan of the Golden Horde. Beginning in his older brother's reign, he spent a great deal of time in Sarai and, over the years, convinced Uzbek that he could be trusted to carry out Tatar policy within Russia. In addition to his energetic collaboration in the expeditions against Tver and Smolensk, he proved, as his nickname suggests, to be a ruthlessly efficient collector of the tribute that Russia paid to the Horde. In return for his services, the Khan gave him an important favour. In 1339, Ivan paid a visit to Sarai and took along his sons and a copy of his will. By affixing his seal to the document, the khan indicated his approval of the contents, above all, the succession of Ivan's son, Simeon, to the grand princely throne.[30]

After 1331, the princes of Moscow held the office of grand prince almost uninterruptedly. Yet, as Ivan discovered, the office of grand prince of Vladimir had limited meaning until the princes who held it gathered the resources needed to give it substance. In order to protect and extend his achievements, his successors had to fight on several fronts. To retain and strengthen the grand princely office, the rulers of Moscow had to maintain good relations with the khans and cope with the growing power of Lithuania. Close ties with the leaders of the church were also a prerequisite for success in the political arena. In addition, the occupants of the grand princely throne faced a continuous battle for the respect of the leaders of the city-republics of Novgorod and Pskov. In moments of crisis, moreover, the house of Moscow could be sure that the rulers of the other important principalities of north-east Russia would challenge their claim to leadership. Finally, within the Moscow principality itself, the ruling prince had to make his authority over his kinsmen and subjects more effective. Unless Ivan's successors successfully carried out these tasks, the gains which he had made might easily slip away.

The first of Ivan's successors, Simeon the Proud (1340–53), appeared to be equal to the challenge. He followed the same policies as Ivan I, but did so in his own manner; for, while Simeon remains rather shadowy, his actions suggest a man of more decisive temperament than his father. He seems to have taken dramatic military and diplomatic measures more often and relied less on court intrigue and financial machinations than his predecessor.

In alliance with the Golden Horde, Simeon responded energetically to the eastward thrust of the Grand Duchy of Lithuania. In 1352, for example, he marched into the territory of Smolensk, a pivotal border principality directly to the west of Moscow, and forced its leaders to recognize his suzerainty. Moreover, in contrast to Ivan I, Simeon was conspicuously successful in forcing the leaders of Novgorod to bow to his will. Even before the city recognized him as its prince, he sent a governor into Torzhok, Novgorod's main outpost near Tver. At first, the republic attempted to resist by sending an army to defend the town. Before long, Simeon confronted the Novgorodians with an overwhelming combination of forces: he came to Torzhok accompanied by Metropolitan Theognostus and almost all of the princes of north-east Russia with their armies. Novgorod had no choice but to make a treaty with the grand prince, recognizing him as its prince with all of the rights that traditionally accompanied that position and granting him additional tax revenues from some of its districts.

Unfortunately for the house of Moscow, Simeon encountered an enemy which no prince could defeat – the Black Death which devastated the Russian lands in 1352 and 1353. Shortly before he died from the plague, the grand prince, in his will, poignantly expressed his sense of desperation, 'And lo, I write this to you so that the memory of our parents and of us may not die, and so that the candle may not go out.'[31] The threat that the entire ruling house of Moscow might die out was very real. Before the plague had run its course, Simeon, both of his sons, one of his two brothers and Metropolitan Theognostus all died.

The Black Death reached Russia from the west. As in Western Europe, the disease struck hard at the urban areas, beginning with Pskov and Novgorod. From there, it spread throughout the Russian lands, so that, for example, according to a later chronicle account, the entire population of Beloozero, far to the north of Moscow, died of its ravages. Moscow itself suffered heavy losses. After the first attack, moreover, the Black Death returned to Russia in 1364–66, this time from the east, and recurred thereafter at intervals of roughly twenty years until 1425, the time of the last serious nation-wide outbreak. Although we have regrettably little hard information about the plague's impact on the Russian lands, the death rate was probably about the same as in Western Europe – approximately one-third of the total population.[32]

Given the paucity of the sources, most historians of Russia have understandably refused to speculate on the economic, social and political consequences of the Black Death. Recent studies, however, have advanced a number of interesting suggestions. Long ago, historians observed that the house of Moscow prospered, in part, because it produced relatively few heirs to subdivide the family lands and political authority. The Black Death helped to prune the family tree. By analogy, Gustave Alef argues that the great noble families of north-east Russia likewise suffered devastating losses in the recurrent epidemics and thus, in many cases, delayed their impoverishment through the subdivision of their lands until well into the fifteenth century. By that time, the grand princes of Moscow had become so powerful that they could exploit the great nobles' weaknesses and easily transform them into servitors.[33]

Looking at the problem from a different vantage point, Lawrence Langer points out that, after the plague, Russian cities suffered from a scarcity of labour. At the same time, the rural population – probably less severely devastated than that of the cities – provided replacements, either free labourers or slaves. Moreover, he argues, Russians like other Europeans expressed their anxiety about the future in acts of religious devotion. The Black Death added fuel to the fire of religious renewal, centred in the monasteries, that had begun before the catastrophe.[34]

In many respects, after the Black Death, political and social life in the Russian lands continued much as before. For Moscow, however, the death of Simeon had nearly disastrous consequences. Ivan II (1353–59), his only surviving brother, followed him as ruler of Moscow and successfully claimed the grand princely throne. Even before his accession, Ivan had displayed calamitous lassitude. As ruler, his ineptness as a military and political leader fully justified his nickname 'the Meek'. In his capacity as grand prince, he offered no resistance when, in 1356, Grand Duke Olgerd (Algirdas) of Lithuania attacked Smolensk and Briansk and captured Rzheva and Belaia. He could not even defend the ancestral possessions of his family: Oleg, the ambitious young ruler of Riazan, seized the district of Lopasnia on the Oka, long a possession of Moscow.

In 1357, this sorry state of affairs came to an end. The change probably resulted from the murder of one regent for the inept Ivan – A. P. Khvost – and the return to Moscow of his successor, the new head of the Russian Orthodox hierarchy, Metropolitan Alexis. On the morning of 3 February 1357, passers-by found Khvost's body in a square. Khvost, the most powerful man at the court of Ivan II, had long played an important and sometimes destructive role in Muscovite politics: Simeon's treaty with his brothers explicitly mentions him as the instigator of quarrels between them, possibly on the side of the future Ivan II. At the time of his death, he held the office of tysiatskii or commander of the militia, a position to which he had apparently been appointed early in Ivan's reign. Many of the circumstances surrounding Khvost's death remain mysterious to this day. One thing seems clear: a conspiracy of rival boyars, probably led by the Veliaminov clan, whose leaders subsequently fled into exile in Riazan, destroyed him because he had concentrated so much power in his own hands.[35]

Alexis stepped into the breach. As metropolitan, he held an office of great power and dignity, above the factional feuds of the court. At the same time, he had deep roots in Moscow's upper class. His father, Fedor Biakont, had entered the service of Prince Daniel and he and his brothers led one of the most prominent boyar clans at court. From the time of his return to Moscow, he seems to have assumed the role of regent. Moreover, it may well have been Alexis who arranged the reconciliation between Ivan and the fugitive boyars that restored harmony to the court and administration. In any case, after 1357, the government of Ivan II began to act more energetically than before. In the following year, for example, its troops recaptured Rzheva from the Lithuanians.

The restoration of stability and confidence came just in time. In 1359 Ivan II died, leaving, as heir, his nine-year-old son, Dmitrii. As contemporaries could clearly see, Metropolitan Alexis became, in effect, ruler of the Moscow principality as well as head of the church. In both of these capacities, he displayed great energy and determination. His intense Muscovite patriotism, however, sometimes blinded him to the needs of the whole Russian Orthodox community and he was not above using ecclesiastical weapons to gain political ends.

Over the course of his reign, Alexis's protégé, Dmitrii Donskoi (1359–89), made important strides towards achieving the goals of the house of Moscow. As ruler of the family principality, he greatly expanded the territory under his control and strengthened his rule over his domains. Moreover, he gave the house of Moscow a far more secure hold than before on the office of grand prince. In that capacity, he successfully asserted his military leadership of north-east Russia and won brilliant victories over the Tatars.

Who was responsible for these triumphs – Alexis or Dmitrii? Alexis undoubtedly made a major contribution. Dmitrii's character is harder to fathom. Unlike several of his predecessors, he was a dashing warrior. At the same time, he could act with greed and duplicity worthy of Ivan I. Moreover, off the battlefield, he seems to have been indecisive: his policy in many areas appears to be unclear or inconsistent.

In the first years after Dmitrii's accession, Alexis had to deal with a world in flux. For more than a century, the Golden Horde had provided an element of coherence in Russian political life. In 1359, however, the murder of Khan Berdi-Beg set off the 'Great Trouble', a long period of turmoil within the Horde. In Sarai itself, repeated coups installed one short-lived khan after another. Moreover, in the early 1360s, an energetic warlord, Mamai, established his own horde in the steppe to the west of the Volga. Since he was not of the royal blood of Chingis Khan, he could not rule in his own name, but had to exercise his authority through a succession of puppet khans. Thus, the princes of Russia had to deal with two competing centres of authority within the Tatar world, both of them unstable. On many occasions this new state of affairs created great confusion within Russia: competing khans sometimes gave patents to the grand princely throne to two rival claimants simultaneously. At the same time, it allowed the Russian princes to set their own policies and fight their own battles with only occasional interference from the Horde.

On the western front, the situation was more predictable. Under Grand Duke Olgerd, Lithuania continued to extend its control over the Russian lands. In the 1360s and 1370s, Olgerd reached into the Chernigov region, south-west of Moscow, establishing principalities for some of his sons and making the native Russian rulers of the area accept his suzerainty. Further east, the Grand Duchy traditionally kept a close watch on affairs in Novgorod and Pskov and, since the time of Prince Alexander, had dynastic connections with the ruling house of Tver.

Within the Russian lands, the balance of political forces shifted in the middle decades of the fourteenth century. Beset by civil war, Tver slipped into temporary eclipse while, in 1348, the leaders of Pskov declared their city independent from Novgorod. In north-east Russia, a new contender for leadership emerged – the principality of Suzdal–Nizhnii-Novgorod, directly east of Moscow. On Ivan I's death, Prince Constantine of Suzdal – younger brother of the Prince Alexander who had shared the grand princely office with Ivan – challenged Simeon the Proud for the throne. In 1341, moreover, during an interregnum in the Horde, Constantine had seized Gorodets and Nizhnii-Novgorod, a thriving trading city at the confluence of the Volga and Oka rivers, which he made his capital. When a new khan, Jani-Beg, emerged from the struggle for power, he ignored the protests of Grand Prince Simeon and allowed Constantine to keep his new territories. The principality of Nizhnii-Novgorod thus became a serious rival to Moscow's position of leadership.

Twice the princes of Nizhnii-Novgorod claimed the grand princely throne on the death of the incumbent. Constantine tried to block the accession of Ivan II and his son, Dmitrii, renewed the claim when Ivan died. Metropolitan Alexis, in effect regent for Prince Dmitrii of Moscow, was equal to the task. After an initial round of negotiations, the current khan in Sarai, Murid, recognized Dmitrii of Moscow as grand prince in 1362. To strengthen its hand further, the government of Moscow approached Mamai's puppet, Khan Abdullah, and received his sanction as well. This sensible step proved costly, however, for Murid, in retaliation, withdrew his patent and recognized Dmitrii of Nizhnii-Novgorod as grand prince. Before long, however, the latter found prudence the better part of valour. After a show of force by the Muscovite army, the ruler of Nizhnii-Novgorod abandoned his claim to be grand prince and, in 1364, made an alliance with his namesake in Moscow. To seal the bargain, he arranged, two years later, for Dmitrii Donskoi to marry his daughter. His large and strategic principality virtually became Moscow's satellite.

Before long, Dmitrii's government faced a still more serious threat to its position of leadership within north-east Russia – a revived Tver led by Prince Alexander's energetic son, Michael. In the late 1360s and early 1370s, Michael mounted a direct challenge to Moscow's pre-eminence. He had formidable assets, above all the diplomatic and military support of Olgerd of Lithuania, his brother-in-law. At the same time, the alliance had its drawbacks: Olgerd's intervention made Michael appear to be the agent of a foreign power and one increasingly drawn to Roman Catholic Europe. In addition, a challenger to Moscow's supremacy could turn to one of the competing governments within the Golden Horde for recognition as grand prince. This weapon too was double-edged. As Dmitrii of Moscow had already discovered, khans could take away their support as quickly as they gave it.

On the surface, Moscow appeared to be far better prepared for the struggle. In particular, the principality of Tver was divided into bitterly hostile appanages. By comparison, Moscow was a haven of peace. Dmitrii's only male relative, Vladimir Andreevich of Serpukhov, cooperated with him and consistently fought with great valour in Moscow's cause.

Paradoxically, Moscow's very strength and aggressiveness helped to provoke the crisis. Under the year 1367, a Tver chronicler made the following entry: 'In the same year Grand Prince Dmitrii walled up the city of Moscow with stones, and began to accomplish many things; he brought all the Russian princes to do his will, and those who did not submit he began to afflict, among them Prince Michael of Tver, and for this cause Prince Michael withdrew to Lithuania'.[36]

Alexis and Dmitrii had many cudgels with which to beat their enemies. Alexis intervened in the continuing struggle between the branches of the ruling family of Tver, supporting the lesser princes in their opposition to Michael. When the ruler of Tver successfully countered that tactic, Alexis took even stronger measures. In 1368, exploiting the aura of his office as metropolitan, he and Dmitrii summoned Michael and his boyars to Moscow. There they took their guests prisoner, keeping them under guard until pressure from the Golden Horde forced their release.

Full-scale war between the rivals quickly followed. In 1368, both sides mobilized and, when Muscovite forces invaded Tver, Michael called in a Lithuanian army which quickly counter-attacked and advanced to the gates of Moscow. The new stone fortifications of the city, however, withstood the siege. Nevertheless, the episode forced Moscow to make a peace in which Tver gained some territory and, in effect, a commitment that Dmitrii's government would not interfere in its internal affairs.

The drama repeated itself in 1370. Taking advantage of Lithuanian entanglements elsewhere, Dmitrii launched an invasion of Tver and overran several towns including Mikulin, the centre of Michael's own domain. In this instance, however, Michael turned not only to Lithuania, but to the Golden Horde as well. He paid a visit to Mamai's court and received a patent as grand prince of Vladimir. Back in Russia, however, he found that he could not enforce his claim to the throne without Lithuanian help. He and Olgerd attacked Moscow with a large army but, once again, failed to take the city.

Michael was not to be denied. In the following year, a second visit to Mamai produced another patent for the grand princely throne. Moscow's leaders responded with a diplomatic offensive on two fronts. Using time-honoured weapons – intrigue and bribes – Dmitrii Donskoi convinced the khan to restore him to the grand princely throne. On the western flank, Metropolitan Alexis wooed away Tver's main ally by negotiating a treaty of peace between Lithuania and Moscow, sealed by the marriage of Vladimir Andreevich, Dmitrii's cousin, to one of Olgerd's daughters. Even though neither of Moscow's diplomatic triumphs lasted long, they served, in the short run, to deprive Michael of his apparent victory.

For four more years, the struggle dragged on; Moscow and Tver fought a bitter and destructive border war, marred by numerous atrocities. In the diplomatic sphere, with the help of deserters from Moscow, Michael of Tver, in 1375, once again received a patent to the grand princely throne from Mamai's puppet khan. He quickly discovered, however, that he could not make good his claim to the throne. Dmitrii of Moscow retained the loyalty of most of the other rulers of the area, including the city fathers of Novgorod. He put together an overwhelming army drawn from many principalities and crushed Michael's forces. Realizing the hopelessness of his position, the latter made peace on 3 September 1375. In the treaty he acknowledged Grand Prince Dmitrii of Moscow as his 'elder brother', agreed not to claim the office of Grand Prince or lordship over Novgorod and gave up independent relations with Lithuania and the Horde. In short, he accepted a status only slightly more exalted than that of a junior member of the house of Moscow.[37]

In ecclesiastical affairs, Metropolitan Alexis struggled to preserve the unity of the Russian hierarchy. He faced formidable opposition. Grand Duke Olgerd of Lithuania was determined to gain control over a united Russian hierarchy or, failing that, to maintain a separate metropolitan as shepherd of his Orthodox subjects. Alexis became metropolitan in the midst of one of the Lithuanian ruler's attempts to do the latter. To thwart Olgerd's plans for a separate west Russian hierarchy, Theognostus had chosen Alexis as his successor as head of a united church. Once installed as metropolitan, Alexis carried on his predecessor's campaign with conspicuous success.[38]

Metropolitan Alexis also used the weight of his ecclesiastical office to support the secular goals of Grand Prince Dmitrii of Moscow, his protégé. His attitude towards political and diplomatic matters grew directly out of the Byzantine tradition of harmony between church and state. When transplanted in Russia, the Byzantine ideal posed serious problems, for Dmitrii ruled only part of Alexis's flock. The other Russian Orthodox Christians lived under the sceptres of independent princes of north-east Russia like Michael of Tver or, even more significantly, non-Orthodox rulers such as Grand Duke Olgerd of Lithuania and King Casimir of Poland. The latter, in particular, could have no sympathy with Alexis's vision of a brotherly union of Russian princes, under Dmitrii's leadership, struggling against their non-Christian neighbours.

The patriarch of Constantinople had the final word on the organization and policies of the Russian church. For years, Patriarch Philotheus consistently supported Alexis's aggressive defence of Moscow's interests, seeing them as identical to his own. A series of his letters, written in 1370, make his attitude clear. He wrote warmly to Dmitrii and Alexis, explaining to the young prince that 'The metropolitan appointed by me is an image of God, and is my representative, so that anyone who is submissive to him . . . is actually submissive to God and to Our Humility'. A general epistle to unnamed Russian princes urged them to remain loyal to Moscow and the metropolitan. The Patriarch had nothing good to say to Alexis's enemies. On one occasion, he solemnly excommunicated Michael of Tver for allying himself with the pagan Olgerd.[39]

Within a few months, Patriarch Philotheus abruptly deviated from his unwavering support of Moscow. The change of direction took place for tactical reasons. Throughout his reign, Philotheus, like his predecessors and successors, consistently attempted to defend and strengthen the entire Eastern Orthodox Church and, in the case of Russia, to keep the Orthodox community united. Suddenly, however, Philotheus realized that unquestioning support of Moscow was not the best path towards these objectives.

Two problems forced him to change direction. First, King Casimir of Poland, a Roman Catholic, had conquered the principality of Galicia, once a part of Kievan Rus, whose population was Orthodox. The king demanded a separate metropolitan for Galicia. In case the patriarch mistook the seriousness of his intentions, Casimir issued a most credible threat. 'And if the grace of God and your blessing are not bestowed upon that man, do not complain against us afterwards. We will be forced to baptize the Russians into the faith of the Latins, if there is no metropolitan in Russia, for the land cannot remain without a law'.[40] In 1371, Philotheus duly consecrated Casimir's candidate as metropolitan.

Olgerd of Lithuania had even more serious objections to Alexis's management of the Russian church. As Tver's ally, locked in deadly combat with Moscow, he protested violently against the metropolitan's partisan use of blessings and canonical dispensations. He also pointed out – quite correctly – that, since his first years in office, Alexis had done little to minister to his flock in the Lithuanian lands. As Olgerd put it, 'He blesses the Muscovites to commit bloodshed. He never visits us. He never goes to Kiev. And when someone kisses the cross to me and then escapes to them, the metropolitan frees him from his allegiance'.[41]

Olgerd's accusations carried weight with Philotheus for two reasons. First, they were obviously true. Second, in the early 1370s, the Grand Duchy of Lithuania was, for the moment, the most powerful force in the political life of the Russian Orthodox community as a whole. Blind support for Moscow no longer made sense.

As a result, Philotheus wrote to Alexis and Dmitrii to chide them for their hostility towards Olgerd and their brothers in the Orthodox faith. His letter to Alexis put the matter bluntly. 'I see nothing good in that you indulge in scandalous conflicts with Michael, Prince of Tver . . . Try to make peace with him, as his father and teacher . . . Your Holiness knows perfectly well that, when we consecrated you, we made you Metropolitan of Kiev and all Russia: not of a part only, but of all Russia . . . '.[42]

In addition, he sent the Bulgarian prelate, Cyprian, to Lithuania in 1373 to pacify the grand duke. Cyprian remained in the Russian lands for two years and, as an experienced diplomat, may well have worked to bring peace to the area. It is entirely possible that he mediated a temporary peace settlement between Moscow and Tver in 1374 and may well have persuaded Olgerd to withdraw his active support of Michael.

In a final act of conciliation, the patriarch appointed Cyprian as metropolitan of 'Kiev, Russia, and Lithuania' in 1375. By so doing, Philotheus hoped to preserve the unity of the Russian Church. The separate metropolitanate was created as a temporary measure, to last only until the aged Metropolitan Alexis died. At that time – in 1378, as it happened – Cyprian would become metropolitan in a united Russian hierarchy. As a foreigner, Cyprian had no partisan commitments in the political struggles within Russia. He was thus better able than Alexis to serve the entire Russian Orthodox community. In practice, however, in pursuing fundamental Byzantine policy, the defence of the Eastern Orthodox community against pressure from surrounding non-Orthodox powers – Lithuania and the Golden Horde – Cyprian, like his predecessors, often threw the weight of his office behind the grand princes in Moscow.

In the second half of the fourteenth century, the size and organization of the principality of Moscow underwent important changes. For one thing, the territory under the control of the house of Moscow steadily expanded. At the very beginning of the young Dmitrii's reign, his government brought the princes of Rostov to heel and annexed the Starodub area east of Suzdal. Moreover, at some time before he wrote his second will in 1389, Donskoi took over the so-called 'purchases' of his grandfather, Ivan I – Galich, Uglich and Beloozero – as well as neighbouring Kostroma. Historians have long debated the meaning of these 'purchases' since no document of Ivan's reign or any other time before 1389 mentions them. The most recent study of the problem convincingly suggests that the person who drafted Dmitrii Donskoi's second will used the word 'purchases' to throw a cover of legitimacy over outright seizures of territory by Donskoi himself. However made, these acquisitions greatly increased the size of the territorial base from which Moscow's rulers struggled for leadership of north-east Russia.[43]

Within Moscow itself, the ruling élite of high nobles or boyars took definite shape. Donskoi and his successors ruled with the support of a small number of clans of noble warriors who served at the court in Moscow and in the grand prince's armies. Their most influential members undoubtedly played a major part in establishing the policies of the grand princely government, particularly at times when the ruler himself was incompetent or a minor.

The composition and political structure of the ruling group of nobles changed frequently. The leading clans of Moscow had begun to gather around the throne at the beginning of the fourteenth century and, in each later generation, new recruits joined their ranks. At the same time, since some clans died out or fell into obscurity, the number of leading families remained fixed at about ten. Moreover, within the ruling élite, some individuals and clans were, at any given moment, more powerful than others: families with matrimonial ties to the ruling dynasty had particularly great influence. Overwhelming power had its risks, however. If an individual or clan threatened to overshadow all potential rivals, the rest of the ruling group would band together to destroy the offender.[44]

Subtle but significant changes took place in the relations between the ruling

49

princes of Moscow and their younger brothers and cousins. In his dealings with his brothers, Simeon the Proud had taken the first steps toward the creation of the appanage or *udel* system. Ivan I's will had stressed the unity of the house of Moscow and its lands. Each of his heirs received a share of the inheritance, but the divisions were conditional: ultimately, the family's lands remained the collective possession of all family members. Simeon's treaty with his brothers, however, sounds a new note. In the agreement, probably made in the late 1340s, the younger members of the ruling house recognized Simeon as their leader and obligated themselves to follow him on military campaigns. For his part, the grand prince promised to consult his brothers on all important matters of state.

The striking novelty in the treaty is the brothers' attitude towards their respective shares of the lands of the house of Moscow. The language of the treaty makes clear that each brother had inviolable possession of his appanage and the right to pass it on to his direct heirs without outside interference. Moreover, each brother had the right to administer his own lands autonomously. The brothers even agreed not to buy up lands in one another's territories. While the treaty may have met the immediate needs of Simeon and his brothers, its provisions had devastating implications for the office of grand prince and the unity of the principality of Moscow whose rulers held it. For, without effective counter-measures, the territory of Moscow could have become fragmented and its rulers fatally weakened.[45]

Dmitrii Donskoi and his cousin, Vladimir Andreevich, the only remaining representative of a younger branch of the house of Moscow, took several steps to deal with this potentially dangerous situation. In many respects, the relationship between these princes reflected the customary legal norms and practices that held sway throughout the Russian lands. Within each principality, the ruling family made a theoretical distinction between the patrimonial possessions of the entire house which could be divided into appanages held as a temporary trust and the patrimonial possessions and rights (votchina) over which individual members and branches of the clan exercised absolute ownership. Thus, in the three treaties between Dmitrii and Vladimir, the grand prince recognized his cousin's absolute right to hold and administer the lands inherited from his father. Each, for example, recognized the right of the other's servitors to change their allegiance without penalty and each promised not to buy land in the other's territory. In one sense, then, the principality of Moscow consisted of two autonomous subdivisions with two capitals – the cities of Moscow and Serpukhov.

On another level, the principality remained a single unit ruled by the entire house of Moscow of which Dmitrii was the head. In the later treaties, Vladimir Andreevich agreed to join his 'elder brother' in time of war. Moreover, although each prince collected the Tatar tribute in his own lands, Dmitrii alone handed it over to the Horde.

In one sense, however, Moscow's position was unique, for the head of the family was also the grand prince of Vladimir. As Presniakov demonstrated, we can see, through the ambiguous provisions of the treaties between Dmitrii and Vladimir, a conscious attempt to build up the dignity and power of the 'elder brother' in his capacity as grand prince. The agreements commit Vladimir to be faithful and obedient to Dmitrii and even to report to him 'whatever you have heard about me, whether it be from the lips of a peasant or a pagan, concerning my goodness or my cunning, or about our otchina and any of its peasants . . .'. The last treaty makes Vladimir's subordination to the grand prince particularly clear. Vladimir agrees to regard Dmitrii not just as his 'elder brother' but 'in place of his father' and to look on Vasilii, Dmitrii's eldest son and heir to the grand princely throne, as 'elder brother' as well.

In his second will, made just before his death in 1389, Dmitrii displayed new attitudes toward his power as grand prince. In many respects, the document follows the traditional lines established by his predecessors. It is essentially a private testament distributing Dmitrii's patrimonial possessions within the Moscow principality among his widow and their sons. Vladimir Andreevich is barely mentioned.

Midway through the will, however, we encounter the startling phrase, 'And lo, I bless my son, Prince Vasilii, with my patrimony, the grand princedom'. In Dmitrii's view, the office was his personal possession, to be passed on to his eldest son! To be sure, the statement is as ambiguous as it is dramatic. Clearly Dmitrii intended to keep the office of grand prince within the house of Moscow. Since he had no younger brothers at the time of the will, it is unclear whether he intended the throne to pass from father to son in future generations. Moreover, it is hard to envision the practical ramifications of Dmitrii's claim. All that the testament itself suggests is that the grand prince has the right to divide the lands pertaining to that office by an act of will. In the clearest example, Dmitrii divided up the 'purchases of Ivan I' among his kin, including his cousin, even though these territories were not, strictly speaking, part of the patrimonial possessions of the house of Moscow.[46]

Important as these changes are, they pale before Dmitrii's most celebrated feat, his rebellion against the Golden Horde. Later chroniclers and historians have often exaggerated the importance of his victories. Nevertheless, Dmitrii's triumphs gave the princes of Moscow great prestige within Russia and made them more clearly than before the military leaders of the nation.

Events outside of Russia largely determined the course of the revolt. The Golden Horde remained divided between the government of the khan in Sarai and Mamai's horde in the steppe directly south of the north-east Russian principalities. A new actor, however, entered the scene from the east. In Central Asia, the greatest Mongol warlord since Chingis Khan, Tamerlane, built an empire. As he consolidated his power, he drew an energetic young Chingisid prince, Tokhtamysh, into his service. Tokhtamysh soon built up his own forces and moved westward into the territory of the Golden Horde. In 1378, he captured Sarai and quickly reunited the Horde under his sceptre.

While these events were taking place, trouble between Russians and Tatars broke out in Nizhnii-Novgorod. The principality guarded the Volga valley and served as the main eastern defence post of the Russian lands. Working closely with Grand Prince Dmitrii in Moscow, the local princes took several steps to strengthen the region's defences. In 1372, for example, they rebuilt the citadel of Nizhnii-Novgorod in stone. Perceiving a threat to his claims to rule the area and collect tribute, Mamai sent troops to the city in 1374. Like the citizens of Tver in earlier days, the people of Nizhnii-Novgorod revolted and massacred or imprisoned any Tatar they could find. Revenge was inevitable, but it was remarkably slow in coming. Mamai's troops sacked the defenceless city twice – in 1377 and 1378.

Tokhtamysh's appearance in the European steppe seriously threatened Mamai's position. He had to make a difficult tactical choice – whether to face the intruder or, first of all, to reduce the unruly Russian principalities to submission. He opted for the second course. In 1378, he sent an army under Begich towards the heart of north-east Russia. Dmitrii Donskoi mobilized against him and, on the Vozha river, the Russian forces won a stunning victory. All Begich could do was ravage the border principality of Riazan in which the battle had taken place.

After this unexpected defeat, Mamai made elaborate military and diplomatic preparations for a campaign to subdue the rebellious Russians. He mobilized a large army and enlisted Moscow's enemies as allies. The new grand duke of Lithuania, Jagiello (Jogaila), agreed to join forces with him. Moreover, Mamai had the cooperation of Oleg of Riazan who found himself in a very difficult position. His domain, like Nizhnii-Novgorod, was constantly exposed to attack from the steppe. In 1378, his subjects had once again borne the brunt of the Tatar attack on the Russian lands. He and his people had little to gain from resistance to Mamai. Moreover, he had old scores to settle with Dmitrii of Moscow, not least the latter's meddling in internal disputes within the ruling house of Riazan.

Mamai's preparations must have frightened the leaders of the Russian principalities. For more than a century, Dmitrii's predecessors had survived by avoiding armed confrontations with the Mongol conquerors. Now a major clash was inevitable. Dmitrii gathered troops from all corners of the territory under his control. Sources of later times claim that he also mustered forces from most other areas of Russia. In all likelihood, however, no troops from Novgorod, Nizhnii-Novgorod or Tver fought under him. Two members of the Lithuanian ruling house – Andrew of Polotsk and Dmitrii of Briansk, sons of the late Grand Duke Olgerd – however, joined forces with Dmitrii against their half-brother and enemy, Jagiello.

In describing Dmitrii's preparations, the Russian chronicles tell how the leaders of the Orthodox Church gave their whole-hearted support to the grand prince's campaign. Some of the well-known stories about the war are clearly literary embellishments of a later time. For example, Metropolitan Cyprian could not have blessed Donskoi before his departure for battle since he was not in Moscow at the time. Equally improbable is the tale that Abbot Sergius of the Holy Trinity Monastery sent two of his monks to fight in the Russian ranks. At the same time, these pious myths are probably an exaggeration of real attitudes. The earliest surviving descriptions of the battle, written by churchmen, present it, in part, as a struggle for the Christian faith against the infidel.[47] It is entirely probable, moreover, that Sergius, the most influential leader of the Russian Church, gave Dmitrii his blessing before a war that was, in any case, unavoidable.

The two armies met on 8 September 1380 on the Kulikovo Pole near the upper reaches of the Don river. The most reliable chronicle accounts give very laconic descriptions of the battle. In the more elaborate works of literature on Kulikovo, however, we find colourful details some of which may well be true. In preparation for the battle, some sources claim, Dmitrii Donskoi disguised himself and one of his nobles put on his clothing and took up his standard. The ruse was successful: the Tatars aimed their heaviest attacks at the presumed Dmitrii who died bravely under the onslaught. The real prince, although wounded, survived to lead his people throughout the fight and afterwards. According to some accounts, the Russian forces used more clever strategy than their opponents. One of the commanders – most likely Dmitrii himself – decided to hold part of the army in reserve when the battle began. Then, when the struggle was at its height and many lives had been lost, these fresh troops, under the command of the valiant Vladimir Andreevich of Serpukhov, sprang from ambush and routed the enemy.

Whether or not these details are true, the sources leave no doubt about the outcome of the battle. Before the Lithuanian army could join Mamai's forces, the Russian troops won a surprising victory. Mamai fled southward in disarray. His fortunes quickly went from bad to worse. In the following year, Tokhtamysh crushed his army on the Kalka river and, when Mamai fled to Kaffa for refuge, the Genoese murdered him.

Dmitrii Donskoi's victory had profound consequences. Later generations saw the battle of Kulikovo Pole as a triumph of the Cross over the Crescent or the Russian people over the Mongol conquerors. Both of these perceptions are skewed at best. Certainly Kulikovo did not free the Russian principalities from the suzerainty of the Golden Horde. On a theoretical plane, the writers of the poems and tales describing the battle stressed that Dmitrii Donskoi revolted, not against the legitimate authority of the khans, but against a usurper of that authority – Mamai.[48] In practice, moreover, the Golden Horde quickly regained the upper hand. Once Tokhtamysh had destroyed Mamai, he turned on his rebellious Russian subjects, mounting a large punitive expedition in 1382. The khan's forces sacked Moscow and re-established his authority over north-east Russia in no uncertain terms. Like his predecessors, Dmitrii gratefully accepted his patent as grand prince.

The victory at Kulikovo, however, greatly increased the prestige of the ruler of Moscow. Those who opposed his policies paid dearly. In the aftermath of the battle, for example, Oleg of Riazan fled his principality. After several confusing and difficult years, Dmitrii made peace with him in 1385, but only on condition that Oleg accept the role of 'younger brother' as Michael of Tver had done ten years earlier.

The battle also gave men food for thought. Over the next two generations, reflections on its meaning crystallized into chronicle accounts, poems and tales proclaiming the victory of Orthodox Christianity, the Russian land and its primary ruler, the grand prince in Moscow.

By 1380, then, the house of Moscow had come a long way. Its princes had established their right to the office of grand prince of Vladimir and assumed the role of first protectors of the Russian Orthodox Church. By a variety of means – above all by winning the trust of the rulers of the Golden Horde – they had, for the moment, beaten back the challenges of other, equally promising regional centres. In small, but significant steps, moreover, the rulers of Moscow had begun to build a solid territorial and institutional foundation which would make the grand prince's power strong and stable. By 1380, Moscow's victory was by no means complete, but its rulers had gathered some of the resources needed for the creation of a powerful kingdom.

REFERENCES AND NOTES

1. Kargalov, *Vneshnepoliticheskie faktory*, pp. 84–111.
2. For a provocative reassessment of Nevskii's policies, see Fennell, *Crisis*, pp. 109–21.
3. Nasonov, *Mongoly*, pp. 11–21, 50; Halperin, *Russia*, pp. 33–43.
4. Fennell, *Crisis*, pp. 116–20.
5. Nasonov, *Mongoly*, pp. 23–34.
6. Vernadsky, *Mongols*, pp. 165–6.
7. Kargalov, *Vneshnepoliticheskie faktory*, p. 170.
8. Goehrke, 'Einwohnerzahl', p. 44.
9. Vernadsky, *Kievan Russia*, pp. 196–201, 212. See also Zernack, *Die burgstädtischen Volksversammlungen*.
10. Ianin, *Novgorodskie posadniki*, pp. 165–75.
11. Ibid., p. 259.
12. Cherepnin, *Obrazovanie*, p. 460.
13. Goehrke, 'Geographische Grundlagen', p. 178.
14. Presniakov, *Formation*, pp. 108–10.
15. Sakharov, *Obrazovanie*, pp. 107–8.
16. Kliuchevskii, *Sochineniia*, vol. 2, pp. 13–15. For the genealogy of the princes of north-east Russia, see Fennell, *Crisis*, p. 176.
17. Kliuchevskii, *Sochineniia*, vol. 2, p.49.
18. Presniakov, *Formation*, pp. 98–9.
19. Meyendorff, *Byzantium*, pp. 92–4.
20. *GVNiP*, pp. 25–6; Cherepnin, *Russkie feodalnye arkhivy*, vol. 1, pp. 293–4.
21. Fennell, *Emergence*, p. 85.
22. Ibid., pp. 87–8; *PSRL* 15:411–12.
23. Presniakov, *Formation*, p. 119.
24. *PSRL* 15:415–16, **25**:168; Fennell, 'Uprising'.
25. *PSRL* 15:49.

26. *TR*, p. 359.
27. Meyendorff, *Byzantium*, p. 157.
28. Presniakov, *Formation*, p. 129.
29. Ibid., pp. 136–7.
30. Cherepnin, *Russkie feodalnye arkhivy*, vol. 1, pp. 12–16.
31. *Testaments*, pp. 191–2.
32. Langer, 'Black Death'; Alef, 'Crisis', pp. 36–8.
33. Ibid., pp. 57–8.
34. Langer, 'Black Death', pp. 62–7.
35. Fennell, *Emergence*, pp. 291–6; Rüss, 'Kampf', pp. 481–9.
36. *PSRL* 15:84; Presniakov, *Formation*, p. 247.
37. Ibid., pp. 248–52.
38. Meyendorff, *Byzantium*, pp. 161–71.
39. Ibid., pp. 188–90.
40. Ibid., p. 287.
41. Ibid., p. 288.
42. Ibid., p. 197.
43. Vodoff, 'A propos des "achats"'. See also Kopanev, 'O "kupliakh"'; Cherepnin, *Obrazovanie*, pp. 509–12, 554–6; Presniakov, *Formation*, pp. 129–34.
44. Shields Kollmann, 'Boyar clan'. See also Veselovskii, *Issledovaniia po istorii zemlevladeltsev*.
45. Presniakov, *Formation*, pp. 143–7.
46. Ibid., pp. 157–64; *Testaments*, p. 212.
47. For example, *TR*, pp. 419–20.
48. Halperin, 'Russian land'.

CHAPTER THREE

Moscow's victory, 1380–1462

Dmitrii Donskoi's triumph over Mamai had ambiguous consequences. On the positive side, the victory at Kulikovo Pole cemented Moscow's claim to political and military leadership within north-east Russia. Never, after that, did the descendants of Prince Daniel relinquish their hold on the office of grand prince of Vladimir.[1] Moreover, although the revolt against Mamai did not directly challenge the suzerainty of the Golden Horde, the victory implanted the vision that, some day, Russia would be free from Tatar tutelage. In his will, Dmitrii Donskoi gave his heirs instructions on how to proceed '. . . if God brings about a change regarding the Horde and my children do not have to give Tatar tribute to the Horde . . .'.[2]

The immediate consequences of the battle, however, provided a frightening reminder of the weakness of the Russian principalities and the fragility of Moscow's position of leadership. As Donskoi and his advisers undoubtedly knew, there was no guarantee that his family's political gains would not be reversed.

In the years between 1380 and 1462, the victor of Kulikovo and his successors struggled to survive and retain their pre-eminence within the Russian lands. It was no easy task. In the late fourteenth century, the grand principality of Vladimir was more of an ideal than a reality. In practice, Dmitrii Donskoi ruled the territory around Moscow, Rostov, Iaroslavl, Kostroma and the 'purchases' – Galich, Uglich and Beloozero. In his capacity as grand prince, he had little, if any, effective control over Novgorod, Tver, Nizhnii-Novgorod–Suzdal and Riazan. Indeed, although they rarely challenged Moscow's hegemony directly, the rulers of the other east Russian principalities showed increasing independence in their relations with Lithuania and the Horde in the late fourteenth and early fifteenth centuries and often styled themselves 'grand princes'. In particular, Tver flourished. Its princes conducted their own foreign policy and regarded themselves as guardians of the Orthodox Church alongside their counterparts in Moscow.[3] Likewise, Novgorod steered its own course by balancing the competing pressures of Moscow and Lithuania. In the early fifteenth century, the republic's oligarchic government achieved considerable stability and, under the patronage of its archbishops, the city enjoyed a burst of cultural creativity.[4] In the aftermath of Kulikovo, Moscow became the first among near-equals.

Donskoi and his successors also had to struggle to maintain their predominant influence over the Russian Orthodox Church. In one sense, they succeeded. Thanks to their loyalty to the Orthodox cause and their determination, the princes of Moscow succeeded in arranging the consecration of a succession of energetic metropolitans whose views and interests harmonized with their own. In another way, they failed. Time and again, the grand dukes of Lithuania tried to establish a separate hierarchy to minister to their subjects of the Russian Orthodox faith. In crisis after crisis, the princes and metropolitans of Russia beat back the challenge and preserved a united hierarchy with its seat in Moscow. In the end, however, the Lithuanian rulers had their way. After 1458, the jurisdiction of the metropolitans of Moscow was limited to the east Russian lands. There they came to depend, even more than before, on the grand princes.

In the eighty-odd years after Kulikovo, the rulers of Moscow had to work for greater control over the people and resources of the grand principality itself. As Dmitrii Donskoi saw clearly, the most important problem was the nature of the relations between the grand prince and the members of his immediate family. In the end, it took a civil war to settle the issue.

For the moment, however, all of these problems were overshadowed by the continuing menace of the Horde; for Donskoi and his allies had wounded it, but not destroyed its power. Within weeks of the battle, Donskoi and other Russian princes welcomed emissaries from the new Khan Tokhtamysh and soon sent their own envoys to his court to pay their respects and offer him rich gifts.[5] The Russian princes, however, ignored his summons to appear before him themselves. Their hesitation in submitting cost them dearly.

In 1382, Tokhtamysh gathered a large army and struck quickly at the heart of Russian resistance. With the help of Oleg of Riazan, who once again was trapped in the Tatars' path, he moved directly on Moscow. With more common sense than valour, Dmitrii Donskoi withdrew northward, leaving the people of his capital to their fate. In their consternation, they turned to a Lithuanian prince, Ostei, to lead the defence of the city. The Muscovites fought desperately against the besieging army, using the traditional weapons – arrows and boiling water – and, according to some sources, firearms as well. In the end, their efforts came to naught. The Tatars lured Ostei out of the fortress with promises of negotiations and killed him. The besiegers then broke into the citadel, massacred many of its defenders and destroyed large parts of the city.

Moscow did not suffer alone. Tokhtamysh sent troops through the neighbouring regions to pillage many smaller towns. Then, having delivered his message in unmistakable terms, he withdrew his army southward, sacking the unfortunate principality of Riazan as he passed.

Dmitrii Donskoi and his rivals within Russia quickly grasped the significance of Tokhtamysh's raid. The rulers of the other major principalities used Moscow's defeat to win back their lost freedom of action. During the Tatar advance on Moscow, Boris, the prince of Nizhnii-Novgorod, threw in his lot with Tokhtamysh and, in effect, became his vassal rather than Moscow's. Michael of Tver went further still, claiming the patent as grand prince of Vladimir. Although Tokhtamysh did not grant his wish, Michael at least succeeded in freeing himself from the humiliating treaty of 1375 in which he had recognized Dmitrii Donskoi's overlordship and in re-establishing independent relations with the Horde. Once again, Riazan took blows from all sides. As soon as Tokhtamysh's punitive expedition left the principality, Muscovite troops moved in, forcing Prince Oleg to recognize Donskoi's suzerainty. Before long, however, Oleg reasserted his independence of Moscow. After a brief invasion of Muscovite territory in 1385, Oleg concluded a peace treaty with Dmitrii, sealed by the marriage of his son to the latter's daughter.

Tokhtamysh's campaign affected the relations between Moscow and Novgorod as well. The leaders of the republic, unable to depend on the military support of the grand prince, called in princes from Lithuania and, as before, set aside certain districts for their support.

As for Dmitrii, after 1382 the prince of Moscow reverted to the role of loyal agent of the khan. Tokhtamysh confirmed him as grand prince of Vladimir. At the same time, the price of leadership was high. The khan forced Dmitrii to collect exceptionally large sums of tribute from the Russian principalities and, as a guarantee of his loyalty, held his son, Vasilii, in Sarai as a hostage. Acting as Mongol tax-collector did little for Dmitrii's popularity. In particular, the citizens of Novgorod, the wealthiest centre in Russia, objected to paying a special tax, the *chernyi bor*, to the Horde. In 1386, the grand prince had to mount a military expedition to force the leaders of the republic to pay up.

The last years of Donskoi's reign also witnessed a decline in the influence of the prince of Moscow over the Russian Orthodox Church. In many respects, Dmitrii had only himself to blame. Well before the battle of Kulikovo, he set off a complex crisis over the succession to the office of metropolitan of Kiev and all Russia.

From Moscow's point of view, Alexis had been an ideal leader of the Russian Orthodox Church. As Dmitrii and his advisers could plainly see, Cyprian, Alexis's designated successor, was a man of very different background and convictions. The new metropolitan's ministry in Lithuania made clear that he sought to serve the entire Russian Orthodox community without tying himself to the political ambitions of any of the region's rulers, including the grand prince in Moscow. From Dmitrii's partisan vantage point, that conviction made Cyprian an ally of the grand duke of Lithuania. Accordingly, Dmitrii did everything in his power to stop him from assuming the office of metropolitan.

With rare exceptions, opposition to Cyprian remained the touchstone of Donskoi's ecclesiastical policy until the end of his life. The grand prince's attitude had implications far broader than a mere clash of personalities, however. By his conduct, Dmitrii made clear that, if he could not put a sympathizer of Moscow on the throne of a united Russian Church, he was prepared, like his Lithuanian counterpart, to accept a division of the Russian hierarchy, provided that the head of the church in the lands of the grand principality of Vladimir supported his political programme.

When Alexis died, Dmitrii put up his own candidate for the metropolitan throne, his own confessor and court official – a parish priest named Michael-Mitiai. The grand prince's nominee was an imposing figure – a large muscular man with a powerful voice who celebrated the liturgy with authority.[6] At the same time, his claims on the office were weak. He was not a bishop and could justify his candidacy only with the false assertion that Alexis had designated him as his successor. Moreover, a number of the most influential bishops and monastic leaders of Russia opposed him. Nevertheless, with the grand prince's blessing, he began to dress and to administer the church as though he were metropolitan. When Cyprian travelled to Moscow to assume the office that he thought was his, Dmitrii's agents arrested and mistreated him before sending him back to Lithuanian territory.

As though ecclesiastical affairs within Russia were not complicated enough, political unrest in Constantinople added to the confusion. While the armies of the Ottoman Turks closed in on the city, pro-Genoese and pro-Venetian factions at the Byzantine court vied for power. Emperor succeeded emperor in rapid succession and patriarchs rose and fell on the changing tides of secular politics. The great Patriarch Philotheus had arranged for Cyprian to succeed Alexis as metropolitan of a united Russian Church. His successor, however, during a very brief term of office, gave his approval to Dmitrii's plans to enthrone Michael. As luck would have it, however, on his way to claim his prize, Michael died on shipboard within sight of Constantinople. At that point, a member of his suite, the Archimandrite Pimen, presented himself as the official Muscovite candidate. The newly chosen Patriarch Neilus consecrated him metropolitan of Kiev and all Russia, leaving Cyprian as head of the Russian Orthodox Church in Lithuania. Moreover, he asserted that, in the event of the latter's death, Pimen would become metropolitan of the entire Russian Church.

On the surface, Dmitrii Donskoi's government had achieved its goal. At precisely that point, however, Dmitrii changed his tack and made peace with Cyprian. Why he did so is unclear. Possibly, Pimen's decision to pass himself off as the grand prince's official candidate offended Dmitrii. Cyprian's role in the events surrounding the battle of Kulikovo Pole may also have contributed to the reconciliation. As a crusader for the unity of the Russian Church, Cyprian consistently worked for good relations between the princes of Lithuania and Moscow in whose domains its members lived. In 1380, he may well have convinced Grand Duke Jagiello not to fulfil his commitment to join forces with Mamai.[7]

Be that as it may, Cyprian moved to Moscow and performed the duties of metropolitan with Dmitrii's full support. When Pimen belatedly returned from Constantinople, the grand prince imprisoned him. After two years, however, Cyprian fell from favour. Once again, it would seem, an international crisis changed his fate. When Tokhtamysh advanced on Moscow in 1382, Dmitrii left the metropolitan in the capital when he retreated to the northern part of his domain. Before long, Cyprian too escaped from the doomed city. Not only did he fail to rally Moscow's defenders, but, while a refugee in Tver, did not stop the local ruler from conducting independent negotiations with the invader.[8] Moreover, once Dmitrii had submitted to Tokhtamysh, Cyprian's belief in reconciliation with Lithuania and resistance to the Golden Horde became an embarrassment to the grand prince.[9] Soon after the invasion, Cyprian left north-east Russia and Pimen emerged from prison to take the metropolitan throne.

Even then, divisions within the Russian Church and instability in Constantinople kept the pot boiling. Over the next seven years, Pimen made several attempts to win the patriarch's unconditional recognition as metropolitan. At the same time, his enemies within Russia worked to convince both the grand prince and the patriarch to depose him. Meanwhile Patriarch Neilus delayed a final decision while investigating the claims and counter-claims of the rival candidates.

In the end, Cyprian's persistence and high standing in Constantinople brought him victory. In 1388 Pimen made a final journey to Constantinople to present his case. Unfortunately for him, before a decision was reached, a new patriarch, Anthony, ascended the throne early in 1389. Anthony moved in the same circles as Cyprian and, not surprisingly, soon decided the festering dispute over the Russian metropolitanate in the latter's favour.

By 1390, the crisis was at last over. Cyprian had outlived his main rivals. Both Pimen and Dmitrii Donskoi had died in the previous year. The new grand prince, Vasilii I, had none of his father's animus toward Cyprian. The two men had met in 1386–87 in Kiev where Vasilii was living after fleeing from captivity in the Golden Horde.[10] Moreover, they shared a common vision of good relations between Moscow and Lithuania. For their part, the leaders of the Russian Church, thoroughly tired of bickering and confusion, rallied around Cyprian when he took up residence in Moscow.

Cyprian's appointment and the crisis that surrounded it significantly changed the relationship between the metropolitan and secular ruler in Moscow. Under Cyprian and his successor, Photius, a Greek by nationality, the head of the Russian Church continued to reside in Moscow and retain close contact with its ruler. At the same time, the two metropolitans made a clear distinction between the needs of the church and the political objectives of the grand princes.

Cyprian, in particular, had a clear programme for revitalizing the Eastern Orthodox community. He aimed to bring the national branches of Orthodoxy closer together by emphasizing their common loyalty and their personal and institutional ties to the ecumenical patriarchate in Constantinople. As Cyprian was well aware, the patriarch's leadership was primarily symbolic at a time when his capital was virtually under Turkish siege. In practice, 'the linchpin of this programme of ecclesiastical diplomacy was the undivided metropolitanate of Kiev and All Russia, with its effective centre in Moscow'.[11]

Cyprian's commitment to the unity of the 'Byzantine commonwealth' is reflected in the celebrated letter written by the patriarch of Constantinople to Vasilii I of Moscow in 1393. The document criticizes the grand prince for forbidding the the metropolitan to commemorate the Byzantine emperor in the liturgy and, as a corrective, reiterates with particular force that the Eastern Orthodox lands are ultimately parts of a universal Christian polity ruled by the emperor.[12] In the words of the letter, '. . . for Christians, it is not possible to have a Church, and not to have an emperor, for the empire and the church have a great unity and a commonality, and it is impossible to separate them'.[13]

Everything that we know about Cyprian indicates that he agreed with the views expressed in the patriarch's epistle. His precise role in the document's composition is less clear, however. Possibly, the new metropolitan protested to Constantinople against a recent decision by one of the grand princes of Moscow to forbid commemoration of the emperor. Perhaps, as John Meyendorff has recently suggested, Cyprian attempted to introduce prayers for the emperor into the liturgy of the Russian Church and complained to the patriarch when Vasilii I refused to accept the innovation.[14] In the end, Cyprian apparently succeeded in bringing the Russian Church to recognize the emperor's symbolic leadership of the whole Orthodox community.[15]

Giving his ultimate loyalty to Constantinople allowed Cyprian to minister impartially to all Russian Orthodox Christians. He maintained his capital in Moscow and collaborated with its grand prince. At the same time, he worked hard to serve the faithful in Lithuanian territory and maintained close contact with the Orthodox hierarchy and the secular leaders of the Grand Duchy.

In his short tenure as undisputed leader of the Russian Church, Cyprian proved to be an able administrator, a skilful diplomat and a scholar of the first rank. Once he assumed office in Russia, he took energetic measures to assert his authority. His handling of the first important crisis within the Russian Church gave contemporaries a clear indication of his methods and the direction of his policies. In 1387, Cyprian plunged into the confused affairs of the church in Tver. For some years, the local prince and some of the clergy had shown open hostility to the bishop, Euthymius, who, as a consequence, had retired to a monastery without vacating his see. Cyprian went to Tver and sorted out the situation by convoking a synod of local bishops which deposed the incumbent and appointed one of the new metropolitan's collaborators as his successor. By his actions, Cyprian made clear that he intended to remain independent of secular political leaders; apparently neither the ruler of Tver nor Dmitrii Donskoi had a voice in the selection of the new bishop.[16]

Cyprian showed equal determination in dealing with the church in Novgorod. Once again, he faced a crisis not of his own making. During the prolonged struggle over the succession to the office of metropolitan, the city government and the archbishop of Novgorod had, in effect, declared their independence from Moscow in ecclesiastical matters. In particular, the

Novgorodians refused to allow the metropolitan to hear appeals against the judgements of the local archbishop. The attitude of Novgorod's leaders deprived the head of the Russian Church not only of his traditional judicial prerogatives, but also of considerable income from legal fees and payments for his subsistence while he held court in the city.[17]

Despite his best efforts, Cyprian failed to bring Novgorod to heel. Neither the metropolitan's pastoral visits to the city nor the stern rebuke of the patriarch of Constantinople shook the Novgorodians' determination to have their own way. Many years later, his successor, Photius, had to fight the same battle with the same outcome. Although they lost this battle, however, both metropolitans made clear that they were determined to be masters in their own house.

Cyprian's protector, Vasilii I (1389–1425), is a shadowy figure. The sources on his long reign give us little sense of his character, except to hint that he was a cautious and indecisive man. In all fairness to Vasilii, however, he faced an array of problems that would have daunted even the most forceful of rulers. In Presniakov's felicitous words,

For Russia, the reign of Vasilii I was a period of instability and painfully strained relations that exhausted the land. Repeatedly conflicts would break out which the grand princely power had neither the energy nor the means to resolve decisively. Moscow swung wildly from one alliance to another, lacking the strength to bring about any definite settlement of the complicated problems arising out of Great Russia's relations with other nations.[18]

For much of Vasilii's reign, Moscow was caught in a vice. To the east and south, Tokhtamysh and later the warlord Edigei made the Golden Horde a formidable power for the last time in its history. To the west, in the course of a chain of dramatic events, the Grand Duchy of Lithuania reached the pinnacle of its power and influence. In 1386, its ruler, Jagiello, married the heiress to the Polish throne, thus creating a dynastic union of the two countries. Before long, however, local resistance within Lithuania took shape around Vitovt (Vytautas), Jagiello's energetic and ambitious cousin. In 1392, the new Polish king was forced to recognize Vitovt as his co-ruler in Lithuania and, in practice, the latter acted as a fully independent ruler, pursuing his own aggressive foreign policy.

At the height of his power, Vitovt aspired to leadership of all of the Russian lands and eventually challenged the Golden Horde for control of the steppe areas north of the Black Sea. The means by which he pursued these objectives, of course, depended in considerable measure on the reactions of his neighbours and rivals.

At first, the young Vasilii I of Moscow posed no threat to his ambitions. In fact, the new grand prince assumed the role of Vitovt's client and junior partner. In the last years of his father's reign, Vasilii had enjoyed Vitovt's protection and, with Metropolitan Cyprian's blessing, became engaged to his patron's daughter, Sophia. The marriage took place in 1391 and established ties of kinship on which Vasilii leaned for support in moments of crisis throughout the rest of his career.

In the 1390s, these three men – Vitovt, Cyprian and Vasilii – formed a 'triumvirate' that dominated political life in the Russian lands. Through most of the decade, for example, both Lithuania and Moscow maintained agents in Novgorod and, in 1397, jointly declared war on the republic after its leaders began to reassert its independence from their control.[19]

While they cooperated on the international scene, both Vitovt and Vasilii I fought ruthlessly to increase their power within their own spheres of influence. In the mid-1390s, Vitovt systematically undermined the positions of the most important of the subordinate Russian princes within his domains.[20]

For their part, Vasilii and his advisers took advantage of political strife in the Mongol world to annex the principality of Nizhnii-Novgorod. In 1392, Khan Tokhtamysh turned his attention to the east: Tamerlane, his former patron, master of Central Asia, inflicted a severe defeat on his armies. Taking advantage of Tokhtamysh's weakness, Vasilii I, on a visit to the khan's court, received his permission to take the throne of Nizhnii-Novgorod. Then, with the help of pro-Moscow renegades within the principality, Vasilii made his claim good, occupying the city and and deposing the local prince.

In certain respects, Vasilii's triumph was less complete than it appears. Several parts of the principality of Nizhnii-Novgorod remained under the control of their own autonomous rulers. Moreover, for a generation, members of the local ruling house periodically attempted to fight their way back on to their lost throne. When their own position was secure, the rulers of the Golden Horde were only too glad to support their claims as a counterweight to Moscow's ambitions. In 1408, for example, the warlord, Edigei, restored the local dynasty whose members ruled the principality until 1414 or 1415 when Vasilii I of Moscow again took over.[21]

Perhaps emboldened by the annexation of Nizhnii-Novgorod, Vasilii's government soon began to fish in other troubled waters. The inhabitants of the valley of the northern Dvina river rebelled against their overlord, the city of Novgorod. The decision of Vitovt and Vasilii to declare war on the republic gave the leaders of the Dvina area their opportunity. In 1397 they invited Vasilii to be their ruler. The prince of Moscow hastened to accept their offer; he sent troops to help the rebels and, to underline his determination, captured a number of other outlying centres of the Novgorod lands as well. In rebel territory, Vasilii began to establish his authority, issuing the judicial Charter of the Dvina Land as a sign of his rule.

Vasilii's northern adventure quickly ended. In 1398, the government of Novgorod recaptured its lost territories and meted out severe punishment to the most prominent of the rebels. Expecting no further help from Moscow, the rest of the population submitted. When Vasilii made a second attempt to take over the area in 1401, his troops encountered bitter resistance and quickly abandoned the expedition.[22]

Vasilii's defeat on the Dvina and his difficulties in maintaining his grip on Nizhnii-Novgorod symbolized the decline of his authority within north-east Russia in the last decades of his reign. While no rival challenged him for the grand princely throne, the rulers of the most important principalities succeeded in consolidating their positions and winning greater freedom from Moscow's control. In 1402, for example, Vasilii made a treaty with the prince of Riazan, promising not to interfere in that principality's internal affairs. At the same time, Tver reasserted its autonomy. Prince Ivan succeeded in reuniting the principality and began to play an independent role in international politics. In 1406, for example, he broke an alliance with Moscow because Vasilii had treated him as an underling rather than an equal. Thereafter Ivan negotiated with Lithuania and the Horde on his own.[23]

In his own dealings with the Horde, Vasilii I behaved far more cautiously than his father, Dmitrii, or his father-in-law, Vitovt. While the latter raised large armies to challenge the Mongol power directly, Vasilii preferred to sit quietly watching the rapidly changing scene in the Horde.

In Vasilii's first years on the throne, a titanic struggle engulfed the Mongol world. Its most powerful leaders, Tokhtamysh and Tamerlane, fought repeatedly for control of a vast area stretching from Central Asia to the steppes of south-east Europe. The first round of fighting ended in 1391 with Tamerlane's decisive victory on the Kondurcha river. Before long, however, Tokhtamysh showed his remarkable powers of recuperation. On the diplomatic front, he made agreements with the major powers of Eastern Europe – Poland, Lithuania and Moscow – settling with Vasilii the fate of Nizhnii-Novgorod. At the same time the khan rebuilt his army and began to raid outlying areas of Tamerlane's domains. A new round of fighting was inevitable.

In 1395 Tamerlane led a large army westward to destroy his rival once and for all. He confronted his enemy's main force just north of the Caucasus and destroyed it. This time, to make sure that Tokhtamysh could not recoup his fortunes, Tamerlane set about devastating his rival's domains. In the course of mopping up the remaining pockets of resistance, Tamerlane turned his army towards Moscow. As his troops advanced northward, Vasilii and his advisers took decisive measures to defend his lands and raise the morale of his subjects. The grand prince gathered an army and advanced to meet the invader while the people of Moscow prepared for another siege. Meanwhile, Metropolitan Cyprian brought the miracle-working icon of *Our Lady of Vladimir* to Moscow. Suddenly, as if by an act of Providence, Tamerlane stopped his advance and withdrew from Russian territory. One later chronicler claimed that a vision of the Virgin defending Moscow with a heavenly host convinced him to turn back.[24] More mundane considerations undoubtedly influenced his decision. At no time did Tamerlane aspire to govern the European steppe, let alone Russia. Once he had destroyed Tokhtamysh's resistance, he was content to return to his Central Asian capital, the rich and sophisticated city of Samarkand.[25] The central territories of the Golden Horde, especially the city of Sarai, however, never fully recovered from his depredations.

The invasion set off a struggle for power within the Horde itself. Edigei, an ally of Tamerlane, emerged as its most powerful leader and drove

Tokhtamysh into exile in Lithuania. From about 1398 until his death in 1419, Edigei dominated the political life of the steppe zone. For a time, he restored the internal coherence of the Horde. Moreover, he beat back Vitovt's campaign to replace its khan as overlord of the region.

At the same time, his power rested on shaky legal foundations. Since he was not of the royal lineage of Chingis Khan, he could not rule in his own right, but, like Mamai before him, had to exercise authority through puppet khans. At times, particularly in his later years, he found that he could not always control his own appointees to the throne.

In his first years of power, Edigei concentrated on the threat from Lithuania and paid little attention to Moscow. While he was distracted, Vasilii I made no attempt to recognize the suzerainty of successive khans under his protection and stopped paying them tribute.

His bravado soon cost him dear. In 1408, Edigei reasserted the Horde's fading authority over north-east Russia. Late in the autumn, he suddenly invaded the territory of Moscow. Just as in 1382, the reigning grand prince retreated to the northern part of his domains to rally his army. On this occasion, however, his capital survived the attack. Edigei's forces looted the areas around the city, captured a number of smaller towns and laid siege to Moscow itself. The garrison held out for several weeks. At that point, on receiving his khan's appeal for reinforcements elsewhere, Edigei agreed to withdraw his forces in return for payment of a large indemnity.[26]

In no sense, however, did Edigei's retreat put an end to Tatar raids on the Russian lands. In 1410, armed bands under the command of a renegade prince of the house of Nizhnii-Novgorod and a Tatar warlord sacked the old national capital, Vladimir, a bloody incident brilliantly re-enacted in the film *Andrei Rublev* (made in 1966). Under such heavy pressure, Vasilii I had to make conciliatory gestures toward the Horde. In 1412, for example, he presented himself to the khan of the moment asking for a renewed patent to the grand princely throne.

Time, however, was on Vasilii's side. In Edigei's last years, internal divisions weakened the Horde and one khan succeeded another in rapid succession. In many instances, the Horde's rulers were clearly clients of neighbouring princes, particularly Vitovt of Lithuania who sponsored the candidacies of the sons of his old ally, Tokhtamysh. By 1420, the Golden Horde, as a political unit, was in its death throes, soon to be replaced by the new khanates of Kazan and the Crimea that emerged from its ruins.

While Edigei struggled valiantly – and ultimately unsuccessfully – to revitalize the Horde, Vitovt made the Grand Duchy of Lithuania the leading power in the Russian lands. Doing so was the least of the grand duke's ambitions. During his long reign, he gave clear indications that he aspired to overthrow the the Golden Horde and, at the time of his death, was in the midst of a campaign to win international recognition as king of Lithuania.

In the face of Vitovt's drive for power, his son-in-law, Vasilii I of Moscow, chose the path of caution. In the 1390s, the two rulers usually cooperated closely with one another and with Metropolitan Cyprian. Nevertheless, as the decade passed, Vitovt's aggressiveness increasingly threatened the harmonious relations of the 'triumvirs'. In 1395, he captured the principality of Smolensk which lay between his domains and Vasilii's. For the moment, however, the ruler of Moscow made no attempt to resist his advance. On the contrary, Vasilii, in effect, accepted the Lithuanian annexation of Smolensk by journeying there in 1396 for a conference with Vitovt and Cyprian.[27]

Before long, Vitovt pursued far bigger game. The struggle for control of the Horde presented him with the perfect opportunity to intervene in its affairs. After Tamerlane's punitive expedition into Europe, his allies, Edigei and a new khan, Timur-Kutlug, took control of the Horde. Tokhtamysh fought a losing battle to save his throne, then fled to Lithuanian territory and asked for Vitovt's help. Seizing the moment, the grand duke began to plan a major expedition against the new rulers of the Horde. In 1397–98, while he made careful diplomatic preparations, his army reconnoitred the steppe zone north of the Black Sea. Then, in 1399, he led his army out for the decisive campaign.

Vitovt met with disaster. On the Vorskla river, Edigei and Timur-Kutlug crushed the Lithuanian army and and its allies. The defeat set clear limits to Vitovt's ambitions. Never again did he try to win a military victory over the Golden Horde. After the battle on the Vorskla, he turned to subtler tactics, choosing instead to use diplomacy and political intrigue to place his candidates on the throne of the khans.

During Vitovt's adventure in the steppes, Vasilii I and the other princes of north-east Russia remained neutral. In the aftermath of his defeat, however, they began to offer open resistance to his advance. The people of Smolensk took the first step. In 1401, they revolted against Lithuanian rule and recalled their former prince. While Vasilii I sat on the sidelines, Vitovt struggled for three years before he succeeded in reasserting his control over the principality.

Given his father-in-law's continued aggressiveness, even Vasilii could not remain neutral for ever. The two finally came to blows over Vitovt's efforts to pull Pskov and Novgorod into the Lithuanian sphere of influence. In 1406, when Lithuanian forces attacked Pskov, Vasilii sent troops to their aid. As a consequence, Lithuania and Moscow fought a fitful border war until 1408. The prince of Moscow also showed his more determined attitude towards his father-in-law by giving temporary asylum to Vitovt's cousin and bitter enemy, Svidrigailo (Svitrigaila).

Before long, the two rulers had to turn their attention to more pressing matters. Vasilii had to deal with Edigei's devastating raid of 1408 and its aftermath while, on another front, Vitovt joined forces with King Jagiello of Poland to inflict a crushing defeat on the Teutonic Knights at Grunewald in 1410. Thereafter, in the second decade of the fifteenth century, the relations between Moscow and Lithuania resumed a more peaceful course. To be sure, there remained points of tension. Vitovt and Vasilii continued to jostle for decisive influence in the affairs of Novgorod and Pskov and both increasingly intervened in the confused political life of the Horde.

In the last years of their respective reigns, Vitovt dominated the political life of the Russian lands and Vasilii I was content to rule in his shadow. Vasilii's second and third wills, written in 1417 and 1423, illustrate the nature of the relationship particularly well. In both documents, the ruler of Moscow named his father-in-law guardian of his wife and children in the event of his death.[28]

While Vitovt's relations with the grand prince in Moscow usually sounded a harmonious note, his ambition brought him into conflict with the metropolitan of the Russian Church. As we have seen, Metropolitan Cyprian aspired to be an impartial pastor to all Russian Orthodox Christians. To a remarkable degree, he succeeded in living up to that difficult ideal. Twice – in 1396 and 1404 – he visited his flock in Lithuania, staying each time for well over a year. He came to know both Vitovt and Jagiello and cultivated good relations with them. On one occasion, he joined the Polish king in proposing that an ecumenical council be held on Lithuanian territory to discuss the reunion of the Roman Catholic and Eastern Orthodox Churches. Moreover, while in Lithuania, he settled local ecclesiastical disputes with the same mixture of firmness and tact that he had shown in his dealings with Tver and Novgorod. At the same time, he remained determined to preserve the unity of the Russian Church and put an end to the surviving traces of a separate west Russian hierarchy.

Photius, Cyprian's successor, found it far harder to maintain the unity of the church. Much of the fault lay with Vitovt. Cyprian died in 1406 – a time of open warfare between Lithuania and Moscow. Seizing the opportunity to make gains on the ecclesiastical front, Vitovt put forward his own candidate for the vacant office of metropolitan. The patriarch, however, refused to follow his lead and, in 1408, with Moscow's prompting, appointed Photius instead. Vitovt greeted the decision with undisguised hostility. Moreover, Photius, a hot-tempered man of authoritarian temperament, quickly made enemies by the rigour with which he collected the revenues and managed the properties that belonged to him as metropolitan. Thus, although, in theory, he was as devoted as his predecessor to the ideal of the Eastern Orthodox commonwealth, Photius quickly gained the reputation of partisan of Moscow's interests and an enemy of Lithuania.

In 1414, Vitovt took decisive steps to create a separate metropolitanate for Lithuania. Accusing Photius of neglecting the Orthodox faithful in his domains, the grand duke refused to allow him to travel to Kiev and expelled his representatives from Lithuanian territory. Vitovt then brought forth Grigorii Tsamblak, a learned and ambitious Bulgarian cleric, as his candidate to be metropolitan in Kiev. The authorities in Moscow immediately protested to the patriarch of Constantinople and, in response, the patriarch excommunicated Tsamblak for his role in the affair. Not to be deterred, however, Vitovt had a synod of local Orthodox bishops confirm his candidate as metropolitan. In 1418, Tsamblak appeared as the grand duke's representative at the Council of Constance in order to discuss problems of church union. Indeed, it is possible that Vitovt had even grander plans for him: some sources suggest that he hoped to reunite the entire Russian Orthodox Church under a metropolitan with his seat in Kiev.[29]

In any event, Vitovt's plans came to naught. Tsamblak disappeared from the scene in 1419 and, in the following year, Photius, true to his ecumenical convictions, immediately made a pastoral visit to Lithuania to reunite the see. In the long run, he succeeded in winning Vitovt's grudging acceptance and, by the time of the death of his patron, Vasilii I, was secure in his position as head of a united ecclesiastical hierarchy in the Russian lands. Over the course of his long and difficult reign, Vasilii I displayed, above all, a talent for survival. In spite of everything, he succeeded in defending the gains of his predecessors on the throne of Moscow. As grand prince of Vladimir, he remained the primary political and military leader of the principalities of north-east Russia. To be sure, the other rulers of the area probably enjoyed greater freedom from Moscow's control than they had at the height of Dmitrii Donskoi's power. None, however, seriously threatened Vasilii's position of primacy. Moreover, in 1425, Moscow was still the seat of the metropolitan of the Orthodox Church in all the Russian lands.

In international affairs, too, Vasilii's accomplishments were essentially negative. His government weathered Vitovt's military and diplomatic offensive. Even so, at the end of his reign, the grand duke of Lithuania was undoubtedly the most powerful ruler in the Russian lands. In a sense, however, Moscow emerged stronger than before because of the precipitous decline in the power of the Golden Horde.

At the same time, as Vasilii's reign demonstrated all too clearly, the gains made by the house of Moscow could easily be lost. In particular, the organization of the principality of Moscow and the relationships between members of its ruling dynasty threatened to undermine the grand princely throne. Like his ancestors, Vasilii I shared the Moscow domain and its revenues with the other members of the family – his older cousin, Vladimir Andreevich of Serpukhov, and his younger brothers. In his capacity as grand prince and head of the family, Vasilii followed the precedent of his father, Dmitrii Donskoi, making arbitrary territorial settlements with each individual in turn. Moreover, like Donskoi, he felt free to dispose of lands that pertained, not only to the family holdings of the house of Moscow, but also to the office of grand prince.[30] Since the implications of customary law were ambiguous and the stakes in family disputes grew higher, the principality of Moscow – the foundation of the grand prince's power – was vulnerable to precisely the same kind of internal strife that had paralysed other Russian principalities in earlier times. For several generations, the small number of adult males in the ruling house had spared Moscow the tribulations of Tver or Riazan. When Vasilii I died, however, the clouds of civil strife were already gathering.

Early in the reign of his son, Vasilii II (1425–62), smouldering tensions within the principality of Moscow exploded into civil war. When he ascended the throne, the new ruler, then ten years old, faced a formidable opponent in his uncle, Iurii of Galich. During the reign of his older brother, Vasilii I, Iurii had shown clear signs of ambition and independence of mind. Sources of the time contain strong hints that the grand prince and his brother did not trust each other. Moreover, Iurii consolidated his hold on his share of the common inheritance of the Muscovite ruling family; he constructed a solid base in the prosperous Galich region, north of the upper Volga, and built up his capital, Zvenigorod, to the west of Moscow, adorning it with fine churches so that it rivalled the grand prince's seat.[31]

As soon as his older brother died, Iurii threatened to challenge his nephew's succession. In the first confrontation, however, the young Vasilii II had two powerful allies – Grand Duke Vitovt of Lithuania, his grandfather and guardian, and Metropolitan Photius, head of the church in Russia. When Iurii gathered an army to oppose Vasilii's accession, Photius intervened decisively. He made a pastoral visit to Galich, urging Iurii to submit and, when the latter refused, withheld his blessing from the recalcitrant prince's subjects. The spiritual arrow hit the mark: the frightened people of Galich put pressure on their ruler to abandon the armed struggle against Vasilii. Tension and uncertainty continued until 1428 when Iurii finally recognized Vasilii as grand prince, in part in response to Vitovt's military pressure on Novgorod and Pskov.

Vasilii II did not enjoy his triumph for long. Death soon deprived him of his principal allies, Vitovt and Photius, and, as soon as they were gone, Iurii, in 1431, claimed the throne of Moscow. Civil war was at hand.

The ambition of the Galich line of the ruling house of Moscow provided the main fuel for the conflagration. At the same time, Iurii based his claim to be grand prince on customary law. In the house of Riurik and within the noble clans of east Russia, primacy within the family usually passed, not from father to son, but from the eldest brother to the second, third and fourth brothers and only then to the next generation. That, at least, was the usual custom. In point of fact, however, Iurii's challenge was anachronistic. For more than a century, the accidents of birth and death had kept the succession within the Moscow branch of the Riurikovichi very simple. In all but two cases, the house of Moscow passed the grand princely throne from father to son. Iurii and Simeon the Proud died without direct male heirs and, in these instances, younger brothers – Ivan I and Ivan II – succeeded. Never, since Moscow's emergence from obscurity, had a ruler's younger brother followed him on the throne in preference to his son as Iurii advocated. Even so, Iurii could point to one important document – the second will of his father, Dmitrii Donskoi – to support his claim to be Vasilii I's rightful heir. Writing at a time when the future Vasilii I had as yet no son, Donskoi had indeed stipulated that, on Vasilii's death, the throne should pass to Iurii.[32]

Regional loyalties also contributed to the conflict. The princes of Galich consistently enjoyed the support of that region and other parts of the north, including independent Viatka. Apparently the leading citizens of the Galich area, rich in furs and salt, wanted to keep control over their local resources. Conflicting personalities and family ambitions also played their part. Not only did the struggle pit the leading members of the house of Moscow against one another; it also brought the clashing ambitions of leading boyars and their clans to the fore.

Like similar dynastic struggles elsewhere in Europe, the Muscovite civil wars, for the most part, directly involved only the upper classes of society, By and large, peasants and townspeople became involved in the struggle as accidental victims of the clashes of their rulers and social superiors.

When Iurii of Galich claimed the grand princely throne in 1431, Vasilii II and his advisers met the challenge. In the time-honoured manner, both princes sent representatives to the khan, Ulug Mehmet, to advance their cause. By all accounts, Vasilii's spokesman, I. D. Vsevolozhskii, did a masterful job, convincing the khan to give Vasilii the patent. As a magnanimous victor, the grand prince gave his defeated uncle the coveted family possession of Dmitrov.

The settlement did not last long. Soon tension exploded into armed conflict. First, Vsevolozhskii deserted to Iurii's camp, apparently because Vasilii and his advisers went back on a promise that the young grand prince would marry his daughter. One slight led to another. According to chronicle accounts, Iurii's son, Vasilii Kosoi, attended the grand prince's wedding to the daughter of the prince of Serpukhov. For the great occasion, Kosoi wore a jewelled gold belt. When he appeared at the celebration, Vasilii's mother demanded that he be stripped of it on the grounds that it actually belonged in the grand princely treasury. Understandably Kosoi returned to his father's court in a rage.[33] Whether or not we take the story literally, it admirably epitomizes the bitterness that divided the courts of Moscow and Galich.

Iurii struck quickly in the spring of 1433. Catching Vasilii off guard, he seized Moscow and the throne. Vasilii had no choice but to recognize him as grand prince and accept his grant of Kolomna as his appanage.

Before long the pendulum swung back. Many nobles refused to recognize the new regime and made their allegiance to Vasilii clear. With his support dwindling, Iurii had little choice but to leave Moscow and its throne to his rival.

Before proceeding, we would do well to examine why the nobles of the court in Moscow behaved as they did. For one thing, a number of them may well have believed that Vasilii – not Iurii – had a legitimate right to the grand princely throne since, up to that point in Moscow's history, an undisputed succession, usually from father to son, had kept the principality united and strong. In addition, they may well have seen the most practical of reasons for remaining loyal to Vasilii even in defeat. Each of the princes of Russia, within the territory of the house of Moscow and elsewhere, had his own group of retainers. If Iurii were to establish himself as grand prince, most nobles of the Moscow court had good reason to fear that members of Iurii's entourage from Galich would replace them in positions of power around the throne. Again and again in the course of the conflict, then, Vasilii – no paragon of effectiveness or personal charm – could count on the support of the nobles of the Moscow court even in moments of defeat and despair.[34]

A period of confusion followed Vasilii's return to power. For one thing, Iurii had made peace with his rival, but his sons were not party to the agreement. Accordingly, Vasilii sent troops against them and sacked Galich. He also began a fatal series of acts of vengeance by imprisoning and blinding Vsevolozhskii, his erstwhile champion.

The tide of battle quickly turned. Early in 1434, Iurii defeated Vasilii and once again seized Moscow. On this occasion, Vasilii's position seemed desperate. He was reduced to the position of a fugitive, trying futilely to rally support in various parts of Russia. Meanwhile, Iurii sat in his capital, holding his rival's mother and wife as hostages, and gaining recognition from some powerful figures, above all, Ivan, prince of Mozhaisk, a cousin of the contenders for power and lord of an important appanage in the principality of Moscow.

Just when Vasilii's fortunes seemed at a low ebb, the nature of the struggle abruptly changed, for Iurii suddenly died. No longer could the princes of Galich claim the throne of Moscow on legal grounds. The struggle became one of conflicting ambitions and loyalties, pure and simple. Iurii's eldest son, Vasilii Kosoi, tried to maintain himself on the Moscow throne. Even his younger brothers, however, rejected his claim and made peace with Vasilii II. Kosoi's position was hopeless: he abandoned Moscow and began to fight a stubborn war of attrition from his base in the north. For two years, he held out. Finally in 1436, Vasilii II captured him and had him blinded, either on grounds that he had broken earlier treaties with his captor or that he had stolen the grand princely treasury when he had fled Moscow.

In one sense, the blinding of Kosoi achieved its purpose. The bloody act effectively destroyed him as a political force and brought the first round of civil war to an end. In another, the atrocity only increased the bitterness that separated Moscow and Galich and led, in the end, to more bloodshed; for the act of revenge did not settle the rivalries – personal and family, political and territorial – that had increasingly come to the fore in the first round of fighting.

The breathing-space allowed Vasilii's government to turn its attention to a long-standing crisis in the church. Since the death of Photius, the office of metropolitan had, in effect, remained vacant. The consensus of local opinion in Moscow, lay and clerical, favoured the appointment of Jonah, bishop of Riazan, who presented himself in Constantinople in 1436 as a candidate for the vacant metropolitan throne.

He and his backers quickly discovered that the emperor and patriarch had priorities very different from their own. By this time, the Ottoman Turks had conquered most of the territory of the Byzantine Empire and were closing in on the imperial capital. In this desperate position, the leaders of the empire responded favourably to diplomatic overtures from the West. The pope and other leaders of Roman Catholicism invited Byzantine representatives to negotiate a reunion of the Eastern and Western churches in return for Western European military aid in stemming the Turkish flood. The prospect of the reunification of Christendom was both alluring and unsettling. Within both communions, especially the Orthodox, suspicion of the other ran deep. As events were to prove, many clerics and ordinary believers in the Greek Church passionately opposed the very idea of union with the hated Latins.

In their campaign for union, the emperor and the patriarch had to build up their forces. Accordingly, they used the vacancy on the metropolitan throne of Russia to advance the career of one of their most energetic and talented agents, Isidore, abbot of the Monastery of St Demetrius in Constantinople. The latter had already taken an enthusiastic part in the preliminary negotiations for an ecumenical council on church union that was soon to meet in Ferrara.

Even though Vasilii II and his advisers must have been bitterly disappointed at the choice of Isidore, they treated him respectfully when he made his appearance in Moscow in the spring of 1437. Within a matter of weeks, the new metropolitan set off for the council in Italy, accompanied by a large Russian delegation representing both Moscow and Tver.

The events that unfolded in Ferrara and Florence, to which the council soon moved, took the Muscovite government and hierarchy completely by surprise. The supporters of union within the Orthodox delegations forged an agreement with the Roman Catholics largely on the latter's terms. After complex negotiations about the precise verbal formulae, the Eastern Orthodox delegates, with significant exceptions, accepted the Latin formulation that the Holy Spirit proceeded not from God the Father alone, as the Eastern tradition taught, but from both Father and Son. They also recognized the pope as the primary leader within Christendom. The Eastern Orthodox Churches would, however, preserve their own distinct liturgies.

Isidore, the head of the Russian delegation, played a very important part in hammering out the agreement and received his due reward – a cardinal's hat and designation as papal legate to Poland, Russia and other areas of Eastern Europe. The native Russians who attended the council reacted very differently, however. While Isidore made a leisurely journey through the capitals of Eastern Europe, the most prominent Russian delegates rushed on ahead. When they reached their homeland, they denounced the union and claimed that they had accepted it only under duress. Two of them who left later written accounts of their experiences – the monk Simeon of Suzdal and the boyar Foma of Tver – made those points with unmistakable clarity. Moreover, Isidore himself gave his Russian flock an indication of things to come when he issued a pastoral letter in Buda in 1440 announcing the union in tactfully vague terms and proclaiming that it was now permissible for Roman Catholics and Eastern Orthodox to make their communion in each other's churches.[35] A storm was brewing in Moscow.

Events moved rapidly once Isidore reached the capital on 19 March 1441. He entered the city preceded by attendants bearing a Latin cross and three episcopal croziers. As his first official act, he celebrated the liturgy in the Cathedral of the Dormition in the Kremlin in the course of which he mentioned the pope first in prayer instead of the Orthodox patriarch and had the act of union read aloud to the worshippers. Vasilii II was scandalized and refused to approach Isidore for his blessing. Instead he ordered the metropolitan's arrest and presented his case to a council of Russian bishops who had already gathered. After brief deliberations, the fathers of the church pronounced the act of union heretical and confirmed Isidore's imprisonment.

All of the main actors in the drama now found themselves in embarrassing positions. Vasilii and his ecclesiastical advisers had no desire to break Russia's ancient tie with Byzantium. At the same time, they were determined to reject the union which the emperor and patriarch supported and to be rid of Isidore who was the latter's hand-picked candidate for the metropolitan throne. Isidore, firmly convinced of the rightness of his cause, sat in a monastery dungeon in the Kremlin facing possible execution at the stake, the usual penalty for unrepentant heretics. Eventually a simple solution presented itself. Isidore escaped, probably with the connivance of the Muscovite authorities. He first fled to Tver where he suffered the identical fate before finally leaving Russian territory altogether.[36]

Isidore's disappearance from the scene left the Muscovite government and church with a larger, but subtler, dilemma. The metropolitan throne was vacant, but to fill it without the patriarch's approval would break the historic tie with the Byzantine Church. Vasilii's regime accordingly hesitated, hoping perhaps that the authorities in Constantinople would return to true Orthodoxy and renounce the union with the Latins. Only in 1448, when domestic political considerations demanded that a metropolitan be consecrated, did a council of Russian bishops choose Jonah of Riazan as metropolitan. The decision, in practice, made the Russian Church fully independent of Byzantium. Intellectually and emotionally, however, it took the Muscovite Church and government years to come to grips with the meaning of their actions.

While the crisis within the church unfolded, changes took place in the political life of the Golden Horde that profoundly affected all of Eastern Europe and the steppe, including Russia. The reign of Ulug-Mehmet, who first became khan in 1419, marked the end of the Horde's unity. In the first years of his reign, Ulug-Mehmet survived a series of civil wars only with the support of Grand Duke Vitovt of Lithuania. Then, after a brief recovery, he had to face the challenge of two rival claimants to the khan's throne. Thus, by the early 1430s, the Golden Horde had split into three distinct hordes, each with its own military force and diplomatic orientation.

Out of the confusion, four sedentary states eventually emerged – the khanates of the Crimea, Kazan, Astrakhan and Siberia. In addition, the Great Nogai Horde maintained the nomadic traditions of the Mongol conquerors in the open steppe beyond the borders of the khanates. Over the next century the rulers of these sedentary states – along with the princes of Moscow – struggled, individually and in combinations, to control these nomads of the grasslands.[37]

The pressure of his rivals forced Ulug-Mehmet northward and, in 1437, he took refuge in Belev along Moscow's border with Lithuania. Vasilii II attempted to drive him back into the steppes. He failed and, for a number of years, the khan remained free to raid Moscow's southern frontiers and, on occasion, the capital city itself. In 1444, he made a decisive move to the east and used a new base, either Nizhnii-Novgorod or Gorodets, to launch raids on the south-eastern lands of the grand principality. Vasilii II, distracted by Lithuanian attacks along the western frontier, mobilized against the khan slowly. His indecisiveness had devastating consequences.

In the following spring, 1445, Ulug-Mehmet sent his sons, Mamutek and Iusuf, on a pillaging raid into Muscovite territory. Once again, Vasilii had difficulty mobilizing his forces and, on 6 July met the enemy near Suzdal with only a part of his army. He suffered a disastrous defeat and was taken prisoner.

The grand prince's sudden misfortune brought all of the seething political and personal rivalries within the Muscovite realm to the surface once again. For the moment, the fate of the grand principality lay in Ulug-Mehmet's hands. The khan withdrew eastward with his distinguished prisoner and weighed the alternatives that faced him. In the past, for the most part, he had tried to establish good relations with Vasilii. At the same time, he may well have carried bitter memories of the grand prince's attempt to dislodge him from his refuge in Belev when he first fled north from the steppe. Be that as it may, Ulug-Mehmet suddenly turned to Vasilii's rival, Dmitrii Shemiaka, younger son of Iurii of Galich, and offered him the grand princely throne. Shemiaka was more than willing to revive his claim to rule. To his misfortune, however, he failed to complete the pact with the khan. The envoys entrusted with the negotiations were long delayed and eventually fell into the hands of Vasilii's troops. As he waited, Ulug-Mehmet apparently concluded that, in the end, Vasilii was the better bet. He released the grand prince.

Four months after being taken prisoner, Vasilii returned to Moscow. His entry was far from triumphal. Much of the city had been destroyed in a disastrous fire. The people were tense: they had lived in uncertainty while the head of state was a hostage and they had no idea what the future held. Without question, Ulug-Mehmet had freed Vasilii only on condition that he pay a staggering ransom. Moreover, the party of 500 Tatars who returned to the capital with the grand prince did nothing to reassure them. Rumours, probably sown by Dmitrii Shemiaka and his partisans, began to circulate to the effect that Vasilii had promised to abdicate in favour of Ulug-Mehmet.

Opposition to Vasilii quickly coalesced. A number of prominent nobles joined a plot to put Shemiaka on the throne. The conspirators struck when the grand prince unwisely went on a pilgrimage to the Holy Trinity Monastery with a small retinue. On 12 February 1446, Shemiaka's troops suddenly occupied Moscow. Shortly afterwards, Prince Ivan of Mozhaisk led a force that took Vasilii prisoner. In revenge for his earlier misdeeds, the conspirators blinded him and had him imprisoned in the northern town of Uglich. His defeat appeared final.

No sooner had Shemiaka seized Moscow, however, than opposition to his rule began to gather. Many leading churchmen and laymen could not accept as legitimate his claim to the grand princely throne. Moreover, the members of Vasilii's inner circle of advisers and servitors did not relish the prospect of being displaced by Shemiaka's supporters. Resistance to Shemiaka took a variety of forms. A number of Muscovite nobles fled to political asylum in Lithuania. Others conspired against the new ruler at home. In particular, the fate of Vasilii's young sons aroused concern. Fearing that they would become the focus of opposition, Shemiaka asked the most prominent leader of the church, Jonah of Riazan, to see to it that they were transferred from their place of refuge, Murom, to Moscow. Once Jonah had carried out his part of the bargain, however, Shemiaka broke his word and had the children imprisoned with their parents. Jonah was outraged and thereafter led the ecclesiastical hierarchy in opposing Shemiaka's regime.

Faced with growing opposition, particularly from the clergy, Shemiaka tried the path of compromise. He met Vasilii in Uglich and agreed to free him and give him Vologda as an appanage in return for recognition of his right to rule. Instead of accepting the settlement, Vasilii II and his advisers took it as a sign of their adversary's weakness. The former grand prince soon journeyed to the St Cyril Monastery of Beloozero where, according to some accounts, the abbot released him from his oath to Shemiaka. From there, he and his growing entourage moved to Tver whose prince had, up until then, behaved with circumspection. Prince Boris chose to throw in his lot whole-heartedly with Vasilii on one important condition – that the latter agree to the betrothal of his son, the future Ivan III, to Boris's daughter.

As Vasilii bided his time in Tver, his strength continued to grow. More and more servitors flocked to his banners: the exiles in Lithuania returned and two of Ulug-Mehmet's sons, Kasim and Iusuf, entered his service. For a time, he attempted to regain his throne through a negotiated settlement with Shemiaka. When diplomacy failed, Vasilii's forces moved on Moscow. In the face of overwhelming odds, Shemiaka withdrew to his domain in the north and, at Christmas 1446, Vasilii's army entered the capital unopposed.

In less than a year the grand prince had seen his fortunes change from defeat and degradation to overwhelming victory. The triumph was no tribute to Vasilii's brilliance as a leader. Despite his lack of attractive personal qualities, however, he succeeded in winning the support of powerful individuals and groups who saw that his cause represented their best interest. For their own reasons, the bulk of the Moscow court nobles, the ecclesiastical hierarchy and the prince of Tver all threw their support to him. Moreover, Shemiaka quickly alienated all but his most devoted supporters. His claim to the throne was a dubious one and, in addition, he achieved a reputation for perfidy, particularly over his handling of the negotiations concerning the future of Vasilii's sons.

From the moment that Shemiaka abandoned Moscow his fate was sealed. At the same time, he still had enough support, particularly in Galich and the adjoining northern regions, to stir up considerable mischief. Vasilii slowly mobilized all of his resources for a final, crushing victory. In strictly military terms, the civil war degenerated into a series of spasmodic campaigns and raids. Proceeding cautiously, Vasilii's army forced Shemiaka to capitulate in 1448 and swear an oath of allegiance to the grand prince. Shemiaka soon repudiated the agreement and continued to resist, with the increasingly open support of the government of Novgorod. Only in 1450 did Vasilii's government mount a major offensive to capture Galich. In the end, Shemiaka had no choice but to seek refuge in Novgorod. There, in 1453, he died, a victim, perhaps, of poisoners in Vasilii's service.

Military campaigns against his defeated rival were the least important of the measures that Vasilii II took to strengthen his hand. Significant changes on the international scene – not all of Vasilii's making – made his position considerably more secure. On the western front, he and Boris of Tver made treaties in 1449 with Casimir IV of Poland and Lithuania, establishing the borders and delineating the spheres of influence of the main principalities of north-eastern Europe. Casimir recognized Moscow's hegemony over Novgorod and Pskov. The principality of Riazan was to be regarded as dependent on both Moscow and Lithuania and Tver was to have friendly relations with both. In 1452, Vasilii cemented good relations with Tver by celebrating the promised marriage of Ivan and Maria, then respectively twelve and ten years old.

On the southern and eastern flank, Ulug-Mehmet's horde finally found a resting-place. Soon after he fortuitously captured Vasilii in 1445, the khan fell victim to strife within his own family. His eldest son, Mamutek, murdered him and moved the horde eastward to Kazan. There he founded the khanate that, for more than a century, was to be a powerful and, at times, troublesome neighbour of the emerging Muscovite state.

After their father's murder, Mamutek's younger brothers fled and, as we have seen, soon entered Moscow's service. They fought faithfully for Vasilii II. In the end, Kasim, the elder of them, had his reward. In 1452 or 1453, he settled in Gorodets Meshcherskii on the Oka river and established his own principality. There he and his successors occupied a strategic position between Moscow and Kazan. The rulers of the khanate of Kasimov – as the principality came to be known – gradually became clients of the princes of Moscow and helped them to play an active and informed part in the political and diplomatic life of the Tatar world of the steppes.[38]

As he mobilized for the final confrontation with Shemiaka, Vasilii's government took a number of steps to increase his prestige and power within the grand principality itself. To begin with, in 1448 Vasilii officially designated his eldest son, Ivan, as his heir and co-ruler. The step speaks well for the grand prince's prudence. Since his own reign had been bedevilled by disputes over the succession, he wanted no doubt as to the identity of his rightful heir. Moreover, now blind and probably weakened in other ways by the harrowing events of his life, Vasilii was less and less capable of playing the part of ceremonial military leader so important in holding the allegiance of the warrior nobles who dominated Russian society. In spite of his youth, the future Ivan III could at least play the symbolic role of military leader of the nation. In the last years of his life, Vasilii saw to it that, in moments of danger, he and his son remained apart so that, if one perished, the other would still be the undisputed leader of the grand principality.

The act of naming Ivan co-ruler had important implications for Moscow's relations with the Golden Horde. Vasilii II made the decision unilaterally, without securing the approval of any of the competing khans. The step, then, amounted to a repudiation of the Horde's overlordship.

At the same time, Vasilii II began to use a new and more exalted epithet, *gosudar*, to describe himself as ruler. The title, which may well be a direct translation of the Greek, *despotes*, implies the power of a householder or lord over his dependants or slaves. Within the Russian cultural world, the word had been used by rulers in Lithuania since the early fifteenth century. In Muscovy itself, it may well be that Shemiaka first used the title and Vasilii took it up like a thrown gauntlet. Whatever its origins, the epithet had a clear purpose – to impress Vasilii's subjects with his power and their obligation to obey him.[39]

In his dealings with the appanage princes – the members of the cadet branches of the ruling house of Moscow – Vasilii proceeded with equal circumspection. Soon after his triumphant return to Moscow, he made treaties with the most important of them, gaining pledges of loyalty in exchange for grants of additional territory from the patrimony of the ruling house. Even Ivan of Mozhaisk, Shemiaka's most stubborn ally, temporarily received territorial concessions in 1447 in reward for a momentary desertion to Vasilii's side. In the end, however, the prince of Mozhaisk was to pay dearly for his misplaced loyalties.[40]

Once the death of Shemiaka assured Vasilii's complete victory, the grand prince began to rule with a determination and ruthlessness that he had never shown before. In particular, Vasilii showed his awe-inspiring qualities in his implacable pursuit of his former enemies in the civil wars. His cousins, the appanage princes, felt his displeasure. In 1454 came the final reckoning with Ivan of Mozhaisk. Vasilii sent troops to his principality and, when Ivan fled to Lithuania, annexed it to the grand prince's personal domain. Two years later, Vasilii of Serpukhov-Borovsk suffered an even worse fate. Up until the final reckoning, Vasilii II had dealt arbitrarily, but fairly, with his cousin, for example giving him some of Ivan of Mozhaisk's former lands. In 1456, the grand prince suddenly had him arrested and confiscated his principality. For whatever reason, Vasilii II regarded his cousin as dangerous. In 1462, when some of the prince of Serpukhov's noble servitors tried to free him from prison, the grand prince had them executed with a savagery that horrified even his hardened contemporaries.

By the end of Vasilii's reign, the traditional pattern of relationships within the ruling house of Moscow had changed dramatically. Like his predecessors, beginning with Dmitrii Donskoi, Vasilii II, in his capacity as grand prince and family head, defined his relations with his cousins and set the boundaries of their territories as he saw fit. More concretely, moreover, by the end of his reign, he had succeeded in eliminating all but one of the surviving appanages, that of Michael of Vereia. At the same time, Vasilii was no revolutionary. He made no attempt to destroy the appanage system as such. Indeed, in his will, as a conventional and concerned father, he created new appanages for the younger four of his five sons.

The boyars who had fought against Vasilii during the civil wars also felt his wrath. During the struggle with the house of Galich, both sides increasingly demanded the loyal service of any noble who held lands in territories under their control. In practice, the right of noble servitors to change liege lords without penalty was severely curtailed and the definition of treason broadened considerably. According to a formula apparently adopted in the 1450s, a disloyal servitor who repented might be pardoned through the mediation of the head of the church if he took a solemn oath that he and all of the members of his family would serve the grand prince unswervingly in future. In practice, those prominent nobles who had not satisfied Vasilii's criteria of loyal service suffered accordingly. The grand prince confiscated their estates after imprisoning them or forcing them to flee into exile.

Nobles who had served Vasilii loyally received their due recompense. The nature of the rewards was calculated not to diminish the grand prince's prerogatives. Vasilii rarely granted his servitors estates on unconditional tenure. Instead, grants of land usually took the form of the right to use a particular estate for the servitor's lifetime, after which it reverted to the original owner, usually an ecclesiastical corporation or a member of the ruling house. More common still were appointments as the grand prince's governor or representative in the provinces. Such posts, customarily held for a year, allowed the holder to collect substantial revenues (kormlenie or 'feeding') for himself from the territory under his jurisdiction.[41]

In settling the score with his enemies, Vasilii II turned on Novgorod and Viatka, regions that had supported Shemiaka. Novgorod had only recently fallen into sin. For most of Vasilii's reign, the republic had recognized the suzerainty of the grand prince in Moscow. In practice, its leaders pursued their own diplomatic course, conducting independent relations with Lithuania, Pskov and Tver. Through most of the Muscovite civil wars, Novgorod remained neutral. Its leaders committed themselves to the cause of the house of Galich only in the final stage of the conflict.[42]

The step proved to be very costly. In 1456, the grand prince led a sizeable military expedition against the great city-republic. The city fathers persuaded Pskov to send help, but, before the sister-city's forces arrived, the disciplined Muscovite army had defeated a larger Novgorodian force. Vasilii then dictated the Treaty of Iazhelbitsy to the helpless metropolis. Novgorod agreed to pay an indemnity of 8,500 roubles to the grand prince and promised never again to harbour his enemies. The treaty prohibited the Novgorodian assembly (veche) from making treaties with foreign powers. Finally – and perhaps most significantly – the agreement specified that only the grand prince's emblem was to appear on Novgorod's coins and official seal.[43]

The grand prince was making clear his determination to exercise Moscow's long-claimed hegemony over the city. At the same time, there is no reason to assume that Vasilii wanted to annex Novgorod altogether: his main concern was to ensure that the city never dabbled in Muscovite affairs again. Even though his ambitions concerning the city appear to have been limited, the treaty's severity caused deep resentment. The city's leaders turned to Casimir IV of Lithuania with a request that he send them a prince to guard the frontiers. On this occasion, the experiment with a prince from Lithuania lasted only one year. It was, however, a sign of things to come. Equally prophetic was Vasilii's response: in 1460, he visited the city in order to reassert his control. Novgorod had reached the final phase of its independence.

Vasilii dealt equally sternly with Viatka, the wild north-eastern frontier area which had consistently supported the princes of Galich. He sent military expeditions which conquered the area in 1459 and added it to the grand princely domain. In the long run, however, Moscow's control over the remote area slipped and had to be asserted again in 1489.

While less dramatic, Vasilii's government made significant gains in its relations with the other principalities of Russia. In connection with his official visit to Novgorod in 1460, the grand prince conducted negotiations with representatives of Pskov. The rulers of Moscow had long claimed hegemony over the city. At the same time, Vasilii was far more favourably disposed towards Pskov than Novgorod since Pskov had remained strictly neutral in the civil wars. Recognizing the legitimacy of Moscow's claims, the city's representatives attempted to have their current prince, a servitor of the grand duke of Lithuania, recognized as Moscow's agent. When the prince in question refused to accept the arrangement and returned home, Pskov accepted a succession of Muscovite nobles as its governors.[44] The leaders of the city, however, retained considerable freedom of action in charting a course between the claims of the grand princes of Moscow and the pressure of Lithuania and the Teutonic Knights to the west.

In the last years of Vasilii's reign, Riazan occupied a very different position. The small south-eastern principality faced one problem above all – frequent raids by the competing Tatar hordes that fought for control of the steppe. Given Riazan's location, only the rulers of Moscow could provide quick and effective military support. It was only natural, then, that Riazan increasingly drifted into Moscow's orbit. In 1456, when its prince died, he left his domain and his minor children under Vasilii II's control. For some years, agents of the grand prince administered the principality. Then, in 1464, Ivan III, true to his father's word, restored the legitimate heir – now his brother-in-law – to the throne.

After a long period of decline, Vasilii's government had succeeded in reasserting Moscow's clear leadership within north-east Russia. During the first half of the fifteenth century, the princes of Tver had acted as independent rulers, conducting their own foreign policy and proclaiming that their realm was a distinct centre of Russian Orthodoxy. Nevertheless, they never directly challenged Moscow's primacy. Indeed, in the later years of Vasilii II's reign, Tver and Moscow became increasingly friendly. A formal alliance between them, forged during the second round of fighting, continued to become stronger thanks to a treaty, concluded in about 1456 and subsequently renewed. Lithuanian influence in north-east Russia had reached a low ebb.

In regaining his throne and consolidating his power, Vasilii, like his predecessors, found particularly staunch allies in the leaders of the Russian Orthodox Church. As we have seen, the Council of Florence and its aftermath left both the grand prince and the ecclesiastical hierarchy in a quandary. There was no metropolitan to exert leadership or help the government weather its political troubles. Yet to appoint one without the approval of the patriarch would mean a break with Byzantium which no one wanted.

Eventually, as Gustave Alef has persuasively argued, the price of inaction became unbearably high. The second round of the civil wars showed clearly that, in order to be strong, the grand principality required united and effective ecclesiastical leadership. In the crisis surrounding Vasilii II's capture and subsequent temporary overthrow, the church had been unable to fill the vacuum of leadership. In the confusion, Jonah, still the obvious native candidate for the metropolitan throne, had gradually emerged as guardian of the grand prince's children and interests. Then, in 1447, Vasilii received a ringing endorsement from the ecclesiastical hierarchy. The fathers of the church condemned Shemiaka in no uncertain terms and stated that if he did not end armed resistance within three weeks he would be excommunicated. The final step in strengthening the church soon followed. In spite of some misgivings on the canonical implications of the step, the leaders of the Muscovite Church agreed to name Jonah as metropolitan. In 1448, the church at last had the strong leader it so badly needed.

Before long, events outside of east Russia pushed the Muscovite Church and the grand princes into a closer dependence on one another. First of all, the Ottoman conquest of Constantinople in 1453 clarified Russian Orthodoxy's relationship to the Greek mother church. Thereafter, Muscovite Russia was the only major state whose government and people were Eastern Orthodox. Even though it took them a long time to draw out the full implications of their new position, Russian churchmen now knew that, from their own perspective, they stood alone in the world. Their chief protector was the Orthodox grand prince of Moscow, heir, by default, of the Byzantine emperor.

The emerging Muscovite state and its church grew together in another sense as well. When Jonah formally became metropolitan, he won recognition from the Russian Orthodox hierarchy in Lithuania as well as at home. In the treaty of 1449, Casimir IV officially accepted his authority. As the years passed, however, the grand duke, like some of his predecessors, increasingly resented the advantage that control of the Russian hierarchy gave the grand prince in Moscow. The dramatic diplomatic successes of Vasilii II's last years may well have fuelled that resentment.

In any case, Casimir abruptly changed direction in 1458. He arranged to have Gregory, a champion of church union and former associate of Isidore, consecrated as metropolitan of the Russian Orthodox Church in his domains, with Kiev as his seat. Political pressure soon forced the rest of the local hierarchy to accept the new arrangements. At last a ruler of Lithuania had achieved the long-standing goal of an enduring separate hierarchy.[45]

Casimir's policy had momentous consequences for the future of the church in north-east Russia. With one blow, the grand duke destroyed the ideal which Cyprian and Photius had defended so passionately – a united Orthodox Church ministering to all East Slavic believers from its centre in Moscow.

Their successors as metropolitans had to adjust to the new reality. Stripped of the dioceses under Lithuanian control, Jonah and those who followed him on the metropolitan throne came to depend more and more on the support of the grand princes of Moscow whose territorial jurisdiction increasingly coincided with theirs. Naturally enough, then, spokesmen for the church began, at last, to draw out the implications of the fall of Byzantium for the grand prince as Orthodox ruler. At the very end of Vasilii II's reign, in the heat of the unsuccessful struggle to stop the creation of the Lithuanian hierarchy, ecclesiastical writers addressed the grand prince with the epithets, 'tsar' and 'samoderzhets' (autocrat). The melding of Moscow's ecclesiastical role and political ambitions had begun.

The reign of Vasilii II marks the triumph over adversity of an entire community. In the last years of his reign, after years of confusion and bloodshed, the power and prestige of the grand prince of Moscow grew by leaps and bounds. Victory gave his government and its supporters, lay and ecclesiastical, an awareness of the potential strength of the realm. The grand prince and his inner circle of advisers made ever more insistent demands on the loyalty and obedience of all of the people of the grand principality. In his relationships with members of his own family, Vasilii acted in a complex and often old-fashioned way. Nevertheless, by the end of his reign, two things had become clear. First, the grand prince was to be the unchallengeable head of the ruling house, endowed with dignities and private wealth that overwhelmed those of his lesser kinsmen. In his will, Vasilii bequeathed to his eldest son, Ivan, the office of grand prince, most of the territory of the grand principality and the exclusive right to collect the Tatar tribute.[46] Secondly, as Vasilii had shown in dealing with his cousins, the grand prince was the sole arbiter of the ruling family's affairs, defining the standards of loyal conduct required of the junior members and punishing those who failed to live up to them.

Towards the other principalities of north-east Russia, Moscow acted with increasing assertiveness. In the ecclesiastical world, the Muscovite Church – more by accident than by design – became autocephalous and, in a broad sense, national.

Moscow's relations with the Tatar world of the steppe also underwent radical change. In Vasilii's time, the grand principality, in effect, ceased to recognize the suzerainty of the Golden Horde, now in disarray. In particular, the future Ivan III became co-ruler in Moscow without the Horde's consent. Moscow was no longer a dependency of the Horde; instead, it became one of the Horde's successors alongside the khanates of Kazan and the Crimea. Future relations with the steppe world would consist of a complex mixture of pragmatic diplomatic manoeuvres and outbursts of warfare.[47]

Thus out of the ebb and flow of the confusing events of the late thirteenth and early fourteenth centuries, Moscow suddenly emerged as the undisputed and increasingly formidable leader of north-east Russia. The incremental steps that Dmitrii Donskoi and his successors took to give their power a solid foundation probably contributed even more to the grand principality's rise than brilliant victories like the triumph on the Kulikovo Pole. And, in his last years, that most unglamorous of rulers, Vasilii II, moved quickly forward on the paths indicated by his predecessors. The stage was set for the triumphs of Ivan the Great.

REFERENCES AND NOTES

1. Cherepnin, *Obrazovanie*, p. 627.
2. *Testaments*, pp. 215–16.
3. Vodoff, 'Place'.
4. Raba, 'Novgorod'.
5. *TR*, p. 421.
6. Ibid., p. 408.
7. Meyendorff, *Byzantium*, p. 224.
8. Presniakov, *Formation*, p. 299.
9. Meyendorff, *Byzantium*, p. 229.
10. Grekov, *Evropa*, p. 189.
11. Meyendorff, *Byzantium*, p. 246; Obolensky, '*Anthropos*', p. 94.
12. Ibid., pp. 264–5.
13. Meyendorff, *Byzantium*, p. 255.
14. Ibid., p. 255–7.
15. Obolensky, '*Anthropos*', p. 96.
16. Presniakov, *Formation*, pp. 302–3.
17. Golubinskii, *Istoriia*, vol. 2, part 1, pp. 311–13.
18. Presniakov, *Formation*, p. 288.
19. Grekov, *Evropa*, pp. 216–19.
20. Ibid., pp. 202–4.
21. Nasonov, *Mongoly*, pp. 138–9, 142–4; Kuchkin, 'Nizhnii Novgorod', pp. 251–2.
22. Cherepnin, *Obrazovanie*, pp. 697–701.
23. Presniakov, *Formation*, pp. 289–91.
24. *PSRL* 11:158–61.
25. Spuler, *Horde*, pp. 134–5.
26. Ibid., p. 144
27. Cherepnin, *Obrazovanie*, p. 709.
28. *Testaments*, pp. 233, 240.
29. Jablonowski, *Westrussland*, pp. 81–2.
30. Presniakov, *Formation*, pp. 312–21.
31. Alef, 'History', pp. 80–7.
32. *Testaments*, p. 215.
33. Alef, 'History', pp. 125–6; Shields Kollmann, 'Kinship', pp. 310–13.
34. Ibid., pp. 301–2.
35. Alef, 'History', pp. 199–202; Cherniavsky, 'Reception', pp. 347–50; Gill, *Council*, p. 359.

36. After his escape from the Russian lands, Isidore devoted the rest of his career to the cause of church union. In 1452, he journeyed to Constantinople as papal legate to proclaim the Union of Florence and, in the following year, lived through the capture of the city by the Turks. He died in Rome in 1464.
37. Keenan, 'Muscovy and Kazan, 1445–1552', pp. xi-xiii, 120–3; Safargaliev, *Raspad*, pp. 260–2.
38. Keenan, 'Muscovy and Kazan, 1445–1552', pp. 3–4, 137–44. See also Vernadsky, *Mongols*, pp. 292–5, 299–302, 316–17; Alef, 'History', pp. 246–54.
39. Ibid., pp. 339–51; Szeftel, 'Title', pp. 62–5.
40. Alef, 'History', pp. 308–15.
41. Ibid., pp. 390–405; Veselovskii, *Feodalnoe zemlevladenie*, pp. 76–7.
42. Bernadskii, *Novgorod*, pp. 237–52.
43. Ibid., pp. 252–63; Alef, 'History', pp. 410–18.
44. Cherepnin, *Obrazovanie*, pp. 830–42.
45. The west Russian metropolitan see became Uniate in 1596 as a consequence of the ecclesiastical Union of Brest. In 1620, the Eastern Orthodox leaders in the Ukraine founded their own metropolitanate of Kiev under the jurisdiction of the patriarch of Constantinople. In the 1680s the patriarch of Moscow took the Kievan see under his jurisdiction. Thereafter, with brief interruptions, the Ukrainian Orthodox hierarchy has remained a part of the Great Russian ecclesiastical structure until the present.
46. *Testaments*, pp. 242–61.
47. Keenan, 'Muscovy and Kazan: remarks'.

CHAPTER FOUR

Building the autocracy, 1462 – 1533

In the reigns of Ivan III (1462 – 1505) and Vasilii III (1505 – 33), the Muscovite monarchy became a strong nation-state and a powerful force in the international relations of Eastern and Central Europe and the Near East. At first glance, the Muscovite state seems to have appeared on the map suddenly in the last decades of the fifteenth century. As historians have long been aware, however, Ivan and Vasilii drew upon the material and human resources so carefully hoarded by their predecessors over the course of a century and a half. In particular, many of their policies and achievements flowed directly from those of Vasilii II, who, in the last years of his reign, greatly increased his prestige and effective power as grand prince of Moscow.

Historians have sometimes classified Ivan as a 'new monarch' alongside his contemporaries in western Europe – Henry VII of England, Louis XI of France and Ferdinand and Isabella of Spain. Like many another historical label, 'new monarchy' has distinctly limited value when used to compare societies as different as those of late medieval Russia and England or Spain. At the same time, the concept can legitimately be used to point to general similarities in the political style and concrete achievements of these rulers of the late fifteenth century.

All of the 'new monarchs' were ambitious and highly successful rulers. They greatly increased their effective power over their subjects by a variety of means – manipulating powerful men and their families, building rudimentary administrative systems and appealing to men's loyalty through the skilful use of political symbols and rhetoric. Moreover, like Ivan and Vasilii, the rulers of France and Spain dramatically expanded the area of the lands under their control. After their reigns, their governments administered large blocks of contiguous territory.

The 'new monarchs'' achievements were far more dramatic than their methods. Instead of instituting dramatic campaigns of reform, they proceeded cautiously, dealing with one problem or situation at a time. Moreover, unlike some of their successors, the 'new monarchs' used existing institutions and practices and well-established political rhetoric in strengthening and justifying their power. While reaching out for new territories or new prerogatives, they insisted that they sought only to restore their ancient and legitimate rights.

These very general characteristics fit Ivan III and Vasilii III remarkably well, if we may judge them by our only source of evidence – their deeds. For the most part, their personal appearance and characters must remain a closed book for us. In spite of the length of their reigns, no authentic portraits and virtually no written descriptions of the men have come down to us. Indeed, as personalities, they made remarkably little impression on the foreign diplomats whom they received. The documents issued in their name were official state papers intended to screen, rather than reveal, the personal qualities of the supposed authors. We know Ivan and Vasilii, then, almost entirely from the principal facts of their biographies and the actions of the government which they led. Thus any statements that we make about their personal beliefs or emotions involve a large element of risk.

A brief review of the career and accomplishments of Ivan III brings a number of words to mind – ambitious, ruthless, cautious, opportunistic. Throughout his reign, Ivan worked for the aggrandizement of his realm and of his office as ruler. When the weaknesses of his enemies gave him opportunities, he was quick to exploit them to the utmost. At the same time, he was no knight in shining armour. When possible, Ivan preferred to pursue his ends by political and diplomatic rather than military means and, when warfare was unavoidable, made sure that the odds were overwhelmingly in his favour.

More than anything else, Ivan III was a master politician. The experiences of his childhood and youth must have made him acutely aware of the rewards of political power and the dangers of losing it. Born in the breathing space between two rounds of civil war, Ivan soon experienced dramatic changes in his fortunes. At the age of six, he fell into the hands of his father's rival for the throne, Dmitrii Shemiaka, and, only after a period of delay and intrigue, was reunited with his parents in their place of confinement. Before long, he shared in Vasilii II's triumphant return to the throne and, in 1448, at the age of eight, became heir apparent and nominal co-ruler of the Muscovite grand principality. When he was twelve, his father married him, in a political match, to the daughter of the grand prince of Tver. Early in life, then, Ivan apparently learned to trust no one and to shape his personal life to the demands of his office.

As a mature ruler, Ivan III seems to have gained men's respect, but not their affection. In so far as we can judge, he chose his advisers and subordinates well: he did not hesitate to dismiss and punish even the most powerful of his courtiers. In his family relationships, politics likewise came first. His own second marriage, to Sophia Palaeologa – niece of the last Byzantine emperor and ward of the pope – was a classic diplomatic union, and a most ambitious one at that. He expected his children to do likewise. In one of the rare glimpses of his private persona in his official correspondence, he appears, chiding his daughter, Elena, for displaying more loyalty to her husband, Grand Duke Alexander of Lithuania, than to the aims of her father's foreign policy![1] When faced with an awkward choice of a successor, Ivan treated both his eldest surviving son and his grandson cruelly in turn, before finally settling on the former, the future Vasilii III. To what degree private emotions, positive or negative, entered into Ivan's choice of his grandson, Dmitrii, and then of Vasilii, we shall never know.

In his conduct of day-to-day affairs, Ivan III reacted pragmatically to the opportunities and dangers that confronted him. But was he more than a mere opportunist? Did he have general goals or ideals which he pursued with any consistency? Some specialists, notably Ivan's biographer, John Fennell, answer in the affirmative. 'His goal was the union of all Russia – of Great, Little and White Russia – under the independent leadership of the grand prince of Moscow, and the creation of a centralized State . . .'[2] While this view may exaggerate the degree to which Ivan consciously pursued a single broad aim, Fennell is surely correct in stressing the remarkable consistency of his military and diplomatic policy. Moreover, the objective of unifying all of the Russian-speaking Orthodox lands under Moscow's leadership complements Ivan's only clear ideological commitments – his firm conviction that Eastern Orthodoxy was the only authentic form of Christianity and his corresponding antipathy to Roman Catholicism.

Vasilii III is an equally elusive figure. We have, if anything, even less direct evidence about his personality and beliefs than his father's. Judging by the only criteria we have – his actions – Vasilii followed closely in Ivan III's footsteps. He too learned the value of power the hard way. During the succession crises at the end of his father's life, Vasilii suffered disgrace and rejection, then suddenly emerged as heir to the throne. Once he became ruler, he fought, above all, to maintain and improve his position, dealing ruthlessly with any threats to his power. When he felt the need, he willingly sacrificed personal loyalties and family ties to the demands of his position as ruler.[3]

Vasilii carried on his father's main policies. He continued the process of unifying the Russian lands with the same single-mindedness and flexibility that his father had displayed. His complex and skilful diplomacy, moreover, had the effect of allowing his government to consolidate its hold on the territories which his father had so rapidly annexed. On the domestic scene he chose his advisers independently and often well, and took a number of small, but important steps to increase the effectiveness of his rule. If he differed from his father it was in his greater openness to new ideas and cultural styles. In his last years, however, political necessity obliged him to give in to the conservative leaders of the church whose pressure put an end to the brief and very limited cultural ferment at the grand princely court.

One of Vasilii's most pressing problems arose from his family life which was as complicated as his father's. Like Ivan, he married twice. His first wife, Solomonia Saburova, a member of a distinguished old family of royal servitors, bore him no heir in twenty years of marriage. As the years passed, personal tragedy produced a political dilemma. How was Vasilii to arrange an orderly succession to the throne? The solution was as obvious as it was elusive – divorce and remarriage. With the support of sympathetic leaders of the church, Vasilii, in 1525, forced his reluctant first wife to take the veil and, less than three months later, married Elena Glinskaia. In 1530, the grand prince's second marriage produced the long-awaited heir, the future Ivan IV.[4]

A glance at a historical atlas reveals Ivan and Vasilii's most dramatic accomplishment. Over the course of their reigns, they brought most lands with a Great Russian-speaking and Eastern Orthodox population under their control. In the process, the Muscovite state expanded its borders explosively so that, in 1533, it encompassed an area more than three times as large as in 1462.[5]

In a number of cases, Ivan III directly followed his predecessors' lead. The principalities of Iaroslavl and Rostov had long been virtually surrounded by the grand princes' lands and their princes had, in effect, acted as servitors of the rulers of Moscow. Nevertheless, they remained technically independent until Ivan's time. In 1463, however, he began the process of absorbing Iaroslavl into his domains and completed it within a decade. Then, in 1474, the last prince of Rostov sold Ivan his ancestral rights.[6]

In the same years, Ivan was stalking far bigger game. At the end of Vasilii II's reign, Novgorod appeared safe in the grand prince's control. In 1456, the republic's leaders had unequivocally recognized the suzerainty of the ruler of Moscow, symbolized by the commitment to use his seal on its documents. They had agreed, moreover, to have no dealings with his enemies. At the same time, the city preserved its internal autonomy and its traditional institutions. Novgorod's economy continued to flourish. The city assembly (veche) still met in stormy sessions to debate the main issues of the republic's policy and try leaders accused of betraying her interests. The oligarchic families whose members served as mayors retained their great wealth and political influence. Indeed, in the course of the fifteenth century, they steadily increased their landholdings in the republic's hinterlands.[7]

Understandably, many of the leaders and citizens of Novgorod chafed under the conditions of the settlement of 1456. In the following years, there emerged a faction within the city which advocated an alliance with Lithuania. At its head stood the strong-willed matriarch, Marfa Boretskaia, widow of a former mayor, who reminded Muscovite chroniclers of all of the evil women of the Bible rolled into one. Marfa and her younger kinsmen and allies aimed, not to exchange Muscovite rule for Lithuanian, but rather to use ties with the Grand Duchy as a weapon to restore the republic's lost freedom of action. Certainly, as the records of their negotiations with the Lithuanians make clear, the anti-Muscovite faction had no intention of betraying Orthodoxy and selling out to Rome as Ivan III alleged. Its leaders were prepared, however, to consider placing the city's archbishop under the jurisdiction of the new metropolitan of Kiev in place of the metropolitan of Moscow.

After years of growing tension, matters came to a head in 1470. The government of Novgorod sent a request to Casimir IV of Lithuania asking for his protection and for a prince to lead the defence of the city. It also requested his help in arranging the consecration in Kiev of the city's new archbishop. Some months later, the city's leaders drew up a treaty with Casimir in which the latter promised to provide military aid in case of a Muscovite attack and to respect the republic's ancient liberties. Whether the grand duke ratified the accord is unknown.[8]

Within a remarkably short time of Novgorod's initial request, Prince Mikhail Olelkovich answered the summons. Younger brother of the prince of Kiev, Mikhail was of impeccably Russian and Orthodox background. Moreover, he quickly became disillusioned with his new office and, within weeks, left Novgorod with his retinue, plundering the southern territories of the republic as he went. Even so, his appearance and the accompanying negotiations set off a dramatic reaction.

After a short period of diplomatic manoeuvring, Ivan III declared war on the republic. Fearing full-scale Lithuanian intervention on Novgorod's side, the grand prince made elaborate military preparations. When, as events transpired, their Lithuanian allies left them in the lurch, the leaders of Novgorod desperately mobilized their forces which, in the end, considerably outnumbered those of Moscow. Strength did not lie in numbers. On the Shelon river, Ivan's well-disciplined cavalrymen easily crushed the Novgorodians, many of whom had little if any military experience. Then, to emphasize his determination, the grand prince executed four prominent leaders of the pro-Lithuanian faction who had fallen into his hands during the battle.

The government of Novgorod had no choice but to make peace. Having made his point, Ivan proved to be a magnanimous victor. The treaty of 11 August 1471 essentially repeated the provisions of the accord of 1456. It stated once again that Novgorod was not to have dealings with the grand prince's enemies, specifically Lithuania, and added the provision that the archbishops of Novgorod could be consecrated only in Moscow. Otherwise Ivan made no attempt to destroy the republic's institutions and traditions.

Observers have often wondered why the grand prince treated Novgorod so generously. In all probability, according to one school of thought, Ivan realized that it would be an enormous undertaking for the rudimentary administration in Moscow to govern the republic's vast territories. Moreover, any attempt to destroy Novgorod's traditional institutions might well unite its people against Moscow. Ideally, then, Ivan would have preferred to leave its traditions intact and its remaining leaders in charge so long as he could be sure that the local authorities would remain loyal to him.[9]

Ivan was soon to find more radical measures necessary. Factional struggles continued to plague the city and some of its citizens turned to their overlord, Ivan, for justice. In response, the grand prince journeyed to the city late in 1475 to assert his authority. He did so quickly and dramatically, arresting several leading citizens and accepting the frantic hospitality of the others. His visit probably strengthened the resolve of the faction within the city which welcomed closer ties with Moscow.

The end of Novgorod's independence came quickly. The final act of the drama opened with an episode that still mystifies historians. Early in 1477, a delegation of relatively obscure Novgorodians appeared at Ivan's court in Moscow and addressed him as 'sovereign' (*gosudar*) rather than the traditional honorific 'lord' (*gospodin*). The meaning of the incident is clear: the new title implied that Ivan was absolute ruler of the republic and could exercise power in it as he chose. The origin of the delegation remains shrouded in mystery. Some scholars suggest that the Novgorodian assembly had temporarily fallen under the control of the pro-Moscow faction and officially voted to bestow the new dignity on Ivan. Others argue that the delegation had no official standing: instead, they suggest, its appearance was the work of individual admirers of Ivan within Novgorod acting, in all probability, with the connivance of the grand prince himself.[10]

Whatever its origins, the delegation set off a chain of decisive events. In response to its offer, Ivan sent two trusted advisers to the city to determine precisely what rights he now enjoyed there. They encountered panic and hostility. The archbishop of Novgorod and its leading laymen insisted that the delegation's offer was invalid and the popular assembly condemned to death several local leaders who had cooperated with the grand prince. In real or feigned fury, Ivan again ordered his army to mobilize.

After elaborate preparations, Muscovite forces descended on the defenceless city and enclosed it in a siege. The Novgorodians only hope lay in negotiation, but, on this occasion, the grand prince was in no mood to compromise. Brushing aside all of the Novgorodians' pleas and arguments, he insisted on exercising his prerogatives as sovereign. The republic's institutions were to be abolished and its lands to be absorbed into the grand prince's domains. To symbolize the end of Novgorod's independence, the bell used to summon the veche was taken down and sent to Moscow.

In the process of conquering Novgorod, Ivan extended his control, not only over the city and its immediate environs but also the republic's vast northern territories stretching as far as the Arctic Ocean and the Urals. Moreover, as sovereign, he became owner of large tracts of land. After complex negotiations, Novgorod's representatives at the peace talks agreed to cede Ivan half of the lands of six of the republic's wealthiest monasteries, ten districts belonging to the archbishop and all of the region of Torzhok. The political implications of Ivan's confiscations are clear. Acquiring the whole of Torzhok effectively sealed off the grand principality of Tver from the outside world. Secularizing some of the holdings of the Novgorodian Church made sense in spite of Ivan's frequent assertions of his Orthodox piety. Traditionally the leaders of the church, particularly the archbishop, were elected by the veche and played an active role in the republic's secular civic life. Ivan undoubtedly viewed them as active opponents of his rule in Novgorod, particularly after their flirtation with the Lithuanian-sponsored hierarchy based in Kiev. In a sense, then, the Novgorodian Church suffered a gentler fate than Ivan's opponents among the laity. When a leading citizen of the republic was imprisoned or executed for treason against the grand prince, he forfeited all of his lands to the crown.

Even after the annexation of 1478, Novgorod knew no peace. In the following year, Ivan returned to the city to break up a conspiracy against his rule. He had over 100 leading citizens executed and imprisoned Archbishop Theophilus in a monastery in the Moscow Kremlin. Several years later, he prevailed on the imprisoned hierarch to resign from an office in which he could not serve and ultimately replaced him with Gennadius, a Muscovite and former abbot of the monastery in which he was held. No longer was the church to be a defender of Novgorod's liberties.

For the rest of the fifteenth century, Muscovite officials kept the former republic under close scrutiny. Several times in the 1480s and 1490s, they arrested thousands of prominent and wealthy Novgorodians. A few suffered the death penalty. For the vast majority, fate was only a little kinder: the government confiscated their property and forced them to move to Moscow or other areas of Ivan's realm far from their former home. In their place, the grand prince colonized the Novgorodian lands with an élite of loyal Muscovites.[11]

The process of pacifying Novgorod led directly to the most dramatic innovations of Ivan's reign. During and after the annexation, his agents confiscated roughly 1.2 million hectares (3 million acres) of populated agricultural land. His government used the opportunity well. It distributed the land to about 2,000 carefully chosen men of various origins. Some were former élite slaves of leading Novgorodian families. More commonly, the new settlers came from Ivan's entourage in Moscow and ranged from a few prominent nobles to impoverished representatives of distinguished boyar clans and obscure cavalrymen.[12]

Even more significant were the conditions under which the new landlords held their estates. Ivan granted them land on conditional (pomeste) tenure. In theory, their estates remained the property of the grand prince. The new tenants enjoyed the rights to them only if they served him loyally and well. A man who failed to fulfil his obligations to his prince would lose his lands. While conditional land tenure was not unknown in earlier times in Russia, the creation of pomeste estates on a massive scale in the Novgorodian lands was an innovation of momentous consequences.

The actions of Ivan's government significantly changed the patterns of landholding in Novgorod. Before the annexation, the majority of local landlords owned very small estates – far too small to support a warrior in service. After the confiscations and redistribution of land, the average layman's estate in the Novgorod lands was larger than before and the majority of landlords, while far from wealthy, could reasonably be expected to support and equip themselves for regular military service.[13]

Moreover, over the course of the following century, the pomeste system became the social and economic foundation of the Muscovite army. It provided a remarkably cheap way of supporting the grand prince's soldiers and guaranteed their cooperation. Indeed, so successful was it that, in the latter half of the sixteenth century, the Muscovite government extended some of its features to the allodial (votchina) estates whose noble owners technically held them unconditionally.

Finally, the confiscations significantly lowered the proportion of church lands to those owned by the laity in the heartland of Novgorod.[14] On the symbolic plane, moreover, the act of confiscating ecclesiastical property made clear that even the church had no exemption from serving the needs of the realm as Ivan defined them.

In pacifying Novgorod, then, Ivan III, cautious though he was, had introduced measures of revolutionary significance for the future of the Muscovite state as a whole.

The annexation of Novgorod set the stage for Moscow's absorption of the remaining east Russian lands. After 1478, Muscovite territory surrounded the grand principality of Tver. For a time, however, relations between the neighbours and ancient rivals remained calm. In the first years of Ivan III's reign, the grand princes of Moscow and the rulers of Tver – now also styled grand princes – continued to cooperate and treat one another as equals, at least on the theoretical level. Tverian troops, for example, took part in Ivan's campaigns against Novgorod.

In the early 1480s, Grand Prince Michael changed the direction of Tver's policy. Like the leaders of Novgorod before him, he tried to preserve the independence of his realm by seeking Lithuanian support. One can hardly blame him. After the annexation of Novgorod, Moscow's political power within north-east Russia was overwhelming. A number of prominent Tverian nobles had already recognized the facts of life and, deserting Michael, had entered Ivan's service.

Once Ivan III learned of Michael's diplomatic overtures to Casimir IV, he took decisive action. After dealing with the unrest in Novgorod, the grand prince invaded Tver in the winter of 1484–85. With no hope of resisting Ivan's army, Michael quickly submitted and agreed to a humiliating peace treaty in which he recognized his inferiority, not only to the grand prince of Moscow but also to the heir to the Muscovite throne. Michael promised to have nothing more to do with Lithuania. The treaty also included a convention stipulating that neither party would lure away the servitor princes of the other.

Within months, Michael's position became hopeless. The trickle of Tverian princes and nobles into Muscovite service became a flood. In contradiction to the recent treaty, Ivan III welcomed the turncoats and rewarded the most prominent of them richly. As his servitors left him, Michael, in desperation, tried once again to open negotiations with Lithuania. Ivan was waiting for just such a step and, when his agents intercepted a Tverian diplomatic courier carrying incriminating messages, he mobilized a large army for the final blow.

The end had come. When Moscow's forces surrounded the city of Tver in September of 1485, the remaining courtiers surrendered the city while Grand Prince Michael fled into exile. To complete the process of annexation, Ivan III granted the former principality to his own heir, Prince Ivan. Tver had ceased to exist as an independent political force.

At the same time, the memory of Tver's former distinctness remained alive.

Unlike the nobles of other annexed territories, for example, many Tverian servitors were not assimilated into the mass of Muscovite cavalrymen. Instead they remained a separate group, registered in their former capital rather than in Moscow. Ultimately, however, Tver became just another part of the Muscovite monarchy.[15]

In the first decades of the sixteenth century, Vasilii III maintained his father's aggressive and opportunistic policy towards the remaining independent east Russian lands. He made the republic of Pskov his first target. In its political organization and social structure, Pskov closely resembled Novgorod, its larger neighbour to the north-east. There was one important difference, however. Pressed on its western border by the Teutonic Knights and Lithuania, Pskov had, for its own good reasons, long been a consistent and loyal ally of Moscow. Its people recognized the grand prince as their suzerain.

Vasilii III, however, may have held a personal grudge against the Pskovians. In 1499, during Ivan III's complex manoeuvres to settle the succession to his throne, he named Vasilii grand prince of Novgorod and Pskov. The leaders of Pskov objected, since the decision would effectively separate the republic from the other domains of the reigning prince of Moscow and his official heir who, at that time, was Ivan's grandson, Dmitrii. The city assembly sent a distinguished delegation to Moscow to register its protest. Ivan angrily insisted on his right to dispose of his patrimony as he saw fit and arrested two of the Pskovian emissaries. The republic had to submit to arrangements that, in the final analysis, were more symbolic than real. The episode can hardly have endeared the Pskovians to Vasilii.

The end of the city's independence came suddenly. In the autumn of 1509, a time of comparative quiet on the international scene, Vasilii III made an official visit to Novgorod. The city government of Pskov took advantage of his presence to complain against the new Muscovite governor of their city whose administration many found oppressive. At first the grand prince encouraged their complaints and, according to one version of the story, elicited petitions and protests from a variety of conflicting factions within the city.

In the end, however, Vasilii ruthlessly asserted his authority. After arresting the prominent citizens of the city who had gathered in Novgorod, he issued Pskov his demands. Following the precedent of the annexation of Novgorod, he insisted that the republic's traditional institutions be abolished and the veche bell removed to Moscow. Pskov was henceforth to be ruled exclusively by the grand prince's governors and officials. Since Vasilii threatened to back his demands with force, the remaining leaders of Pskov had no choice but to accede to them. On 13 January 1510, the veche bell, symbol of the republic's independence, was taken down amid general mourning.

To complete the annexation, Vasilii and his advisers had only to destroy the power of Pskov's traditional leaders. During an official visit to the city, the grand prince held a great reception to which he invited local officials, merchants and representatives of other groups in the population. At the height of the festivities, he arrested them and sent them into exile in central Russia along with their families and those in custody in Novgorod. Vasilii also ordered the local population removed from the central section of the city. There he settled cavalrymen from Novgorod who were to act as his garrison. In time, moreover, he had about 300 families of merchants moved to the city to replace those whom he had deported.

Vasilii's policies had exclusively political roots. The deportations were intended to remove possible leaders of opposition to his direct rule, not to undercut the city's thriving economy. For decades after the annexation, Pskov continued to prosper. Moreover, the exchange of population may have had unintended cultural consequences, spreading Pskovian traditions to the Muscovite heartland.[16]

The absorption of the last independent east Russian principality was little more than a formality. By the end of Ivan III's reign, half of Riazan had fallen into the grand prince's hands. The remainder prolonged its shadowy existence on the border between Muscovy and the steppe. Once again, Vasilii III struck suddenly. In about 1520, he arrested the last prince of Riazan on the grounds that he had betrayed Russian interests by negotiating with the khan of the Crimea – the Mongol successor state on the north coast of the Black Sea. It is, of course, possible, that he, like the leaders of Novgorod and Tver before him, tried to preserve his freedom of action by seeking a counterweight to Moscow's overwhelming might. In any case, the grand prince confiscated his principality. As elsewhere, the Muscovite government deported its leading citizens and replaced them with loyal agents of the crown.

Moscow now ruled all of the once-independent lands of northern and eastern Russia. In the process of expansion, Ivan III and Vasilii III transformed Muscovy from an ambitious principality into a nation-state of enormous size. The very extent of their territorial gains, however, posed grave problems for their government. For how was the small and rudimentary Muscovite administration to govern such vast territories? The answer is not to be sought in dramatic institutional reforms, but in the slow and sometimes erratic process of building a corps of loyal and effective servants of the crown and creating structures through which they could function effectively. In the long run, as we shall see, the princes and their advisers were remarkably successful in finding simple, but efficient ways of governing their vast domains.

The struggle to unify the Russian lands under Moscow's control led directly to the heart of Ivan's and Vasilii's western diplomacy – relations with the Grand Duchy of Lithuania. Although it had long been a powerful rival of Moscow's rulers, Lithuania was a tempting target. Many of the grand dukes' subjects spoke some variety of East Slavic and professed the Eastern Orthodox faith. Moreover, the central government in Vilna had little control over the more remote corners of the huge realm which it claimed to rule, including the west Russian lands along the border with Muscovy.

Ivan III used a variety of methods to take advantage of the opportunity. In the diplomatic sphere he tried the time-honoured tactic of making friends with the potential enemies of his foe. Beginning at the end of the 1470s, Ivan's government began negotiations with the rulers of Moldavia, Hungary and the Holy Roman Empire. In concrete terms, only the talks with Moldavia led to a formal alliance, sealed, in 1483, by the marriage of Ivan's son to the daughter of its prince.[17]

Along the frontier, Ivan's government worked by fair means or foul to convince the Russian princes and nobles who lived on the Lithuanian side to change their allegiance and, if possible, bring their estates with them. From the beginning of the 1470s, some responded voluntarily to the call. To encourage or force others to follow them, raiding parties from Muscovy ravaged the Lithuanian border areas in the late 1480s. The undeclared war undoubtedly had the blessing of Ivan III and proved incontrovertibly that he and his agents had more power over the population of the Lithuanian frontier region than its nominal ruler, the grand duke. The campaign of terror succeeded. Several prominent local princes changed their allegiance to Moscow's side, lands and all. Before long, moreover, some of them began to use the same vigilante methods to force their neighbours and kinsmen to do likewise.

In 1492, Ivan's government changed its tactics. Taking advantage of the death of Casimir IV and the accession of his son, Alexander, as grand duke, regular Muscovite armies overran the principality of Viazma, directly west of Moscow. Under the circumstances, the new regime in Lithuania had no choice but to sue for peace.

In its eagerness to reach a settlement, the government of Lithuania made sweeping concessions. The treaty of 1494 gave Muscovy legal right to what it had already seized – Viazma and the lands of the princes who had deserted to Moscow. Perhaps even more significantly, during the peace negotiations, Ivan III referred to himself bluntly as 'sovereign of all Russia (*gosudar vseia Rusi*)'. By using this honorific, Ivan, in effect, claimed the right to rule all of the Russian lands, presumably including those presently in Lithuania. In spite of the threatening implications of the title, the Lithuanian negotiators accepted its inclusion in the final treaty.

To secure the peace, the Lithuanians proposed a dynastic marriage between Grand Duke Alexander and Ivan III's daughter, Elena. Ivan agreed to the match, but insisted repeatedly that Elena be allowed to practise Eastern Orthodoxy unhindered. After he received guarantees on that score, the bride journeyed to Vilna where the marriage took place in 1495. The ceremony was symbolic of things to come; it took place in a Roman Catholic church and, as it proceeded, the bride's bumptious Muscovite attendants conducted their own private rites. From Ivan's point of view, his daughter's marriage was anything but a guarantee of peace. If his subsequent conduct is any indication, Ivan expected Elena to act as his agent at the Lithuanian court. Moreover, the issue of her freedom to practise her religion provided a ready pretext for future hostilities.[18]

In the late 1490s, Ivan's government made careful diplomatic preparations for renewed warfare, doing all in its power to see that Lithuania would fight alone. Moreover, the grand prince took careful note of reports that Elena was

94

being persecuted for her faith. Finally, in 1500, amid allegations of a general campaign against the Orthodox in Lithuania, several prominent Russian princes deserted to Moscow. The most notable of them were the direct descendants of Vasilii II's enemies, Ivan of Mozhaisk and Dmitrii Shemiaka, who controlled extremely large tracts of land along the frontier.

Armed with these advantages, Ivan III declared war. In a carefully coordinated attack, Muscovite forces moved westward and captured several important fortresses well inside Lithuanian territory. The main Muscovite army soundly defeated its counterpart in battle on the Vedrosha river. In the following months, Ivan's troops continued to advance, but Lithuanian resistance gradually stiffened and, in 1502, the Muscovites failed in their attempt to take Smolensk, the pivot of Lithuania's eastern defences.

By the beginning of the following year, both Ivan and Alexander, weary of fighting, opened peace negotiations. From beginning to end of the discussions, however, the two rulers took irreconcilable positions. Alexander consistently demanded that Ivan, as the aggressor, return all of the territory which his armies had occupied. Equally stubborn, Ivan III not only refused, but also claimed the remaining Russian lands under his rival's control as his patrimony. Moreover, by harping on the alleged persecution of the Orthodox in the Grand Duchy, he, in effect, gave himself a *carte blanche* for further meddling in Lithuania's internal affairs. Under the circumstances, there could be no real peace settlement. The best that the negotiators could do in 1503 was to agree on a truce for six years. Even so, Ivan III had won a spectacular victory. He had conquered one third of Lithuania, adding to his realm a wide band of territory including much of the Smolensk region, Briansk and the regions of Chernigov and Novgorod-Severskii to the south. Neither he nor his successors ever relinquished these lands.[19]

In this, as in other spheres, Vasilii III followed in his father's footsteps. Given the continuing hostility between Moscow and Lithuania and the impending end of their truce, he had little choice. Once Sigismund succeeded his brother Alexander on the Lithuanian throne in 1506, both sides began to prepare for war. Once again, Russian grandees in the Grand Duchy played a prominent role. M. L. Glinskii, the most ambitious and flamboyant of them, rose in revolt in 1508 and began a search for support from abroad. Vasilii III was only too glad to oblige. He offered Glinskii his protection and sent troops into Lithuania in support of the revolt. Before long, however, Grand Duke Sigismund suppressed the rebellion, forcing Glinskii to seek refuge in Moscow.

The confusing events of 1508 led to a temporary resolution of the conflict between Lithuania and Moscow. In order to free himself to consolidate his power at home, Sigismund proposed a peace treaty recognizing Moscow's rule over the territories conquered by Ivan III. Equally in need of respite, Vasilii III gladly accepted the offer.[20]

Within a few years, tensions again rose to breaking-point. Once again, the unfortunate Grand Duchess Elena, Vasilii III's sister, unwittingly contributed to the brewing conflict. In 1512, the new government of Lithuania threw her into prison where she soon died. Her fate gave her brother the pretext he needed to begin military operations.

In the autumn of the same year, Muscovite troops moved across the frontier and again laid siege to Smolensk. The defenders of the massive fortress beat back two Russian attempts to capture it, thanks, in part, to the inadequacy of the besiegers' artillery. At last, in 1514, a third attack succeeded. After offering the defenders generous terms, Vasilii III triumphantly claimed his prize.

The capture of the city rounded out Muscovy's gains on the western front. Soon after Smolensk fell, a Lithuanian victory at Orsha stopped the Russian advance. All that remained was to conclude a truce, in 1522, which established the Muscovite–Lithuanian frontier for the rest of the sixteenth century.[21]

In their European diplomacy, Ivan III and Vasilii III fought to gain international recognition of their importance as rulers. In this regard, negotiations with the Habsburg rulers of the Holy Roman Empire were particularly important. From the beginning of his dealings with their ambassadors, Ivan III insisted on being treated as the emperor's equal. For one thing, he made clear that, if the Habsburgs contemplated a matrimonial alliance, they would have to accept the union of children of the two rulers. Ivan's daughter would marry only her equal, the emperor's son.

Ivan also made increasing use of the title tsar. The equivalent of the terms 'emperor' or *basileus*, the word – derived from the Latin *caesar* – implies that the bearer is a fully sovereign ruler, not the vassal or dependant of another prince. Understandably, medieval Russian sources consistently referred to the Byzantine emperors and the khans of the Golden Horde as tsars. In a domestic Russian context, writers of polemics had, before Ivan III's time, occasionally referred to one of his predecessors as tsar. Ivan, however, was the first prince of Moscow to apply the title to himself in official documents. As was his custom, he proceeded cautiously, at first using it only occasionally in dealings with obvious inferiors. The pretensions of the Habsburgs stimulated him to take a risky step; beginning in 1489, he insisted on calling himself tsar in negotiations with them. For a long time, the emperors resisted the claims. In the end, the rulers of Moscow made their point: in the treaty of 1514, Emperor Maximilian accorded Vasilii III the title his father had sought and the recognition of equality that it symbolized.[22]

At some time in the 1490s, Ivan III adopted another symbol of suzerainty and equality with the emperors. As Gustave Alef has convincingly argued, the Muscovite government began to use a double-headed eagle on its state seal in imitation of the Habsburgs. As befitted an Eastern Orthodox state, however, the Muscovites copied a Byzantine version of the emblem.[23]

Increasingly, then, the governments of Ivan III and Vasilii III forced the major powers of Eastern and Central Europe to take Muscovy seriously as a negotiating partner and potential ally.

Moscow's relations with her eastern and southern neighbours had even greater importance than her western diplomacy. She shared the heritage of the Golden Horde with the Tatar khanates of Kazan and the Crimea. The

Muscovite rulers and their diplomats knew intimately the political system and traditions of the world of the steppe. Moreover, they kept themselves informed of the course of day-to-day events in the khanates and the open steppe between them.

Knowledge of the Tatar world was essential, for the khanates could be valuable allies or the most dangerous of enemies. Russians and Tatars shared a common interest in the security of the trade routes to the eastern Mediterranean and the Middle East. Moreover, Muscovy and the khanates all needed to channel the restless energy of the the nomads of the steppe. On the negative side, the warlord aristocrats who dominated the political life of the khanates had a vested interest in a state of undeclared war with Russia and the other societies north of the grasslands. The slave trade played an important part in the khanates' economy; in the sixteenth and seventeenth centuries, thousands of Russian and Polish peasants passed through the slave markets of the Crimea and Turkey. Thus, even when Muscovy and the khanates were officially at peace, Tatar raiding parties might well strike unprotected frontier districts and carry off much of their population.

Muscovy and her Tatar neighbours also shared a common dilemma. Which of them had inherited the mantle of the Golden Horde? From time to time after the mid-fifteenth century, the rulers of the khanates claimed that they had the right to collect tribute payments from the Russian lands. This the Muscovites denied. By the mid-sixteenth century, however, they recognized that, in moments of weakness, they had no choice but to pay significant sums of ransom or blackmail which they discreetly labelled 'presents' (*pominki*).[24] The legal and practical state of relations between Russia and the Tatar world remained extremely fluid from the mid-fifteenth to the mid-sixteenth centuries.

Under Ivan III and well into Vasilii's reign, Muscovite policy followed the same general lines. By and large, their governments cultivated good relations with the Crimea in order to control the steppe between them and put joint pressure on Lithuania. Moscow's dealings with Kazan were more complex. From time to time, her diplomats and warriors dabbled in the confusing politics of the khanate in support of a particular claimant to the throne. On other occasions, relations between the two neighbours were harmonious.

In the first years of his reign, Ivan III gave primary attention to Kazan. In 1468, he intervened in the political struggles within the khanate, supporting the attempts of his old ally, Kasim, to overthrow his nephew, Ibrahim, who had become khan in violation of the usual order of succession. In that year and again in 1469, Muscovite armies advanced into Kazan territory towards the capital, but, in the end, Khan Ibrahim beat back the challenge to his rule.[25]

Before long, Ivan's government received a dramatic threat from an unexpected quarter. After decades of decline, the nomads of the open steppe reappeared as a powerful political force menacing the khanates and Muscovy alike. In about 1460, the energetic Khan Ahmed took control of the Great Horde, the nomadic remnants of the Golden Horde. His neighbours quickly learned of his determination. In 1468, his forces raided the Riazan area. Four years later, with a larger army, he attacked the Muscovite frontier post of Aleksin, near the Lithuanian border.

Ahmed caused even more trouble in the Crimea. In the late 1470s, the khanate temporarily collapsed under pressure from two directions. As part of its policy of seizing control of the Black Sea littoral, the Ottoman Empire, in 1475, captured the southern coast of the Crimea and its most important commercial cities. In the following year, Ahmed invaded the peninsula from the north and drove the khan, Mengli-Girey, from his throne. The latter fled to the Turks and, only after a three-year interregnum, regained his throne with their help.

By that time, Ahmed had become a formidable figure. He commanded a fighting force that probably outnumbered any other in the Tatar world. Moreover, he took with the utmost seriousness his conviction that he was the primary heir of the former khans of the Golden Horde. He thus saw himself as suzerain of all of the Horde's successors.[26] Although of impeccable Chingissid lineage, however, Ahmed was, in the final analysis, the last of the great steppe warlords whose power depended on his personal charisma and his ability to lead his horde to victory. After he was murdered, his heirs slowly but surely lost control of his forces and of the steppes which they had once controlled.

In 1480, Ahmed embarked on an adventure that has provoked debate ever since – a large-scale invasion of Muscovy. The khan laid the groundwork for his invasion carefully: besides mustering his own forces, he made an alliance with Casimir of Lithuania. When all was in readiness, Ahmed moved his troops northward towards the point where the southern frontier of Muscovy touched Lithuania in order to join forces with his ally.

His campaign caught Ivan III at a difficult time. Apart from his recurring troubles in Novgorod, Ivan had to deal with the rebellion of two of his younger brothers, Andrew the Elder and Boris. Eventually, through persistence and tact, Ivan was able to unite the armed forces of his realm. He also received welcome support from Mengli-Girey of the Crimea who agreed to an alliance against their common enemy.

In the light of such elaborate preparations, the military operations of the combatants seem almost comical. Even contemporary Muscovite chroniclers and polemicists could not understand the unheroic conduct of Ivan and his enemies. In the fall, the two armies stood on opposite sides of the Ugra river, a tributary of the Oka. Ahmed's troops made one serious attempt to cross, but were beaten back. After that, the khan was content to carry on negotiations while his troops plundered the surrounding areas. For his part, Ivan had no need for chivalric gestures. As winter approached and still no Lithuanian army appeared, Ahmed retreated quietly into the steppe. Ivan III's prudence had saved Muscovy from a devastating invasion with almost no loss of life.

While the course of the events of 1480 is clear, their meaning is not. What were Ivan and Ahmed fighting about? According to one school of thought, the grand princes of Moscow had continued to pay tribute to the Horde until Ivan III renounced the practice shortly before the invasion. Ahmed attacked in order to restore his ancient rights.[27] Other scholars, whose view I find convincing, argue that, in practice, the rulers of Moscow had long since stopped regular payments of tribute, preferring to keep the revenue in their own treasury. Ahmed's demands that Ivan III recognize his suzerainty and resume tribute payments were echoes of an era long since past.[28] The 'stand on the Ugra' did not end the 'Tatar yoke' because, under less dramatic circumstances, it had ended decades earlier. At the same time, even the most sceptical of scholars recognize that the events of 1480 soon assumed great symbolic significance. In the minds of later Russian writers, the failure of Ahmed's campaign showed unmistakably that Muscovy's ruler had become a fully independent sovereign.

Whatever its theoretical implications, Ahmed's campaign and his subsequent demise had only a limited practical effect on Muscovy and the Tatar khanates. His failure to reassert the political leadership of the nomadic hordes of the steppe, by implication, strengthened the neighbouring sedentary states, especially the Crimea. On a more mundane level, Moscow's relations with the khanates retained their familiar contours. In the last decades of Ivan III's reign, his government and the Crimean regime of Mengli-Girey maintained good relations. The grand prince and the khan reached a consensus on the treatment of Kazan where factional struggles kept political life in turmoil.

The root of Kazan's problems lay in a disputed succession to Khan Ibrahim. For most of the 1480s, two of his sons, Ali-Khan and Mohammed-Emin, struggled for the throne. The latter had several valuable assets. Important political forces within Kazan regarded him as the legitimate ruler. In addition, Mohammed-Emin's mother, Nur-Sultan, was a forceful and astute politician in her own right. When she married Khan Mengli-Girey of the Crimea, she threw the diplomatic weight of his realm on to her son's side of the balance. Mohammed-Emin also enjoyed the support of Ivan III whose armies marched on Kazan in 1487 and boosted him on to the throne.[29]

During his long and often-interrupted reign, Mohammed-Emin usually stayed on good terms with Ivan and Vasilii III. On several occasions, the intervention of the Muscovite army gave him victory over domestic opposition within Kazan. At the same time, it is an exaggeration to claim that he was a vassal of the grand prince or that the khanate was Moscow's protectorate. On one occasion, for example, Mohammed-Emin turned against Muscovy, attacked Nizhnii-Novgorod and later defeated a punitive expedition sent against him. Moreover, as the grand princes' government found out over and over, no outside power could force the Kazanis to accept a khan who lacked the support of at least some of the leading noble clans which dominated the political life of the khanate.

The shape of steppe politics changed significantly in the second decade of Vasilii III's reign. After many years of cooperation with Muscovy, Khan Mengli-Girey of the Crimea changed direction and, in 1513, made an alliance with the grand duke of Lithuania. The reasons for the change are not immediately evident. In broad terms, however, the 'diplomatic revolution' reflected political changes in the steppe world. Once the Great Horde had declined into insignificance, the Crimea and Muscovy no longer needed one another's help in controlling the political life of the open steppe between them. Moreover, from the Crimean point of view, Muscovy's steady advance to the south and west brought her borders uncomfortably close to the centre of the khanate.

Once the Muscovite–Crimean alliance collapsed, relations between the powers quickly went from bad to worse. Both dabbled in the affairs of Kazan, trying, by diplomacy, intrigue and the judicious use of force, to win the local grandees' support for their candidate for the throne. After the death of Khan Mohammed-Emin in 1518, Vasilii's government brought forth Shah-Ali and quickly orchestrated his accession. Before long, however, the new khan proved to be something of a liability. Raised in Muscovy, Shah-Ali was unquestionably a willing tool of Russian interests. At the same time, his personal background and character won him far more enemies than friends. He came from a branch of the clan of Chingis Khan whose members were traditionally mortal enemies of the ruling house of the Crimea. Moreover, Shah-Ali was an exceptionally sinister figure – at once ruthless, greedy and cowardly.[30] Before long his discontented subjects turned to the Crimea for a more suitable ruler. As a consequence, a succession of *coups d'état* punctuated the history of Kazan in the late 1510s and 1520s. Before long, Vasilii's government realized that its best interest lay in abandoning Shah-Ali's candidacy and dealing with claimants to the throne more acceptable to the Kazanis. In 1525, the grand prince's new policy brought important gains: after a Muscovite army advanced on Kazan, the new khan, Safa-Girey, son of the late ruler of the Crimea, made peace with Vasilii and agreed that henceforth Russian merchants would conduct their trade, not in his capital, but in Nizhnii-Novgorod. With this provision of the settlement, Vasilii proclaimed his government's determination to control commerce on the Volga.[31]

In addition, as Crimean–Muscovite relations degenerated, raiding parties from the peninsula began to attack the southern frontiers of Muscovy. The most devastating invasion, in 1521, brought Crimean forces under Khan Mohammed-Girey's leadership right to the outskirts of Moscow itself. The raid, launched while much of the Muscovite army was engaged on the western front, caused great physical and emotional damage: the raiders looted the areas through which they passed and carried off large numbers of captives.[32] Fortunately for the Muscovite government, the Crimeans made no attempt to press their advantage: indeed, by the late 1520s, relations between the two powers were comparatively peaceful once again. Nevertheless, the episode served as a vivid reminder of two constant features of Muscovy's military and diplomatic posture – that the country's southern borderlands were never completely safe from Tatar incursions and therefore that, if possible, the grand princes' government had to avoid simultaneous warfare on the western and southern frontiers. The ever-present threat from the south and east meant, moreover, that the rulers of Muscovy had, at all times, to keep their subjects ready for war.

Ivan III and Vasilii III made major contributions to the institutional development of the Muscovite monarchy. Their triumphs in the domestic sphere were far less dramatic than their victories on the battlefield or at the conference table. Yet, by providing the means for mobilizing the resources of their domain, the domestic policies of Moscow's rulers made their military and diplomatic victories possible.

The most striking feature of the Muscovite government in their time was the great power of the ruler. Herberstein, the Austrian visitor to Vasilii's court, wrote of him, 'in the sway which he holds over his people, he surpasses the monarchs of the whole world . . .'.[33] As Herberstein's further comments make clear, an observer from Central Europe was astounded, above all, by the grand prince's power over the nobility. He could make them serve him on his terms and, if displeased with them, could treat them in a harsh and arbitrary manner. As we shall see, the explanation for the monarch's broad power lies not so much in the efficiency of his government as in the lack of barriers to his exercise of it; for no estates or corporate organizations limited the grand princes' freedom of action and no constitutional norms defined their authority.

Yet Ivan and Vasilii also resembled the 'new monarchs' of Western Europe in that they increased their power to rule their subjects slowly, in small, incremental steps. Instead of making grandiose pronouncements of their intentions or making systematic reforms of the administration's structure and methods, they chose to deal with people – individually and in families and groups. Even so, Ivan and Vasilii introduced important new principles and procedures into the process of governing their rapidly expanding realm.

Ivan and Vasilii had no choice but to develop new methods and styles of governing. The annexation of the rest of northern and eastern Russia posed three unavoidable problems. First, they had to find ways, however simple, of administering the vast territories under their rule. Second, the Muscovite government had to deal with the ruling élites of the annexed territories. Were the former rulers and high nobles of the once-independent principalities to be destroyed through execution or exile? Or would they be absorbed into the grand princes' court and administration and become members of the political and social élite of a united Muscovite state? Finally, to what extent would that administration make allowances for the distinct political and legal traditions of the annexed areas?

Moreover, the government's need to defend Russia's frontiers and its increasing appetite for territory and international recognition forced its leaders to begin systematically mobilizing the country's manpower and material resources, particularly the former. For the comparative economic and social backwardness of the Russian lands forced the grand princely administration to depend, above all, on the creation and maintenance of a large and well-disciplined corps of servitors to meet its obligations. At the same time, to rule through individuals and groups of men involved recognizing their social, economic and emotional needs and coming to grips with the traditions that they shared.

The administration of Ivan III and Vasilii III was thus a curious mixture of the old and the new. On one hand, the number of the grand princes' courtiers, officials and military retainers grew dramatically. With some important exceptions – notably Novgorod and Pskov – the rulers of Muscovy tried to absorb the élites of the other Russian lands. In addition, the government greatly increased the number of noble cavalrymen who formed the core of the army. One result of the rapid increase in the number of royal servitors is self-evident: while still very significant, personal relationships played a less important role than before in the functioning of the administration and the army. A century earlier, Dmitrii Donskoi probably knew his most important servitors by sight: Ivan III did not.[34]

On the other hand, power still flowed through personal channels. Under Ivan and Vasilii, a very small number of courtiers and favourites dominated the government and established the main lines of royal policy. These men – usually members of genealogically distinguished and well-established noble clans – achieved power primarily through their close personal ties with the grand princes and one another, ties regularly reinforced by intermarriage.[35] In this sense, the political life of the Muscovite court followed long-established patterns. Now, however, the stakes in the struggle for power at court were greater and the rewards for success richer than before.

As in earlier times, the grand prince and his closest advisers constituted the nerve centre of the administration. Almost all of the latter held the rank of boyar, signifying membership in the Boyar Duma, the informal council that advised the ruler on matters of state and heard the most important judicial appeals. To be a boyar was an exceptional privilege: in the reigns of Ivan III and Vasilii III, there were at most fifteen at any one time and usually far fewer.[36] Within this select group, some men wielded much more influence than others: some boyars repeatedly carried out vital administrative and diplomatic tasks, while others did little that would justify their exalted rank.[37] Moreover, there is a good deal of truth in I. N. Bersen-Beklemishev's oft-quoted remark that Vasilii III made important decisions '. . . alone with two or three others in his bedchamber'.[38] Much the same could probably be said of his father.

Outside of the very narrow circle of royal advisers stood the members of the ruler's court (dvor). Courtiers in Muscovy served a variety of practical and ceremonial functions. Collectively, they constituted '. . . the reservoir from which the appointees to military or higher court positions were selected . . .'.[39] From this pool of manpower, the grand princes and their advisers picked the generals who commanded their armies and the officials who represented the ruler in the provinces. Moreover, the mass of courtiers, in effect, constituted the grand prince's bodyguard and accompanied him on the most important military campaigns. Finally, much of the royal administration was a direct extension of the grand prince's household. The major domo (*dvoretskii*), equerry (*koniushii*) and treasurer (*kaznachei*) all played significant parts in the administration of the realm as a whole. At the same time, they shared administrative functions with the officers of the royal government as such and, when an official of the household enjoyed unusually great power, he most often owed it to the ruler's favour rather than the prerogatives of his office.[40]

The personnel of the Muscovite court reflected the grand princes' overwhelming power within north-east Russia. Ivan III and Vasilii III had little trouble luring or dragooning princes and boyars from other areas of Russia into their army and court. Service in Moscow gave Russian nobles a chance to share in the rewards of victory – commands in the most powerful army in north-east Europe, influential and lucrative offices and a share in the rustic glamour of the grand princes' capital. Ivan and Vasilii played these cards with great skill; to mention only one example, Ivan III lured away two of the generals of the prince of Tver by offering them lucrative governorships.[41] On other occasions, he used far rougher methods to bring men into his service. At the same time, Ivan did not neglect the descendants of the non-titled aristocratic clans whose members had, for generations, loyally served his forefathers in Moscow. Throughout his reign, these non-titled aristocrats, whom Ivan trusted far more than the newcomers to his court, received the most important administrative posts and military commands, including most of the seats in the Boyar Duma.

The arrival of many distinguished immigrants posed serious problems both for the grand prince and for his established courtiers. How were the newcomers – often men of royal blood – to be integrated into the corps of royal servitors? Ivan III's handling of the dilemma shows his remarkable political sagacity. He gave his new aristocratic servitors social recognition and places in his army and administration. Once they were safely in Moscow's camp, however, the newcomers received comparatively minor posts while tried and true servants of the grand prince led his armies and administered the realm. Only when Ivan had thoroughly tested them did he reward some of them with really vital responsibilities.[42] One sign of his concern about the loyalty of his new servitors was the policy which he adopted in the 1480s: after that time, instead of bringing new noble subjects – Tverian boyars and princelings from the Lithuanian frontier, for example – to Moscow, he made them serve him from their ancestral homes. Vasilii was as cautious as his father and, in his later years, even used an additional method – formal oaths of loyalty – to control prominent aristocratic courtiers.

The old families of the court reacted to the newcomers with equal reserve. We can well imagine their feelings towards rivals for their coveted positions around the ruler's throne and at the head of his armies. In most cases the immigrants had to wait a generation or two before well-established court clans would make marriage alliances with them.[43]

In the long run, many of them succeeded in gaining entry into the club. In the last years of Ivan's reign, a number of immigrant princes forced their way into the inner circle and more joined them under Vasilii. By the time of Ivan IV's accession in 1533, the evolving court aristocracy of Muscovy had become a complex blend of princes and non-titled servitors.[44]

Being a member of Ivan and Vasilii's court meant fighting for a share in a limited fund of rewards. Since Russian aristocrats were nobles of the sword and few showed special aptitude for technical administrative tasks, most had to compete for a limited number of suitably high military commands and provincial governorships and appropriately exalted diplomatic assignments. Although the sources of the period give us relatively little information about the struggle for power at court, they indicate some of the weapons used in the fight. Marriage alliances, especially with the ruling dynasty and its close relatives, helped less favoured courtiers rise to high rank and served as the best defence of those already close to the throne. Conspicuous success in battle or in peacetime service stood a man in good stead. Moreover – it need hardly be said – the grand princes' leading servitors fought one another with the familiar weapons of courtiers everywhere – intrigue and calumny.

At the Muscovite court, the leading families and individuals usually maintained a fragile balance of power which guaranteed to all access to office and its rewards. Their position was never entirely secure, however. It might be threatened from two quarters: the grand princes' courtiers might fall from the ruler's favour or be eclipsed by the shadow of an all-powerful clan or favourite.

Muscovite society knew 'overmighty subjects'. Their position, however, was radically different from that of their Western European equivalents, for Russian magnates built their bastions within the court and the royal administration. There they drew down not only the suspicion of their royal master, but also the jealousy of their fellow courtiers. The emergence of an overwhelmingly predominant man or family united the other clans of the court in opposition to the upstart.

A well-known episode from the last years of Ivan's reign provides the best example. A complex succession crisis of his own making dogged the grand prince. After the death of his eldest son in 1490, Ivan wavered, unable to choose between two possible successors, his second son – the future Vasilii III – and his grandson, Dmitrii, son of the deceased. The struggle between the two contenders and their backers – to which we shall soon return – lasted several confusing years. In 1499, in the midst of the struggle, Ivan III arrested his most powerful courtier, Prince I. Iu. Patrikeev, along with his two sons and his son-in-law, Prince S. I. Riapolovskii. The grand prince sentenced them all to death: in the end, only Riapolovskii was executed, but the Patrikeevs suffered a severe enough fate – forcible tonsure as monks and confiscation of their property.

How can we explain Ivan's actions? In their perplexity, historians have advanced many theories and hypotheses. Recently, however, approaching the subject from slightly different angles, Gustave Alef and Nancy Shields Kollmann have come to the same convincing conclusion. The Patrikeevs fell because they were too powerful. The clan, one of the very first families of princely immigrants, entered the ruling circle through a marriage with a daughter of Vasilii I in 1418. From then on the power of the Patrikeevs steadily increased until, by the end of the civil wars, they became the mightiest noble family in Muscovy. Under Ivan III, their influence continued to grow. In the years just before their destruction, they and their allies constituted a majority in the Boyar Duma, had a virtual monopoly of prestigious diplomatic assignments, and increased their already considerable wealth by acquiring confiscated land in Novgorod. As the grand prince's most powerful adviser, Prince Ivan Iurevich probably had great influence over the selection of military commanders and provincial governors.

In the face of such overwhelming power, rival courtier clans banded together to bring the mighty down. In all probability, their spokesmen gained Ivan's ear, perhaps by threatening to throw their support to Vasilii – then out of his father's favour – in his struggle to win recognition as the heir apparent. Whatever the validity of these suggestions, Ivan evidently decided to destroy the Patrikeevs to preserve the tranquillity of his court and realm.[45]

The annexation of huge territories and the need to mobilize the manpower and material resources of their realm forced Ivan III and his son to expand and strengthen its system of administration. Under their precedessors, the grand princes' household managed what we would consider affairs of state as well as the rulers' private and family business. Whenever possible, men dealt with government affairs orally, face to face. The closest equivalent of modern bureaucrats were the secretaries of the grand and appanage princes, men who were usually slaves. In the reigns of Ivan and Vasilii, however, the new demands forced the rulers gradually to distinguish between their official and private capacities. Moreover, the sheer size of the country and the growing complexity of governmental operations forced the princes and their agents to make extensive use of written records. The result was the emergence of an embryonic bureaucracy and its small staff of state secretaries (*diaki*), who, at any particular time, numbered far fewer than fifty.

The transition from household management to state administration was a complex and subtle one. Historians who have given the subject special attention differ widely in their assessment of the timing, detailed process and meaning of the change.[46] Suffice it to say here that, up to the end of Vasilii III's reign, the great officers of the royal household such as the major-domo and treasurer continued to play a very important role in the administration and at court. Often one noble family's members served again and again in the same office – the Cheliadnins as major-domos and the Khovrins as treasurers, for example – suggesting that the clan cultivated an expertise in that particular aspect of administration. Moreover, some historians speculate, their administrative departments – the Great Court and the Treasury – formed the kernel from which the other branches of the bureaucratic administration eventually sprang. Among their subordinates we find a number of the most prominent state secretaries.

The process of separation was slow. The majority of Vasilii's diaki worked in the management of the royal estates. At the same time, a growing minority – including some of the most distinguished – carried out only state functions and some of the estate managers performed governmental functions as well.[47] Even though its formal structure was simple, the embryonic bureaucracy performed demanding tasks – maintaining land cadastres and records of noble estates held on service tenure, and drawing up diplomatic papers.

The diaki made up a new élite of skill, rather than of birth. The late A. A. Zimin identified more than 200 of them for the period from Ivan's accession until Vasilii's death. As far as we know, they were of varied social origin – some may well have come from the clergy or the urban population, while others were the descendants of earlier élite slaves. What made them special was their training. Literate from childhood but not bound to serve in the army, the future secretaries served a long apprenticeship at court or in the provincial administration, learning how to draft documents and keep records.

The most outstanding secretaries were impressive men indeed. Expert diplomats like Fedor Kuritsyn and Elizar Tsypliatev apparently had considerable influence at the royal court. At the same time, their power rested on shaky foundations. Unlike the grand princes' noble courtiers, the secretaries did not enjoy the support of powerful families or the protection of a long tradition of service to the ruler. Their only weapons were their talent and the favour of the prince. As a group they were indispensable: individually, even the most influential of them lived in peril. Over the years, then, service as a state secretary tended to become hereditary: in a number of cases, diaki passed their expertise and their wealth to their sons. At the same time, the most prominent secretaries of all held their positions for relatively short periods of time before falling into obscurity or disgrace.[48] In the struggle for power at court, they were understandably no match for their aristocratic rivals.

Under Ivan III and Vasilii III, the administration of the provinces made effective use of very limited resources. Fortunately, the grand princes' aspirations and pretensions were also limited. For one thing, in spite of its imposing appearance on a map, Muscovy was far from united. Domestic tariff barriers divided one region from another. In many areas local traditions remained strong: a number preserved their own systems for measuring land. In particular, Novgorod had its own currency, distinct from Muscovite, and many features of local political life continued the traditions of the independent republic.[49] In response, the grand princes created special departments or named particular officials to administer a number of newly annexed territories – Novgorod, Tver and Riazan, for example.[50]

For another, the rulers of Muscovy had a limited choice of potential officials and no money with which to pay them. Thus emerged the system of provincial administration that lasted until the reforms of Ivan IV. Like their predecessors, Ivan III and Vasilii III chose nobles from their court and sent them to be governors of particular towns or rural areas. Their obligations were simple, but very demanding. The namestniki and volosteli, as they were called, had to organize the defence of their assigned territory and maintain law and order. They were also expected to dispense justice, maintain roads and collect certain revenues for their royal master.[51] By and large, Ivan and Vasilii chose courtiers of the second rank for the job. In times of war or civil unrest, however, they sometimes sent a member of their inner circle to a particularly important or strategic place such as Novgorod.[52] Governors usually served very short terms – a year or two at most – before returning to the capital.

The central government maintained its agents in the provinces at very little cost. While on assignment, the governors lived on kormlenie, the supplies of food and services provided by the local population. In addition, the namestniki collected judicial and other fees for their service. The system had obvious advantages and dangers: it was simple and cheap, but it gave the governor extensive power over the people in his jurisdiction. At the same time, regulations – most notably the Beloozero Judicial Charter – legally limited the fees and favours which the governor could extract from the local population and required that its representatives take part in the proceedings of the namestnik's court.[53] In spite of these formal safeguards, documents of the sixteenth century, written to justify the abolition of kormlenie, claim that the governors abused their privileges shamelessly. How many of them did so in fact is hard to determine.[54] Moreover, emphasizing the corruption of the system distorts the conditions in which the governors functioned. For every rapacious governor of a rich city, there were scores who attempted to perform their herculean duties in poor and remote villages.

The problem with the traditional system of provincial administration was not that it was a pit of corruption or a bastion of aristocratic privilege, but that it was too rudimentary to meet the increasingly complex needs of the state. One sign is the tendency of the grand princely administration to define the governors' rights and duties more and more precisely. Another clear indication of the problem is the creation of the office of *gorodovoi prikazchik* in the reign of Vasilii III. These new officials from Moscow took over some of the governors' functions, particularly collecting taxes, maintaining public order and seeing to it that the provincial nobles fulfilled their obligation to serve in the grand princes' armies. In effect, then, these 'city overseers' increased the central administration's effective power over the local population and served as a check on the governors' power.[55] They were also harbingers of still more dramatic changes in the royal administration under Ivan IV.

Waging war was the most important function of the grand princes' government. The demands of the foreign policy of Ivan III and Vasilii III forced their regimes to make their army a more powerful and efficient fighting force. In harmony with their style of rule, the two princes proceeded from conventional assumptions and traditional practices. The government introduced few important innovations in military affairs. Nevertheless, over the course of their reigns, Muscovite military power increased spectacularly.

Under their predecessors, the grand princes' cavalry armies consisted of their own retinues of warriors supplemented by units provided by the other rulers of north-east Russia. Therein lay the rub. Whatever inter-princely treaties might say, the grand prince, as commander of Russia's armies, depended on the voluntary cooperation of the other independent princes and even the cadet members of his own house. In moments of crisis, troops from Tver or Vereia might – or might not – appear for muster when the grand prince summoned them. The experiences of Dmitrii Donskoi before Kulikovo and Vasilii II before the disastrous battle of Suzdal showed all too clearly the unreliability of troops who were not under the grand prince's direct command. Ivan and Vasilii were determined, above all, to make the army a trustworthy instrument of their will. Thus, whether based in the capital or the provinces, the warriors of Muscovy came under the direct control of the grand prince and his officials.

The rapid growth of the royal army had wide-ranging consequences. Ivan III and Vasilii III chose boyars and other prominent courtiers to command their armies while limiting their own participation to the most important campaigns or essentially ceremonial occasions. In other words, the grand princes gradually ceased to be warriors and became leaders of a nation at war. Moreover, organizing a large and complex fighting force required more sophisticated administrative techniques: chancery officials had to keep elaborate lists of commanders and men and the posts to which they were assigned. Means had also to be found to equip and support the warriors, especially the lesser nobles who made up the rank and file of the cavalry army.

As we have seen, Ivan found a bold solution to this problem in the course of pacifying conquered Novgorod. The pomeste system of conditional landholding creatively addressed several issues at the same time. It provided economic support for Ivan's cavalrymen. In addition, in newly annexed areas, the *pomeshchiki* served as Moscow's occupation force and garrison. Finally, the new system of land tenure gave the ruler more effective control over his warriors. A family could retain control of a pomeste estate only if it could provide a suitably equipped cavalryman for the army. A widow with small children, however, might be allowed to keep all or part of her late husband's estate as a form of pension on the assumption that her sons would eventually repay the government with their service. A warrior who failed to serve satisfactorily could lose his estate: in the first generations of the system's operation, a number undoubtedly did.[56]

The many advantages of the pomeste system led to its spread from Ivan's laboratory in Novgorod to other areas of his realm. Where and when it was introduced elsewhere is hard to determine, however, for almost all of the surviving evidence on landholding in the fifteenth and sixteenth centuries comes from Novgorod itself. Clearly Ivan and Vasilii's governments introduced pomeste holdings into the old heartland of Muscovy. Former residents of Novgorod and Viatka who were exiled there received new estates on conditional tenure.[57] Moreover, a detailed study of the Pereiaslavl district, north of Moscow, shows that pomeste estates began to appear there in the reign of Vasilii III. They were created from the confiscated estates of disgraced nobles or from the so-called 'black lands', tracts nominally owned by the grand prince but controlled, in fact, by the peasants who occupied them.[58] Pereiaslavl was apparently typical of much of the country. According to historians' traditional wisdom, however, the Muscovite government eventually ran into a serious barrier to the expansion of the system. It had at its disposal only a limited quantity of populated land in those parts of the country where it made sense to settle its servitors. We will return to this contention in other contexts.

In the late fifteenth and early sixteenth centuries, the Muscovite army included forces that were not fully integrated into its command structure. The remaining appanage princes – younger brothers or cousins of the ruling grand prince – continued to maintain their own military retinues. By their actions, Ivan and Vasilii made clear, however, that the appanage warriors owed ultimate loyalty to them. Moreover, over the course of time, the most energetic and ambitious nobles learned to avoid service in the appanages since the rewards paled beside those to be gained in the grand prince's retinue. The military servitors of the great lords in the Novgorod–Severskii area along the southern section of the Lithuanian frontier occupied a similar position.

From the time of Vasilii II, a number of Tatar warlords entered Muscovite service bringing their retinues with them. They occupied a unique place among the grand princes' warriors, for many of them and their followers preserved their own cultural and religious traditions. Indeed, some of them regarded themselves, not as immigrants, but as refugees, waiting for an opportunity to return to Kazan in triumph.[59] While in Muscovy, they performed invaluable service particularly as shock troops.

In the army, as in other areas of national life, Ivan and Vasilii used well-established methods and techniques to maximum advantage. In their time, technological innovation was rare. By and large, Muscovite warriors still fought on horseback with bows and arrows in the Mongol manner. Change took place mainly in the artillery. The Italian military engineers imported by Ivan III brought modern firearms to Moscow and taught local masters to cast cannon in bronze rather than iron as before. Smaller firearms, however, played only a marginal role in Muscovite military operations until well into the sixteenth century.

One area cried out for improvement – the defence of the southern and eastern frontiers against Tatar incursions. In Ivan III's time, the Muscovite government responded pragmatically to threatened invasions and, in times of peace, left much of the border undefended. Vasilii III's government, however, began to assign large bodies of troops to the southern frontier to be prepared in case an invading army should suddenly appear.[60] From there, a series of further steps led to the elaborate system of defence works that, in the seventeenth century, finally assured the safety of Muscovy's agrarian heartland.

Taken as a whole, the military reforms of Ivan and Vasilii strengthened not only the army but the power of the grand prince as well. The pomeste system kept much of the lesser nobility under the ruler's thumb. Moreover, the fact that the grand prince's army had become the only major fighting force in the Russian lands narrowed the options available to the high nobility. Increasingly the cream of Russia's warriors concentrated, not on resisting the ruler's power, but on fighting one another for the best command posts in his army.

In discussing the domestic policies of Ivan III and Vasilii III, we must not forget the extent to which their personal relationships with their close relatives affected the history of their reigns. Historians have devoted a great deal of attention to two related issues – the succession to the grand princely throne and the rulers' relations with their younger brothers and cousins, the appanage princes. Over the years, intelligent and erudite scholars have put forward a wide variety of complex theories to explain the family history of the ruling dynasty.

The most stimulating treatments of these issues share several assumptions. Their authors generally agree that relationships within the ruling house meant far more than ordinary domestic arrangements or family quarrels. They therefore look for an explanation of crises within the grand princely family in the sphere of national politics – in considerations of foreign policy or in the struggle against decentralizing tendencies within Muscovy. By and large, moreover, authors of monographic studies of the problem often assume that events, close in time, were bound together in a single chain of cause and effect.

Our purposes are more limited. We aim to outline Ivan's and Vasilii's relations with their families and to offer a few simple hypotheses about the source and significance of the main events. Above all, we must bear in mind that, in examining the grand princely family circle, we are entering a realm of private emotions as well as public policy – an area in which we will never understand all mysteries.

In the last years of his reign, Ivan III had to settle on a successor. Until 1490, the choice had been clear. When the grand prince's eldest son and namesake died in that year, however, matters became more complicated. There were two obvious candidates – Ivan's second son, Vasilii, and his grandson, Dmitrii. Although of different generations, the two were nearly the same age: Vasilii was only four years older than his potential rival. Apart from their personal qualities, each candidate had something to recommend him. Vasilii was Ivan's oldest surviving son while Dmitrii, as the son of the eldest son, had an even better claim if the principles of primogeniture were to be observed.

Tension over the succession suddenly came to the surface in 1497. Apparently Ivan decided to name Dmitrii as his heir. Historians have advanced many reasons for the grand prince's decision. The simplest explanation is probably the best: at that time, Vasilii was eighteen and his future status had to be decided.[61] Whatever the motive, Vasilii and his supporters prepared to fight back. A small group of men was arrested and executed, allegedly for plotting Dmitrii's murder. The most recent studies show that the chief conspirators were courtiers of lesser rank or declining status – men who had little hope of appointment to high positions and no connections to the dominant faction at court.[62] The tragic episode left Vasilii and his mother, Sophia Palaeologa, in disgrace.

Very soon thereafter, Ivan proceeded to make his grandson his official heir. On 4 February 1498, the metropolitan solemnly crowned Dmitrii as co-ruler in a ceremony closely modelled on the Byzantine coronation rite for a caesar (junior co-emperor). Even then, however, matters were far from clear. Apparently Dmitrii, now in his mid-teens, exercised very little real authority. Moreover, Vasilii never completely disappeared from the scene and soon his star was again ascending. In 1499 his father proclaimed him grand prince of Novgorod and Pskov, a decision which the citizens of the latter vigorously protested because it removed them from Ivan's direct control. Whatever else it may have meant, Vasilii's appointment effectively undercut his rival's position as co-ruler, since it removed a large and important part of the realm from his nominal jurisdiction.

Vasilii soon took a dramatic and dangerous step to improve his position. In April of 1500, early in the war with Lithuania, he rose in revolt against his father and led his troops to Viazma near the battle lines. The precise details of the episode are not clear. Vasilii was probably in contact with the Lithuanian authorities and may have carried his rebellion to the point of battle with his father's forces.[63] In any case, he got what he wanted. After submitting to his father, Vasilii was made co-ruler and unquestioned heir while Dmitrii and his mother, Elena of Moldavia, fell into disgrace and died in prison.

How are we to understand these confusing events? Since we are dealing with the intimate relationships and private emotions of people long dead, we cannot hope for a fully satisfactory explanation of the crisis. Nevertheless, we can offer two suggestions that shed some light on the problem. First, as recent scholarship has indicated, there is a link between Vasilii's struggle to gain the succession and the battle of the less favoured court clans to oust the Patrikeevs from their pre-eminent position. Vasilii and the aggrieved courtiers had a common interest in upsetting the existing structure of power at court. Together they succeeded in putting such pressure on Ivan III that he restored Vasilii and abandoned the Patrikeevs.[64]

Secondly, in the face of crisis, Ivan III tended to behave with great caution. When a member of his immediate family rebelled against his authority in time of war, as Vasilii did, he chose the path of conciliation rather than risk full-scale civil war. Later, under more secure circumstances, Ivan might well have exacted retribution. Time was on Vasilii's side, however. After 1500, Ivan's grip on affairs of state apparently loosened somewhat and, even if he wished to do so, he died before he had the opportunity to reinstate Dmitrii as his heir.

Much of the discussion of Ivan's family relationships centres on the fate of the appanage princes. As we have observed, the princes of Moscow traditionally provided a living for all of their sons by willing them some territory within the realm. At the same time, the grand princes increasingly saw to it that the eldest son inherited not only the right to the throne, but a share of the family's land far larger than those of his younger brothers. Nevertheless, the younger brothers – the appanage princes – were significant figures in their own right.

Into the sixteenth century, the rulers of the appanages had substantial power over the inhabitants of their principalities. They had the right to tax their subjects, provided that they forwarded the Tatar tribute to the grand prince, and could dispense 'low justice', that is, judge all but the most serious crimes. They maintained their own armies and staffs of administrators. Moreover, the appanage princes inherited a tradition of family solidarity according to which the grand prince was expected to consult them on questions of war and peace. In addition, if one of them died, all of the survivors assumed that they would receive a share of the deceased's lands.

The prerogatives of the appanage princes have led a number of historians to see them as dangerous opponents of the grand princely power, champions of regional autonomy or 'centrifugal forces' in the body politic. This view exaggerates their significance, however. We should bear in mind that the grand princes of Moscow created the appanages. Moreover, by the fifteenth century, many of these principalities, although theoretically held in hereditary tenure, existed only for the lifetime of their first ruler before reverting to the crown. After the civil wars, few of the appanage princes actively opposed the grand prince even momentarily: most quietly collaborated with their elder brother or cousin on the throne of Moscow.

Even so, the appanage princes did have the power to stir up considerable trouble. They commanded armies which they were expected to contribute to the national defence. Refusal to do so could severely dislocate the grand prince's military efforts. Moreover, as cadet members of the royal family with their own courts, they could act as magnets for the ruler's opponents or protectors of his enemies. At the same time, even their nuisance value was limited. The grand princes' domain, army and court were all very much larger than those of their younger brothers. Consequently, the most gifted and ambitious nobles of Russia naturally gravitated to Moscow where the rewards for service were potentially far greater than in the appanages. Moreover, Ivan III succeeded in making the point that the warriors of the appanages ultimately owed their allegiance to him.

To illustrate the situation, let us examine the concrete relationship of Ivan III and Vasilii III with the appanage princes. On the eve of Vasilii II's death, there was only one remaining appanage, the principality of his cousin, Prince Michael of Vereia. By the terms of his will, Vasilii created four more to provide for his younger sons.

In his dealings with all five of the appanages, Ivan III showed his customary persistence, using any opportunity to whittle away the authority of their princes and, if possible, to absorb their lands into his domain. His treatment of the principality of Vereia provides an excellent example. Although Prince Michael had remained steadfastly loyal to Vasilii II during the civil wars, Ivan systematically undercut him. In a series of treaties, the grand prince eventually forced him to recognize that he was inferior in rank to all of Ivan's brothers.

Ivan also made him yield some of his lands and promise, at his death, to will the northern territory of Beloozero to the grand prince. Finally, in 1483, Prince Michael's son and only heir fled to Lithuania, thus, in Ivan's eyes, committing treason. Within months, Ivan forced the young man's father to will him his entire principality. When the old prince died in 1486, the grand prince absorbed Vereia into his own holdings.[65]

Ivan III treated his younger brothers with equal ruthlessness. Like his immediate predecessors, he decided the fate of the appanages unilaterally. In particular, he insisted, whenever he could, that any appanage principality whose prince died, reverted to the crown in its entirety. When Prince Iurii, the oldest of Ivan's younger brothers, died in 1473, the grand prince took over his principality. After the annexation of Novgorod, Ivan's surviving younger brothers received no share of the spoils.

The rising tension within the ruling family exploded into open conflict in 1480. Two of Ivan's younger brothers, Andrew the Elder and Boris, rebelled against him. They led their armies westward towards Lithuania, hoping to win the support of Casimir IV and to force Ivan to treat them with greater respect. The rebels held one strong card: Ivan needed their troops as he mobilized to meet Khan Ahmed's impending invasion. In other respects, Andrew and Boris had little room to manoeuvre. Once it became obvious that the Grand Duke of Lithuania would not give them active support, they could do nothing but wander aimlessly around the western districts of Muscovy while their soldiers terrorized the population. A compromise extricated the parties from a situation of mutual weakness. Andrew and Boris renewed their allegiance to their elder brother and contributed their armies to the war effort in return for the grant of additional lands for their appanages.

As soon as the crisis was over, Ivan returned to the attack. When his youngest brother died, he once again took over the deceased's entire principality. After the revolt, relations with Andrew the Elder remained tense. In 1491, another crisis erupted: when Andrew refused to appear for muster, Ivan had him arrested for treason and confiscated his principality. Boris fared better: when he died, his two sons inherited shares of his appanage. Thus, in Ivan's last years, only one of the five original appanage principalities remained intact.[66]

At his accession, Vasilii III faced exactly the same situation as had confronted his father. In settling his affairs, Ivan III created new appanages for all four of his younger sons. Thus, Vasilii had to deal with five appanage princes, including Fedor of Volok, his uncle Boris's heir.

Vasilii followed in Ivan's footsteps. He made clear that, as grand prince, he could treat his junior kinsmen as he pleased. In one well-known episode, for example, he took the Volokolamsk Monastery under his personal protection even though it was located in Prince Fedor's principality. Vasilii prohibited his younger brothers from marrying until he himself had heirs. When they died childless, he absorbed their principalities into his domain one by one. By the time of his death, only one appanage remained.[67]

From this brief survey, it is difficult to see how the appanage princes seriously threatened the power of the grand prince or stood at the head of 'centrifugal forces' in the body politic. By the mid-fifteenth century, the creation of appanages expressed the grand princes' emotional and practical need to provide a living and a position of dignity for their younger sons. As time passed, the practice became increasingly anachronistic.

Historians' theories about the appanages reflect a very real problem, however. Under Ivan III and Vasilii III, the rudimentary royal administration had very limited control over large areas of the country. The central government's authority was refracted through other institutions and jurisdictions. As a result, successive regimes – including that of Ivan IV – tried different methods of increasing their effective control over the inhabitants of their vast domain. Only in the seventeenth century did their successors solve the problem.

Given the limited resources at their disposal, Ivan III and Vasilii III achieved remarkable things. They greatly increased the territory under Muscovite control and – even more important – created a simple but effective system of administration. Moreover, they transformed the warriors of north-east Russia into a corps of servants of the crown, above all by making clear that power, prestige and wealth could reasonably be sought only in Moscow. After their reigns were over, there could be no doubt that Muscovy was, in every sense, a major power.

REFERENCES AND NOTES

1. See Fennell, *Ivan*, pp. 264–6.
2. Ibid., p. 17. See also Vernadsky, *Russia*, pp. 13–15.
3. Zimin, *Rossiia*, pp. 417–18.
4. Ibid., pp. 67, 295–7.
5. Alef, 'Reflections', p. 76.
6. Cherepnin, *Obrazovanie*, pp. 825–30.
7. See Bernadskii, *Novgorod*.
8. *GVNiP*, pp. 130–2.
9. Bernadskii, *Novgorod*, p. 286; Fennell, *Ivan*, pp. 46–7.
10. Ibid., p. 49; Bernadskii, *Novgorod*, p. 298.
11. Based on Bernadskii, *Novgorod*, pp. 264–313; Fennell, *Ivan*, pp. 29–60; Vernadsky, *Russia*, pp. 42–63.
12. Veselovskii, *Feodalnoe zemlevladenie*, pp. 287–97.
13. Shapiro et al., *Agrarnaia istoriia. Vtoraia polovina XV v.*, pp. 328–35.
14. Ibid., p. 333.
15. Fennell, *Ivan*, pp. 60–5; Presniakov, *Formation*, pp. 376–8; Cherepnin, *Obrazovanie*, pp. 887–95.
16. Zimin, *Rossiia*, pp. 112–23; Vernadsky, *Russia*, pp. 140–9.
17. Fennell, *Ivan*, pp. 106–31; Bazilevich, *Vneshnaia politika*, pp. 239–81.
18. Fennell, *Ivan*, pp. 132–63.
19. Ibid., pp. 211–86; Bazilevich, *Vneshnaia politika*, pp. 432–542.
20. Zimin, *Rossiia*, pp. 79–94.
21. Ibid., pp. 150–68.

22. Szeftel, 'Title', pp. 70–5; Zimin, *Rossiia*, p. 157.
23. Alef, 'Adoption'.
24. Fisher, 'Muscovy'.
25. Keenan, 'Muscovy and Kazan, 1445–1552', pp. 144–50; Fennell, *Ivan*, pp. 19–28.
26. Safargaliev, *Raspad*, pp. 267–72.
27. Fennell, *Ivan*, pp. 72, 87–8; Bazilevich, *Vneshnaia politika*, pp. 118–68.
28. Keenan, 'Muscovy and Kazan: Remarks', p. 43; Vernadsky, *Russia*, p. 77.
29. Keenan, 'Muscovy and Kazan, 1445–1552', pp. 177–80.
30. Zimin, *Rossiia*, pp. 194–5.
31. Keenan, 'Muscovy and Kazan, 1445–1552', pp. 263–4; Zimin, *Rossiia*, pp. 265–6.
32. Ibid., pp. 241–7.
33. Herberstein, *Notes*, vol. 1, p. 30.
34. Alef, 'Reflections', pp. 76–7.
35. Shields Kollmann, 'Kinship', pp. 420–2.
36. Alef, 'Reflections', pp. 106–7; 'Aristocratic politics', p. 93.
37. Zimin, *Rossiia*, pp. 409–11.
38. *AAE*, vol. 1, p. 142.
39. Alef, 'Aristocratic politics', p. 95.
40. Zimin, *Rossiia*, pp. 407–8.
41. Alef, 'Crisis', p. 53.
42. Ibid., pp. 52–6.
43. Shields Kollmann, 'Kinship', pp. 475–9.
44. Alef, 'Aristocratic politics', pp. 85–93.
45. Ibid., pp. 80–1; Shields Kollmann, 'Kinship', pp. 482–521.
46. Brown, 'Early modern bureaucracy', Ch. 1.
47. Zimin, 'Diacheskii apparat', pp. 281–5.
48. Zimin, *Rossiia*, pp. 410–14.
49. Pronshtein, *Novgorod*, Ch. 5.
50. Zimin, *Rossiia*, pp. 405–7.
51. Dewey, 'Decline', pp. 22–5.
52. Alef, 'Reflections', pp. 83–91.
53. *Muscovite Judicial Texts*, pp. 1–6; Dewey, 'White Lake Charter', pp. 74–9.
54. Dewey, 'Decline', pp. 33–9.
55. Ibid., pp. 28–9; Zimin, *Rossiia*, pp. 415–17.
56. Veselovskii, *Feodalnoe zemlevladenie*, pp. 305–9.
57. Alef, 'Muscovite military reforms', pp. 98–100.
58. Alekseev, *Agrarnaia i sotsialnaia istoriia*, pp. 147–50, 165.
59. Zimin, *Rossiia*, pp. 404–5.
60. Alef, 'Military reforms', p. 78.
61. Shields Kollmann, 'Kinship', p. 515.
62. Ibid., pp. 511–15; Alef, 'Aristocratic politics', p. 80. Shields Kollmann's attempts to tie the conspirators to particular court factions are strained: her critique of earlier scholarship is excellent.
63. Kashtanov, *Sotsialno-politicheskaia istoriia*, pp. 147–69.
64. Alef, 'Aristocratic politics', pp. 80–3.
65. See Fennell, *Ivan*, pp. 307–15.
66. Ibid., pp. 289–307.
67. Zimin, *Rossiia*, pp. 397–402.

CHAPTER FIVE

The Eastern Orthodox Church in Muscovy

Long before Moscow emerged as the political centre of north-east Russia, the Eastern Orthodox Church directed the spiritual and cultural life of the nation. Being Russian meant, more than anything else, adhering to the Orthodox faith.

Eastern Christianity has many alluring features, above all its tradition of public worship. At the centre of the faith stands the Divine Liturgy, the celebration in word and gesture of God's revelation of himself to men. From earliest times, services in the great churches of Constantinople, Kiev and Vladimir appealed to all of the worshippers' senses through movement, music, painting and incense, making them intensely aware of the divine presence among them. The worship of the Western Church never achieved the magnificence and emotional power experienced in the Christian East.

Although identical with Roman Catholicism on many points of doctrine and practice, Eastern Orthodoxy had other features to appeal to new converts. Each major cultural community worshipped in its own language and had its own organizational structure within the Orthodox commonwealth. In this respect, Russians were particularly fortunate, for, by the time of their conversion, the Bulgarians and other Slavs already celebrated the liturgy and read Christian devotional writings in a language akin to their everyday speech. Moreover, conversion gave them immediate access to the artistic traditions of the Byzantine world. Within a generation or two, the new Russian Church began to build sanctuaries of remarkable complexity and sophistication. As in the West, the hierarchy of bishops formed the backbone of the institution. Until the middle of the fifteenth century, Russian Christians recognized the patriarch of Constantinople and, more generally, all of the Orthodox patriarchs together, as the ultimate source of authority within Christendom. Even after that, the secular and ecclesiastical leaders of Muscovy treated the patriarchs, then subjects of the Ottoman Turks, with great respect. Within the Russian lands, a metropolitan held authority over the local archbishops and bishops. The size of the Russian hierarchy remained remarkably stable over the years; in the three centuries between the Mongol conquest and the Stoglav Council of 1551, the number of bishops and archbishops increased very little – from fifteen to sixteen.[1] Of much greater significance was the division of the Russian hierarchy into western and eastern branches in the mid-fifteenth century. After several attempts, as we have seen, the rulers of Lithuania finally succeeded, in 1458, in arranging the creation of a second metropolitan to serve as shepherd of the Russian Orthodox in their domain.[2] Seven of the existing episcopal sees fell under his jurisdiction.

Until the split, the Orthodox hierarchy was the main unifying force within the East Slavic lands. During the centuries of political fragmentation and strife before and after the Mongol conquest, the church alone united all Russian believers in a single community. In other respects as well, the church enjoyed a special status during Mongol rule. In accord with their flexible and tolerant attitude towards all religions, the conquerors extended their protection to the leaders of the church, granting them exemption from taxes in return for prayers for the Mongol emperor. Moreover, Russian churchmen were able to maintain close institutional and cultural ties with Constantinople and the rest of the Orthodox world.

Within the East Slavic lands, the metropolitan clearly had jurisdiction over the rest of the hierarchy. At the same time, in practice each bishop had a free hand in administering his own diocese. With the help of a staff of officials and agents, many of them laymen, he supervised the work of the parish clergy and collected fees and fines both from them and from the laity. Moreover, like his Roman Catholic counterpart, an Orthodox bishop had extensive judicial authority. The church alone could try its own people accused of any crimes other than murder or flagrant robbery and had exclusive jurisdiction over issues of belief and morality, such as heresy, sorcery, adultery, divorce and marriage. The boundary between the legal spheres of the church and the secular arm was not easy to define precisely, however. For example, the hierarchy unquestionably had jurisdiction over priests and deacons and monastics; but what was the legal status of peasants living on church lands or laymen living in monasteries? Throughout our period, church and state wrestled with the problem without finding a satisfactory solution.[3]

The members of the hierarchy supported themselves and their staffs with their administrative revenues and the income from their estates. From earliest times, the Russian metropolitans and bishops owned tracts of land worked by the peasants who lived on them. In most cases, however, we do not know the extent of their holdings. Data from a much later time – 1678 – suggest, however, that the hierarchy, as early as the late fifteenth and sixteenth centuries, held large quantities of land; the monasteries, however, owned very much more.

Without question, the two most powerful members of the Russian hierarchy, the metropolitan and the archbishop of Novgorod, owned many properties scattered over a wide area. The pattern by which the metropolitans built up their holdings is particularly revealing. At the time when Peter moved his seat to Moscow, he administered the lands that had formerly belonged to the archbishops of Vladimir. His immediate successors, particularly Alexis, the politically astute native of Moscow, increased their portfolio of landholdings dramatically. The acquisition of these estates, located within the territory of the Moscow principality, reflected the close ties between its rulers and the metropolitan throne in the middle decades of the fourteenth century. For decades after Alexis's death, however, the resources of the metropolitans remained stable. Only in the mid-fifteenth century under Jonah, the close political ally of Vasilii II, did the metropolitans' campaign of acquisitions begin again. Over the next century, especially in the early 1500s, Jonah and his successors grew much wealthier, in many cases buying land from lesser nobles in their service. In about 1550, the metropolitan of Moscow owned estates, of unknown size, in fourteen different districts of the realm.[4] Likewise the cathedral chapter of St Sophia in Novgorod gradually acquired extensive estates scattered throughout the territory of the republic. Even after the conquering Ivan III confiscated much of their land, the archbishops – later metropolitans – of Novgorod retained large holdings; in 1678, after the return of a few of their confiscated estates, their lands had a population of over 1,800 peasant households – a figure far smaller than those for the wealthiest monasteries and aristocratic clans of the tsar's court, but still remarkable, especially considering the sparse population of the Novgorodian lands.[5] Clearly the metropolitans, archbishops and bishops enjoyed the best that Muscovite society could offer.

The parish priests under their tutelage lived in a completely different world. It was their duty to celebrate the liturgy, give instruction and set moral standards for the laity among whom they served. This was no easy task. For the vast majority of priests, life presented a number of insuperable problems. One was economic. Unlike bishops, parish priests were obliged, by tradition, to marry. That placed them under pressure to provide for their families, a risky undertaking at best. In the countryside, village communities usually provided for their priest by setting aside a plot of land for him to farm. In addition, for performing baptisms and weddings, blessing homes and burying the dead, he received offerings, which, in spite of bishops' injunctions to the contrary, he probably regarded as regular fees. Since the number of parishes in the Muscovite Church proliferated out of all proportion to the need, priests sometimes served tiny congregations which could not, by these means, offer them adequate support. To the consternation of the church's leaders, many parishes could not support a priest at all![6] Understandably, priests greatly preferred appointment to those parish churches which received an endowment income (*ruga*) from the monarch or another wealthy patron.

The expectation that parish priests would be married men presented the hierarchy with a problem to which its members devoted inordinate attention – what to do with priests who became widowers. The situation arose frequently, for in Muscovy, many people died young, not least women in childbirth. To a bereaved layman, the church held out the prospect of a second or third marriage. By a rigid interpretation of the canons, however, the leaders of the church insisted that a priest who had lost his first wife could not remarry. Moreover, they repeatedly stipulated that, in order to avoid scandal, a widower priest should leave his parish and enter a monastery or give up

Socially as well, the monastic communities dominated entire regions of the country. With hundreds of monks and many more dependent peasants and lay servants, they were among the largest institutions in a society with a sparse population and comparatively rudimentary forms of organization. Only the larger cities and towns rivalled them as centres of social activity.

Moreover, the leaders of the most important monasteries often exercised enviable influence in the world outside of the cloister. St Sergius was not the first abbot, nor the last, to advise the rulers of this world. On occasion, rival princes vied for the moral support of his most powerful successors. Eastern Orthodox tradition gave princes and nobles still another reason for maintaining good relations with the leading monastics of the realm. Since canon law required that bishops and other members of the hierarchy be monks, today's abbot might well be tomorrow's metropolitan.

In medieval society, monasteries were, almost by default, the main centres of social welfare, learning and culture. In times of famine, their stores might feed the hungry and, during war or civil strife, they offered shelter.[22] They also attempted to provide medical care: the Holy Trinity and St Cyril monasteries kept collections of medical treatises and maintained small hospitals and almshouses for the care of the local population.[23] The monasteries' charitable activities, of course, fell far short of the need. In addition, they sometimes had a distinctly ambiguous effect. A peasant who borrowed grain to tide him over a crisis might well end up hopelessly in debt to the monastery that made the loan. Still the communities were small islands of charity in a world where it could be found virtually nowhere else.

Just as in Western Europe in earlier times, the Muscovite monasteries acted as centres of education and the arts. In the centuries before 1600, men copied manuscripts, wrote edifying and polemical treatises, and painted icons mainly in the monastic communities and the courts of the metropolitan and the archbishop of Novgorod. The Holy Trinity and St Cyril – Beloozero Monasteries and the cloisters in and around Moscow, in particular, were renowned for their large libraries of manuscripts and the quality of the work carried out in their scriptoria and workshops.[24] Even after the tsars' court had emerged as a patron of the arts, the monasteries remained guardians of the cultural heritage of Orthodox Russia.

The Byzantine movement of mystical revival known as hesychasm inspired many of the greatest leaders of Russian monasticism. Emerging from the monasteries of Mt Athos in the first decades of the fourteenth century, hesychasm exerted deep influence on the intellectual and spiritual life of the Byzantine Empire and its people. Its advocates like Gregory Palamas taught that the Christian believer can achieve mystical communion with God by self-discipline and contemplation. In particular, through the cultivation of quietness and the focusing of his spiritual energies, he can reach an experience of God's presence as uncreated light. As aides to contemplation, the Byzantine hesychasts practised the incessant repetition of the 'Jesus prayer' and exercises to control breathing. Such was the impact of the movement in Byzantium that, by 1350, its teachings were the subject of public debate and its advocates became a potent force in the governing of the church and the political struggles of the empire.[25]

Hesychast teachings quickly spread to the Russian lands. There too they exerted profound influence, but in far subtler ways than in Byzantium. The 'Lives' of the great monastic leaders – SS Sergius and Cyril – emphasize their practice of mystical quietness and their firm self-discipline in pursuit of communion with God. At the same time, we see no trace in Russia of the more dramatic manifestations of hesychasm. Russian mystics of later generations laid great stress on the practice of the 'Jesus prayer', but Yoga-like breathing exercises had no place in their spiritual arsenal. Moreover, the public furore that accompanied the emergence of the movement in Byzantium had no echo in Muscovy.[26]

For at least a century and a half, however, hesychasm quietly simmered below the surface of Russian religious life, inspiring writers, painters and mystics. The life and teachings of Nil Sorskii are a case in point. By origin a Muscovite, Nil became a monk in the St Cyril Monastery. At an early stage in his career, he travelled to the spiritual centres of Orthodoxy – Constantinople and Mt Athos. Nil returned to St Cyril, but, in approximately 1480, withdrew from the community for reasons that are not entirely clear, and founded his own hermitage on the Sora river. There disciples joined him and, over the next twenty years, he wrote several compositions setting out his ideal of the monastic life. Drawing on teachings of the 'desert fathers' of the early church and the Byzantine hesychasts, he urged his disciples to devote themselves to rigorous self-discipline and contemplative quietness, using a number of the now-familiar hesychast techniques. In Nil's view, mystical communion with God was the essence of the monastic life. Forms of community organization and the external elements of worship were, by implication, of secondary importance. At the same time, Nil's teaching and practice made clear that he had a marked preference for a particular kind of monastery, the skete or small idiorrhythmic community which combined the best qualities of the large cenobitic cloisters and the individual hermit's life while avoiding the dangers of both. Moreover, simplicity of life was the essence of the monastic profession: churches, for example, should not be lavishly decorated. Rather than depend on others, each monk should work to support himself.[27]

In the generation after Nil's death in 1509, his later disciples and admirers, above all Vassian Patrikeev, went much further than their mentor in their demands for monastic poverty and simplicity. In polemical writings, Vassian – or perhaps others using his name – directly attacked the practice by which monasteries owned large estates. Wealth, whether held individually or collectively, endangered the soul. In addition, the administration of properties distracted monks from their real calling and made them oppressors of the peasants who lived on their estates. Such views brought him into conflict with many leaders of the Russian Church who believed that, while individual monks should not own property, monasteries as communities had the right to do so.[28]

Nil Sorskii was by no means the only monastic reformer of his generation: Joseph of Volokolamsk strove just as whole-heartedly to rekindle the fire of St Sergius and his early disciples. The lives of the two centemporaries centre around one remarkable similarity. Like Nil, Joseph left the community in which he had been tonsured – in this case the Monastery of St Pafnutii of Borovsk – and struck out on his own. According to tradition, conflict within the monastery prompted his action: in 1477, Pafnutii chose Joseph to succeed him as abbot, but the latter's strictness in enforcing the rules of common life and communal property aroused the opposition of many of the brothers. After much reflection, Joseph founded his own community where the traditions of cenobitic monasticism would be observed in all their purity. His rigour drew disciples to him and, in time, the Volokolamsk Monastery, like so many others, became a citadel of the faith.[29]

Historians have sometimes exaggerated the differences between Nil and Joseph. In their own ways, both aimed to live a disciplined life devoted to bringing themselves and their disciples to a more intense experience of God's presence. Indeed, there is considerable evidence that Joseph's followers admired Nil's teachings and that the two men collaborated in defending the Orthodox faith against heresy.[30] At the same time, their preaching and practice revealed important differences of emphasis. To begin with, there are no traces of hesychast aspirations or practices in Joseph's writings. Moreover, his 'rule' differs from Nil's in its emphasis on the practical day-to-day details of monastic life and the necessity of maintaining discipline and order in the community through external sanctions rather than its members' striving for purity of spirit. Finally, Joseph's ideal of a monastery was a large cenobitic community which had the resources necessary to worship God with appropriate magnificence and minister to the needs of the world outside. Icons and other works of art – and, for that matter, landed property – were blessings to be enjoyed without shame as long as they were owned by the whole community and dedicated to God's service.

In the last years of the reign of Ivan III, Joseph devoted much of his energy to a struggle against heresy. It was the latest round of a perennial battle. Obolensky has suggested, for example, that the Bogomil or Cathar heresy spread to the Russian lands in Kievan times.[31] During Moscow's rise to pre-eminence, heresy most often raised its head in the city-republics of Novgorod and Pskov. To judge by the attacks of the defenders of orthodox Christianity, Russian heretics were few in number, but intelligent and articulate and therefore disproportionately influential. One such group, the *strigolniki*, came to light in 1375 when several of them were executed in Novgorod. Like similar groups in the Roman Catholic world, the strigolniki criticized the abuses in the church of their day. They focused particular attention on simony, the practice whereby members of the hierarchy accepted payments for ordaining or consecrating men to ecclesiastical office. This practice, in the opinion of the strigolniki, destroyed the hierarchy's claims on the allegiance of believers. What, beyond this, the Novgorod heretics taught is hard to determine. They may have extended their critique of the Orthodox Church to a rejection of the priesthood and of the sacraments of confession and the Eucharist. There is little doubt that they were highly critical of contemporary priests whom they described as drunkards and friends of drunkards.

After 1375, the stream of heresy again flowed underground until early in the following century. In 1416 and again in 1427, Metropolitan Photius wrote pastoral letters attacking strigolniki who had appeared in Pskov. The new group of heretics may have carried their assault on the authority and traditional teachings of the church even further than their Novgorodian predecessors: the good metropolitan was convinced that the Pskov heretics rejected not only the authority of the priesthood and the legitimacy of the monastic life, but also the resurrection of the dead.[32]

Photius's successors faced equally dangerous enemies of the faith. About the time of the city's conquest by Moscow, heretics once again appeared in Novgorod, known, this time, by the pejorative label of Judaizers. According to Joseph, their outspoken enemy, a Jew named Zechariah arrived from Lithuania in 1471 in the train of Prince Mikhail Olelkovich and converted some of the local population to Judaism. Most modern scholars reject the literal truth of this story. There is no doubt, however, that, by 1488, Archbishop Gennadius of Novgorod was locked in a struggle to extirpate the heretical views of some local priests and their followers. Moreover, heresy spread to Ivan III's court in Moscow, probably in the mid-1480s after the prominent diplomat, Fedor Kuritsyn, returned from a mission to Hungary. It penetrated the ruling family itself: Ivan's daughter-in-law, Elena of Moldavia, was its most prominent adherent and patron.

Reconstructing the beliefs of the Judaizers is no easy task, for their views have come down to us, in large measure, in the polemical denunciations of their opponents. Ia. S. Lure, the leading scholar of the movement, argues that they were members of a typical 'pre-reformation' movement which, like its counterparts elsewhere in Europe, attacked the institutional power of the church and rejected some of its traditions and teachings. Like the strigolniki before them, the Judaizers repudiated the authority of the hierarchy because of the practice of simony and criticized the veneration of icons and other human creations. They also attacked monasticism and some of the teachings of the church fathers. It is possible that their views were even more radical than this: the writings of their opponents suggest that they did not believe in the doctrine of the Trinity nor in the authority of any of the writings of the Apostles and church fathers other than the New Testament.[33]

Joseph's accusation that the heretics of his day had adopted Jewish beliefs and practices still causes controversy. In Lure's opinion, the charge was simply a tactical manoeuvre of a medieval polemicist, an attempt to attach to his opponents a label that would establish once and for all their wickedness in the eyes of the faithful. Other historians, however, suspect that there was at least a small flame under the clouds of polemical smoke. Pointing, in particular, to the one important Judaizer composition that has come down to us – Fedor Kuritsyn's *Laodicean Epistle* – Fairy von Lilienfeld and others argue that the author respected Jewish learning and drew on medieval European alphabetic mysticism and cabalism, often associated with Judaism.[34] Whatever the merits of these scholars' detailed arguments, there is nothing unreasonable about their basic hypotheses. Christians in many times and places have looked to the Old Testament and later Jewish tradition for inspiration and guidance without necessarily becoming Jews.

We can identify only a handful of Judaizers, mainly parish priests and officials of the grand prince's court. Nevertheless, the heretics aroused the consternation of the Orthodox Church's leaders and presented Ivan III with a painful dilemma. From the beginning, Gennadius and Joseph saw the Judaizers as a menace to the souls of the faithful and demanded their extirpation. In 1488, Gennadius subjected some of the Novgorod heretics to public humiliation for attacking icons: he paraded them through the city, mounted backwards on horses, wearing birch bark dunce caps – later burned while still on their heads – labelled 'This is the army of Satan'. Two years later a church council excommunicated and anathematized the leaders of the Novgorodian group. Beyond such measures, however, the fathers of the church could not go. Only the secular ruler, Ivan III, could order the imprisonment or execution of heretics as the council of 1490 urged. This he would not do. In exasperation, Gennadius appealed to him to follow the pious example of the king of Spain.[35]

For a number of years, Ivan hesitated to institute a Russian version of the Spanish Inquisition. His reluctance probably sprang from several sources, above all his close relationship with leading heretics like Elena and the Kuritsyn brothers. Two events, not directly connected with ecclesiastical problems, undercut his resistance to the pressure of the church's militant leaders. In about 1500, Fedor Kuritsyn disappeared from the scene. Two years later, when, as we have seen, Ivan disinherited his grandson, Dmitrii, and arrested the boy and his mother, Elena, the Judaizers' fate was sealed. A church council condemned the remaining members of the Moscow group in 1504 and Ivan III promptly sent them to the stake.[36]

As men like Gennadius were well aware, the Russian Church and government dealt with heretics just as any ecclesiastical and political authorities in Europe would have done. At the same time, the crushing of the Judaizers consolidated the leadership of those in the church who wanted, by any means necessary, to maintain uniformity of belief and practice within Russian Orthodoxy. Within a generation, Joseph and his successors destroyed opponents of impeccable orthodoxy such as Vassian Patrikeev and the learned monk from Mt Athos, known in Russia as Maxim the Greek.

The crusade against heresy and dissent in the church led to a new flurry of investigations and trials early in the 1550s. In 1554, the leaders of the church excommunicated Artemii, former abbot of the Holy Trinity Monastery, a self-proclaimed disciple of Nil Sorskii, Vassian and Maxim. Although the case against him centred on petty or narrowly technical issues, he had, in reality made enemies by insisting, like his mentors, that monks must lead a life of strict asceticism and by demanding that the government of Ivan IV confiscate the estates of wealthy monasteries. Two men arrested for heresy at about the same time – Matvei Bashkin, a minor noble, and Feodosii Kosoi, a runaway slave – held even more shocking views. Both were accused of rejecting the authority of the church and its traditions and questioning a number of orthodox Christian doctrines. Each, in his own way, moreover, attacked the injustices of the society of his day: Bashkin condemned slavery and Kosoi rejected all social inequality, earthly political authority and war. Contemporary accusers charged that Bashkin and Kosoi had fallen under the influence of Protestant teaching.[37] These allegations may well contain a measure of truth. In the 1550s, radical Protestant ideas were spreading rapidly in neighbouring Poland and Lithuania. Kosoi's views, as they have come down to us, may well be a mixture of convictions he held before his arrest and positions which he adopted only after he fled to Lithuania.

After these episodes, the triumph of the Orthodox hierarchy over critical and heretical opinions was complete. For the next century, few traces of unorthodox thought appeared on the surface of Muscovite religious life. In another sense, however, the victory of the church's 'inquisitorial' leaders proved hollow. The bishops and abbots of the Russian Church were not equipped to deal with threats far more serious than heresy. One such danger was the interference of the secular ruler in the church's affairs, a problem symbolized most dramatically, as we shall see, by Ivan IV's assassination of Metropolitan Filipp. Another came to a head in the mid-seventeenth century in the revolt of cultural and religious conservatives, even more determined than the church's leaders to preserve Russian Orthodoxy in all its purity.

Muscovite Christianity produced another – very different – kind of eccentric, the fool in Christ (*iurodivyi*). A type of saint virtually unknown in Western Christendom, the holy fools fascinated foreign visitors to sixteenth-century Muscovy, who described their repulsive dress and conduct and the awe in which Russians, from the tsar down to the poorest peasant, held them.[38]

Iurodstvo was a form of sanctity particularly prone to abuse. Undoubtedly some self-styled fools in Christ were charlatans while others were insane. In its purest form, however, the tradition of iurodstvo had an ancient and honourable history. The direct ancestors of the holy fools of Russia, the hermits of the early Christian East, had performed dramatic feats of asceticism, giving glory to God by making themselves foolish in the eyes of men. From them, the tradition of striving for Christian humility through self-humiliation passed through the Byzantine Church to the newly converted Russian lands.

Perhaps the most imposing of all of the holy fools were those who appeared in Muscovy between the fifteenth and sevententh centuries, especially in times of political or cultural strife. Two of Ivan the Terrible's contemporaries, St Basil the Blessed and Nikola of Pskov, revealed the iurodivyi in all his glory. Their outrageous dress and conduct – going nearly naked in the dead of winter, for example – made them the centre of popular attention for both good and ill. Once in the ring, so to speak, as divinely inspired clowns, they suffered men's scorn. At the same time, their severe way of life implicitly condemned the comfortable, lukewarm faith of ordinary believers and the hypocrisy and corruption of contemporary society. In addition, their role as jesters of the Lord allowed them to play the prophet with impunity – to condemn the sins of all of their contemporaries. Beggars and princes alike felt the sting of their tongues. Both Vasilii and Nikola attacked Ivan IV to his face and lived to tell the tale. Popular tradition, recorded by the Englishmen, Giles Fletcher and Jerome Horsey, credited Nikola with saving Pskov in 1570 from the wave of executions and confiscations of property that had just taken place in Novgorod. Suddenly confronting Ivan on the outskirts of the city, the holy fool denounced him as a devourer of Christian flesh and demanded that he leave Pskov in peace. When divine portents – varying from one story to the next – confirmed his message, the tsar abruptly returned home.

Ivan's stunned silence before the 'foul creature' reflected the profound respect of contemporaries for these practitioners of 'guerrilla theatre' in the name of Christ. His subjects paid the holy fools of Moscow their highest tribute when they renamed the magnificent Cathedral of the Veil on Red Square in honour of St Basil the Blessed, a popular usage that has endured until today.[39]

The tension between the aspirations of the Eastern Orthodox Church and the needs of the Muscovite monarchy came to the surface in the controversy over the monasteries' right to acquire and manage large estates. Beginning in the last century, generations of historians have described the 'church lands crisis' in essentially the same terms. In the reign of Ivan III, so the story goes, two factions contended for power within the Russian Church – the group around Joseph of Volokolamsk which defended the right of monasteries to own lands and the 'non-possessors', Nil Sorskii and his disciples, who argued that monastic landholding was spiritually dangerous and morally unacceptable. The secular ruler, Ivan III, had a strong interest in the debate. While establishing control of conquered Novgorod, he had confiscated large tracts of land from the archbishop and the monasteries and redistributed them to his noble servitors on conditional pomeste tenure. From Ivan's point of view, the pomeste system was the ideal way to provide a living for the thousands of noble cavalrymen who made up the Muscovite army. His government therefore wanted to extend it to the rest of his realm. Unfortunately for him, the church, with its vast landholdings, stood in the way. The situation made the 'non-possessors' Ivan's natural allies within the church. It was also, according to some historians, the reason why Ivan refused to execute the leading Judaizers who were also critics of monastic landholding.

The simmering conflict suddenly flared up at the ecclesiastical council of 1503, called initially to deal with problems of church discipline such as the status of widower priests. One sixteenth-century account related that Nil Sorskii and his followers unexpectedly proposed that the council '. . . request the sovereign that the monasteries not own villages'. Another source credits

Ivan himself with desiring to confiscate lands from the monasteries.[40] Whoever took the initiative in raising the issue, the outcome of the conflict was clear. The Josephites, whose ranks included the overwhelming majority of the church's leaders, bitterly opposed the proposal. Ivan III, realizing that he needed the political and ideological backing of the bishops and abbots of the realm, made a strategic retreat in the face of their intransigence.

The result, according to this interpretation, was a compromise. Ivan and his immediate successors undertook no systematic confiscations of church lands. Moreover, they cooperated with the Josephites in their campaign to destroy the 'non-possessors' and extirpate heresy. For their part, the princes of the church supported the political pretensions of the rulers of Muscovy and, in recognition of the government's needs, agreed to accept a series of enactments, culminating in a decree in 1580, committing the church not to accept any new bequests of land without the express consent of the monarch.

Some historians have recently raised serious objections to this traditional view of the situation. First of all, Lure argues, the polemical writings of Nil Sorskii and Joseph do not reveal them to be mortal polemical enemies; while their attitudes towards the monastic vocation differed considerably, they shared a number of opinions – relentless opposition to heresy, for example – and cooperated with one another on certain occasions. In his recent studies, Donald Ostrowski goes even further, arguing that the most reliable evidence does not support the traditional picture of two distinct and mutually exclusive factions or parties within the church – the Josephites and 'non-possessors'. In their polemical writings, some presumed 'non-possessors' made clear that they did not object to monastic property as such, while some well-known 'Josephites' were as sensitive as Nil or Vassian to the spiritual risks that monks ran when they owned and administered lands. In addition, many prominent clergymen of the period cannot, with confidence, be assigned to either camp.

Moreover, Ostrowski and others argue, there is no indisputable proof that the council of 1503 ever discussed the issue of the monastic lands. The council undoubtedly took place, but its protocols make no mention of the problem of church landholding. As many scholars concede, the sources which link that question to the council are literary in nature and come down to us only in copies of the mid-sixteenth century at the earliest. For these reasons, Ostrowski concludes that polemicists of the 1550s wrote the stories about the council of 1503 putting their own views into the mouths of men like Nil and Vassian whom they admired. There was, it follows, no discussion of the monastic lands in 1503 and thus no conflict from which Ivan III had to retreat.[41]

Finally, studies of the changing patterns of landholding in Muscovy suggest that, in Ivan III's time, the government felt little pressure to confiscate monastic estates throughout the realm. For one thing, until the latter half of the sixteenth century, it had significant amounts of crown or 'black' land at its disposal in the central regions of the country.[42] Moreover, it was in the decades after 1503 that the leading monasteries of Russia made their most spectacular gains as landowners: they acquired new properties at a particularly feverish pace in the reign of Ivan IV, above all in the late 1560s and 1570s.[43] Finally, at no time before the eighteenth century did the rulers of Russia seriously consider secularizing monastic lands throughout the country as Henry VIII did in England. At the same time, as his policy in Novgorod demonstrates, Ivan III and his successors confiscated individual ecclesiastical properties from time to time – and did so with impunity.[44]

At present, many features of the problem of ecclesiastical landholding and its political, economic and spiritual implications remain unclear. To mention only one example, more research is needed on changing patterns of landholding in sixteenth-century Muscovy, especially in the area immediately around Moscow. All the same, thanks to recent studies, we can, I believe, offer a number of tentative conclusions and working hypotheses. First, there was indeed a 'church lands crisis' in sixteenth-century Muscovy, but it took place later and was less dramatic than has often been thought. Beginning in the late fifteenth century, reformers like Nil and Joseph presented their views on how best to realize the ideals of Christian monasticism. In time, attention focused on the question of monastic landholding. Towards the end of his life, Joseph explicitly defended the right of cenobitic monasteries to own property and his followers maintained that position. From the beginning, Nil's advocacy of apostolic poverty implied that monks should not be engaged in the ownership and management of large estates. Over the years, his disciples took an increasingly militant position: Vassian Patrikeev directly attacked monastic landholding because it contradicted the teachings of Christ and the Apostles and led to the exploitation of the peasants who lived on the land.[45] In the end, by the 1550s, at the very latest, critics of ecclesiastical wealth – as yet not clearly identified – demanded that the tsar intervene and confiscate estates from wealthy monasteries.

At about the same time, early in the majority of Ivan IV, the tsar and his advisers began to worry about the rapid increase in the size of the great monasteries' estates, particularly in the central regions of Muscovy where the government needed land for its military servitors. The solution, embodied in the tsar's decrees and the resolutions of church councils, was a simple one: the monasteries were to stop acquiring new properties, but could retain those which they already owned. At first, these pious statements of good intention had little effect. The monasteries went right on adding to their holdings. In fact, Ivan IV was their greatest benefactor: he himself gave generously to his favourite monasteries and his reign of terror frightened many nobles into generous bequests. Finally, the decree of 1580, issued at a time of rapidly mounting social and economic crisis, had the desired effect. Thereafter, the monasteries acquired new estates relatively rarely under special circumstances. The question of ecclesiastical landholding remained moot until the eighteenth century when Peter I and Catherine II attacked it with a ruthlessness which earlier Russian rulers probably could not have imagined.

In the fifteenth and sixteenth centuries, leaders of the Eastern Orthodox Church in Muscovy wrestled with a problem of inescapable urgency. As the

Byzantine Empire, the fountain-head of Orthodoxy, disappeared beneath the onslaught of the Ottoman Turks, what was the role in the Christian community of the Russian Church and its protectors, the rulers of Moscow? The dilemma linked two issues inseparably. How the leaders of the Russian Church viewed their position within Christendom determined the nature of their relations with their fellow Eastern Orthodox and with the church in the West. Moreover, in theoretical terms, the rulers of Moscow, like other medieval Christian princes, presented themselves, first and foremost, as supporters and defenders of the faith and the church which embodied it. If the position of the Russian Church changed, so, by definition, did the secular rulers' standing in the Christian world. It was the task of Russian churchmen to justify these changes with appropriate arguments and symbolic statements.

The Byzantine tradition provided comprehensive explanations of the place of the Orthodox Church and the emperor in human affairs. These theories emerged as relations between the Eastern Orthodox and Roman Catholic Churches gradually deteriorated, a process that reached its denouement in 1054 when the pope and the patriarch formally excommunicated each other. Issues of doctrine, liturgical practice and discipline separated East and West. To mention only two questions that still complicate ecumenical relations in the twentieth century, the Orthodox believe that the Holy Spirit proceeds from the Father alone and encourage their parish priests to marry. In the Roman communion, priestly celibacy is the rule and the Latin Creed states that the Spirit proceeds from both the Father and the Son (*filioque*). Probably an even more important cause of the schism was the rivalry of two claimants for primacy in the Christian world, Rome and Constantinople. During the painful process of separation and self-definition, the Eastern Orthodox came to regard their church as the sole guardian of the Christian faith, pure and undefiled. The papacy, of course, returned the compliment!

Byzantine convictions found concrete expression in the myth of the transfer of empire (*translatio imperii*). God ordained that all Christians be united in one church which cared for their souls, and one polity whose ruler governed their lives in this world. When the Roman emperor, Constantine, accepted the faith, his realm, which encompassed the entire Mediterranean world, became a universal Christian empire. In Byzantine eyes, however, the Western Church and its political protectors gradually drifted away from the true faith. Only in the Christian East centred in Constantinople – the New Rome, founded by Constantine himself – did the faith survive unsullied. Thus the Byzantine emperor was Constantine's only true successor, the universal Christian monarch, protector and sustainer of the church. Here too East and West collided, for Roman Catholic rulers – first the Carolingians, then the Holy Roman Emperors – also claimed the mantle of Christian empire.

Within the Eastern Orthodox community, the Byzantine self-image proved to be remarkably ambiguous, both in theory and in practice. From the time of the conversion of the Russian lands, the Greek Church remained in close touch with her Slavic daughter. The patriarch of Constantinople installed each new metropolitan of the Russian Church. At the same time patriarchs sometimes clashed with Russian princes over the choice of candidates for the metropolitan throne. Moreover, the political implications of the relationship were not entirely clear: as Patriarch Anthony complained in his pastoral letter of 1393, the Russian Church did not automatically accord the Byzantine emperor recognition as the political leader of the Christian community.

Problems also arose on the theoretical plane. For, if the Byzantine ruler could claim, thanks to the purity of his faith, to be the universal Christian emperor, what was to prevent another Eastern Orthodox prince from making the same claim? If the centre of Christendom had already moved from Rome to Byzantium, why could the mantle of empire not be passed on once more? At the end of the fourteenth century, a writer at the Bulgarian court hailed his royal patron, John Asen Alexander, as a Christian emperor (tsar) and called his capital, Trnovo, the new imperial city. This idea – that the Orthodox world had a new centre – soon reached the Russian lands in the baggage of South Slavic immigrants, above all Metropolitan Cyprian.[46] Before long, changing circumstances would force Muscovites to adapt it for their own purposes.

The fall of Constantinople in 1453 – and the Council of Florence which preceded it – shocked Russian leaders profoundly. In the face of this catastrophe, Dimitri Strémooukhoff has argued, Muscovite thinkers had to adjust their interpretation of Christian history and Russia's place in it. They had to choose one of three possible solutions: 'to admit that the fall of Byzantium was not final, and that the imperial city would be freed by the Russians; to admit the supremacy of the Holy Roman Empire of the West; or, lastly, to set up Moscow herself as a definite empire, the successor to that of Byzantium'.[47]

Like the Bulgarians before them, they selected the last of these alternatives. The texts which describe and interpret the Council of Florence present their initial response most dramatically. Although based on the eyewitness testimony of Russian participants, Simeon of Suzdal and Foma of Tver, these accounts of the negotiations for a church union with Rome probably took their final form after 1453. Simeon's *Tale* tells the story of the council in stark black and white. By entering into union with the Roman heretics, the Byzantine emperor and his church betrayed the true Christian faith. Enslavement to the Turks was just punishment for their apostasy. After the council, undefiled Orthodoxy survived only in Russia. Credit for preserving the true faith belonged primarily to the grand prince of Moscow, Vasilii II. It was he who saw through Metropolitan Isidore's machinations and vigilantly defended Orthodoxy. Thus, since the Byzantine emperor had failed in his duty as protector of the faith, Vasilii II of Moscow had replaced him as the one true Orthodox prince on earth, 'the God-chosen . . . God-crowned tsar of Orthodoxy and of all Russia'.[48] Such sentiments were not restricted to Moscow. Foma's account reached the same basic conclusions: in his version, however, his sovereign, Grand Prince Boris of Tver, replaced Vasilii II in the hero's role.

The eclipse of the Byzantine Empire also contributed to a radical institutional change in the Russian Church. As we have seen, domestic political crisis in Muscovy forced Vasilii II to install Jonah of Riazan as metropolitan in 1448 to fill the vacancy created when Isidore was deposed. The grand prince and the new head of the church realized, to their considerable embarrassment, that the nature of the appointment was unprecedented. Nevertheless, they justified the unilateral decision of the grand prince and the Russian bishops by pointing out that the Turkish conquest had left the Orthodox world without an emperor and had immobilized the patriarch. The grand prince and the bishops, they argued, had no choice but to act alone.

The questionable legality of Jonah's installation gave the Grand Duke of Lithuania, Casimir, the perfect excuse to create a separate metropolitanate for his Eastern Orthodox subjects. Earlier metropolitans of Moscow – whether Russians, Greeks or South Slavs – had fought vigorously to preserve the institutional unity of the Russian Orthodox Church. On this occasion, however, Jonah was in no position to assert his authority in Lithuanian territory. He and his patron, Vasilii II, had no choice but tacitly to accept the coexistence of two separate Russian Orthodox hierarchies.

Thus, in the mid-fifteenth century, the Eastern Orthodox Church in Muscovy became autocephalous in fact, if not in theory. Moreover, it became a national church in the sense that the political and religious communities were now identical; in other words, the grand prince's subjects and the metropolitan's flock were one and the same. The fates of church and state were inextricably intertwined, for better or worse.

Vasilii II's successors made the protection of Eastern Orthodoxy a central element of their political rhetoric. Again and again, Ivan III justified his aggressive policies towards Novgorod and Lithuania as the defence of Orthodox lands and peoples from the menace of Roman Catholicism. He and his diplomats and chroniclers ingeniously combined this argument with a second, less pious but equally sweeping, assertion – that as heir of the grand princes of Kiev, Ivan had a legitimate claim to all of the Russian lands.

Ever the practical politician, Ivan III used many means to present himself to his subjects and the outside world as the Orthodox emperor. Whenever diplomatic circumstances permitted, he and his representatives referred to him as tsar. In this regard, the campaign to force the Habsburg emperors of Roman Catholic Europe to recognize Ivan and his successors as their equals received highest priority. In addition, the grand prince repeatedly used his family life to present his political message. Whatever its practical results, his marriage to Sophia Palaeologa, niece of the last Byzantine emperor, undoubtedly reinforced Ivan's symbolic claim to the Byzantine inheritance. The coronation of his grandson, Dmitrii, as his co-ruler and heir in 1498 made his point with particular bluntness.[49]

For their part, Russian churchmen continued to work out the implications of Muscovy's role in Christian history. The most striking new departure of Ivan III's reign is found in a very unlikely context – Metropolitan Zosima's commentary on the paschal canon which he issued in 1492. As it approached, the date of Columbus's historic voyage had ominous significance for Russian believers; for, in the Eastern Orthodox calendar, it was to be the year 7000. As the time drew near, many Muscovites believed prophecies that the end of the world would come with the new millennium. This conviction had important consequences. For one thing, when the end did not come, the Judaizer heretics attacked the leaders of Orthodoxy for leading their flock astray. Moreover, those leaders were completely unprepared for continued life in this world: no one had compiled calendars of liturgical observances for the new age.

Zosima stepped into the breach and, in meeting this obvious need, allowed himself to speculate on Russia's role in a world that still existed after all. He placed the ruler of his own day, Ivan III, in a broad historical context. Constantine, he recalled, founded Constantinople, the New Rome, and Grand Prince Vladimir baptized Russia. Ivan III, their heir, was thus 'the new Emperor Constantine of the new Constantinople – Moscow'. Zosima's statement was the first to call Moscow an imperial city.

At roughly the same time, the circle of learned men around Archbishop Gennadius of Novgorod elaborated its own version of the doctrine of the transfer of empire, the *Tale of the White Cowl*. The composition was a by-product of the group's primary function, to arm the Russian Orthodox Church for the struggle against the Judaizer heresy. One obvious chink in the church's armour was the fact that it lacked a complete Slavonic translation of the Bible. Gennadius therefore commissioned his group of scholars to supply the missing books, some of which had to be translated from the Latin Vulgate version with the help of a Roman Catholic, the Dominican friar, Benjamin. The editing of apocalyptic writings, previously inaccessible to Russians, probably inspired them to speculate about the place of Orthodox Russia in the divine scheme of things.

The *Tale of the White Cowl* presents the pattern of universal history from an ecclesiastical and Novgorodian point of view. The rambling story has a simple core. The original Christian emperor, Constantine, gave the bishop of Rome a white cowl as symbol of the purity of the Christian faith. When Rome deserted the true faith, the cowl passed to the patriarchs of Constantinople. Then, when Byzantium in turn fell into apostasy and ruin, the archbishops of Novgorod inherited the cowl. Russia, in the words of the tale, had become the 'Third Rome'.[50]

The circumstances from which the *Tale* emerged are significant for two reasons. First, the story was written in Novgorod, on Russia's frontier with central Europe. There Orthodox churchmen were unusually cosmopolitan, open to inspiration from the Roman Catholic world as well as from the Byzantine heritage. Archbishops of Novgorod – above all, Gennadius and Macarius, later to be metropolitan early in the reign of Ivan IV – sponsored the development of ideological statements and liturgical observances glorifying Orthodox Russia and her rulers in words and gestures drawn from both Eastern and Western Christian traditions.

Second, some scholars argue, the *Tale* served, among other things, to defend the position of a church under siege. Not only did Gennadius have heretics to fight; he also had to watch while Ivan III confiscated ecclesiastical lands in his archdiocese. The *Tale*, then, sent a two-edged message to Novgorod's ruler, the grand prince. He could indeed rejoice that the city, and Russia generally, was now the only home of the authentic Christian faith. At the same time, that fact, by implication, obliged him, as a true Christian ruler, to treat the church and its possessions with respect.[51]

Other ecclesiastical theorists sounded equally ambiguous notes. In compositions dating from about 1510, after he had patched up a long-standing quarrel with Grand Princes Ivan III and Vasilii III, Joseph of Volokolamsk praised the latter as the God-ordained Christian emperor and autocrat (*samoderzhets*) of the whole Russian land.[52] In a very familiar passage, he addressed his sovereign in the words of the sixth-century Byzantine theorist, Agapetus; 'for by nature the Emperor is like all men, but in his power, he is like the Almighty God'.[53] There was a catch to Joseph's hymns in praise of the Muscovite ruler, however. They occur in tracts whose primary purpose was to urge Vasilii III to extirpate heresy from his domains. In effect, Joseph demanded that, since the grand prince was the Orthodox emperor, he act the part!

The doctrine of the 'Third Rome' received its first full elaboration in the work of Philotheus of Pskov, another writer from Russia's western borderlands. In the one composition that can with confidence be attributed to him – a letter written to the grand prince's representative in Pskov, M. G. Misiur Munekhin, in about 1523 – Philotheus applied the biblical prophesies of Daniel, Ezra and Revelations to Russia's new position in the world with a thoroughness and rigour that far surpassed the theoretical statements of his predecessors.[54] In one passage, he briefly retold the story from the twelfth chapter of Revelations of the woman who fled into the desert and there escaped from a flood let loose by the dragon which pursued her. Interpreting the woman as a symbol of the Christian church escaping from unbelief, he concluded that: '. . . all Christian states are drowned because of the unbelievers. Only the sovereign of our realm alone stands by the Grace of Christ.' Thus, now that Rome and Byzantium had fallen into apostasy, the ruler of Muscovy had become '. . . the only tsar for Christians in the whole world . . .', and his capital, Moscow, the centre of Christendom. At the climax of his work, Philotheus encapsulated his theories in a slogan of striking power: '. . . two Romes have fallen, the Third stands and there shall be no Fourth'.[55]

Philotheus's words and images quickly entered the mainstream of Russian ecclesiastical thinking. Identical or very similar statements can be found in two other compositions, traditionally attributed to him, and occur again and again in later compilations. The popularity of his teaching about the Third Rome should not blind us to two of its features. First, the theory springs from speculation about the fate of the Orthodox faith: its sources are religious and so are its main implications. While the doctrine provides the rulers of Muscovy with a theory justifying their power, it contains no concrete political or diplomatic programme and no recommendations on the form which their government should take. If anything, by stressing the Russian tsars' role as defenders of the only remaining citadel of true Christianity, the Third Rome theory implies that they should accept the moral tutelage of the church.[56] Second, the implications of Philotheus's teaching were not entirely optimistic. God had given Russia and her rulers a heavy burden of responsibility; for they were the last guardians of the faith. If they failed and the Third Rome fell, there would be no Fourth. Thus, as later generations were acutely aware, the fate of the entire universe depended on the purity of Russian Orthodoxy. If Russia lapsed into apostasy, the end of the world would inevitably follow.

The development of the ideas of the transfer of empire and of the special destiny of Muscovite Russia reached its zenith in the work of Metropolitan Macarius and his circle. In the literary compilations and ceremonies which Macarius and his staff created, these now-familiar notions became fused with the well-established conviction that the prince of Moscow should, by right, rule all of the Russian lands and the new note that it was his duty to lead a crusade against Islam.

The imperial and national ideas received their most dramatic and unprecedented expression in Ivan IV's coronation as tsar in 1547. Although several of Ivan's predecessors had used the imperial title in a variety of contexts, none had ever been formally invested with it. The ceremony closely resembled the Byzantine coronation rite in the last centuries of the empire and its ideological climax, the metropolitan's homily, explained the divine origin of the tsar's office and his obligations as guardian of Orthodoxy in terms taken from Agapetus and other Byzantine writers as well as Joseph's earlier Russian adaptation of their ideas.[57]

At roughly the same time, Macarius took other steps to glorify the Russian heritage and to strengthen the church which embodied it. In 1547 and 1549, ecclesiastical councils canonized a total of about thirty-seven native Russians; the group, about twice as large as the list of all previously recognized East Slavic saints, included monks, hierarchs and national military heroes. Soon thereafter the Stoglav Council sought to bring rigour to the discipline and uniformity to the practices of Russian Orthodoxy.[58]

On the literary front, Macarius and his assistants had long been active. Earlier in his career, while archbishop of Novgorod, he had begun the *Great Menology*, an encyclopaedia of edifying readings which included not only saints' lives, but a bewildering variety of other ideological and devotional writings. A second work, the *Book of Degrees of the Imperial Genealogy* (the *Stepennaia Kniga*), gradually took shape, achieving its final form in the early 1560s, shortly after Macarius's death. Both compositions draw on a wide variety of sources – Byzantine, Russian and even some from the Roman Catholic world, reshaped to fit a rigidly Orthodox context.

In their learned compilations, Macarius and his associates blended all of the ideas with which we are now familiar – the tsar as Orthodox emperor and Moscow as the Third Rome and ruling centre of all of the Russian lands. To emphasize the ancient pedigree of the Muscovite Church, they retold the legends that the Apostle Andrew had originally brought the Christian faith to Russia. Moreover, the editors repeatedly underlined the connection between the ruling house of Moscow and the grand princes of Kiev, especially St Vladimir, baptizer of the Russian lands.

To their ideological concoctions, Macarius and his associates added comparatively new myths stressing the distinguished ancestry of Ivan IV and his house. One, best expressed in the *Tale of the Princes of Vladimir*, traced the tsar's ancestry back to the Roman emperor Augustus. The obvious absurdity of the claim did not take away its attractiveness. To understand its appeal, we should bear in mind that fantastic stories of national origins and fabulous family genealogies enjoyed wide popularity in many parts of Europe in the sixteenth and seventeenth centuries. Other myths elaborated the Muscovite ruler's connections with his Byzantine and Russian predecessors: one told how the Byzantine Emperor, Constantine Monomach, had given a crown to the Kievan prince, Vladimir Monomakh. That, in reality, the crown came from Central Asia and the princes in question ruled half a century apart was beside the point.[59]

All of the arguments, myths and symbolic statements in the great compilations of Macarius's circle redounded to the glory of the Muscovite tsardom and, even more important, of the Russian Orthodox Church which gave legitimacy to the new empire. In these writings and the works of art associated with them, Muscovite ecclesiastical culture reached its fullest and most elaborate stage of development.

That culture was the creation of a minuscule élite within Muscovite society. A small number of churchmen wrote and copied the texts in which the theories of Orthodox empire found expression. Moreover, in all probability, their impact at first did not extend beyond the ecclesiastical hierarchy, the most important monasteries and the tsars' court.

Nevertheless, over the course of time, the theories explaining the uniqueness of Russian Orthodoxy and the autocrat who protected it filtered down into the consciousness of millions of people. It is difficult to determine precisely when these rather esoteric theories took hold in the popular imagination. Clearly, however, by the middle of the seventeenth century, many ordinary Muscovites accepted these ideas as axiomatic and thousands were prepared, if necessary, to die in the struggle to restore true Orthodoxy and the Christian tsardom, which, in their view, were destroyed in the 1650s by the reforms of Patriarch Nikon.

One channel through which the churchmen's theories reached a wider public was the ceremonial life of the tsar's court. For men and women who could not read the thousands of intricate pages of the *Great Menology*, Muscovite churchmen created dramatic public rituals in which the tsar acted out the ideal of Orthodox empire. By the time of Tsar Alexis in the mid-seventeenth century, public participation in the liturgy, pilgrimages and ritual acts of charity took up a great deal of the ruler's time and energy. In all probability, Macarius and his group could claim credit for weaving this liturgical tapestry. They certainly seem responsible for developing the great

Palm Sunday procession, adapted from much earlier Roman Catholic theory and practice, in which, before thousands of his subjects, the tsar walked from Red Square into the Kremlin leading the horse on which the head of the church, representing Christ, rode in triumph. It is hard to imagine a more striking statement of the doctrine that the tsar was God's annointed and protector of the faith.[60]

Even after the coronation of Ivan IV, there remained one obvious flaw in the structure of the new Christian empire. A full century after the fall of Byzantium, the head of the Russian Church, the metropolitan of Moscow, remained nominally subordinate to the patriarch of Constantinople. Yet, it was absurd for an empire not to have its own patriarch. In Moscow's case, the situation was doubly anomalous. First, the local church had been autocephalous in practice since the consecration of Metropolitan Jonah in 1448. Second, in the sixteenth century, the leaders of the Greek Church in the Ottoman Empire looked to the rulers of Muscovy, the last powerful Orthodox sovereigns, for moral support and hand-outs. Finally, in 1589, a solution was found. Following lengthy negotiations during a visit to the tsar's court, Patriarch Jeremiah of Constantinople agreed to help in the creation of a new office, patriarch of Moscow, and consecrated the current metropolitan, Job, as its first holder. At last, the Muscovite Church had won recognition as an independent and equal member of the international Orthodox community.[61]

The creation of the patriarchate illustrates the complexity of the relationship between church and state in Muscovy. On the surface, the decision served the interests of the church, strengthening its leadership and glorifying Russian Orthodoxy. At the same time, it was primarily the work of a lay political leader, Boris Godunov, regent for Tsar Fedor, and increased the prestige of the imperial government as well as the church.

The ambiguity lies at the heart of the Byzantine tradition. Ideally, in the Eastern Orthodox view, emperor and patriarch, church and state, should function inseparably, like two sides of a coin, and in close harmony (or *symphony*). In the real world, of course, the interests of the leaders of church and state often clashed; in Byzantium, when this happened, the secular arm predominated more often than not. In Muscovy, the outcome of such conflict was, if anything, even more predictable.

Still, to underestimate the influence and power of the Muscovite Church would be a grave mistake. Over the course of the fifteenth and sixteenth centuries, its spokesmen created the ideological formulas which described the position of Russian Orthodoxy in the Christian world and, by extension, legitimized the claims and pretensions of the Muscovite monarchy. Moreover, in the mid-sixteenth century, the church was the only guardian of men's souls and consciences; for, over the preceding decades, militant leaders like Joseph, Gennadius and Macarius had silenced all public expressions of doubt and criticism from within the community. By the time of Ivan IV, the Muscovite monarchy and the church were united in an ideological crusade against

Roman Catholic neighbours to the west and Muslims to the south and east. Inside the realm, ecclesiastical corporations, particularly the most prestigious monasteries, owned very large estates and acted as the country's main centres of learning. In the arts, only the royal court itself, served, in considerable measure, by ecclesiastics, could rival them.

Wealth and cultural achievement had their price, however; for, as the ideological pronouncements of the period make clear, it was the tsar who ultimately governed the affairs of the church. The secular ruler, for example, had the final say in the selection of each new metropolitan.[62] Those whom the tsar exalted, he could also bring down. Of the men who served as metropolitan from Iona's consecration in 1448 until the creation of the patriarchate in 1589, fewer than half died in office as we would normally expect. Ruling monarchs or cliques of courtiers acting in their names deposed four heads of the church and one – Filipp – suffered martyrdom in 1568 on Ivan IV's orders.[63]

The princes of Moscow got what they wanted from the church by whatever means necessary. Vasilii III, for example, replaced Metropolitan Varlaam with Daniel in order to receive absolution for breaking his oath of safe-conduct to Prince Vasilii Shemiachich.[64] Daniel lived up to his promise: in 1525, he gave Vasilii III permission to rid himself of his barren first wife by forcing her into a convent and blessed his second marriage. The royal 'divorce' had many implications: for one thing, it gave Daniel and the rest of the hierarchy still another weapon in their struggle to silence the leading critics of the church's wealth and power, Vassian Patrikeev and Maxim the Greek, who opposed the grand prince's action as a breach of canon law.[65] The fact that Daniel, in turn, soon fell from power is little consolation: indeed, his fate provides still more evidence of the church's vulnerability to secular interference.

In spite of everything, the Orthodox Church remained capable of acting as the voice and conscience of the people of Muscovy. In particular, when the crises of the early seventeenth century – traditionally known as the Time of Troubles – destroyed the political order of the Muscovite state and unravelled its social fabric, the church displayed its moral authority. In the absence of any other unquestionably legitimate leader, its head, Patriarch Hermogen, rallied the faithful to defeat the Polish invaders and restore the monarchy. Hermogen's stand cost him his life, but, as so often happens, his martyrdom contributed even more to the cause than his exhortations. The Orthodox tradition of Russia also ministered to men's minds in their hour of need. The teachings about Orthodox Russia's role in world history provided a framework in which they could interpret the cataclysmic events through which they were living. The people of Muscovy, many concluded, were suffering for wavering in their loyalty to Orthodoxy and its guardians, the legitimate Christian emperors. Only by returning to their fundamental allegiance to the church and the autocracy could the nation be restored. Thus, in the experiences of the Time of Troubles lay both the foundations of the seventeenth-century church's glory and the roots of the tensions that ultimately split it apart.

REFERENCES AND NOTES

1. Golubinskii, *Istoriia*, vol. 2, part 2, pp. 26–33.
2. Jablonowski, *Westrussland*, p. 84.
3. *Stoglav*, pp. 197–9; Kollmann, 'Moscow Church Council', pp. 451–4, 474–84.
4. Veselovskii, *Feodalnoe zemlevladenie*, pp. 330–90.
5. Grekov, *Novgorodskii dom*, pp. 235–304 and appendices.
6. *Stoglav*, pp. 246–7.
7. Ibid., pp. 48–9, 91–4, 134–5; Kollmann, '*Stoglav* Council'; Golubinskii, *Istoriia*, vol. 2, part 2, pp. 77–94; *Rude & Barbarous Kingdom*, pp. 214–16, 228–9.
8. *Stoglav*, p. 141. For an imaginative re-creation of the rites that so shocked the fathers of the church, the reader should see Andrei Tarkovskii's film, *Andrei Rublev*.
9. Obolensky, 'Popular Religion', pp. 51–2.
10. Zguta, *Russian Minstrels*, pp. 31–43.
11. Kliuchevskii, *Sochineniia*, vol. 2, p. 247.
12. *TL*, p. 434.
13. Smolitsch, *Russisches Mönchtum*, pp. 86–93. For St Sergius's vita in English, see Zenkovsky, *Medieval Russia's Epics*, pp. 262–90.
14. Smolitsch, *Russisches Mönchtum*, pp. 95–8.
15. Makarii, *Istoriia*, vol. 4, pp. 138–49.
16. Alekseev, *Agrarnaia i sotsialnaia istoriia*, pp. 94–6.
17. Rozhkov, *Selskoe khoziaistvo*, p. 403; Novoselskii, 'Rospis', pp. 88–95. A chetvert was normally equivalent to 4.1 acres or 1.66 hectares, Muscovite tax assessors taking a multiple of the assessment of one field in a three-field arrangement.
18. Kopanev, *Istoriia*, pp. 140–1.
19. Zimin, *Krupnaia feodalnaia votchina*, pp. 170–88.
20. *Ocherki istorii SSSR. Konets XV v.*, pp. 46–52, 219–33.
21. Kliuchevskii, *Sochineniia*, vol. 7, pp. 5–32; Smith and Christian, *Bread and Salt*, pp. 34–9. Elsewhere in Russia, producers usually extracted salt from the brine from saline springs.
22. Smolitsch, *Russisches Mönchtum*, pp. 295–7.
23. Zguta, 'Monastic medicine', pp. 63–70.
24. Rozov, *Kniga*, pp. 108–26; Vzdornov, *Iskusstvo*, pp. 8–9, 63–112, 134–5.
25. Meyendorff, *Byzantium*, pp. 96–107.
26. See Bushkovitch, 'Limits' and Prokhorov, 'Isikhazm'.
27. Lure, *Ideologicheskaia borba*, pp. 295–345; Lilienfeld, *Nil Sorskij*, pp. 133–57. For an English translation of Nil's 'rule', see Fedotov, *Treasury*, pp. 90–133.
28. Kazakova, *Vassian Patrikeev*, pp. 78–86, 255–71, 287–92. The polemical literature criticizing monastic wealth needs further examination. See, for example, Sinitsyna, 'Eticheskii i sotsialnyi aspekty', for a fresh look at Maxim the Greek's views on the issue.
29. Zimin, *Krupnaia feodalnaia votchina*, pp. 37–54.
30. Lure, *Ideologicheskaia borba*, pp. 331–7.
31. Obolensky, 'Popular religion', pp. 53–4.
32. Kazakova and Lure, *Antifeodalnye ereticheskie dvizheniia*, pp. 34–71, 251.

33. Lure, *Ideologicheskaia borba*, pp. 127–85. Lure's hypothesis that the name 'Judaizers' actually refers to two separate groups of heretics – the Novgorod and Moscow circles – with distinctly different beliefs has not convinced most of his colleagues.

34. Lilienfeld, "Häresie"; for Lure's thoughtful response, see his 'Ideological movements'.

35. Kazakova and Lure, *Antifeodalnye ereticheskie dvizheniia*, pp. 130, 472–3.

36. Lure, *Ideologicheskaia borba*, pp. 407–26.

37. Zimin, *Peresvetov*, pp. 153–214; Klibanov, *Reformatsionnye dvizheniia*, pp. 265–302.

38. There are traces of folly in Christ in the life of St Francis of Assisi.

39. Likhachev and Panchenko, *'Smekhovoi mir'*, pp. 93–182; Fedotov, *Sviatye*, pp. 205–19; *Rude & Barbarous Kingdom*, pp. 218–20, 268–9.

40. Lure, *Ideologicheskaia borba*, p. 413.

41. Ostrowski, 'Fontological investigation'.

42. Alekseev, *Agrarnaia i sotsialnaia istoriia*, pp. 13–41, 168–85.

43. Rozhkov, *Selskoe khoziaistvo*, pp. 402–29.

44. Ostrowski, 'Church polemics'; M. B. McGeehon, 'The problem of secularization'. In *Council of 1503*, pp. 164–88.

45. Kazakova, *Vassian Patrikeev*, pp. 255–7.

46. Schaeder, *Moskau*, pp. 19–20.

47. Strémooukhoff, 'Moscow'. In *Structure*, p. 111.

48. Cherniavsky, 'Reception', p. 353.

49. Schaeder, *Moskau*, p. 53.

50. Strémooukhoff, 'Moscow'. In *Structure*, p. 113.

51. Labunka, 'Legend', abstract, p. 2. See also N. Andreyev's similar argument in 'Filofey'. Other parts of Andreyev's article, however, have been superseded by A. L. Goldberg's 'Tri 'poslaniia" which, by analysing the extant manuscripts, argues that Philotheus of Pskov probably did not write the 'Letter to Ivan Vasilevich' attributed to him by later copyists.

52. *Poslaniia Iosifa Volotskogo*, pp. 229–32; Lure, *Ideologicheskaia borba*, pp. 474–9.

53. Joseph of Volokolamsk, *Prosvetitel*, p. 647; Sevčenko, 'Neglected Byzantine source'.

54. Goldberg, 'Tri 'poslaniia".

55. Translations quoted from Andreyev, 'Filofey', p. 28.

56. Philipp, 'Begründung', pp. 115–18.

57. Miller, 'Coronation'.

58. Miller, 'Velikie Minei Chetii', pp. 265–6.

59. Ibid., pp. 268–369.

60. Crummey, 'Spectacles'; Labunka, 'Legend', pp. 220–77 argues that Macarius further developed a ceremony originally adapted by Archbishop Gennadius.

61. Ammann, *Abriss*, pp. 230–6.

62. Makarii, *Istoriia*, vol. 6, pp. 47–322; Golubinskii, *Istoriia*, vol. 2, part 2, pp. 23–4.

63. Kartashev, *Ocherki*, vol. 1, pp. 362–451.

64. Zimin, *Rossiia*, pp. 254–5.

65. Ibid., pp. 277–8.

CHAPTER SIX

The reign of Ivan the Terrible

The reign of Ivan IV, the Terrible (1533–84), was a time of great accomplishments and ruinous disasters for the ruler of Moscow and his subjects. Ivan's government continued the mobilization and consolidation of the nation's resources, particularly through creative reform of the royal administration and armed forces. In war, he used the weapons forged by his predecessors – a powerful army, a solid diplomatic position and a sense of national mission – to win brilliant victories. What began so well, however, ended in tragedy. By the end of Ivan's life an aggressive foreign policy led to humiliating defeat, domestic reform had degenerated into a bloody reign of terror, and serfdom had begun to swallow up the Russian peasantry.

The reign, then, presents us with a mixed pattern of light and shadow, of triumph and tragedy. Since Ivan's own time, observers have wrestled with a single question more than any other. To what extent does the motley pattern of triumphs and setbacks mirror Ivan's own personality? Historians have long been tempted to see Ivan IV as a 'Renaissance prince', a brilliant, complex and mercurial ruler, like Henry VIII, who was exhilarated and burdened by the demands of his office.[1]

In recent times, however, this traditional picture has come under attack. Historians who attempted to portray Ivan's personality and outline his ideas on government relied heavily on his exchange of letters with Prince A. M. Kurbskii, a Muscovite aristocrat who deserted to Lithuania. Edward L. Keenan, however, has argued that these documents are not genuine, but instead the invention of a seventeenth-century writer or writers.[2] From that point, Keenan has gone on to sketch quite another picture of Ivan – that of a chronic invalid, incapacitated by the drugs and alcohol with which he deadened the pain of a chronic disease. He was no intellectual on the throne; indeed, he may not have been literate. Given his physical and mental limitations, he could not possibly have played a leading role in the conduct of governmental affairs which, fortunately for Russia, usually fell into the hands of his advisers.[3]

Keenan's arguments and hypotheses have stirred up a storm of controversy. Many well-informed scholars reject his views about the origin of Ivan's letters:

143

the correspondence, they argue, is a genuine work of his time and, in some sense, of his pen. If they are right, they have also preserved the essential outlines of the traditional portrait of Ivan as an intellectual – an erratic, irascible and provincial one, to be sure – on the throne.[4] Moreover, I am convinced, we have a good deal of credible evidence apart from his correspondence from which to reconstruct Ivan's personal qualities and political style.

The controversy over the letters of Ivan IV and Kurbskii is only one of many disputes about the events of the reign and their meaning. Given the confusing state of the literature at present, how can we describe Ivan and discuss the events of his reign? First of all, we can restrict our discussion, as much as possible, to facts and explanations that are generally accepted by reputable historians of the period. Secondly, when we enter areas of controversy – as we inevitably shall – we will chart the areas of disagreement among the specialists and, on occasion, suggest possible resolutions of the conflict. Finally, we will emphasize, not what men of the time may have written, but who they were and what they did.

Fortunately, we know many things about Ivan as man and ruler. A well-publicized twentieth-century autopsy of his remains shows that he was a man of imposing stature who, in his later years, suffered from a severe deformity of the spine. His physical suffering led him to take heavy doses of drugs and made him extremely irascible, as contemporaries knew only too well. How his affliction affected his performance as ruler is harder to gauge. Ivan must surely have found it difficult to carry out the onerous practical and ceremonial responsibilities of a ruler. But did he cease to rule at all? Even a man in Ivan's condition might well make the most important decisions governing Muscovy's foreign and domestic policy. Certainly foreign visitors to his court assumed that he did.

In the sixteenth century, Western and Central Europeans assembled their first comprehensive picture of Russia and its ruler. It came from a variety of sources – diplomats' reports, merchants' and voyagers' accounts and popular tales. Geographically, the foreign sources on Ivan's reign fall into two categories – the English and the Germanic. In both, the authors saw Russia from a particular vantage point. For Englishmen, Muscovy appeared, above all, as a trading partner; in the German-speaking world, Ivan's Russia was a ruthless enemy engaged in savage warfare against his German neighbours. Apart from their instinctive biases, foreign writers about Muscovy faced other problems as well. A number had never visited the country about which they wrote. Those who did, particularly the diplomats, lived in conditions of comfortable house arrest while guests of the tsar. Only a favoured few merchants and mercenaries in Russian service had much freedom to observe the country on their own. Like many other historical sources, then, foreigners' accounts of Muscovy are far from ideal.

For all of their weaknesses, contemporary foreign writers left many valuable comments on Ivan IV. Observers of all nationalities agreed on certain characteristics of his personality and manner of ruling. Ivan created an imposing impression, presiding at court functions in magnificent regalia. Behind the glamour lurked a mercurial personality: those who dealt with him, particularly in his later years, feared his sudden outbursts of temper. Anger easily led to violence. Accounts of Ivan's reign are full of tales of his sadistic cruelty. A number, unfortunately, are true, not least the lurid account of his murder of his eldest son.

Not all of the foreigners' comments are disparaging. Sir Jerome Horsey, an English visitor to Ivan's court, described him as 'of ready wisdom' as well as 'cruel, bloody' and 'merciless'.[5] German writers, not Ivan's greatest admirers, likewise described him as an intelligent man with a prodigious memory as well as many disagreeable traits. Ivan's intense devotion to the rituals of Eastern Orthodoxy also impressed his contemporaries. A few of them even claimed that he was curious about the beliefs and practices of other branches of Christianity.[6] Antonio Possevino, the Jesuit diplomat and missionary, wrote a long description of his public disputation with Ivan on the practices of the Roman Catholic Church. To be sure, as Possevino describes it, the 'debate' was a missing – not a meeting – of minds. Ivan struck his Jesuit visitor as, above all, stubborn and his questions and observations as trivial or ill-informed. Even in this most optimistic of descriptions, then, Ivan hardly qualifies as a competent theologian. At the same time, Possevino presents the Russian ruler as a forceful, lively and inquisitive – not to say temperamental – man.[7]

As seen by foreign contemporaries and by Russians of subsequent generations, then, Ivan IV was a strong-willed, often cruel, man who really exercised political authority in Muscovy, both for good and for ill. In the final analysis, however, his personality and political style are far less important than the events of his reign and the policies of his government.

Ivan IV inherited the throne under most difficult circumstances. When his father died in 1533, he was only three years old. During his final illness, Vasilii III did his best to arrange an orderly succession. He left his widow and their children in the care of her ambitious uncle, Mikhail Glinskii, and another kinsman, D. F. Belskii. The dying grand prince made the leading nobles of the court responsible for the affairs of state.[8]

Vasilii's arrangements could not save Muscovy from a long and difficult regency. Within a year, for example, rivals at court had Ivan's guardian, Glinskii, arrested. Thereafter, until Ivan came of age in 1547, the most powerful aristocratic clans engaged in a chaotic and brutal struggle for power. One after another, they seized control of the government only to fall victim to the intrigues of their rivals. The principal contenders were the Glinskiis and Belskiis, Ivan's relatives through his mother, and the Shuiskiis, princes from Suzdal who dominated the Boyar Duma at the time of Vasilii's death. Each of these clans apparently did all in its power to improve its position. The contending factions made matrimonial or strictly tactical alliances with other court clans and probably tried, as well, to draw less prominent courtiers and officials into their camp. The feuding clans had also to take into account the members of the royal family in whose names they aspired to rule.

Even if we ignore the autobiographical statements attributed to him, Ivan IV's childhood and youth must have been confusing and difficult. As nominal head of state, the young prince had to play the central part in long and wearisome official ceremonies. As the years passed, he must, like Louis XIV in a later generation, have been struck by the discrepancy between his ceremonial majesty and his lack of real power. He surely realized that his name and authority were indispensable to the courtiers who dominated the royal government, but it was they who ruled, not he. At the same time – despite later allegations to the contrary – he probably received good treatment from the men and women around him since they needed his favour. When and how Ivan began to take political action in his own right is not clear. Many historians assume that, by his mid-teens, Ivan actively intervened in the struggles around him, ordering the executions of courtiers who lost his trust.

In the first years of the regency, however, the pivotal figure at court was Ivan's mother, Elena Glinskaia. As factional intrigues swirled around her, she and her reputed lover, Prince Ivan Ovchina Telepnev-Obolenskii, headed a government that proved to be remarkably resolute and effective. Under their leadership, the regime fought a successful border war with Lithuania and consolidated its power on the domestic front.

Once Elena died in 1538, the political life of the Muscovite court lost all coherence. The Shuiskiis, already strong, arrested Obolenskii and assumed control of the government. Their triumph did not last long, however. In the course of confusing infighting, they lost out to the Belskiis. The latter, in turn, gave way to a coalition led by the Vorontsovs, a well-established family of non-titled royal servitors. The Vorontsovs and their allies held sway until 1546, when their leaders were executed, probably at Ivan's own command. At that moment, the political carousel completed a full circle. On the eve of his coronation, the young prince's maternal relatives, the Glinskiis, once again dominated the court.[9]

During the chaos of feuds, disgraces and executions, the dominant court clans made no attempt to weaken the royal administration, for they had no interest in doing so. Whatever their place of origin, the Glinskiis, Shuiskiis and their fellows had chosen to serve the princes of Moscow and had moved their residences to the capital. Having thrown in their lot with the Muscovite monarchy, they aimed, not to weaken it, but to control it for their own ends. At the same time, the regimes of the regency period gained a deserved reputation for corruption as the ruling boyar clans did everything that they could to enrich themselves and reward their allies. Moreover, the rapid changes in political leadership made it difficult to follow consistent policies, particularly after Elena Glinskaia disappeared from the scene.

Nevertheless, in spite of the distractions of the factional struggles at court, the regimes of the regency period, acting in their own interest, took measures to strengthen the royal government. For example, they attacked the last of the appanages created by Ivan III. As soon as Vasilii III died, the regents arrested his younger brother, Iurii of Dmitrov, and left him to die in prison. Andrew of Staritsa, the last remaining brother, suffered the same fate after

Elena Glinskaia's government goaded him into a revolt in 1537. Her regime also established a single system of coinage for all of Muscovy and built or renovated fortifications in many parts of the realm.[10] After her death, her successors began to reorganize the administration of the provinces – a series of reforms which we will examine in another context.

Ivan's minority formally ended in 1547. In January of that year, Metropolitan Macarius, the head of the Russian Church, crowned him as tsar. Ivan's coronation was a momentous step. For the first time, a Russian ruler was invested with the title of emperor, implying both complete national independence and theoretical superiority to all other political authorities on earth. Investing the young monarch with the imperial title culminated the campaign of the ecclesiastical theorists to demonstrate that universal Christian monarchy had passed to Russia, and that her ruler alone could legitimately claim to be the one true Christian emperor.

On a more practical plane, the coronation met the needs of at least two groups in Muscovite society. Macarius and the other leaders of the church had every reason to sponsor a symbolic statement that brought greater glory to Russian Orthodoxy. Most historians assume, for example, that the metropolitan was responsible for the composition of the ceremony at which he presided. In the lay world, the glorification of their young kinsman on the throne strengthened the hand of the Glinskiis, the dominant faction at court. Indeed, the very extent of the Glinskiis' triumph may have led to their downfall.

Exactly three weeks after his coronation, Ivan IV took his final step into manhood. He married Anastasia Iureva-Zakharina. The bride's family – known in later generations as the Romanovs – had long played an important role at the Muscovite court and been represented in the Boyar Council since the time of Ivan III. Her father was a council member and her uncle had occupied prominent positions under Vasilii III. Moreover, her brother and cousin received boyar rank in connection with the marriage.[11] Custom dictated that royal in-laws occupy high ceremonial positions at court. The Romanovs were not merely courtiers, however: they were a gifted, energetic and ambitious clan and their representatives continued to exercise leadership and enjoy great influence at court long after Anastasia died.

Ivan's adult reign began on a frightening note. On 21 June 1547, fire broke out in the centre of Moscow and quickly spread through the wooden city. Within a matter of hours, most of the central districts lay in ruins. The devastation was so great that the royal family withdrew to its nearby summer residence of Vorobevo.

The fire set off smouldering resentment against the Glinskiis. Within the inner circles at court, the overweening power of the tsar's maternal relatives led to the emergence of a broad coalition determined to overthrow them. At its centre were the Shuiskiis and Ivan's new in-laws, the Romanovs. In the alleys and markets of Moscow, bitterness over the Glinskii regime's corruption stimulated imaginations. Rumours circulated that the tsar's grandmother, Anna Glinskaia, was a witch who had started the great fire by making a potion from human hearts and sprinkling it on the city. Whether or not the Glinskiis' enemies at court and in the streets actively collaborated is a matter of dispute. They certainly shared a common goal – the destruction of the all-powerful favourites.

Five days after the fire, rebellion broke out in Moscow. The capital quickly slipped from the government's control as rioters coursed through the streets looking for Glinskiis. Ivan IV's uncle, Iurii, sought sanctuary inside the Cathedral of the Dormition in the Kremlin. The rebels found him there, dragged him outside and lynched him. Three days later large numbers of Muscovites, with their own executioner in tow, marched out to Vorobevo to demand the surrender of the other leaders of the Glinskii clan. Ivan IV came out to face his mutinous subjects and, in time, the crowd dispersed even though its demands were not met.

The experience was surely harrowing for all concerned. Ivan himself must have been thoroughly frightened. The remaining Glinskiis – the tsar's grandmother and his uncle, Mikhail – completed their own fall by attempting to flee to Lithuania some months later. As for the rebels, the government quietly sought out and punished their leaders once it had restored order. The only real winners in the struggle of 1547 were the Glinskiis' rivals at court. After it was over, the Romanovs and their allies consolidated their position around the throne.[12]

In the years after the uprising, Ivan IV's government showed remarkable energy and determination. The tsar and his advisers made a number of important domestic reforms and embarked on an ambitious foreign policy. Before discussing the government's actions, however, we should examine its composition.

Who ruled Russia in the years of the reforms? The question is by no means easy to answer. Even historians of seventeenth-century Russia, who have far more documentation at their disposal, cannot describe, with any certainty, the tsars' part in setting national policy. In many instances, it is impossible to determine who advocated particular domestic reforms or changes in foreign policy. The outlines of sixteenth-century politics are murkier still. Historians have long debated the composition of the so-called 'Chosen Council', the inner circle around the young Ivan's throne.[13] Leaving aside their more imaginative hypotheses, we can offer a few observations.

Ivan's inner circle was a remarkably motley group. His in-laws, the Romanovs, occupied prominent positions at court and undoubtedly exercised great influence. Beside them stood men who owed their positions to their talents or to the tsar's favour. Aleksei Adashev – the man usually regarded as head of the government – came from a far less eminent noble family which had recently moved to Moscow from Kostroma. His father had enjoyed a distinguished career in royal service and, during Ivan's minority, had carried out important diplomatic assignments. At the same time, the Adashevs were outsiders to the social world of the court, and Aleksei's formal rank never truly reflected the power that he wielded. In essence, he was a royal favourite, but one whose personal qualities more than justified his high standing. In addition, like his immediate predecessors, Ivan relied heavily on his most prominent chancery officials, especially Ivan Viskovatyi who made major contributions to the conduct of foreign policy. The final figure who almost certainly belonged to Ivan's inner circle was the most enigmatic one. Later narrative sources credit Sylvester, a priest of the Cathedral of the Annunciation in the Kremlin, with great influence over the young tsar and thus over the policies of his government. At the same time, his position as a clergyman in politics was, at best, anomalous and his reputed influence in secular affairs is not reflected in the documents through which the government transacted its business.[14]

What of Ivan himself? Did the young ruler contribute significantly to the making of governmental policy? Or did the members of the inner circle rule in his name? We cannot be sure. One thing is clear, however; several of the members of the inner circle owed their positions to their personal connections with the tsar. Whether he ruled or not, the young Ivan IV occupied the central position in the political constellation of his time.

As soon as it took shape, Ivan's inner circle launched a campaign of reforms. Its objectives were most ambitious. Judging by their actions, the tsar and his advisers aimed at making the royal administration more efficient and less corrupt, bringing consistency and order to the church and the royal courts, and strengthening the army. In pursuit of these goals, the government mobilized the lesser nobility and merchants by consulting their representatives on important matters of state and giving them a central part in the administration of the provinces.

To open the campaign, Ivan made a number of symbolic gestures, expressing his government's intentions. According to one chronicle, for example, the tsar addressed a combined meeting of the Boyar Duma and a church council on 27 February 1549 and demanded that the great nobles stop oppressing the lesser nobles and peasants as they had during his childhood. When the boyars promised to obey him, the story continues, Ivan decreed that henceforth provincial governors were not to sit in judgement of lesser nobles in their jurisdictions unless the latter were accused of major crimes.[15]

The meeting of 1549 was the first of many occasions on which the tsar publicly met with ecclesiastical and lay leaders to announce his government's policies. The composition of such gatherings apparently varied. Sometimes, as in 1549, they consisted only of the Boyar Council and the leaders of the church. On other occasions, the government reached out to include members of the lesser nobility who happened to be in Moscow and perhaps even merchants and artisans from the capital.

Over the course of the 1550s and 1560s, these meetings evolved into the *zemskii sobor* or 'assembly of the land'.[16] At the height of its development, this institution bore a rough resemblance to the national estates of the monarchies of Western Europe. We should not stress the parallel too much, however. Except on rare occasions in the seventeenth century, the zemskii sobor was not a representative institution. Instead – as Kliuchevskii pointed out long ago – Ivan's government created it as a means of mobilizing the support of its leading servitors. In the sixteenth century, the sobor did not so much decide issues of national policy as lend its support to decisions that the tsar and his advisers had already made.[17]

Actions soon followed words and gestures. In the early 1550s, Ivan's government made a large number of detailed technical reforms which fall into two categories – housekeeping in state and church and preparation for war with Kazan. In putting its house in order, Ivan's government, in 1550, issued a new law code (*Sudebnik*). The act of promulgating a legal codex symbolized the regime's determination to deal energetically with pressing issues of national life. At the same time, the Sudebnik did not represent a radical departure from previous practice. Like the Code of 1497, from which it drew many provisions, the Code of 1550 was, in essence, a procedural manual for conducting investigations and trials. Moreover, its concrete provisions were generally conservative. In certain particulars, the Sudebnik reflected the general drift of Ivan's policies. Several of its articles attacked the corruption of officials. Others aimed at strengthening the central administration's control over the provincial governors (namestniki) and, in certain respects, freed the newly created district elders from their jurisdiction. The Code also reflected the government's desire to keep accurate records of the landholdings of the church and the nobility and to limit the scope of the monasteries' immunities.[18]

Ivan's government also took steps to bring greater order into the practices of the Russian Church. According to the Stoglav, the official record of the event, the tsar summoned a church council which met in his palace early in 1551. Ivan asked the church fathers a number of detailed questions about abuses in their administration and the liturgical and moral failings of their flock. For their part, the assembled ecclesiastics promised to deal with the problems to which the tsar had pointed.[19]

How literally can we take the Stoglav's statements about Ivan's role in the council?[20] That a secular ruler preside over an ecclesiastical council is fully consistent with Christian tradition particularly in the Eastern Church. Even if Ivan did not literally give the speeches ascribed to him, the document reflects his government's concern to reform many areas of national life including the church. Other official acts of the same year make this policy clear. In May, the government prohibited the hierarchy and the monasteries from buying estates from nobles and forbade several categories of nobles from willing land to monasteries in return for prayers for their souls. Any land acquired in violation of these stipulations would be confiscated by the tsar.[21]

Other, more radical reforms aimed at strengthening the central royal administration. The key to change lay in its structure. Since the fifteenth century, the rulers of Muscovy had gathered around themselves a small corps of officials who specialized in carrying out assignments requiring particular expertise. Over the course of time, such bureaucrats became more numerous and worked in increasingly highly organized offices with well-defined duties and procedures. In the opinion of A. A. Zimin, Ivan IV's government completed the process of forming the central bureaucratic chanceries (*izby*, later *prikazy*) in the late 1540s and 1550s. Each of these offices had a single director and performed one particular administrative function. Among the first were the Petitions Chancery, the Brigandage Chancery, which supervised the government's campaign against highwaymen, and the Post Chancery, which managed its system of post horses and relay stations. Three of the new chanceries formed the central core of the administration. The Foreign Office took care of international affairs, the Razriad kept records of the tsar's warriors and issued orders for muster, and the Pomestnyi Prikaz maintained registers of noblemen who held estates on conditional pomeste tenure.[22]

The reorganization and refining of the central administration gave Ivan and his advisers a powerful weapon for mobilizing for war and bringing the country under more effective control. For the next century and a half, the system of prikazy grew dramatically in size and complexity. Until the reforms of Peter the Great, however, the bureaucracy retained the essential shape and qualities that Ivan's government had given it.[23]

In preparation for an all-out assault on Kazan, the regime attacked several weaknesses in the army. First it tackled the most destructive feature of mestnichestvo (precedence ranking). Ivan's early campaigns against Kazan fell into disarray in large measure because the aristocratic commanders of the Muscovite army in the field wasted time and energy in quarrels over precedence and even refused to perform their duties for fear that doing so would lower their future standing and that of their family. This, as the royal government quickly realized, was no way to run an army![24] Something had to be done. At first, the government tried simply prohibiting further disputes among officers. When the problem recurred in the campaign of 1550, Ivan promulgated a set of regulations governing the relationships between military commanders in the field.

In order to understand the tsar's decree on mestnichestvo, we must consider the organizational structure of the Muscovite cavalry army while on campaign. A full army consisted of five regiments – the great or central, the advance guard, the rearguard, the right wing and the left wing. Ivan's decree worked on the assumption that a precedence dispute would normally involve only two commanders at a time. It stipulated that, while in the field, all other officers were to recognize the commander-in-chief of the great regiment as their superior. The commanders of the right wing, and the advance and rear guards were to treat one another as equals. The commander of the left wing was to have the same relationship to the commanders of the advance and rear. The commander of the right wing, however, was to be the superior of the one on the left. In broader terms, the decree specified that a man's military posting under these arrangements could not serve as a precedent for future disputes.[25]

The decree was a very tentative step in the direction of reform. The measure clarified the lines of authority among the commanders of an army in the field. Beyond that, it remained a statement of good intentions. In no sense did the decree attack the whole system of mestnichestvo which played so central a part in the life of the aristocratic clans of Ivan's court. Moreover, in practice, it did little to stop litigious generals from making fools of themselves and endangering the lives of their men. The military records from the remainder of the sixteenth century report many such quarrels.

In preparation for the assault on Kazan, Ivan's government created a new military force to complement the noble cavalry that could cause so much trouble. Since it had been formed for steppe warfare, the Muscovite army stressed mobility and made little attempt to exploit the power of firearms. By the late fifteenth century, to be sure, the tsar's forces included artillery and gradually added foot-soldiers with hand-guns. In 1550, Ivan IV ordered the formation of six companies of musketeers (*streltsy*). These men, recruited in large part from the earlier foot-soldiers, served throughout the year and received a salary from the royal treasury. In battle, the streltsy usually fought on foot and provided much of the concentrated firepower needed to capture fortresses like Kazan or compete against contemporary European armies. As hoped, the new units contributed greatly to the conquest of Kazan and became an essential, permanent element in the armed forces of Muscovy. From the beginning, moreover, since the streltsy lived in urban centres, they took on the role of garrison troops and police.

Finally, in the autumn of the same year, Ivan's government drew up a list of 1,000 noble servitors to whom it proposed to grant lands near Moscow. The purpose of the project was clear enough. An estate near the capital was a great boon to one of the tsar's servitors. A prominent courtier who lived in the city could easily get provisions for his city household from his nearby lands. A less privileged member of the cavalry could live on such an estate and still report for duty within a few hours. It is scarcely surprising, then, that the Muscovite government wanted as many noble servitors as possible to own land near the capital.

By the mid-sixteenth century, finding and distributing such land were no easy matters. Nobles and monasteries already owned much of the populated arable land in the central regions of the country. For this reason, historians disagree about the fate of the project of 1550. A. A. Zimin makes a strong case that, in spite of its good intentions, Ivan's government could not carry out the reform for lack of available land. As he points out, relatively few of the men named in the project are listed in the cadastres of the Moscow region in subsequent decades.[26] Whatever its concrete achievements, the government's motive was clear – to strengthen the upper echelons of the service nobility.

Equipped with an army even stronger than before, Ivan's government made a remarkable advance in foreign policy – the creation of an empire. The conquest of Kazan was the turning-point. In the late 1540s and early 1550s, Muscovy's policy towards the khanate, once pragmatic, became increasingly aggressive. Even in the last years of Ivan's minority, his government showed that it aspired, at the very least, to achieve hegemony over the khanate to the east. In 1545, a large Muscovite army advanced to the very walls of Kazan before withdrawing.

With Ivan's coming of age in 1547, his policy took on a still more aggressive tone. From that time, his government aimed to conquer Kazan and absorb it into his domains. Under the energetic leadership of Metropolitan Macarius, the church played an important role in mobilizing the community for the struggle. For one thing, ecclesiastical councils canonized a number of native saints, some of whom, like Alexander Nevskii, symbolized the Orthodox Russian community victorious in war against the enemies of the faith and the motherland.[27] Moreover, in their official statements, government and church portrayed relations with Kazan as a crusade – a struggle between Orthodox Christians and Moslems whom they branded 'Godless hagarenes' or 'saracens'. Orthodox Russia could achieve peace and security only after the Cross had completely vanquished the Crescent. The authors of public statements and the court chronicles used such rhetoric to mobilize support within Muscovy for the war. In its essence, it accurately captured the determination of the Muscovite government and its ecclesiastical supporters to deal decisively with Kazan. At the same time, crusading rhetoric obscured many features of the domestic and military situation. Such language obviously had no part in the negotiations between Muscovy and her Tatar ally, the Nogai confederation, whose leaders provided vital support for the Russian plans of conquest.[28]

Muscovite military power and the internal problems of the khanate combined to bring Kazan down. The latter were urgent and profound. It was difficult enough to reconcile the interests of the landed aristocracy of the khanate and the international Moslem merchant network for whom the city was a valuable entrepôt. The Islamic clergy also had a distinct view of Kazan's best interests. In addition, the great aristocratic clans which dominated Kazan's political life could not agree on the best way to counteract the pressure of her enemies.

Ivan IV and his advisers repeatedly took advantage of the khanate's instability. In 1546, when conspirators overthrew Khan Safa-Girey, Ivan sent his perennial candidate, Shah-Ali, to occupy the throne. Other leading Kazani nobles, however, continued to support the ousted ruler. Recognizing the insecurity of his position, Shah-Ali fled to Muscovite territory, taking a number of his supporters with him. Safa-Girey returned to power, but under conditions that alienated many grandees. He surrounded himself with favourites from his native Crimea and executed several prominent nobles who plotted against him.

The restlessness of the non-Tatar nationalities of the khanate also played into Moscow's hands. Most importantly, the Cheremiss of the right or high bank of the Volga revolted against Kazan's rule and asked for Muscovite protection. Ivan IV was only too glad to oblige. He sent an army into the region and made it a staging area for expeditions against Kazan itself. Moreover, the taxes paid by the area's inhabitants now went into Ivan's treasury.

As the khanate's troubles mounted, Moscow's military pressure increased. Ivan and his generals led large armies towards Kazan in the winters of 1547–48 and 1549–50. In both cases, however, unseasonably warm weather made it impossible to transport arms and supplies over melting ice and snow. Neither expedition reached its goal. The Muscovite government quickly learned its lesson. In 1551, it founded the fortress of Sviiazhsk in Cheremiss territory on the Volga. The new town served both as a supply depot and listening-post close to Kazan.

Continuing instability and mounting desperation within the khanate gave Ivan the chance to take it under his effective control without outright military conquest. When Safa-Girey died leaving his two-year-old son as heir, leading political figures in Kazan began to look for a more desirable alternative. In 1551, a delegation approached the Muscovite government asking support for another attempt to enthrone Shah-Ali. The Kazanis involved were prepared to hand over the young khan and his mother and to release all Russian prisoners in their custody. Aleksei Adashev, Ivan's chief negotiator, added a heavy new condition to the list. As ruler of Kazan, Shah-Ali was to recognize Moscow's annexation of the Cheremiss country.

On the surface, Ivan's government had painlessly achieved its objective. Its insistence on the annexation of Kazani territory, however, quickly undermined the settlement. Shah-Ali and his supporters tried unsuccessfully to convince Ivan to drop the condition. Moreover, the new khan discovered that he was powerless to repatriate some of the Russian prisoners in the hands of his subjects. His position quickly became untenable once again.

At that point, Kazani exiles at Ivan's court proposed a more radical solution – to replace Shah-Ali with a Muscovite general who would serve as governor. Thus, in effect, Ivan's representatives would take control of the political machinery of the khanate while leaving the power of the local aristocracy intact. The scheme foundered – as it probably would have in the long run – when a few of the exiles, fearing Muscovite intentions, returned to Kazan and urged the population to fight to keep Muscovite troops out of the city.

Ivan and his advisers now had no choice but direct and massive use of force. After a delay for mobilization, a large Muscovite army invested the city. The Kazanis offered desperate resistance, but, in the end, Ivan's troops forced their way into the citadel and, on 4 October 1552, the tsar entered the city in triumph.

Even after the capital had fallen, the khanate was not conquered. For five more years, bitter resistance continued in the hinterland. At last, the entire territory of Kazan lay in Moscow's grasp.[29] Moreover, the advance down the Volga led directly to the annexation of the shadowy khanate of Astrakhan at the mouth of the river.

The results and meaning of the conquest of Kazan were profound. At one stroke, Muscovy became an empire, the ruler of highly organized communities with cultural traditions radically different from her own. From that time forward, successive Russian governments would wrestle with the problem of controlling and governing alien peoples within their borders.

As is well known, the conquest gave Muscovy control of the Volga highway to the Middle East and opened the way to Siberia and, ultimately, the shores of the Pacific. In even broader terms, the events we have described marked an important turning-point in the ancient struggle between the agriculturalist and the nomad, between the peoples of the forest and the steppe. Now the agricultural way of life was advancing and, in time, Russian peasants would conquer the grasslands with their ploughs.

Finally, the conquest gave Ivan and his people a profound sense of accomplishment. The expansive rhetoric of the chroniclers and the dizzying exuberance of St Basil's Cathedral, built to celebrate the event, vividly express the joy of leading circles in Moscow. Victory also posed a dilemma. How should Muscovy next use her growing military might? Was an attack on the Crimea – a more remote and more dangerous Tatar state than Kazan – the logical next step? Or should the tsar turn his forces westward toward the decaying feudal state of Livonia, key to the Baltic shore? On the answer rested the fate of Ivan's policies and the fortunes and lives of many of his subjects.

Within a year of the conquest, Ivan IV's own life hung in the balance. On 1 March 1553, the tsar fell gravely ill. Realizing that he might die, he tried to secure the succession for his infant son, Dmitrii. His attempt to put his affairs in order set off a short, but serious crisis within the ruling circles at court. Some of the boyars immediately agreed to swear allegiance to Dmitrii even though, as contemporaries put it, he was still in diapers. Others hesitated. The prospect of an infant monarch provided all too vivid reminders of the instability of Ivan's own childhood. As a result, Adashev's father and other prominent nobles expressed their willingness to accept Ivan's son, but voiced the fear that, if he came to the throne, the real rulers of Russia would be his mother's kin, the Romanovs. According to an interpolation in the official court chronicle, Ivan forcefully assured them that such would not be the case.

Yet a third group of boyars, mostly from princely clans, momentarily looked to another candidate, Ivan's cousin, Vladimir Andreevich of Staritsa. Although of very limited intellect and energy, Vladimir was at least an adult of royal blood. If Ivan and his baby son were to die, he would be the only credible heir to the throne. Moreover, his ambitious mother gave force and direction to his cause. Even so, his candidacy quickly collapsed. Apparently the boyars who had considered supporting him soon submitted to Ivan IV's wishes and, in the end, Vladimir Andreevich and his mother reluctantly swore allegiance to the infant prince. With their submission, the crisis ended. Soon Ivan returned to health and, on the surface, life at court resumed its normal pattern. From that time, however, the tsar kept his cousin under close surveillance.[30]

In spite of its short duration, the crisis of 1553 had serious consequences. It profoundly embittered the relations between Ivan and the Staritsa branch of the ruling family. Moreover, the experience of momentary powerlessness seems to have obsessed Ivan in his later years. Otherwise it is difficult to explain why, many years afterwards, the tsar or someone close to him bothered to interpellate a detailed and self-serving account of the events into the official court chronicle.

After this brief interruption, Ivan's government returned to the path of domestic reform. He and his advisers continued to restructure the administrative and judicial system on the local level – a process begun by the transitory regimes which had ruled during his minority. The regents had attacked an urgent problem. Banditry flourished in many parts of the country and both the governors (namestniki) sent out from Moscow and local leaders were unable or unwilling to put an end to it. Thus, beginning in 1539, the central government issued charters to the population of particular districts (guby), especially in northern Russia, instructing them to select officials (starosty) who were to be responsible for assembling posses and, on their own authority, arresting and hanging highwaymen and other notorious characters. Rather than reporting to the provincial governor, the district elders were to be accountable directly to officials in Moscow who led the campaign against brigandage.[31]

These ruthlessly simple arrangements worked, above all, to the advantage of the royal administration in Moscow. Its officials undoubtedly increased their ability to supervise the administration of justice in the provinces since the district elders were strictly accountable to them. The reform placed the local nobles in an ambivalent position. On the one hand, they gained sweeping powers to deal with troublemakers and presumably had official sanction to lord it over the local population at large. Moreover, the local leaders were presumably happy to see the government take more effective measures against highwaymen. At the same time, as their oath of office made clear, the elders' responsibilities were onerous. For their part, the great nobles of the court who served as provincial governors can hardly have regretted losing functions that brought them nothing but trouble.

Ivan's government clearly saw the advantages of the new system, for, over the next decades, it introduced district elders to more and more areas of the country. Moreover, the idea that the royal government would function more effectively if it made local élites responsible for their own fate produced an even more sweeping reform of the local administration within a few years.

In the mid-1550s, Ivan and his advisers applied this principle in two distinct ways. First, they extended the system of local judicial officials (gubnye starosty) to more and more areas of Muscovy and further refined and broadened the elders' judicial prerogatives and responsibilities.[32]

Second, they created a new group of officials, drawn from leading elements of the local population, to serve as tax collectors. Like the guba elders, they at first appeared in a few particular localities, ostensibly in response to the petitions of local leaders.[33] In 1555, Ivan's government transformed these officials (zemskie starosty) into a radically new system of administration. In the next few years, governors (namestniki) disappeared from most parts of the country. In their place, representatives of the local populace took charge of tax collection.

Once again, apparent decentralization served to increase the effectiveness of the central bureaucracy. Unlike the old governors, the prominent local merchants or wealthy peasants who received the onerous job of collecting taxes from their fellow citizens had little to gain from cheating the royal exchequer. Moreover, the local elders worked under the tight supervision of the central bureaucracy in Moscow. Finally, the taxpayers paid dearly – twice the previous rate – for the privilege of taxing themselves.

In the northern regions of Muscovy, the government found particularly rich soil for the new system. There economic prosperity had created the merchants and prosperous peasants who made ideal recruits for the treasury's army of agents. From the point of view of these local leaders, however, the reform was surely a mixed blessing. They escaped from the governors' power, but at a high cost in money and trouble.

By way of contrast, Ivan's noble courtiers – the men who had normally served as governors – probably saw the change as a boon. They no longer had to spend time administering remote and often poor districts. In addition, in return for the loss of the right to maintain themselves (kormlenie), they received payments in money from the treasury's increased revenue.[34]

The abolition of kormlenie had obvious military implications as well, for it freed the tsar's leading warriors from administrative duties and allowed them to concentrate on fighting. For this reason, Ivan's court chronicle linked the changes in the local administration with a strictly military reform, the 'decree on service' of 1556.

For many generations, all Muscovite nobles had been obliged to fight in the grand princes' army when summoned. The 'decree on service' set norms for the nobles' military obligations. According to its provisions, the owner of any estate – whether held on hereditary or conditional pomeste tenure – had to appear for muster himself and bring with him one fully equipped cavalryman for every 100 chetverts (about 165 hectares or 410 acres) of good land which he owned. If a landowner complied with the decree, he would receive a payment of money to support his entourage; if he refused, he was to be fined accordingly.[35]

Seen together, the reforms of the provincial administration and the army exemplify the accomplishments of Ivan IV and his advisers. The policies which they adopted greatly improved the firepower and discipline of the Muscovite army. Their actions also increased the central administrative chanceries' capacity for mobilizing men and collecting revenue for war. Indeed, paradoxically, the very success of Adashev and the other reformers led to the collapse of their regime and brought an end to their campaign of gradual reform, for it raised the question of how next to use Muscovy's increased military might.

Towards the end of the 1550s, questions of foreign policy increasingly preoccupied Ivan and his advisers. Serious differences of opinion split his inner circle. The Adashevs argued for a war to neutralize and, if possible, conquer the Crimea. The idea had much to recommend it. Such a policy was a logical extension of the seizure of Kazan. The political structure and economic foundations of the Tatar khanates made peace along the frontiers with them virtually unattainable. If a state of war between Christian and Moslem was inevitable, why not accept this reality and attack the centre of Tatar power directly? On the other hand, the conquest of the Crimea would surely be no easy task. Geographically, the peninsula was a virtually impregnable fortress and lay much further than Kazan from the centres of Muscovite power. A series of probes against the Crimea, culminating in Daniil Adashev's unsuccessful expedition in 1559, seemed to prove that a southern strategy was beyond Muscovy's military capacity.

By that time, Ivan IV had already chosen a different alternative. Accepting the advice of his 'foreign minister', Ivan Viskovatyi, the tsar turned his army westward. For many years, his government had shown an intense desire for closer diplomatic and commercial contacts with the countries of Central and Western Europe. In 1547, for example, the tsar sent Hans Schlitte, a German in his service, back to Central Europe to recruit doctors, scholars and artisans.[36] Then, in 1553, Richard Chancellor's fortuitous arrival on the coast of the White Sea opened direct commercial and diplomatic ties with England. The relationship with Queen Elizabeth's realm proved both invigorating and frustrating. The primary source of difficulty lay in the trade route itself: the White Sea, an arm of the Arctic Ocean, is frozen for much of the year and the northern waters off Britain and Norway always treacherous. Understandably, Ivan and his advisers continued to look for a safer and more direct avenue to Europe.

Livonia, they believed, offered answers to many of Muscovy's problems. The region had a strategic location on the eastern coast of the Baltic, and its highly developed cities had long functioned as important centres of international trade. By the sixteenth century they had gained a monopoly over Russian exports through the Baltic. The Livonian countryside was fertile and productive. Conquest of the area would give Muscovy ports within easy reach of Western Europe and, like Kazan, might well provide lands to distribute to Ivan's warriors.

So great a prize appeared to be available at very little cost. Institutionally, Livonia was a survival of an era long past. Founded by the crusading Order of the Livonian Swordbearers, later joined by the Teutonic Knights, it had, by the sixteenth century, become a hodgepodge of conflicting political forms, religions and nationalities. At the centre of political life remained the Livonian Order of Knights, still the area's main defence force. By the mid-sixteenth century, however, many erstwhile knights had become Lutheran and settled down as country squires lording it over Estonian or Latvian peasants. Moreover, just as elsewhere in the Holy Roman Empire, the principal Roman Catholic bishops acted as secular rulers of their sees and the main ports were, in effect, free cities, ruled by merchant oligarchies. Beside the increasingly powerful and centralized Muscovite monarchy, Livonia appeared helpless.

There was only one catch. Livonia had not one, but a host of rapacious neighbours. For one thing, in the previous decades, Polish influence in the area had increased dramatically. As Ivan and Viskovatyi surely realized, then, any Muscovite move against the area might well provoke counter-measures by Sweden, Denmark or Poland–Lithuania. If Muscovy were to seize the prize, she would have to do so quickly.

After carefully creating a pretext for war, Ivan sent his troops into Livonia in January of 1558. In a lightning advance from the south, Muscovite forces took Dorpat (Tartu) and, in the north, seized the coastal fortress of Narva. At this point, however, disputes in Moscow destroyed the army's momentum. Under pressure from Adashev, Ivan's government, in 1559, concluded a six-month truce with the Livonian Order in preparation for the unsuccessful Crimean expedition of that year. The pause in the fighting gave the knights a chance to improve their military and diplomatic posture. The master of the order and the archbishop of Riga put themselves under the protection of Sigismund II of Poland. In the same year, another interested party, Denmark, intervened by seizing the large island of Ösel (Saaremaa). The partitioning of Livonia had begun.

Once war resumed, the Muscovite army, after initial difficulties, continued its victorious advance. In 1560, Ivan's troops destroyed the army of the Order near Fellin (Viljandi) and occupied that pivotal fortress in the very centre of Livonia. Once again, however, Muscovite triumphs set off frantic responses. The cities on the northern coast accepted Swedish rule and, in 1561, the last master of the Livonian Order ceded his lands to Poland.

Polish intervention dramatically changed the nature of the conflict. Instead of merely fishing in Livonia's troubled waters, Muscovy now faced full-scale warfare all along the frontier with her powerful neighbour to the west. In the first stage of the conflict, Ivan's troops gained the upper hand, capturing Polotsk in 1563. A year after that dramatic victory, however, the Muscovite army suffered a serious defeat on the Ulla river and its advance bogged down.

As victory turned into stalemate, political tension built up within the Muscovite court. In the early 1560s, Ivan IV simultaneously underwent a change of political direction and a serious personal crisis. To begin with, he destroyed two men – Adashev and Sylvester – who had once been his close advisers. In 1560, the tsar assigned Aleksei Adashev and his brother, Daniil, to command posts in the army in Livonia and, later in the year, confiscated their estates and disgraced them. Aleksei was lucky enough to die of natural causes a few weeks later, but Daniil had still more to suffer. He was executed in 1563 along with some of the Adashevs' relatives by marriage. Sylvester, who had lost Ivan's confidence, retired to a monastery.

In late summer of the same year, Ivan suffered a personal tragedy. His wife, Anastasia, unexpectedly died. Generations of historians have speculated that the tsar loved his consort deeply and was profoundly moved by the loss. Even though tradition may have cast an excessively romantic glow over the relationship, the fact remains that Ivan's family life changed dramatically from that time on. In about a year, he took the first of his numerous later wives, Maria Temriukovna, a Circassian princess from the northern Caucasus whose father had recently entered Ivan's service. Moreover, contemporary reports and later legends recount that the social life of the Muscovite court took on a bawdy quality unknown before.

In the years that followed, Ivan began to lash out at the aristocratic clans of his court. The tsar lived within a spider's web of family relationships. Ties of kinship or marriage linked many of the powerful court clans – princely and non-titled – to one another. These interlocking family groupings monopolized the highest commands in the army and filled almost all of the places in the Boyar Council. Economically, their power rested on ownership of estates held on unconditional tenure. Any Muscovite ruler had to reckon with them when making appointments or charting national policy.

Ivan's impatience with the high nobles of his court and the tension created by war with Poland came to the surface in 1562 when he disgraced several prominent aristocrats on suspicion of disloyalty. I. D. Belskii, for example, was accused of planning to defect to Poland. The fate of the victims varied greatly. D. I. Kurliatev and his son were forced to take monastic vows and the Vorotynskiis lost their ancestral principality near the Lithuanian frontier. Others, like Belskii, were soon pardoned.

The tsar's forgiveness had its price. Men restored to favour had to sign formal declarations of their future loyalty witnessed by large numbers of fellow courtiers. Such written oaths of loyalty were not new. Beginning in the 1560s, however, Ivan IV made much more extensive use of the practice than his predecessors and the guarantors were more numerous and varied than before.[37]

In 1563 and 1564, the political thermometer continued to rise. In addition to the purge of the Adashevs, Ivan IV ordered the execution of a number of his courtiers. N. V. Sheremetev, a general from one of the most ancient and distinguished non-titled clans, probably perished at this time as a scapegoat for the Muscovite army's defeat on the Ulla.[38] Moreover, according to an oft-quoted story, Ivan had Prince M. P. Repnin killed because that distinguished gentleman refused to take part in a drunken masquerade at the court and rebuked the tsar for his unseemly conduct. In reality, Prince Repnin may have died because Ivan suspected him of treason or because of his family connections with other disgraced aristocrats. In any event, his murder, after he had been dragged out of a church, provided one more proof of the tsar's increasing impatience and brutality. Not all of the victims of Ivan's wrath, however, were men as eminent as Repnin and Sheremetev: some of those purged were comparatively obscure members of the court.

In the same years, Ivan moved against his cousin and potential rival, Vladimir Andreevich of Staritsa. For years the relationship between the two had remained stable and peaceful on the surface. Now, however, when one of the servitors in the Staritsa appanage denounced Vladimir Andreevich and his mother for plotting against Ivan, the tsar disgraced them. He forced the energetic princess to enter a convent and surrounded her son with new servitors of his own choosing. At that point, Ivan and his cousin were reconciled: as a condition of the settlement, Vladimir Andreevich ceded Ivan some of his lands in exchange for the town of Romanov on the upper Volga, some distance from the rest of the Staritsa appanage. By removing its strongest leader from the scene, scattering its servants and dividing its lands, the tsar had prepared the cadet branch of the dynasty for destruction.[39]

As the war in the west reached stalemate and the tone of Muscovite political life became more menacing, a number of Ivan's soldiers defected to the enemy. Most were relatively minor figures who would have remained obscure but for their treason. One, however, was a man of real significance. On 30 April 1564, Prince A. M. Kurbskii slipped out of Dorpat and fled to Wolmar where he entered Polish service. The scion of a line of princes of Iaroslavl, Kurbskii had family connections with a number of other prominent clans at the Muscovite court. For years he had held responsible positions of command in the army, particularly in the first years of the Livonian War. There may, moreover, be some truth to the later stories that he was a close friend of the tsar. Be that as it may, his defection was a boon to King Sigismund and, at the very least, a grave embarrassment to Ivan.

Why Kurbskii fled is a matter of dispute. Some historians stress his fear of disgrace and execution either because of his failures in the field or his connections with other disgraced courtiers. Recent events in Moscow undoubtedly gave many aristocratic commanders food for thought. Others emphasize his dreams of power and wealth in Polish service.[40] Both explanations may tell part of the story. Kurbskii was not the first man to try to draw profit from impending disaster: nor will he be the last.

Once in Sigismund's camp, Kurbskii became the central figure in a circle of Muscovite *émigrés*. From there, most scholars still believe, he wrote letters attacking Ivan's baseless cruelty towards his leading servitors and protesting his own innocence. In return, Ivan composed a long and blistering epistle in which he lashed out at Kurbskii and his former advisers. An autocrat, Ivan argued, is answerable to God alone and may treat his subjects, however distinguished, exactly as he likes. Paradoxically, even if we accept Keenan's argument that these letters are compositions of a later time, they testify to Kurbskii's stature and the importance of his defection; for why, otherwise, would a later falsifier want to put his own words into Kurbskii's mouth?

The gathering storm broke in all its fury in December of 1564. Ivan IV left Moscow to celebrate the feast of St Nicholas in one of his suburban residences. This was no ordinary excursion or pilgrimage. When he departed, the tsar took along his wife and children, a number of his courtiers and his treasury. His subjects became increasingly uneasy when, instead of returning to his capital, Ivan journeyed northward past the city to the Holy Trinity Monastery before finally settling in his hunting lodge at Aleksandrova Sloboda.

On 3 January 1565, after a long silence, Ivan made a startling pronouncement. In an epistle to Metropolitan Athanasius, head of the church, he explained that he had left Moscow out of anger at the boyars and chancery officials and the leaders of the church. Since his childhood, he alleged, the boyars had not fought to defend their country and had oppressed the rest of the population. The clergy had angered him by interceding for those who had fallen into his disfavour. Since he could not tolerate any more of their treasonous deeds, the tsar intended to abdicate the throne and go where 'God directed him'.

Although contemporaries noticed in Ivan signs of extreme nervous tension, there was method in his apparent madness. As he surely expected, his dramatic gestures and statements caused consternation among his subjects. The leaders of the royal administration and the church appealed to the metropolitan to intercede with Ivan and, within hours, a delegation set out for Aleksandrov bearing petitions begging the tsar to remain on the throne and deal with traitors as he wished.

In response, Ivan announced his plans 'to create for himself an oprichnina', a separate administration and court to do his bidding. In order to support himself and the men who would serve in these new institutions, the tsar set aside substantial areas of the country, the districts of Suzdal, Mozhaisk and Viazma and most of the far north including the valley of the northern Dvina river. The Boyar Council was to administer the remaining areas of the country (the *zemshchina*) and report only the most important matters of state to Ivan. Thus, Muscovy suddenly found itself with two administrations, two armies and two separate groups of territories, one ruled directly by Ivan IV and the other by the aristocrats of his old court. Ivan's great experiment had begun![41]

The oprichnina remains the most controversial episode of Ivan's reign. For generations, historians have argued with one another about the details of the tsar's experiment and, even more vehemently, about its basic direction and purpose. Even its name was confusingly archaic, for, in much earlier times, the word 'oprichnina' referred to a widow's portion of her late husband's estates. Why did Ivan create an oprichnina for himself? What did he hope to achieve by dividing up his realm and its administration? The statements attributed to Ivan give us little help in answering these questions: the tsar spoke of his need to destroy his enemies – sometimes roughly equated with the high nobility – and to protect Muscovy from treason.

Ivan and his advisers have made the historian's task very difficult, for they left behind remarkably little reliable information about the oprichnina. The main court chronicle breaks off soon after its inception. Moreover, once the oprichnina was abolished, many of the records of its operations were apparently destroyed deliberately. In spite of the problems, a number of painstaking recent studies have reconstructed what Ivan did in the stormy years after 1564.[42]

Determining Ivan's objectives and evaluating his success in reaching them is more difficult still. For roughly a century, historians of the reign have split into two camps. Some, following the lead of S. F. Platonov, see the oprichnina as a continuation of Ivan's earlier reforms with more violent methods. In their opinion, the core of the tsar's domestic policy after 1564 was a systematic attempt to strengthen his authority by destroying the power of the aristocratic clans whose members dominated his court and administration. Other scholars, whose views I find more congenial, regard Ivan's experiments not as projects of conscious social engineering, but as expressions of a paranoid personality's search for security in a threatening world. The issue of aristocratic power was real, they argue, but Ivan's attempt to deal with it was neither realistic nor consistent. The debate continues and each new study contributes new facts or insights to the discussion.[43] Nevertheless, much about Ivan's character and policies in later life is still mysterious and will perhaps always remain so.

Once Ivan's leading subjects had acquiesced to his demands, he and his new advisers – above all, Aleksei Basmanov – turned to organizing his state-within-a-state, centred in Aleksandrova Sloboda. They had picked out the oprichnina's scattered territories with a clear purpose – to provide generous revenue and supplies for the tsar's new court and entourage.[44] The northern Dvina valley and the White Sea coast were a particularly good choice; the region, populated chiefly by townspeople and peasants, was enjoying a period of prosperity, in part because the river was the main artery for trade between the interior of Muscovy and Western Europe.

As the years passed, Ivan added new patches of territory to his private principality. Most of the new acquisitions lay well to the north of Moscow – the Kostroma area and part of Iaroslavl, the Beloozero district, and part of the city of Novgorod and two of its northern rural dependencies. In keeping with his desire to keep his hand on the pulse of commerce, Ivan also saw to it that the headquarters of the English traders and the enterprises of the Stroganovs, the leading native entrepreneurs, came under his direct jurisdiction. And to keep abreast of events in Moscow, he set aside a section of the city to the west of the Kremlin and built a fortified residence there.[45]

In the lands set aside for the oprichnina in central Muscovy, Ivan undertook a review of the nobility. Those who satisfied him of their loyalty became members of the oprichnina's army. They took an oath to inform the tsar of any plots against him and put on the black uniform of the *oprichniki* complete with a small broom symbolizing their master's determination to sweep treason from the realm. Those who failed the test had their lands confiscated: they had to move to new estates in territories outside of the oprichnina.

The tsar's criteria for accepting or rejecting a man appear to have been entirely personal. Over the course of the oprichnina's existence, men of many backgrounds served in Ivan's private army and court. Some came from aristocratic clans and many more from the lesser nobility. On occasion, some members of a prominent family served in the oprichnina, while others did not. In short, as V. B. Kobrin has convincingly argued, the social composition of the oprichnina court and that of the zemshchina were virtually identical.[46] The only significant difference between the two parallel courts was the presence in the oprichnina of a scattering of foreign adventurers, several of whom later wrote accounts of their experiences.

Ivan proved as good as his word when he announced that he intended to destroy his enemies. Early in 1565, a new wave of executions rocked Moscow. The most prominent victims were men of impressive personal qualities and exalted lineage. First to fall was A. B. Gorbatyi, a Suzdal prince and leader of the army that conquered Kazan. He perished along with his teenage son and his son-in-law, P. P. Golovin, a courtier distinguished in his own right. Soon Ivan turned on an old nemesis, Prince S. V. Rostovskii, whom he had briefly imprisoned many years earlier after his son was arrested attempting to flee to Lithuania.[47] Rostovskii was murdered on the tsar's orders.

The executions of 1565 reveal several of Ivan IV's characteristic methods of operation. First, when he suspected a man of disloyalty, he attacked his entire family, executing male kinsmen along with the primary victim. Indeed, on a number of occasions during the oprichnina's existence, Ivan ordered the execution even of the retainers and servants of the primary victims. Second, he often chose exceptionally brutal and terrifying methods of execution. For example, his executioners impaled Prince D. F. Shevyrev. Foreign contemporaries, hardened to the sight of public executions, were none the less horrified by Ivan's cruelty. Undoubtedly, his subjects were equally frightened.

Many more of Ivan's subjects felt his disfavour in less dramatic ways. Soon after founding the oprichnina, the tsar uprooted about 200 nobles and banished them to the region of Kazan. There the exiles had to find new lands to replace their previous estates, confiscated by the tsar. As the cadastres of the area make clear, most only managed to carve out very small holdings to which they received conditional title.

Who was exiled to Kazan? R. G. Skrynnikov's recent study shows that princes from the regions of Starodub, Iaroslavl and Rostov made up the largest single component of exiles. A few of them – like F. I. Troekurov – were distinguished military commanders. Others had very large estates and staffs of retainers. Many of the exiled princes, however – the numerous Gundorovs, for example – were, in every sense, obscure figures. Moreover, a significant number were not princes at all; a few came from distinguished non-titled families and considerably more from the lower echelons of the court.[48]

What do these findings mean? Returning to earlier theories, Skrynnikov argues that Ivan IV saw these princes as a threat to his power because of their concentrated landholdings in their regions of origin and their influential positions in the royal administration and at court. His explanation is open to at least two major objections. First, it is based on several unprovable assumptions. We simply do not know, for example, whether or not most of the exiled Starodub princes actually owned ancestral lands in that area. Second, as S. B. Veselovskii repeatedly observed, imputing to Ivan IV policies of conscious social engineering implies a consistency that we do not see in his concrete actions. Some princes in the affected regions, for example, were not exiled at all. Moreover, the tsar pardoned most of those who were banished within about a year. For a number, the amnesty came too late; they could not regain control of their family property even though they had the right to do so and, if they did, the estate was probably in ruins by the time they recovered it. Other princely families survived the exile well and, in later generations, enjoyed great wealth and power.

After their initial steps to deal with their enemies, real or imagined, Ivan and his advisers turned their attention to foreign policy. By the mid-1560s, hope for a decisive victory in Livonia had evaporated. Poland–Lithuania, Sweden and Denmark had all intervened in the struggle and carved out their own spheres of influence. Although wary of one another, all three shared a determination to keep Muscovy from dominating the area. Moreover, they enjoyed an advantage that Russia did not possess in spite of her army's might: all three succeeded in winning the cooperation of leading individuals and groups in the local population. Ivan IV's attempts to build a base of support within Livonia invariably foundered on religious differences, the incompatibility of Muscovite autocracy with Livonian traditions of corporate rights, and the tsar's growing reputation for sadistic cruelty.

In this increasingly complex and unpromising situation, Ivan's government sensibly decided to simplify its options and solidify its position. In 1564, Muscovy made a seven-year truce with Sweden, thus strengthening her hand in dealing with Poland. At the same time, her diplomats began a series of peace negotiations with Polish representatives. It soon became obvious, however, that the two sides were far apart.

By 1566, Ivan stood at the crossroads. Still flushed by Muscovy's early victories, he and his advisers rejected even the most generous Polish terms – a return to the status quo before the war. The decision posed a serious political problem – how to convince Ivan's leading subjects of the need to continue a long and costly war. The tsar responded in two ways. His government retreated from the militant policies of the oprichnina's first year. Many victims of Ivan's disfavour – Prince M. I. Vorotynskii and most of the exiles in Kazan – received clemency and were allowed to reclaim their confiscated estates.

Moreover, in 1566, Ivan summoned a zemskii sobor to deal with the latest Polish peace offer. The resulting meeting of the estates turned out to be the most representative and significant of the entire sixteenth century. Three hundred and seventy-four men attended, including members of the church hierarchy and the Boyar Council as well as representatives of the royal bureaucracy, the urban population and the rank-and-file nobility. How the delegates were chosen is not clear. In all probability, most of the noble representatives happened to be in Moscow already when the assembly was announced. In any case, Ivan's government consulted, not with representatives of society as a whole, but, by and large, with its own leading officials and servitors.

From Ivan's point of view, the sobor brought mixed blessings. As expected, the delegates supported his decision to reject the Polish proposal for peace. Doing so meant, in addition, accepting the burdens of service and taxes that continued warfare would inevitably bring. At the same time, the zemskii sobor of 1566 provided a focal point for opposition to the oprichnina. Many nobles in the zemshchina petitioned Ivan to end his experiment. Their protest angered the tsar: according to one report, he ordered the arrest of the petitioners and publicly humiliated their leaders. Three of them, including Prince V. F. Pronskii, were executed.

Resistance appeared in another, rather unexpected, quarter as well. The head of the church, Metropolitan Athanasius, retired to a monastery, probably in protest against the tsar's policies. When Ivan's first choice as successor had to be rejected for the same attitude, he turned to Filipp, abbot of the Solovetskii Monastery and a member of the non-titled Kolychev clan. At first, Filipp too expressed strong opposition to the oprichnina, but, in the end, took office on condition that he did not interfere with Ivan's conduct of the affairs of state.

The appearance of open opposition to royal policy gave the oprichnina new life. For several years after 1566, Ivan IV displayed exaggerated concern for his own safety. Suspecting conspiracy in Moscow, he spent more and more time in Aleksandrova Sloboda, protected by his bodyguard and elaborate security measures. At the same time, he began to build up Vologda, the entry point into the northern Dvina river basin, as a major fortress and cultural centre. He became obsessed with the need to escape from the dangers of leadership in one way or another. On a lengthy visit to the St Cyril Monastery of Beloozero, he expressed the desire to retire there and take monastic vows. Moreover, in 1567, he asked a startled Anthony Jenkinson to secure Queen Elizabeth's pledge of asylum in England should he be forced to flee his realm. All of these statements and gestures suggest that, at the height of the oprichnina, Ivan suffered from acute delusions of persecution.

Developments in the real world gave his paranoid imagination much food for reflection. In 1569, the Union of Lublin transformed the dual monarchy of Poland–Lithuania into a unitary kingdom. Henceforth the enemy whose overtures Ivan had scorned would be stronger than before. Moreover, the newly united kingdom served as a staging ground for Muscovite exiles. In the same year, a small Polish force captured the important border fortress of Izborsk because Russian defectors, masquerading as oprichniki, tricked the defenders into opening the gates. In addition to his troubles on the western front, Ivan had to divert part of his army to ward off a combined Ottoman Turkish and Crimean army which attempted to capture Astrakhan. Finally – and far more frighteningly – Ivan learned that a conspiracy of Swedish nobles had overthrown King Erik XIV in 1568. The spectre of a legitimate monarch, even a mere Vasa, overthrown by his 'boyars' must have struck fear into Ivan's heart. Moreover, the coup boded ill for Muscovy's relations with Sweden since it brought Ivan's old enemy, John III, to the throne.

In response to such pressure from within and without, Ivan IV let loose a new wave of terror, singling out and destroying people whom he regarded as threats to his power. While even the wisdom of hindsight does not give the historian unequivocal answers, many of the alleged conspiracies against him were probably figments of the tsar's imagination. All the same, we can see certain general patterns in Ivan's choice of victims. First, just as in later times, the reign of terror took on a momentum and logic of its own. Fear impelled men to denounce one another. Malicious accusations or false confessions under torture implicated new groups of victims who, in turn, led their torturers to still more suspects. Finally, the last to suffer torture and death were the leading exponents of the terror themselves.

Second, Ivan and his entourage frequently lashed out at targets that had once threatened the power of the monarchy but did so no longer. Ivan III had dealt ruthlessly with the appanage princes of the royal family and had systematically subdued Novgorod and assimilated it into the Muscovite system of administration. Yet Ivan IV felt compelled to fight these same battles all over again. The reason for his obsession probably lay in events of his childhood which made these distant threats a reality in his own life and imagination. Ivan's official court chronicle, for example, gives considerable attention to the 1537 revolt of Prince Andrew of Staritsa against the regency government and his attempts to enlist the nobles of Novgorod in his cause. Other passages in the chronicle or its later revisions likewise point to the appanage princes or Novgorod as a danger to the royal authority.[49]

Once the terror began, one group of victims followed another at regular intervals. The first to fall were the leaders of the zemshchina, above all, I. P. Cheliadnin-Fedorov. Responsibility for their fate lay, in part, with the government of Poland. Once hostilities between the two countries resumed in 1567, King Sigismund attempted to undermine the Muscovite war effort by writing secretly to several leaders of the zemshchina, inviting them into his service. The boyars in question quickly informed the tsar of the intrigue, but the memory of the incident must have festered in his mind. In the following year, rumours circulated that Fedorov and other boyars wanted to replace Ivan with his cousin, Vladimir Andreevich. Whether true or not, the reports stirred Ivan to action. First, he sent the oprichniki around the country to pillage Fedorov's estates and systematically murder his retainers. The master's turn soon followed. In September 1568, Fedorov, four Kolychevs and several other representatives of prominent boyar clans mounted the scaffold. Other distinguished victims soon followed them. Before the purge ended, about 150 nobles and chancery officials perished, to say nothing of their servants.[50]

The identities of the victims of the Fedorov affair are significant for at least two reasons. First of all, the most prominent of them came from the most distinguished non-titled clans of the Muscovite court and the highest echelons of the royal bureaucracy. In other words, Ivan attacked his own leading servitors – precisely the men who should logically have helped him rule. Second, the tsar and his followers chose their victims quite indiscriminately. In this and later purges, many of those executed were obscure men and women. At the same time, there was a certain method in Ivan's madness. When the tsar turned on a prominent noble like Fedorov, he systematically annihilated his entire family and all of his retainers who, in some mysterious way, must have shared in his guilt.

Metropolitan Filipp's turn soon followed. Outraged by Ivan's conduct, the leader of the Orthodox Church withdrew from Moscow without resigning his office. Several sources, moreover, describe angry public confrontations between tsar and metropolitan. Filipp had more than enough reasons to be angry. By almost any standard, Ivan's behaviour was immoral and certainly inappropriate for the lay protector of the Orthodox faith. Moreover, the tsar had destroyed several of Filipp's kinsmen and many others in the social milieu from which he had come. Once the metropolitan raised his voice, his fate was sealed. With the help of collaborators within the higher clergy, Ivan hastily convoked a court which convicted Filipp of moral turpitude. The oprichniki then humiliated the fallen leader by publicly stripping him of his regalia before imprisoning him in a monastery. There, on his master's orders, Maliuta Skuratov strangled him.[51]

Filipp's deposition and death admirably illustrate Ivan's ambivalent attitude towards the Orthodox Church during the oprichnina and after. The tsar cultivated good relations with his favourite monasteries and, in the oprichnina court, adopted some monastic observances, with strange and grimly comic results. Yet to be a leader of the church was dangerous: Filipp was only the most prominent of a number of bishops and abbots who lost their lives at the tsar's hands. At the same time, the destruction of Filipp and other individual hierarchs did not mean a frontal attack on ecclesiastical power, as some historians have suggested. The martyrs made their sacrifice, but, in many ways, the church as an institution thrived. In particular, the monasteries of Muscovy were acquiring land in unheard-of quantities thanks to the terror which the oprichnina inspired in the hearts of wealthy nobles. Some aristocrats, fearing execution, took the tonsure and, in beginning their new life, gave land to their community. Many more made grants in return for the monks' and nuns' prayers for the repose of their relatives' souls or their own.

Vladimir Andreevich of Staritsa, the tsar's cousin, met his fate next. Had Ivan not had scruples about the destruction of a member of the royal family, Vladimir Andreevich might well have perished long before 1569. The memory of the crisis of 1553 apparently still gnawed at the tsar's mind. The oprichnina's reign of terror put the prince of Staritsa in a particularly vulnerable position. The investigation of Fedorov's 'conspiracy' turned up allegations that the plotters planned to put Vladimir Andreevich on the throne. At that point, Ivan decided that his cousin had to be eliminated. Members of the oprichnina entangled him in a fantastic plot to poison Ivan with the help of the royal cook. They then condemned him to death and forced him and his wife and youngest child to drink poison. Oprichniki also took his mother from the nunnery and murdered her. Ivan spared only Vladimir's two grown daughters as bait for future royal marriages and his eldest son to whom he later restored his father's appanage.

The fall of the house of Staritsa led Ivan directly to a far more imposing target – Novgorod. Long after Ivan III conquered the former city-state and absorbed it into his domain, it remained wealthy and vitally important. With a population of at least 30,000, Novgorod was the second city of Muscovy and a centre of international and domestic trade and artisan production. Even after Ivan III's draconian treatment, the city retained some of its unique institutional traditions. Moreover, the court of the archbishop acted as a window open to cultural influences from Central Europe.[52]

At the same time, Novgorod had changed greatly since the days of its independence. The tsar's government commanded the heights of local society. All of the leading officials of state and church – the governors, chancery officials and the successive archbishops – came from Moscow as the representatives of the central authority. Moreover, many nobles and merchants in Novgorod were the descendants of settlers brought in by the Muscovite administration to replace leading citizens of the republic who had been deported. Thus, to see Ivan's attack on the city as a campaign against the 'remnants of feudal separatism' is misleading at best.[53]

Sources of the time, Russian and foreign alike, leave no doubt why Ivan turned on Novgorod: he suspected Archbishop Pimen and the rest of the people of conspiring to hand their city over to the Poles. Some versions of the allegation add a second, apparently contradictory, indictment – that Novgorod wanted to have Vladimir Andreevich as tsar. These reports were highly improbable for several reasons. For one thing, Pimen had always worked closely with Ivan, for example collaborating in deposing Metropolitan Filipp. Moreover, the surviving fragments of evidence suggest not that the people of Novgorod were engaged in a gigantic conspiracy, but rather that false documents, perhaps planted by Polish agents, convinced Ivan of their treason.

In short, Ivan's attack on Novgorod arose from his excessive suspiciousness and gullibility. Rumours of treason may well have triggered individual and collective memories of the city's former independence and more recent role in revolts against the royal authority, including several episodes in Ivan's childhood. Moreover, it was a time of war and Novgorod occupied a strategic position on Muscovy's north-western frontier. The fall of Izborsk in 1569 may have convinced him that many commanders and officials in the border zone were traitors: when his troops retook the fortress, he had a number of the defenders executed.

Once he had decided to punish Novgorod, Ivan showed no mercy. In December 1569, he secretly gathered a large force of oprichniki as though for an important campaign. Any territory through which the tsar passed felt the blows of his rage and the ravages of his brutal and greedy followers. The expedition moved westward through Tver and other centres, executing selected victims and terrorizing the population in each. Finally, early in January 1570, Ivan set up his court in Novgorod and launched a reign of terror. His agents arrested many prominent residents of the city and brought them to his headquarters where they were questioned under torture. After the interrogations, they executed the victims in conspicuously cruel ways, including dragging them to the Volkhov river and stuffing them through holes in the ice. Often entire families of victims died together.

Ivan and his henchmen attacked all of the leading groups in Novgorodian society, beginning with the church. He had Archbishop Pimen imprisoned in a monastery far from his see where he soon died. During the sack of the city, the oprichniki arrested many monks and systematically plundered churches and monasteries. Ivan also lashed out at the leaders of secular society: his victims included a number of prominent local nobles, chancery officials and merchants.

From Novgorod, the tsar moved on to Pskov. There, once again, he and his followers began by arresting local ecclesiastical leaders, above all the abbot of the Pskov Monastery of the Caves, and confiscating church plate. Pskov, however, was spared many of Novgorod's tribulations. Ivan took no formal action against its laypeople, perhaps because his government had recently deported a number of local merchants whom he suspected of disloyalty. In a sudden, and seemingly miraculous, change of heart for which contemporaries gave credit to Nikola, the fool in Christ, Ivan abruptly left Pskov, just as his followers were beginning to plunder the city, and returned to Aleksandrova Sloboda. The Novgorod expedition was over.

The cost of the venture was incalculable. In Novgorod, the formal processes of torture and execution alone claimed nearly 2,200 lives.[54] According to the reports of foreigners who served in the oprichnina, moreover, Ivan's troops had a free hand in dealing with the rest of the population. The oprichniki scoured Novgorod and the surrounding countryside, looting, raping and killing. What they could not carry away, they destroyed. Thus, even though contemporary reports exaggerate the number of victims of the sack of Novgorod, it is entirely probable that thousands of men, women and children died of cold, hunger or the sword as a result of Ivan's campaign.

The sack of Novgorod had an important part in its decline from a great city into a run-of-the-mill provincial town. Being attacked by its own ruler cost the community dearly in lives and property and must have been a shattering psychological blow. At the same time, as Skrynnikov has sensibly observed, it is unfair to blame Ivan IV for all of Novgorod's troubles. Even before his punitive expedition, the interconnected scourges of crop failure and epidemic disease killed off many people in the city and its hinterland. Moreover, natural catastrophes and high taxes kept up the process of depopulation after the departure of the oprichniki.[55] As increasing numbers of inhabitants died or fled from the Novgorod area, its economy declined and its glory receded into the past.

Back at his headquarters, Ivan continued to pursue his obsession with Novgorod's treason. He and Maliuta Skuratov supervised the torture of the associates of Archbishop Pimen and many others brought back under arrest. The pain which they inflicted brought predictable results – the denunciation of still more 'traitors'. This time, however, the trail led back to the heart of the royal administration and to Ivan's entourage itself.

On 25 July 1570, the oprichniki treated the people of Moscow to a chilling spectacle. Foreign observers who described the scene left little to the imagination. Into a square prepared for public torture and executions, Ivan and his bodyguards led about 300 prisoners. Some the tsar spared. For the benefit of the crowd which his followers had summoned, Ivan began to harangue the others, singling out two of the most prominent officials of the zemshchina, Ivan Viskovatyi and Nikita Funikov, the royal treasurer. When both kept their dignity and refused to confess their guilt, Ivan ordered them killed. The oprichniki hacked Viskovatyi to pieces and boiled Funikov alive. More than 100 others perished in equally horrible ways.

In the end, like later reigns of terror, the oprichnina devoured its own leaders. In 1570, Ivan executed Aleksei Basmanov, the chief architect of the policy, along with one of his sons and several kinsmen. The tsar spared Basmanov's other son, Fedor – his homosexual lover according to contemporary gossip – but removed him from power.[56] Then, in the following year, a number of members of the oprichnina's Boyar Council went to their deaths. When Maliuta Skuratov died in battle at about the same time, the last of the important leaders of the oprichnina passed from the scene.

Meanwhile the Livonian venture went from bad to worse. In order to extricate himself from the morass, Ivan attempted to find a trustworthy local agent through whom he could dominate the area. In 1570, he and his diplomats seemed to have found a solution at last. Prince Magnus, younger brother of the king of Denmark and lord of the island of Ösel, eagerly sought Ivan's support against their common enemy, Sweden. For his part, the tsar received Magnus in Moscow, recognized him as 'king of Livonia' and promised him the hand of one of Vladimir Andreevich's surviving daughters.

From the beginning, Magnus proved to be a poor risk. He failed his very first test: in 1570, at the head of an army of Muscovite troops and his own retainers, he laid siege to Reval, the most important Swedish fortress in Livonia. After several months of futility, however, he had to abandon the attempt. Thereafter Magnus's fortunes waned as he gradually lost the confidence of the leading citizens of Livonia and of his patron in Moscow.

Still worse was to follow. At the beginning of the 1570s, the Muscovite government had to face a strategic nightmare, simultaneous warfare on its western and southern borders. Early in 1571, while much of the Russian army was engaged in the west, Khan Devlet-Girey of the Crimea struck at the heart of Muscovy with a large force of Tatar cavalry. Moving with lightning speed, the invaders outflanked the troops sent against them. Within a few days, the Crimeans reached Moscow, occupying and pillaging the outskirts of the startled capital. Fire broke out in the occupied districts and, fanned by high winds, spread to the rest of the largely wooden city. The result was a catastrophe of the first magnitude. Thousands of people died, many suffocated in the shelters where they had hastily taken refuge.[57]

The disaster completed Ivan's disillusionment with the oprichnina. He had already broken with its first leaders and now the private army that he had created to protect him from his enemies had proved powerless to defend the capital of his realm.[58] The tsar ordered the execution of several of its leaders whom he held responsible for the defeat. Moreover, in planning for the next round of fighting, he and his advisers turned away from the concept of two armies and two administrations. In 1572, when Devlet-Girey tried to repeat his recent triumph, he encountered a large and well-prepared army drawn from both the oprichnina and the zemshchina. Once again, the Tatars' speed allowed them to outflank the Muscovite forces, but, this time, the Russians regrouped and, under the leadership of Prince D. I. Khvorostinin, defeated the invaders in a series of fierce battles at Molodi and drove them back into the steppe.[59]

Now that Muscovy had a united army, Ivan proceeded to liquidate the oprichnina. His government reunited his own principality with the rest of his realm and absorbed his private chancery into the regular royal administration. Indeed, the tsar decreed that none of his subjects should so much as mention the oprichnina again. At last the experiment was over.

What had the oprichnina accomplished? It destroyed many people of all social groups, from aristocrats to the poorest artisans and peasants. Moreover, its operations contributed to the economic decline and social dislocation of much of Muscovy, particularly the Novgorodian lands. As a programme of political reform or enforced social change – if it was ever intended as such – it was a dismal failure. After 1572, just as before, the tsar ruled in collaboration with the aristocratic clans of his court. Many individual aristocrats perished alongside their fellow citizens of humbler rank, but, in most cases, their surviving kinsmen succeeded in preserving their clans' position next to the throne. Moreover, the very idea of dividing the land, army and administration of Muscovy into two parts made any consistent and rational policy impossible from the start.

The meaning of the oprichnina is to be sought, above all, in the realm of psychology. Ivan IV created it to keep himself and his realm safe from enemies, real and imagined. And, in the end, his desperate search for security destroyed his subjects' confidence in the order and predictability of life. Years of absurd denunciations, sudden arrests and blood-curdling executions left Muscovite society numb and made Ivan IV the terrible and awe-inspiring figure of literature and legend.

After the abolition of the oprichnina, Ivan displayed less energy and ambition than before. For one thing, his physical disabilities probably grew steadily more crippling. Moreover, he and his subjects surely felt exhausted after the dramatic events of the recent past. In his last years, his government showed little inclination to undertake new ventures or make dramatic reforms.

At the same time, obsession with his own security remained the keynote of his domestic policy. Throughout the last decade of his reign, Ivan continued to designate particular groups of servitors as his own retinue or 'court (*dvor*)' and to set aside certain areas of the realm for his own support. The details of these arrangements are shadowy and the division of land and manpower seems to have been far less dramatic than in the oprichnina.

In 1575, a full revival of the oprichnina seemed imminent. As he so often did, Ivan turned on his former favourites and destroyed them. Once again, one purge led to the next. First, he ordered the execution of the leaders of the government, Prince B. D. Tulupov and V. I. Umnoi-Kolychev, along with their close relatives. As in 1570, the victims suffered the greatest pain and humiliation that Ivan's torturers could devise. Tulupov, for example, was impaled.

Next to fall into the net was Ivan's German physician, Eleazar Bomelius, a sinister figure in the eyes of his contemporaries. If their reports can be trusted, his professional services included preparing poisons to dispatch the tsar's enemies. Bomelius was arrested while attempting to flee from Muscovy. Before he died under torture, he gave testimony implicating a number of prominent individuals. As a result, Leonid, the new archbishop of Novgorod, was deposed and arrested. He soon died under mysterious circumstances leading to a variety of rumours, among them the story that, dressed in a bearskin, he had been torn apart by hunting dogs. A number of other men, notably P. N. Iurev-Zakharin, a maternal kinsman of Ivan's grown sons, also lost their lives in the purge.

Stranger events by far soon followed. In the autumn of 1575, Ivan IV announced his abdication and placed Semen Bekbulatovich on the Muscovite throne. The former tsar began to style himself 'Ivan of Moscow' and took on the attributes of an appanage prince. Like those cadet members of the royal family in bygone days, he controlled his own autonomous principality centred in Moscow, and commanded his own army.

The enthronement of Semen mystified contemporaries. With the advantage of hindsight, writers of more recent times generally agree on the meaning of the episode. Once again fearing conspiracies among his courtiers, Ivan abandoned the central ceremonial position at court where he was an easy target and retired to the shelter of his own residence and bodyguard. As a replacement, Semen had much to offer. A converted Tatar khan, he carried in his veins the royal blood of Chingis Khan. The charisma of the Mongol imperial dynasty made him an ideal head of state. At the same time, he had served Ivan loyally and shown little aptitude for leadership. He would feel no temptation to transform his ceremonial position into one of real power.

Ivan IV left no doubt who really ruled Muscovy; he made clear to English diplomats that they were to deal with him. Moreover, although his communications with 'Tsar Semen' sounded a note of abject humility, the content of his petitions revealed the real relationship between nominal subject and sovereign. In the first of them, for example, Ivan demanded that he be given a free hand to recruit servitors into his guard, but that 'the tsar' had no right to summon any of Ivan's men to his banner.

Just when the new reign of terror appeared to be gaining momentum, however, it abruptly ended. Within a year of his abdication, Ivan took back the throne, sending Semen out to pasture with a pension and the nominal title of grand prince of Tver.[60] Why the tsar suddenly abandoned his last experiment in government is not clear. In all likelihood, the increasing intensity of the Livonian War distracted him from domestic affairs.

Warfare dominated Ivan's last years. When the attempt to establish a vassal kingdom in Livonia failed, the Muscovite government launched a final campaign to conquer the area. Opportunity knocked in 1574. The throne of Poland became vacant and the ensuing election campaign paralysed the commonwealth. Ivan IV added to the confusion by presenting himself and his second son, Fedor, as candidates. In the end, Stefan Bathory, prince of Transylvania, won the crown. Although he ultimately proved to be a formidable adversary, the new king had first to struggle until 1577 to bring his own domain under control.

Ivan seized his chance. Turning toward the Swedish zone of occupation, his army captured Pernau and Hapsal in 1575 and 1576. Then, in the following year, they struck at both of the principal cities of the region – Reval and Riga. Muscovite forces drove back both Swedes and Poles until they held virtually all of Livonia. The greatest prizes – the dominant port cities – still eluded them, however. Moreover, their success drove their enemies, Sweden and Poland, back into one another's arms.

Before long the tide of battle turned. Under Bathory's determined leadership, a large Polish army counter-attacked and captured Polotsk in 1579 and Velikie Luki in 1580. At the same time, Swedish forces began to advance eastward to threaten Muscovy's toehold on the Gulf of Finland.

By that time, Muscovite society could no longer bear the burden of warfare against a coalition of enemies. Natural calamities and years of high taxes had already lowered the population of parts of the country, particularly the Novgorod lands. In the early 1580s, these scourges struck again, worsening an already difficult situation. Not only did the peasants suffer: the minor nobles who depended on their labour found it increasingly difficult to live from their estates while in military service. Understandably, even though foreign invasion threatened Muscovy, the government had trouble making noble cavalrymen appear for muster and keeping them in the ranks.

One response was to put additional limits on the church's right to acquire land. Edicts of 1572 and 1580 forbade the monasteries to accept any more bequests. Moreover, the latter added the stipulation that any former patrimonial estates of princes in the monasteries' control ultimately belonged to the crown. By implication, then, the monarch could confiscate these lands if necessary.[61]

Another measure restricted the peasants' traditional right to move from one settlement to another in the St George's Day period late in the autumn. Here too the connection between the problems of the peasantry and the plight of the lesser nobles is clear. In protecting their own interests, the peasants frequently used their 'right of departure' to move from the land of a poor noble to the estate of a more powerful and more generous lord, most often a monastery. To protect the livelihood of its warriors, the government, in 1580 or 1581, instituted the 'forbidden years', suspending the peasants' right to move for the year in question. As the years passed, such decrees became increasingly frequent. The full enserfment of the peasantry was not far away.[62]

On the battlefield, the Muscovite army continued to lose ground. In 1581, the Swedes finally took Narva and continued their advance along the coast of the Gulf of Finland. Further to the south, the Polish offensive continued. The ancient Russian city of Pskov lay in the king's line of march. Ivan's government rushed to reinforce the garrison before the expected assault. When the attack came, the defenders, including the men and women of the city, resisted valiantly and, in the end, compelled the Polish army to abandon the siege.

While his army fought a rearguard action, Ivan tried desperately to find a diplomatic solution for his problems. He sent an emissary to Rome, hinting that, if the papacy helped to mediate a peace settlement, he might be open to proposals for church union. In response, Antonio Possevino came to Muscovy, conducted his celebrated theological disputation with Ivan and, more to the tsar's taste, helped Muscovy and Poland put an end to the war that was now exhausting them both. Early in 1582, the two powers concluded the ten-year Truce of Iam Zapolskii which restored pre-war borders.

On the northern front, the Swedes fought on for another year before concluding the Truce on the Pliussa river. Its terms represented a distinct setback for the Muscovite government: the Swedes took over all of Muscovy's coastline on the Gulf of Finland except a small salient at the mouth of the Neva river.

Twenty-five years of struggle for Livonia cost Muscovy dearly. Many lives were lost and much treasure wasted. These, however, are only the most obvious of war's costs. The Livonian War put an end to the reforming activity of Ivan's government and put the tsar and his subjects under great strain. In that sense, the war helped to trigger the outbreaks of terror that punctuated Ivan's later years.

Domestic tragedy also stalked Ivan in his last years. After the death of his first wife, the tsar's domestic life was unstable and confused. Six times he remarried and, on the eve of his death, was engaged in negotiations for the hand of Mary Hastings, cousin of Elizabeth I of England. Many of his later unions tied him to the court favourite of the moment and ended when the wife in question died or took the veil.

Ivan IV seemed more fortunate in his heirs. His eldest surviving son, also named Ivan, was a vigorous man in his early twenties. As happens in many families, the strong-willed father and his son clashed as the latter grew to maturity. Complicating the young prince's position were his close ties to his mother's clan, the Romanovs, who fell from favour in the last decade of the reign. The father did not help the situation by interfering continually in the heir's domestic life. Ivan IV arranged three marriages for his son and promptly broke up two of them. A quarrel over the third wife proved fatal to the younger Ivan and ultimately to the peace of the whole realm. On 9 November, 1581, the tsar entered his daughter-in-law's chambers and chastised her for being unsuitably dressed, considering her advanced pregnancy. Hearing his angry shouts, his son rushed to his wife's defence and, in the ensuing scuffle, suffered a fatal blow to the head. Within hours, the young princess had a miscarriage. Thus, in one outburst of rage, Ivan destroyed his heir apparent and his grandchild.[63]

The consequences for Russia were incalculable. Ivan's remaining adult son, Fedor, became his successor. According to contemporary observers at the Muscovite court, he had none of the qualities needed to exercise leadership of so large and complex a realm. Apart from him, however, Ivan's only heir was Dmitrii, the very young child of an uncanonical seventh marriage. Neither age nor undisputable legitimacy qualified him for the throne.

When Ivan died on 19 March 1584, he left his weak heir a devastated country. Over the course of his reign, a thriving economy had fallen into depression and important areas of the country had suffered a catastrophic loss of population. In other respects, the situation was equally bleak. After brilliant success on the battlefield, Ivan's armies had suffered defeat in Livonia. Moreover, the conditions under which peace had been made virtually guaranteed the renewal of hostilities at an early date. On the domestic scene, Ivan's majority began with significant reforms, but his obsession with his own security led him into destructive experiments and reigns of terror. In the end, his government had done virtually nothing to change the structure of political power in which the monarch ruled with and through an intricate network of aristocratic clans. Instead, he had lashed out indiscriminately, destroying individuals and households, and demoralizing the rest of the ruling élite.

When Ivan died, then, Muscovy was an exhausted and deeply troubled country. The perceptive English visitor, Giles Fletcher, looked at Russia's future with foreboding. As he suggested, Ivan's subjects were to pay dearly for his sins.[64]

On a still more profound level, however, Ivan IV and his predecessors had created the institutions and, even more important, moulded the modes of public behaviour and patterns of thought that allowed Russian society to survive even crises as devastating as the 'Time of Troubles' that engulfed Muscovy under his immediate successors.

REFERENCES AND NOTES

1. For a stimulating discussion, see Cherniavsky, 'Ivan'.
2. Keenan, *Apocrypha*. Keenan's argument rests on detailed study of particular texts and manuscripts and on the hypothesis that in sixteenth-century Muscovy there were two entirely distinct cultural spheres – ecclesiastical and lay – and thus that no layman of Ivan's time could have written epistles in a churchly style.
   At present the battle lines of the controversy remain drawn and the war appears destined to last a long time. Both Keenan's supporters and his many opponents can present strong arguments in their favour. Moreover, both camps tend to depend, to some extent, on a closed circle of arguments so that dialogue between them is virtually impossible.
3. Keenan, 'Vita'.
4. See, for example, Skrynnikov, *Perepiska*; *Perepiska Ivana Groznogo*; Rossing and Rønne, *Apocryphal?*
5. *Rude & Barbarous Kingdom*, p. 313.
6. Kappeler, 'Ivan', pp. 163–9.
7. Possevino, *Moscovia*, pp. 67–75.
8. Zimin, *Reformy*, pp. 225–7.
9. Ibid., pp. 248–78.
10. Ibid., pp. 234–41.

11. Ibid., pp. 277–8.

12. Ibid., pp. 294–310; Shmidt, *Stanovlenie*, pp. 75–119.

13. Grobovsky, *'Chosen Council'*.

14. Smirnov, *Ocherki*, pp. 202–63.

15. *PRP*, vol. 4, pp. 575–6.

16. Shmidt, *Stanovlenie*, pp. 120–261.

17. Kliuchevskii, *Sochineniia*, vol. 2, pp. 373–95.

18. Zimin, *Reformy*, pp. 348–65; Dewey, *'Sudebnik'*.

19. *Stoglav*.

20. For a careful discussion of the sections of the Stoglav which are ostensibly statements or questions of Ivan IV himself, see Kollmann, 'Moscow Church Council', pp. 163–86.

21. *PRP*, vol. 4, pp. 523–4.

22. Zimin, *Reformy*, pp. 328–33, 421–2, 449–60; see also Brown, 'Early modern Russian bureaucracy', pp. 57–60.

23. Some historians question the appropriateness of the word 'bureaucracy' to describe the central administrative apparatus of Russia before the middle of the nineteenth century. Although the central chanceries of Muscovite Russia were a far cry from the most efficient modern bureaucracies, I believe that the word none the less serves as a useful label for them.

24. Shmidt, *Stanovlenie*, pp. 262–307.

25. *PRP*, vol. 4, pp. 582–3.

26. Ibid., pp. 581–2; Zimin, *Reformy*, pp. 366–71.

27. Ibid., pp. 276–7, 328–9.

28. Keenan, 'Muscovy and Kazan', pp. 5–6.

29. Ibid., pp. 305–49; Nolde, *Formation*, vol. 1, pp. 24–62.

30. *PSRL*, 13:522–6; Zimin, *Reformy*, pp. 407–17; Veselovskii, *Issledovaniia po istorii oprichniny*, pp. 278–90.

31. *PRP*, vol. 4, pp. 176–88; Zimin, *Reformy*, pp. 253–8.

32. *PRP*, vol. 4, pp. 179–88; 356–70; Zimin, *Reformy*, pp. 418–22.

33. *PRP*, vol. 4, pp. 188–97.

34. Nosov, *Stanovlenie*, pp. 240–526; Zimin, *Reformy*, pp. 422–36; Keenan, review of Nosov.

35. *PSRL* 13:268–9; Zimin, *Reformy*, pp. 437–40.

36. Donnert, *Russland*, pp. 316–20.

37. Veselovskii, *Issledovaniia po istorii oprichniny*, pp. 123–6.

38. Zimin, *Oprichnina*, pp. 109–10.

39. Ibid., pp. 104–6.

40. Ibid., pp. 112–19; Skrynnikov, *Rossiia nakanune 'smutnogo vremeni'*, pp. 72–80.

41. *PSRL* 13:391–5; Zimin, *Oprichnina*, pp. 127–34; Skrynnikov, *Rossiia nakanune 'smutnogo vremeni'*, pp. 83–7.

42. Veselovskii, *Issledovaniia po istorii oprichniny*; Sadikov, *Ocherki*; Zimin, *Oprichnina*; Skrynnikov, *Nachalo* and *Oprichnyi terror*; and Kobrin, 'Sostav'. Additional research on the oprichnina is still needed. In particular, it would be valuable to know more about the changing composition of the ruling élite at court in order to understand why Ivan IV devastated some prominent clans and spared others.

43. For a review of the literature, see Crummey, 'Ivan'.

44. Veselovskii, *Issledovaniia po istorii oprichniny*, pp. 156–63.

45. Ibid., pp. 167–77.

46. Kobrin, 'Sostav'.
47. *PSRL* **13**:237–8.
48. Skrynnikov, *Nachalo*, pp. 271–98; *Rossiia nakanune 'smutnogo vremeni'*, pp. 89–94.
49. On the official chronicle and the interpolations in it, see Kloss, *Nikonovskii svod*; Alshits, 'Ivan Groznyi'; and Andreyev, 'Interpolations'.
50. Skrynnikov, *Rossiia nakanune 'smutnogo vremeni'*, pp. 113–16.
51. Zimin, *Oprichnina*, pp. 246–57.
52. See Tikhomirov, *Rossiia*, pp. 279–316; Pronshtein, *Novgorod*.
53. Skrynnikov, *Oprichnyi terror*, pp. 27–30; compare with Zimin, *Oprichnina*, p. 305.
54. Skrynnikov, *Oprichnyi terror*, p. 64.
55. Ibid., pp. 72–6.
56. Skrynnikov, *Rossiia nakanune 'smutnogo vremeni'*, pp. 138–39; Zimin, *Oprichnina*, pp. 442–4.
57. Ibid., pp. 451–60.
58. Veselovskii, *Issledovaniia po istorii oprichniny*, p. 195.
59. Skrynnikov, *Rossiia nakanune 'smutnogo vremeni'*, pp. 152–5.
60. Skrynnikov, *Rossiia posle oprichniny*, pp. 5–39; *Rossiia nakanune 'smutnogo vremeni'*, pp. 162–71.
61. Ibid., pp. 180–1.
62. Hellie, *Enserfment*, p. 96.
63. Skrynnikov, *Rossiia nakanune 'smutnogo vremeni'*, pp. 171–6, 194–5.
64. *Rude & Barbarous Kingdom*, pp. 105–6, 140.

CHAPTER SEVEN

The arts and culture

Even the casual visitor to contemporary Moscow encounters the artistic monuments of Muscovite Russian culture. The golden cupolas of the Kremlin and the riotous shapes and colours of St Basil's Cathedral – all works of the fifteenth and sixteenth centuries – draw the eye like a magnet. Elsewhere in the city, parish churches and chapels of the Muscovite period stand in the shadow of stark modern office buildings and apartment houses. The sense of communion with Russia's medieval heritage is still more intense in the icon collection of the Tretiakov Gallery, the overpowering interior of the Dormition Cathedral in the Kremlin and, outside of Moscow, in museum-towns like Suzdal and Rostov.

Reminders of Muscovy are everywhere; yet much of the cultural legacy of the Muscovite monarchy remains a closed book even to cultivated Russians. In the Soviet Union and abroad, the public sees medieval Russian life and culture largely through the re-creations of artists of the nineteenth and twentieth centuries. Mussorgskii's opera, *Boris Godunov,* the historical paintings of Repin and Vasnetsov, the plays of A. K. Tolstoi and films such as Eisenstein's *Ivan the Terrible* and Tarkovskii's *Andrei Rublev* immediately come to mind. Until the end of the last century, however, the painting, literature and architecture of medieval Russia received little attention. Old Russia had no artist like Shakespeare whose works remain an inescapable part of contemporary culture. Educated Russians study samples of medieval literature in school, but, in later life, their reading of the classics very rarely extends back in time much beyond Pushkin.

Muscovite architecture and icon painting have a more serious following within the contemporary cultural élite. Beginning late in the nineteenth century, artists, critics and political authorities joined to preserve and restore the most important buildings of earlier periods. Under the last two tsars, there was even a fashion – fortunately short-lived – to imitate Muscovite styles of the sixteenth and seventeenth centuries in new structures. The so-called Church of the Saviour on the Blood in Leningrad, built on the spot where Alexander II was assassinated, is an outstanding example of this unfortunate trend. Far more important is the fact that many fine cathedrals and churches and even a few palaces of the Muscovite period have been carefully restored and are now open to the public. Not all of the monuments of medieval Russian architecture, however, have survived the vicissitudes of life in the twentieth century. A number of churches of incalculable artistic significance were destroyed in the Second World War, some fell victim to anti-clerical zeal and many still suffer the effects of decades of neglect. Still, on balance, the efforts to restore Muscovy's architectural heritage and make the general public aware of its importance have been remarkably successful.

Icons, too, have won recognition as major works of art. Orthodox believers, of course, always venerated them as devotional objects. Only at the end of the last century, however, when contemporary painters rebelled against naturalism and began to take colour, shape and line seriously for their own sake, could critics and scholars begin to appreciate the talent of the best icon painters and the grace and emotional power of their work. In recent decades, art historians in many countries have written brilliant studies of icons and major museums around the world have displayed them prominently. In the 1960s and 1970s, a passion for icons gripped the Soviet cultural élite: museums sent teams to remote villages to search for new samples, the most fashionable Muscovites and Leningraders flocked to special exhibits of their discoveries, and icons – usually of recent vintage and poor quality – became a staple of the black market. Yet, in spite of its less desirable features, the fad had real significance. Now that scholars have restored and displayed so many fine examples of medieval Russian painting, it is inconceivable that cultured people will ever again dismiss icons as quaint and primitive.

In their own day, medieval Russian works of art served many functions. The beauty of the churches, icons, poems and stories undoubtedly appealed to men and women just as it does today. On another level, each work of art also served as means of convincing people to be faithful to Eastern Orthodoxy and loyal subjects of the secular rulers of the Russian lands. Church buildings spoke of the glory of God and icons retold stories from the Bible and the lives of the saints in a way that even the illiterate could understand. Chronicles, tales and saints' lives glorified the princes and warriors who fought for the Christian faith and the Russian land and praised the men and women who distinguished themselves in God's service. As the centuries passed, the leaders of the church and the rulers of the Muscovite monarchy made increasingly systematic and self-conscious use of the arts in order to win men's loyalty and obedience.

Thus, as it has come down to us, Russian élite culture, from the fourteenth to the seventeenth century, was largely the creation of a small number of artists and writers in the service of the church or the tsars' court. These men worked – often with remarkable creativity – within the intellectual framework and artistic canons of the Eastern Orthodox tradition. Doing so meant respecting the doctrinal teachings of Orthodoxy, choosing suitably edifying themes, and expressing them in an artistic manner calculated to instruct and elevate the reader or viewer. At the same time, it would be a mistake to exaggerate the piously didactic qualities of medieval Russian culture or the Christian humility and self-effacement of the artists who created it. Literature, in particular, teems with the stuff of real life – acts of reckless chivalry, wanton cruelty and self-indulgence as well as courageous self-sacrifice and devotion to God. In the end, however, with very rare exceptions, artists worked within the broad framework of the Eastern Orthodox tradition.

Alongside this élite ecclesiastical culture, Muscovite Russia had a lively popular tradition which blended Christian and non-Christian elements in a continually changing synthesis. Unfortunately, the sources of the time give us only occasional glimpses of the cultural life of ordinary laymen. Élite culture and the popular tradition undoubtedly fertilized one another: we can see traces of folk art and oral literature in some of the most sophisticated artistic creations.[1]

The ecclesiastical high culture of medieval Russia differed considerably from its Byzantine prototype and from the Latin culture of Western Europe in the High Middle Ages. The arts, especially icon painting, displayed creativity unsurpassed anywhere else in medieval Europe. Intellectual life, however, stagnated. Part of the problem was linguistic: since few Russian ecclesiastics knew Greek and even fewer Latin, they were cut off from direct contact with the heritage of classical antiquity. Far more significantly, Georges Florovsky argues, learned Russian churchmen lacked the inquisitiveness necessary to make use of the Byzantine heritage, much of which was accessible through translations.[2] To mention one example, Muscovite bookmen copied compilations of Byzantine canon law, but they made no attempt to study them analytically as Western scholars did. In this sense, medieval Russian culture was one-sided. Its greatest accomplishments are nevertheless worthy of profound appreciation and respect.

This chapter makes no claim to be a survey of literature or the arts in Muscovite Russia between 1304 and 1613.[3] Its objective, instead, is to describe the main currents in the development of literature, architecture and icon painting, integrating these three whenever possible in order to examine the values which they shared and the techniques in which they expressed them. Choosing this goal means slighting some of the arts – fresco painting, for example – and ignoring others such as music and most of the decorative arts altogether. Moreover, for a variety of reasons, the discussion will concentrate on a very small number of important examples of each period, region or style and ignore many other, equally significant, works of literature and art. Hopefully, however, getting to know a few masterpieces will whet the reader's appetite for more of the treasures of medieval Russian culture.

In 1300, Russians could look back on more than two and a half centuries of impressive cultural achievement. Indeed, one could well argue that, after 1304, the painters, builders and writers of the Russian lands never surpassed and, in most cases, failed to live up to the standards of their Kievan predecessors. Since another volume in this series will describe the main features of Kievan civilization, our discussion of the subject will be extremely brief.

The culture of Kievan Rus was cosmopolitan in two senses. First of all, the

Russian lands belonged to the Eastern Orthodox community and had close contacts with Byzantium and the South Slavic countries. The whole Orthodox world shared a common fund of literary subjects and genres, architectural styles and iconographic themes. Thus, it is not always possible to tell whether Greek or native artists painted the earliest icons preserved in Russia and designed the great churches of Kievan times. Moreover, the very question is misleading, for it projects modern concepts of nationality back into an age when such distinctions were far less important than they are today. Second, much the same can be said of the use of the word 'Russian', which we associate with the Great Russian ethnic group of modern times, to categorize the medieval culture of the East Slavic lands. The cultural achievements of Kievan Rus are part of the heritage of all of the East Slavic nationalities – Ukrainians, Belorussians and Great Russians. Yet, since the English language does not contain an adjective such as 'Rusian' (pertaining to medieval Rus), we have no convenient alternative to 'Russian', misleading though it is.

Moreover, Kievan culture was not narrowly ecclesiastical. Literature and the decorative arts exhibited a wider variety of themes and motifs than in later Muscovite times. The chroniclers gave a great deal of attention to worldly events, many far from edifying, and painters and sculptors juxtaposed sacred themes with images drawn from nature or daily life.

In 1300, the most dramatic reminders of the legacy of Kievan Rus were its cathedrals and churches. Ecclesiastical architecture flourished in the Russian lands almost from the moment of conversion. In the mid-eleventh century, the builders of the first national cathedral, the St Sophia of Kiev, adapted contemporary Byzantine styles to produce a large structure of remarkable complexity. The present exterior, rebuilt in the baroque manner in the seventeenth century, bears virtually no resemblance to the original structure which had five apses, a large central cupola and twelve smaller ones, and complex porches and arcades surrounding the central core.[4] The interior, although often redecorated, still retains much of its original magnificence: the visitor is surrounded by the images and colours of the frescos, painted on every available surface, and overpowered by the commanding mosaic of Our Lady, the Divine Wisdom, in the central apse behind the altar.

By the time of the Mongol invasion, great churches also dotted the landscape of the future Muscovite monarchy. Novgorod had its own St Sophia, the symbol and nerve-centre of the city-republic. Completed in 1050, the cathedral projects an image radically different from its Kievan prototype. The St Sophia is imposing in its simplicity. The plain exterior walls reflect the division of the interior into five aisles and the five main cupolas form a single cluster, with the largest in the centre. Frescos once warmed the simple, well-lit interior, but most have suffered fatal damage in war or at the hands of clumsy restorers. The Novgorodian striving for austerity appears on a much smaller scale in the Church of Our Saviour in Nereditsa, built in 1198. This tiny structure, well outside the city, was almost completely destroyed during the Second World War, but has been rebuilt. Its design is extremely simple and its execution comparatively crude. The floor plan is virtually a square, divided into three aisles by four pillars which hold up a single large cupola. The exterior walls have virtually no decoration: until the war, however, the interior was covered with brilliant frescos, now tragically lost for ever.[5]

When the princes of north-east Russia rose to pre-eminence in the second half of the twelfth century, they undertook major building projects to adorn their capital, Vladimir. Except for one tower, the palaces of Andrei Bogoliubskii and Vsevolod III have long since disappeared. Several great churches, however, still testify to their ambition and artistic taste.

The architecture of Vladimir has qualities all its own. Its builders had a fine sense of proportion and their choice of building material, soft white stone, allowed them to decorate their work with graceful carving. Their most imposing creation is the Cathedral of the Dormition built, beginning in 1158, on a bluff above the Kliazma river. Andrei Bogoliubskii intended the church to be the religious centre of the Vladimir–Suzdal area and the symbol of his political and ecclesiastical independence of Kiev. Originally a large, light building of simple design with three apses and a single cupola, the cathedral took on its present appearance between 1185 and 1189 when it was rebuilt after a fire. At that time, the restorers added two additional aisles, porches and four more cupolas on the corners of the expanded building. The cathedral creates a heavier, more solid impression than it must once have done, but the effect is lightened by the restrained carving – blind arcades and false columns on the façade, the apses, and the supporting drums of the cupolas.[6]

There are even lovelier examples of the Vladimir style. The nearby Cathedral of St Dmitrii, which dates from the 1190s, preserved the simple and harmonious design of the original Dormition Cathedral – three aisles with three apses and a single cupola. The most striking feature of St Dmitrii's is the elaborate carving on the north wall and the drum of the cupola. A row of saints stands guard over the north door and above them we see a profusion of shapes – human figures, lions and mythical beasts, birds, plants and abstract designs. In spite of its richness, however, the decorative carving is not distracting, but rather enhances the harmonious effect of the entire structure.[7] The quality of the carving and the elaborate arched doorway are reminiscent of the best Romanesque architecture of Western Europe: indeed, it is possible that some Western craftsmen worked in Vladimir.

The Church of the Veil on the Nerl river, on the eastern approaches to Vladimir, may well be the most beautiful of all medieval Russian buildings. Prince Andrei built it in 1165 on an artificial mound above the river flats as a memorial to one of his sons. Even today the little church stands in splendid isolation, visible far across the flat landscape. Its design is extremely simple and the decorative carving restrained. At the same time, there is nothing ordinary about it: the proportions are exceptionally fine and the comparatively high façade with its delicate ornamental columns and the tall cupola combine to give an impression of lightness and grace. The onlooker feels as though lifted up towards heaven.[8] In future generations, Russian builders rarely, if ever, achieved this ethereal effect again.

Painters of icons and frescos in the Russian lands likewise reached great heights of achievement long before 1300. Icons, devotional pictures painted on wooden panels, had a central place in the religious observances of Eastern Orthodox believers. Worshippers carried them in processions, venerated them in churches and made them the focal point of private devotions at home. As the centuries passed, the number of icons in places of public worship grew steadily. By the end of the fifteenth century, in Russian churches a partition-like screen or stand of icons (*iconostasis*) separated ordinary worshippers from the altar which only the clergy could approach. The structure and iconographic arrangement of the icon stand were always the same. Three small double doors allowed the clergy to move from the altar to the central section of the church where the worshippers stood. Immediately above the doors, at the very centre of the icon stand, was the *Deesis*, the group of icons centred on Christ in Majesty with Our Lady on his right and John the Baptist on his left. The icons in the row above the *Deesis* retold the life of Christ.

Russian icon painters followed well-established traditions in choosing and presenting their subjects. Many of their works portrayed the central figures of the faith – Christ, the Mother of God and the saints. Other icons were inspired by written texts, such as hymns.[9] Moreover, tradition dictated the manner in which a particular figure or scene was to be presented. In the Annunciation, for example, the archangel stands on the left side of the picture gesturing dramatically toward the Virgin on the right as he explains that God has chosen her to bear Christ. Even the choice of colour was not entirely free: the Virgin's wrap is almost always dark red or purple. The painter's range of choices was so narrow that, in comparatively recent times, inexperienced provincial artists sometimes worked from patterns much like those used by dressmakers.

In spite of the stylized nature of the genre, however, the most imaginative painters found in it almost limitless possibilities for creative expression. They discovered that slight changes in the arrangement and line of the figures and nuances of colour could make a great difference in their work's effect on viewers. Thus, icons on the same subject can create radically different impressions: a Christ in Majesty, for example, can appear fierce and judgemental or compassionate according to the artist's treatment. An individual artist or school of painters could develop a distinct and easily recognizable style of expression. In this variety and creative power lies the enduring appeal of icons.

By the time of the Mongol invasion, Russian churches contained icons of the highest quality. The most influential, *Our Lady of Vladimir*, was probably brought to Russia from Byzantium. In its new homeland, it quickly developed a reputation as a worker of miracles and as symbol of Our Lady's protection of the faithful. Apart from its allegedly supernatural qualities, the icon fully deserves the adulation accorded it. The painting belongs to the iconographic category, *The Mother of God of Tenderness*, in which the Virgin holds the Christ child in her arms and inclines her head towards him as he snuggles against her cheek. The composition of *Our Lady of Vladimir* is refined, the facial features delicate and the colouring subtle. Although the treatment of mother and child is a far cry from the naturalism of the High Renaissance, the stylized figures project an intense sense of human warmth and love. At the same time, the artist reminds us that this is no mere earthly family but God incarnate and his Mother. Like the representations of the Virgin in medieval Western art, *Our Lady of Vladimir* shows the viewer the compassionate, forgiving side of God's nature. Russian painters copied and adapted it again and again.

Native artists, too, produced works of extraordinary skill and power. The *Ustiug Annunciation*, probably painted in Novgorod in the late 1100s, ranks alongside any icon ever made. The artist reproduced the traditional arrangement of the figures with special finesse: he painted the facial features, the archangel's gesturing hand, his hair and wings and the folds of the garments with great delicacy. One feature of the composition is unusual and striking: an embryonic Christ appears fully formed on the Virgin's breast. Perhaps most impressive of all is the artist's use of colour: the Virgin's robe is a brilliant blue and her wrap an intense dark red, while the angel's figure and robes, in contrast, range subtly from white, through flesh and earth tones to brown. Later Russian painters sometimes equalled the achievement of this remarkable, unknown artist, but never surpassed it.[10]

The literature of the Kievan period is remarkable for its richness and variety. The compositions that have come down to us represent many genres – chronicles, epic poems, saints' lives, and sermons – often woven together in a single text. The predominant literary manner was, in D. S. Likhachev's phrase, 'monumental historicism'. Writers concentrated on the deeds of princes and the lives of monastic saints. Moreover, in describing their heroes, they presented them as ideal types, using stock epithets appropriate to their social position rather than as individuals with unique traits of appearance or character.[11]

Like icon painters, however, the most gifted writers used conventional techniques to produce works of remarkable communicative power. The largest and most complex work of the period, the so-called *Russian Primary Chronicle* or *Tale of Bygone Days*, is an excellent case in point. Monks compiled the chronicle in stages over many decades and in 1116 finished the redaction that has survived until today. Although outwardly a chronicle, it is, in fact, a literary anthology which brings together smaller compositions of many genres and styles.[12] Two episodes, both of which narrate the bloody consequences of interprincely feuds, will serve as examples.

The story of the martyrdom of Princes Boris and Gleb at the hands of their older brother, Sviatopolk, has many of the features of a saint's life. On the central events – the young princes' murder – the writer builds a structure of edifying commentary, much of it quoted from Scripture. His most significant and moving contributions, however, are his description and interpretation of the heroes' martyrdom. Friends warn both Boris and Gleb of Sviatopolk's treachery, but both accept their fate without resistance. Indeed, in his devotions just before his death, Boris likens his self-sacrifice to Christ's sacrifice on the cross. Thus, suggests the writer, by refusing to resist evil, the victim of political conflict became a martyr to the Christian faith. The hymn to the fallen princes which concludes the story drives the point home even more clearly, praising them in elaborate rhetorical formulae as authentic Christian martyrs from the newly converted Russian nation and as intercessors in heaven for their faithful countrymen.[13]

The *Primary Chronicle* narrates a second story of vindictive cruelty in an entirely different manner. In 1097, after an abortive peace conference, Princes Sviatopolk II and David of Vladimir in Volynia joined forces to destroy Vasilko of Terebovl. They lured him to Kiev and, on David's insistence, imprisoned and blinded him. The author tells the story tersely. Tension mounts as the conspirators' plans unfold and reaches its height in a bloodcurdling scene in which an assassin cuts out Vasilko's eyes while four warriors sit on a paving stone on his chest to stop his desperate resistance. With a few deft touches, the writer arouses the reader's sympathy for the victim. As he is taken across the countryside in a wagon, a priest's wife weeps for him while washing his blood-stained shirt. Then, when Vasilko regains consciousness and realizes what has happened to him, he laments that he has not died and 'stood before God in this bloody shirt'. Unlike Boris and Gleb, however, Vasilko elicits the reader's pity only as a victim of wanton violence and treachery; indeed he soon returns to the field to wreak vengeance on his enemies.[14]

The Mongol conquest did not destroy the cultural achievements of Kievan Rus. At the same time, the initial shock of the invasion and the impact of later punitive expeditions temporarily slowed the cultural development of the Russian lands. To mention the most obvious example, there are very few buildings in Russia which date from the second half of the thirteenth century, although construction did not stop altogether. In addition, the Mongols deported Russian artisans and, as a consequence, some highly specialized crafts such as enamelling disappeared completely from the Russian lands. By the beginning of the fourteenth century, however, we see clear signs of cultural as well as political and economic revival.[15] The writers, painters and architects of the new age continued the traditions of Kievan times, but adapted them to new conditions and changing artistic tastes.

During the centuries of the 'Mongol yoke', the Russian lands had two predominant cultural centres – the north-east region from which Moscow emerged as national capital and the city-republics of the north-west, Novgorod and Pskov. The latter two cities played the major part in passing the Kievan heritage on to future generations: their inhabitants preserved the majority of the earliest works of Russian literature and art that have survived until modern times. Moreover, the republics developed their own vigorous artistic life.

The cultural style of Novgorod and Pskov reflects their political and economic structure. Commerce and artisan production formed the cutting edge of their economies. In both, oligarchies governed a concerned and volatile citizenry. Moreover, a goodly number of those citizens were probably literate:

in Novgorod, archaeologists have uncovered many fragmentary texts carved on birch bark whose messages range from commercial transactions to declarations of love.[16] The most important patrons of the arts, however, were the leaders of the church, in particular, archbishops of Novgorod such as Euthymius II in the mid-fifteenth century and Gennadius and Macarius after the republic fell to Moscow.

The Novgorodians and Pskovians were practical, down-to-earth men and women who appreciated good craftsmanship and simple, direct forms of expression. Living on Russia's western border in regular contact with people of many nations, they valued good ideas and effective artistic techniques, whatever their source. Long before the reign of Peter the Great, Novgorod and Pskov served as a 'window to the West' – and, for that matter, to the Orthodox lands of the eastern Mediterranean as well.

The Church of Our Saviour on Ilina Street is a fine example of Novgorodian architecture of the fourteenth century. The builders, who erected it in 1374, achieved a fine blend of simple solidity of design and elegance of decoration. The stucco-covered brick structure follows familiar patterns: it is, in essence, a square surmounted by a single cupola. However, the unknown architect introduced interesting, characteristically Novgorodian, variations on the theme. All four outer walls are divided into three clear subdivisions, reflecting the fundamental structure of the building's interior. The roof of the church is gabled on all four sides. Delicate decoration lightens the effect of the basic symmetrical design: abstract geometric patterns 'run' around the drum of the cupola, and window openings, niches and raised abstract designs add interest to the façades.[17]

Our Saviour's combines beauty and practicality in the best tradition of the city-republics of the north-west. A number of other Novgorodian churches of the thirteenth and fourteenth centuries share many of its features. So do the parish churches of Pskov. Usually very simple in design, the latter are, if anything, even more solid and closer to the ground than their Novgorodian counterparts.[18]

The Church of Our Saviour presents striking testimony to Novgorod's receptiveness to cultural currents from the rest of the Eastern Orthodox community. The interior contains fragments of magnificent frescos painted, in 1378, by Theophanes the Greek, an outstanding representative of the Palaeologan artistic revival in the Byzantine Empire. Working quickly on a damp plaster surface, Theophanes used simple means to create images of great expressive power. With a few brush strokes in basic colours – most often white and shades of brown – and extensive use of dramatic highlighting in white, he vividly conveyed the essential qualities of the people whom he portrayed – the ascetic rigour of the saints of the desert and the serenity of the angels in the *Old Testament Trinity*.[19] Theophanes's work heralded a new wave of heightened emotion and a striving for deeper spirituality in the painting and literature of Russia.

The best Novgorodian icons have none of the subtlety of Theophanes's frescos. Works of great skill, they speak plainly to the viewer. The icons of

Novgorod are celebrated for their use of blocks of brilliant colour, especially red, their simple composition and their fine drawing, emphasized by dark outlines around the figures. The well-known icon of the *Prophet Elijah*, probably painted early in the fifteenth century, is an excellent example of the style. Set against a bright red background and the dark brown of his cloak, the stern face of the prophet stares out at the viewer. The artist emphasized the severity of the image by sharply outlining Elijah's head and face and, in particular, his eyes. The onlooker has no trouble remembering that the prophet was a direct descendant of the pre-Christian, Slavic god of thunder. The Novgorodian tradition in painting had deep roots and survived long after the republic fell to Moscow. A sixteenth-century representation of another popular theme, *St George and the Dragon*, displays many of the same characteristics as the Elijah. Once again, the composition is simple and highly effective. In this case, the curve of the saint's body extending through the hindquarters of the horse dominates the picture. Again the colours are dazzling. The fiery red of St George's cloak and the subtler shade of his armour and shield, repeated throughout the picture, stand out sharply against the gold background.[20] In sharp contrast, the best-known icons of Pskov are comparatively subdued in colour and unsophisticated in design, but have a vigorous and charming folkloristic quality all their own.[21]

The Novgorodians' love of directness of expression extends to literature as well. The chronicles of the city record the main events in its history precisely and laconically. Even a story as complex as the account of the uprising of 1418 is told in remarkably few words. A man named Stepanko started the uproar by seizing a member of the oligarchy in the street. As he did so, he shouted to passers-by to help him right some wrong which the boyars had inflicted on him. The crowd that gathered beat the accused boyar severely and threw him into the river. However, much to the crowd's consternation, a fisherman rescued its victim. Then, when Stepanko and the boyar gathered supporters to continue their feud, public order collapsed and the city lurched towards civil war. Only the intervention of the archbishop, the only leader of Novgorod with undisputed moral authority, restored domestic peace to the city. Such a brief retelling does a grave injustice to the chronicler's skill; for, in a few short sentences, he gives a lively account of the events of the crisis and explains precisely where they occurred. His narrative is much more than a police report, however: in terse phrases, he interprets the events, branding the upstart tradesman or artisan, Stepanko, a tool of the devil and making the archbishop the hero of the story. In short, the tale of 1418 is a fine piece of storytelling.[22]

Novgorod's cultural achievements reflected her people's pride in her traditions and way of life. Understandably, then, the city's culture was especially rich in the middle decades of the fifteenth century when its people struggled against the noose which the princes of Moscow slowly tightened around the republic's independence. A dramatic example of this creative tension is the icon of the *Battle of the Novgorodians with the Suzdalians*, probably painted just before Ivan III conquered the city. In four distinct scenes, the icon retells the story of Grand Prince Andrei Bogoliubskii's siege of the city in 1169. The archbishop of the day took the icon of Our Lady of the Sign, the protectress of Novgorod, from its accustomed place and mounted it on the walls of the besieged city. Bogoliubskii's troops shot their arrows at the icon and, as punishment for this irreverent behaviour, the Virgin gave the victory to the Novgorodians who stormed out of the citadel to avenge her.[23] In the face of a far more serious threat from the east, the memory of this past triumph – and of Our Lady's protection – must have brought the people of Novgorod comfort.

At the turn of the fourteenth and fifteenth centuries, Russian ecclesiastical culture reached remarkable heights of artistic achievement, above all in the icons and frescos of Andrei Rublev. This extraordinary outburst of creative energy occurred in unpropitious political circumstances. Dmitrii Donskoi's victory over the Mongols at Kulikovo Pole in 1380 had raised the national morale and reinforced Moscow's claims to leadership of the Russian lands. In concrete political and military terms, however, the famous battle accomplished very little. Within the Russian lands, political strife remained the order of the day. Thus, the film director, Tarkovskii, was right in picturing the world of *Andrei Rublev* as one of poverty, political discord and capricious violence.

In these trying circumstances, the Eastern Orthodox Church underwent a remarkable spiritual and artistic revival. Beginning in the main religious centres of the Byzantine Empire, the hesychast movement and the so-called 'Palaeologan Renaissance' in the arts brought new life to literature, painting and spirituality in all lands of the Orthodox community. Literature flourished not only in Byzantium, but also in Bulgaria and Serbia, linguistically natural bridges to Russia. During the fourteenth and early fifteenth centuries, the Orthodox lands remained in close touch with one another. Greek and South Slavic writers and painters – men like Theophanes the Greek – settled in the Russian lands and Russian churchmen visited the other centres of Orthodoxy.

A number of features of this international movement sprang from hesychasm. Theophanes's frescos in the Church of Our Saviour in Novgorod reflect the hesychasts' striving for a more intense and authentic experience of God's presence and their determination to see through the mundane details of life to comprehend the essence of man's nature and the divine order of things. In literature, hesychasm made writers throughout the Orthodox world aware of the power of language. The struggle of authors everywhere to find 'the right word' took on added significance since, in hesychast teaching, words were as real as the realities for which they stood. As they were well aware, choosing the wrong word on a matter of faith could instantly plunge one into the darkest heresy. On the positive side, words had the power to bring people into closer communion with God. Thus, throughout the Orthodox lands, particularly in Serbia, writers of devotional works harnessed the power of language in an ornate literary manner often known as 'the weaving of words'.

The outstanding Russian master of this international style was Epiphanius the Wise. A monk from Rostov, Epiphanius travelled to many centres of Eastern Christendom, including Jerusalem and Mt Athos, before settling in the Holy Trinity Monastery. In the course of his apprenticeship, he mastered the literary techniques of the Orthodox revival and used them to compose his masterpieces, the lives of two recently deceased older contemporaries, SS Stephen of Perm and Sergius. The former tells how, after a long period of preparation and study, Stephen went as a missionary to the Komi (or Permians) and converted many of them to Christianity. Sergius's *Life* relates how, against heavy odds, the saint founded the Holy Trinity Monastery and guided its growth until it became a major centre of the faith and he a man whose moral authority extended far beyond its walls.[24]

These compositions, written in 1396–98 and 1417–18 respectively, epitomize the 'weaving of words'. In each case, Epiphanius embellished the story with complex literary devices – many adapted from the Psalms – calculated to stir the reader's emotions and create a halo of sanctity around the central figure. For one thing, in order to underline the exalted nature of his subjects, Epiphanius used an ornate rhetoric and esoteric vocabulary very different from ordinary speech. Complicated compounds, neologisms and plays on words abound in his writings.

Moreover, the structure of his prose is very complex and has a strong rhythmic pulse. Epiphanius built many passages, often rhymed, around extended sets of parallel constructions or rhetorical questions and long chains of similes or metaphors. As a consequence, his writing, while extremely wordy, has an almost hypnotic power which captivates his readers.[25]

In addition, Epiphanius took a flexible approach to the traditional structure of the saint's life by weaving in fragments of other genres. The best example is the moving and highly unconventional conclusion of the life of Stephen; it consists of three formal laments in which the new converts, their church and the author himself mourn the saint.[26]

Like any writer of hagiography, Epiphanius concentrated his attention on the character and actions of his heroes as exemplars of Christian virtue. At the same time, he made no attempt to analyse the personalities of Stephen and Sergius as a modern novelist would. His aim, instead, was what D. S. Likhachev has felicitously called 'abstract psychologism' – to present the reader with the heroes' most important characteristics, much as Theophanes the Greek did in his frescos. Epiphanius often used lists of descriptive epithets to convey the hero's image to the reader. A number of other devices – among them, editorial comment, descriptions of the heroes' actions, and lengthy speeches which he put into their mouths – also helped the author create his verbal portrait. Epiphanius painted his characters in simple colours – black or white, good or evil. In contrast to Stephen's steadfastness and gentle determination, for example, Pam, the Permian shaman, appears manipulative and cowardly.[27]

Following the path of international literary convention, Epiphanius reached the goal for which he set out. Through a creative use of stylized literary devices, he preserved vivid images of Stephen and Sergius. To this day, his biographies remain the primary sources of information on the personalities and activities of these giants of the Russian monastic revival of the fourteenth century.

While Epiphanius's writings reach a limited readership of professors and students, the paintings of Andrei Rublev are familiar to many thousands of art lovers. This was not always the case. Rublev's name and works enjoyed great respect in the sixteenth and seventeenth centuries, but his icons gradually disappeared from view behind elaborate metal covers and layers of new paint and varnish applied by well-intentioned restorers. Only in the twentieth century have some of his paintings recaptured a measure of their original splendour and reclaimed their rightful place among the masterpieces of world art.

Little is know for certain about Rublev's life. A monk, like virtually all early Russian writers and artists, he lived in the Holy Trinity and Andronikov Monasteries near Moscow. By the time of his death in 1430 at about the age of sixty, his icons and frescos adorned both of these monasteries and the cathedrals and churches of Moscow, Vladimir and Zvenigorod. During his lifetime he enjoyed the respect and support of ecclesiastical leaders and lay patrons.[28] As a charter member of a small artistic élite, he was probably in close touch with the other leading painters of his day, including the celebrated Theophanes.

The best way to know Andrei Rublev is through his paintings, for he distilled the traditional themes and techniques of the icon and the fresco into a highly individual manner. Two of his best-known icons – the *Saviour* and the *Trinity* – provide excellent examples.

The *Saviour* is a variant of the theme, 'Christ, the all-powerful' in which Christ represents the omnipotence and righteous judgement of God. Rublev apparently painted it in about 1410 for a cathedral in Zvenigorod, the residence of Iurii of Galich, brother of Vasilii I and, later, rival of his nephew, Vasilii II. Even though it survives in a badly damaged condition, it is an arresting work. Through his penetrating eyes which dominate the icon, Christ looks out at the viewer. The face reflects the awe-inspiring power of God, but it is, at the same time, an intensely human face, full of compassion as well as determination. In other words, in the *Saviour*, Rublev expressed the doctrine of the Incarnation, the conviction that Christ was both God and man, with a subtlety that few artists have ever approached.[29]

Rublev's *Trinity* is so celebrated – and rightly so – that any description or commentary seems superfluous. Surprisingly little, however, is known for certain about the circumstances in which it was painted. Art historians agree only that Rublev painted it in about 1411 for the Holy Trinity Monastery.[30] The icon depicts the *Old Testament Trinity*, the three angels who visited Abraham and Sarah and predicted that, in their old age, they would have a son. In Christian iconography, depictions of the scene of the angels at dinner served to represent the Trinity, the three persons of God. Rublev's treatment stresses the doctrinal implications of his theme by showing only the angels and leaving Abraham and Sarah out of the icon altogether.

Words cannot do justice to the skill and refinement of Rublev's work. The bodies of the three angels are gracefully curved and their features delicate. Moreover, together they form, in the centre of the icon, a circle, symbol of eternity. The circle, in turn, draws attention to the cup on the table symbolizing God's self-sacrificing love. Each angel holds a staff which leads the eye outward to one of the objects – the house, the tree and the mountain – in the background of the picture.[31] In the *Trinity*, Rublev's use of colour is even more striking than the beauty of the composition. Like other works of his, the icon has a hazy quality. Moreover, even in their present slightly faded condition, the intense blue, dark red and gold retain their freshness and contrast wonderfully with the diaphanous effect of the outer garments of the angels on the left and right of the picture. It reflects no dishonour on later Russian icon painters that none ever matched this achievement.

Living in trying times, Epiphanius the Wise and Andrei Rublev used established genres and stylized means of expression with brilliant creativity. The extent of their accomplishments is most evident when we compare their best work with the creations of subsequent generations. Later writers and painters in Muscovy employed many of the same techniques and motifs, but applied them more mechanically, with less flexibility and inspiration.[32]

Literature and the visual arts clearly reflected the rise of Moscow to leadership of the Russian lands. Moreover, in their turn, writers, architects and painters contributed to Moscow's victory over its rivals. Poets praised the princes of Moscow as the military leaders of Russia and their chroniclers recorded their triumphs in war and diplomacy. As the world outside of Muscovy changed rapidly, other writers wrestled with the meaning of the new patterns of international politics, especially the fall of the Byzantine Empire and the rise of its conquerors, the Ottoman Turks. Some of the ideas which emerged from their musings have been discussed in an earlier chapter. Finally, for their part, the architects, builders and painters who rebuilt and decorated the Moscow Kremlin created the visual embodiment of the pretensions and growing real power of the rulers who lived within its walls.

One of the earliest reflections of Moscow's rise was the 'Kulikovo cycle', the poem and tales celebrating Dmitrii Donskoi's victory over Mamai in 1380. The time and circumstances in which these three works – the *Zadonshchina*, the *Chronicle Tale about the Battle of Kulikovo*, and the *Story of Mamai's Battle* – were written are still hotly disputed. At one extreme are scholars who argue that all of the texts date from the 1380s and 1390s, beginning with the composition of the *Zadonshchina* roughly one year after the battle. At the other end of the spectrum, M. A. Salmina argues that all three date from the end of the 1440s or later, with the *Chronicle Tale* first in order of composition. Many of the contending scholars' arguments are highly technical and need not concern us.[33]

The convictions of the authors of the 'Kulikovo cycle' and the literary means which they used to express them are much less controversial. The

Plate 1.   *Ustiug Annunciation.* Novgorodian (?). Late 1100s.

Plate 2.   The Cathedral of the Dormition, Vladimir. 1185 – 1189.
Plate 3.   (right) The Church of the Veil on the Nerl, Bogoliubovo
(near Vladimir). 1165

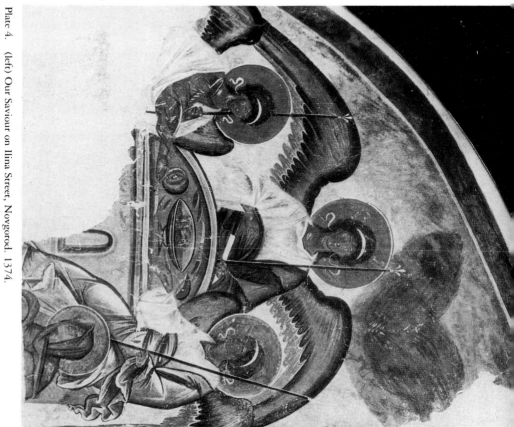

Plate 4. (left) Our Saviour on Ilina Street, Novgorod, 1374.
Plate 5. Theophanes the Greek, *Old Testament Trinity*. Fresco in the Church of Our Saviour on Ilina Street, 1378.

Plate 6. *Elijah.* Novgorodian. Early fifteenth century.

Plate 7. Andrei Rublev, *Saviour,* c.1410.

Plate 8. The Kremlin, Moscow.

Plate 9.   Andrei Rublev, *Trinity*. c. 1411.

Plate 10.   (right) Dionysius, *Crucifixion*. 1500

Plate 11.   (left) The Cathedral of the Dormition, Moscow. 1475 – 1478.

Plate 12.   St George and the Dragon, Novgorodian. Sixteenth century.

Plate 13.   (left) The Church of the Ascension, Kolomenskoe (near Moscow), 1532.
Plate 14.   The Cathedral of the Archangel Michael, Moscow, 1505 – 1508.

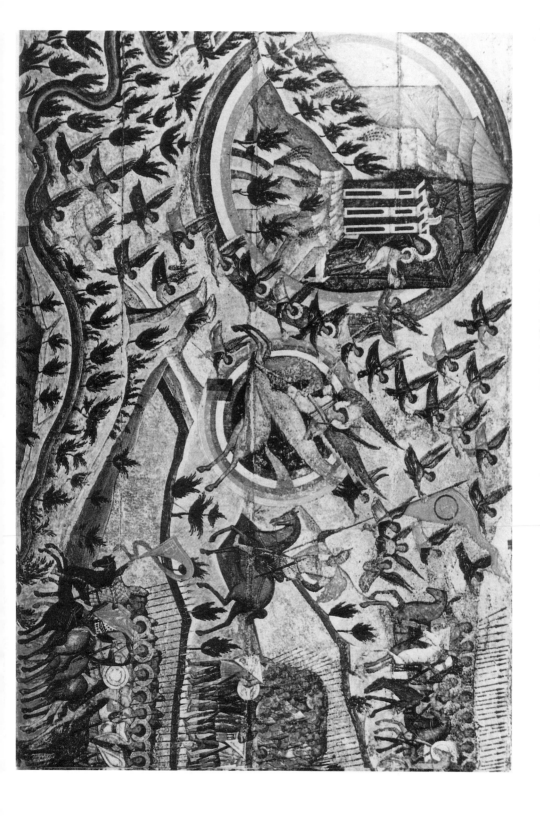

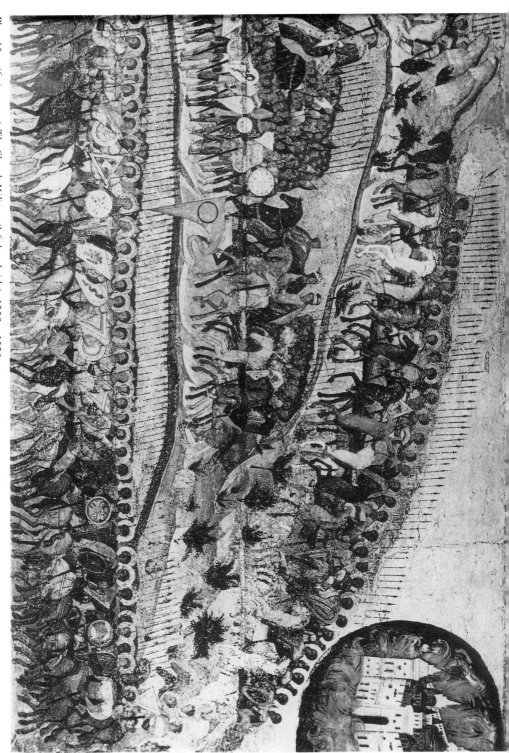

Plate 15.   (facing page) *The Church Militant* (left-hand side), 1552 – 1553.

Plate 16.   *The Church Militant* (right-hand side).

Plate 17.   The Cathedral of St Basil, Moscow. 1555 – 1561.

Zadonshchina is a poem in prose which combines flights of striking imagery with passages of plain narrative. In some respects, it belongs to the genre of the 'military tale' (*voinskaia povest*). Like its precursors, it narrates the story of a military campaign, beginning with the preparations, reaching a climax in the decisive battle and concluding with reflections on the outcome. In other ways, however, the poem is radically different from earlier military tales; where their writers employ a simple narrative style, its author uses many dramatic and occasionally far-fetched metaphors and engages in extended digressions reflecting on the meaning of the events he describes.[34]

Through the brilliant imagery of the *Zadonshchina*, the author's message shines clear. He characterizes Dmitrii Donskoi's campaign against Mamai as the defence of the 'Russian land' and carefully enumerates the many regions from which warriors came to do battle in the national cause. He contrasts the Russian victory with the devastating defeat at Kalka, harbinger of the Mongol conquest, and interprets it – rather optimistically – as the end of Mongol overlordship. Echos of the glories of Kievan Rus resound throughout the poem; the author compares Dmitrii to its great leaders such as St Vladimir and Iaroslav the Wise. Ultimately, however, the spotlight falls on Donskoi himself. With the help of his cousin, Vladimir Andreevich, the grand prince of Moscow mustered the warriors of the Russian land and led them to a glorious victory. Moscow, in the poet's eye, had become the leader of the nation.[35]

The other Kulikovo texts, the *Chronicle Tale* and the *Story*, present the same political message. They view Donskoi's campaign in quite a different light, however, interpreting it primarily as a Christian crusade against Islam. Even though the author of the *Zadonshchina* sometimes equated the struggle to free the Russian land with the defence of the Christian faith, this theme played a comparatively minor part in his work. For the writers of the two other texts, however, Moscow and its prince, Dmitrii, appear primarily as leaders in the defence of Orthodoxy. To underline this aspect of their message, they used a number of literary devices familiar to a reader of Epiphanius's lives of the saints; the characters in the story interrupt their campaign with long reflective speeches, prayers and tales of miraculous visions.[36]

The 'Kulikovo cycle' testifies to a growing awareness of Russia's national identity and mission among writers and their readers, most of them ecclesiastics. The works also bear witness to an increasing acceptance of Moscow as the military command post of the Russian lands. But to what period does their testimony apply? When did learned clerics formulate the ideas which they express? Even if we choose to avoid detailed textological argument, we cannot altogether escape the vexed question of the dating of the Kulikovo texts. While it is inconceivable that participants in the battle of Kulikovo did not tell of their adventures, the literary compositions of the 'cycle' harmonize best with the political and ideological circumstances of the mid-fifteenth century when, out of bitter and bloody civil war, the Muscovite monarchy under Vasilii II began to raise its political authority and pretensions to unheard-of heights. Salmina's argument that the *Chronicle Tale* was written in 1448 and the *Story* at some time thereafter makes good sense. The time of the composition of the *Zadonshchina* is more problematical. It may well also be a work of the mid-fifteenth century as Salmina argues; if not, it was almost certainly written after 1408, the date of the earliest surviving chronicle account of the battle, a simple and forceful narrative from which all of the more elaborate literary reworkings of the story in some measure derive.[37] In writing the Kulikovo texts, then, Muscovite authors transformed a dramatic historical event into a myth which reflected the achievements and aspirations of the descendants of those who fought against Mamai.

Later in the fifteenth century, in the time of Ivan III, Muscovite writers and translators turned their attention to the world outside of Russia. Their eyes fell, naturally enough, on the most important international event of mid-century, the fall of Constantinople to the Turks, and, more broadly, the conflict between Christian and Moslem powers all along their common frontier. Two compositions – the *Tale of the Conquest of Constantinople by the Turks in 1452* and the *Tale of Dracula, the Voevoda*, about a real Romanian ruler, Vlad IV Țepeş of Wallachia (1456–62 and 1477) – illustrate the characteristic features and range of this literature.[38]

These tales are a far cry from the elaborate rhetorical concoctions of Epiphanius the Wise or the 'Kulikovo cycle'. The Muscovite writers who composed them or adapted them from foreign prototypes told their stories simply. Their primary objective was to present the reader with a clear exposition of interesting and important events. Both authors made clear that their accounts were trustworthy because they were based on their own personal experience and the testimony of other eyewitnesses. Moreover, while both authors made clear their allegiance to Eastern Orthodox Christianity, neither placed the struggle of Christian against Muslim nor Orthodox against Roman Catholic at the centre of his account. The author of the Russian *Tale of Dracula* – probably Fedor Kuritsyn, the well-known diplomat and Judaizer heretic – condemned the hero for acquiescing in a forcible conversion to the Roman Church; his story, however, places the heaviest emphasis, by far, on Dracula's spectacular acts of cruelty and his insistence on his right, as absolute ruler, to perpetrate them.

What, then, was the purpose of the writers of these tales of foreign lands? For the most part, they were content to provide their readers with good stories and, in Dracula's case, a good scare. Both tales could have served as pretexts for political and social commentary, but their authors, by and large, passed up the opportunity. The vivid and matter-of-fact tale of the conquest of Constantinople contains no speculations about Russia's possible role as the 'Third Rome'. The Dracula stories, set concretely in the Wallachia of Vlad IV, provide more food for thought. The central character's statements about his right to reward and punish men according to his whim suggests a discourse on tyranny. But does the author implicitly praise or condemn Dracula's tyrannical rule? Historians disagree. It makes most sense to read the tale, like the others of the type, as a work of entertainment. Dracula's court banquet among corpses rotting on stakes belongs, not on the pages of Machiavelli, but in a modern horror film.[39]

The fifteenth century was a great age of chronicle writing throughout the Russian lands. In most instances, the identity and location of the compilers of the chronicles are a matter of speculation. Many appear to be the work of churchmen – monks of the St Cyril – Beloozero Monastery or secretaries of the archbishop of Rostov, for example. The rulers of Moscow, however, were not willing to leave the keeping of historical records entirely to ecclesiastics. Under Ivan III, the grand prince's chancery in Moscow produced compilations in 1472, 1479 and the 1490s from which a number of surviving chronicle texts derive.[40]

Ivan's scribes shaped their narrative to glorify their patron. The story of the grand prince's expedition against Novgorod in 1471 provides an excellent example. The writers told the story in a simple, prosaic manner. In spite of the subject, however, the account lacks dramatic tension; it is rambling and contains extensive digressions and editorial comment. Evidently the authors' goal was not to tell an exciting story, but to present a political message. This they did most effectively. They portrayed Ivan III as rightful suzerain of Novgorod and as champion of Orthodoxy, underlining the latter role with details of the grand prince's devotions and consultations with leaders of the church. In the chroniclers' view, Novgorodian opposition to Ivan arose from the machinations of a small clique which, in proposing to accept a prince from Lithuania, intended to desert Orthodoxy for Roman Catholicism. Thus, as Ivan explains in the narrative, the Novgorod expedition was an Orthodox crusade against apostasy. Everything in the story redounds to Moscow's glory. Although the chroniclers ridiculed the military ineptness of the Novgorodians, they managed to praise the Muscovite warriors for their bravery on the grounds that they were badly outnumbered. Moreover, they concluded, the conquest of the city was the best possible outcome for the Novgorodians themselves, for most of them happily accepted Ivan's overlordship.[41]

The grand princely chronicles did not always paint Ivan in such flattering colours. The best-known account of Khan Ahmed's invasion of 1480 openly criticizes the grand prince and his consort, Sophia Palaeologa, for their cowardice during the confrontation on the Urga. Fearing a surprise attack by the other, the chroniclers claimed, both Ivan and Ahmed slipped away from the battlefield without fighting. For her part, Sophia fled from Moscow when the capital was in no danger of attack. How can we account for the presence of so unfavourable an account in the court chronicle? In all probability, its compilers took the story directly from a non-Muscovite source, possibly a Rostov ecclesiastical compilation, and failed, for some reason, to revise it.[42] Such slips were rare, however. Ivan III and his successors found chronicles a powerful literary and ideological weapon in the struggle to rule the Russian lands.

The rebuilt Moscow Kremlin served the same function far more effectively.

While few men would ever read the court chronicles, many thousands could see the awe-inspiring creations of Ivan III's architects. Long before Ivan's birth, earlier grand princes of Moscow systematically built up the Kremlin as a political and religious centre of the Russian lands. In 1326, Ivan I constructed a Dormition Cathedral named after the great church in Vladimir, the previous national cathedral of north-east Russia. Subsequent rulers of Moscow built additional chapels and churches and commissioned artists like Theophanes the Greek and Andrei Rublev to decorate them. They also began to collect the finest icons and liturgical objects from other parts of Russia; in 1395, for example, Metropolitan Cyprian brought the icon, *Our Lady of Vladimir,* from the old capital to protect Moscow from Tamerlane.[43] All of these acts emphasized the Moscow rulers' message: their city was the new political and religious capital of the Russian lands.

The glorification of Moscow and its Kremlin reached its apogee in the construction projects of Ivan III and his immediate successors. The new Kremlin, which today is still the architectural showpiece of the Soviet capital, bears witness to two important elements in Muscovite political and cultural life in Ivan's time. First, it is a monument to the nascent imperial self-image of the Muscovite monarchy. It is no accident that the same sovereign who built it also made intermittent use of the title 'tsar' and adopted political symbols such as the two-headed eagle.[44] Second, the rebuilt Kremlin testifies to the openness of Ivan's court to technological skills and artistic tastes from Italy through channels established by the grand prince's marriage to Sophia Palaeologa. Italian engineers and architects supervised the rebuilding of the fortress walls and the construction of most of the Kremlin's principal buildings.

Set on a low bluff above a bend in the Moscow river, the Kremlin with its massive towers and cluster of golden cupolas dominates its surroundings. It took on its present appearance in a very short period of time. The first step in Ivan III's campaign was the complete reconstruction of the Dormition Cathedral between 1475 and 1479. Next in order came the smaller Cathedral of the Annunciation, which served as the ruling family's private chapel, and the Church of the Deposition of the Robes connected to the metropolitan's residence. The construction of both began in 1484 under the direction of Russian architects. Between the Cathedrals of the Dormition and Annunciation on the great Kremlin Square, the Italians, Marco and Piero Antonio Solari, began work on the Palace of Facets in 1487. This solid rectangular building with a faceted façade, reminiscent of such contemporary Italian structures as the Palazzo dei Diamanti in Ferrara, served primarily as the setting for formal court ceremonies and receptions. At the same time, the Solaris oversaw the reconstruction of the outer walls of the Kremlin. Once again, their work reminds the onlooker of their homeland, in this case, the great citadels of northern Italy. The massive brick walls, interrupted at regular intervals by imposing towers, each one individually designed, effectively sheltered the heart of official Moscow from enemy attack and projected an awe-inspiring image of the authority of its prince. As in so many other spheres,

Vasilii III continued what his father had begun. Early in his reign, he hired Aleviso Novi to build the imposing, yet light and graceful Cathedral of the Archangel Michael which, in time, came to serve as the imperial family's burial crypt. Here too the Italian touch is clear in the shell-shaped gables and the delicate decorative columns that adorn the façades. Vasilii also began work on the so-called Bell Tower of Ivan the Great whose completion in 1600 brought the great age of Kremlin building to a close.[45]

The Dormition Cathedral (*Uspenskii Sobor*) remains the Kremlin's focal point and *pièce de résistance* just as Ivan and his architects intended. Construction of the new building began in 1472. Unfortunately the structure collapsed on the verge of completion and Ivan had to begin again in 1475, after replacing the original native architects with an Italian builder known as Aristotle Fioravanti. From the beginning, the grand prince made clear that his new cathedral was to resemble the great church of Vladimir in more than name alone. He sent Fioravanti to inspect the prototype before beginning his work. The resulting church is a fascinating mixture of traditional Russian and Italian features, with the former predominant. Like its precursor, the Moscow cathedral has five cupolas grouped together with the largest in the centre. The basic structure is simple and traditional – a rectangle divided lengthways into three aisles leading to three apses at the eastern end. Fioravanti placed his own distinct stamp on his work. The Dormition Cathedral is exceptionally well proportioned. The central cupola and apse, for example, are clearly larger than the others but not so much so as to overpower them. The architect decorated the building's façades simply and delicately. A row of graceful columns runs across the middle of the south wall facing the Kremlin Square and full-length rectangular pillars adorn the apses. Worshippers enter the sanctuary from the great Kremlin Square through a dramatic portal surmounted by a large mosaic centred on an image of the Virgin and Child, powerfully reminiscent of *Our Lady of Vladimir*. The sense of balance and harmony extends to the interior as well. Although later decoration makes the effect difficult to appreciate now, the sanctuary was once spacious and full of light since only four circular pillars supported the roof. From the beginning, the cathedral's royal patrons took great pains to see that their handiwork was suitably magnificent. The collecting of icons continued until the icon stand of the Dormition Cathedral became a veritable gallery of masterpieces of Byzantine and Russian painting.[46] Moreover, in about 1481, Ivan III hired the leading artist of his day, Dionysius, and a group of associates to paint frescos on the interior walls. The fragments which survive, above all the depiction of the Visit of the Magi, testify to Dionysius's maturing skill as a painter.[47] All in all, as intended, the magnificence of the Dormition Cathedral redounded to the glory of God and of Ivan III, his anointed ruler of the Russian lands.

In the official culture of the reigns of Ivan III and Vasilii III, the glorification of Moscow and its ruler went hand in hand with 'Counter-Reformation' tendencies. The leaders of the Eastern Orthodox Church suppressed heterodox currents of thought among the faithful and strove for uniformity of belief and practice. The successful struggle of Archbishop Gennadius of Novgorod and Joseph of Volokolamsk to extirpate the Judaizer heretics is a particularly dramatic case in point. Moreover, as the work of Gennadius's circle of scholars demonstrates, the leading members of the hierarchy gladly used any available political or intellectual weapon to beat back the enemies of traditional Orthodoxy.[48] Throughout the sixteenth century, Muscovite church leaders followed their example. Metropolitan Daniel was particularly vigilant in this regard. He kept a careful eye on the tiny and deeply divided group of 'humanist' thinkers at the court of Vasilii III and, on two occasions – in 1525 and 1531 – had Maxim the Greek, the talented and resolutely Orthodox scholar and translator, condemned for heresy and imprisoned.[49] In the ideological fortress of Muscovy, unity had to be preserved at any price.

In these circumstances, we should not look for literature of striking originality. The most impressive literary achievement of the time was the composition the so-called *Nikonian Chronicle*, the most comprehensive and most blatantly partisan of all of the great Muscovite compilations. The editors – of whom Daniel himself may have been the first – saw the rise and triumph of Orthodox Moscow as the unifying principle and culmination of his history.[50]

In the visual arts, the mobilization of Russian Orthodoxy produced its most impressive results in icon and fresco painting, especially the work of Dionysius and his school. During his long life, Dionysius won widespread recognition as a worthy successor of Andrei Rublev. At the same time, attributing particular icons and frescos to him is no easy matter: a layman, he often worked with his sons and other painters on joint projects. He and his collaborators carried out commissions in many important centres of Muscovite political and religious life – among them the Dormition Cathedral of the Moscow Kremlin and the Ferapontov Monastery near Beloozero where a brilliant cycle of frescos has been preserved in all its glory.[51]

Dionysius's best icons are among the finest ever painted.[52] They stand out, above all, for the fine sense of line and proportion in their composition and their rich and varied colour. At the centre of the *Crucifixion* is the curve of Christ's body on the cross. The groups of figures in the lower right and left of the picture, with their intensely coloured robes, underline the significance of the pale and fragile central figure.[53] In *Metropolitan Peter*, a visual saint's life, the artist drew attention to the hero by placing him against a white background, thus changing and intensifying the colours of his face and vestments and of the cartoon-like scenes from his life which run around the icon's borders.

Several characteristics of Dionysius's manner suggest that he consciously followed in Rublev's footsteps. Both artists strove to inspire the viewers of their work by presenting the central figures in gracefully elongated form as exemplars of Christian ideals. Both aimed at an impression of serene harmony and a mood of quiet contemplation. In other respects, however, the works of the two masters are distinctly different. Dionysius's compositions display more concern with strictly decorative considerations than Rublev's and his use of colour, although dazzling, is less nuanced. Moreover, Dionysius's icons lack the sense of character and emotional intensity of his predecessor's; nothing in his work approaches the power of Rublev's *Saviour*.

Several new tendencies characteristic of fifteenth-century painting link Dionysius with the 'Counter-Reformation' tendencies in Muscovite ecclesiastical culture. One is the artist's evident concern for formal order. Second, some of his work reflects a trend towards 'monumentalism': a number of his icons and many frescos – the visual hymns to the Mother of God, for example – are exceedingly complex in composition, with large numbers of figures. Dionysius's mastery of composition allowed him to group them so that the main lines and focal points of his paintings remain clear; under the brush of lesser artists, such masses of figures simply numb and overwhelm the viewer. In addition, some of his paintings provide examples of the didacticism which became increasingly characteristic of Russian art in the sixteenth century. Icons and frescos illustrated the words of hymns or proclaimed Orthodox doctrine in clear allegorical statements. Even the *Crucifixion*, austere in its simplicity, contains symbolic figures, in the air on both sides of the cross, representing the vanquished Old Testament synagogue and the victorious New Testament church.[54]

Thus Dionysius stood at a crossroads in the development of Russian painting. The brilliance of his simplest and most conventional icons make him a worthy heir of the greatest artists of earlier times. By reflecting the artistic fashions of his own day, he also became a harbinger of the future. Yet Dionysius's skill and his grounding in artistic tradition saved him from the excesses of formalism, busyness or sentimentality into which most of his successors fell. No later Muscovite artist matched his achievement.

In the reign of Ivan IV, writers, architects and painters created monuments to the glory of the Orthodox tsardom of Muscovy. Chronicles, icons and frescos proclaimed again and again the familiar messages: Muscovite Russia was the one remaining citadel of true Christianity; Ivan IV, its tsar, worthily followed in an unbroken succession which could be traced back to the emperors of Byzantium and ancient Rome; and he was, with brilliant success, fulfilling his obligation to lead the armies of Christ against the enemies of the Cross.

The official art of Ivan IV's time emerged from the imperial court and the entourage of the metropolitan working in close harmony. In all probability, Metropolitan Macarius personally supervised or commissioned much of the work: without question, his staff produced the great literary compilations of the period and he appears in the documentary account of the so-called 'Viskovaty affair' as defender of the theological orthodoxy of controversial new icons.[55] The degree of Ivan IV's personal involvement in sponsoring the arts is a far more controversial matter.

The creators and sponsors of the official art of the mid-sixteenth century aimed at consistency and uniformity in style and content. To a remarkable extent, chronicles, genealogies, icons and frescos – particularly those inspired by the conquest of Kazan – say precisely the same things with the same symbols. The central figures of the *Tale of the Princes of Vladimir*, for example, appear again and again. Vladimir Monomakh, the Kievan prince who supposedly brought the imperial regalia from Byzantium to Russia, plays the central role in the decorative panels on the imperial throne in the Dormition Cathedral in the Moscow Kremlin, appears prominently in the icon, *The Church Militant*, and has an important part in the *Book of Degrees*.[56]

In literature, the imperial manner appears most clearly in the compilations of Macarius's circle, the *Great Menology* and the *Book of Decrees* and in the official chronicle compiled at the tsar's court. The authors of the mid-sixteenth century strove for an elevated and dignified rhetoric worthy of their exalted subjects. What they created was a complicated and stilted style far more mechanical and less moving than Epiphanius's elaborate verbal creations. In their writing, they favoured complex grammatical constructions, a pretentious vocabulary and rhetorical devices such as repeated exclamations. At the same time, the most dramatic passages in the court chronicle and several separate tales show that Muscovite writers had not entirely lost the knack for vivid storytelling.[57]

Although also wordy in the extreme, the polemics of the period have a far sharper cutting edge. The best of them, the letters attributed to Ivan IV – most of which, I still believe, are, in some sense, his creations – display an impressive talent for invective. Passages of pompous formal rhetoric alternate startlingly with earthy colloquialisms. At times, indeed, Ivan appears to use the formal ecclesiastical style to parody the pretensions of his polemical targets. A number of passages in the letters have an intense, breathless quality because the author wrote in a kind of shorthand without primary verbs or other crucial grammatical elements. Throughout the tsar's correspondence, moreover, runs a streak of bitter, sarcastic humour aimed at people as diverse as Queen Elizabeth and Vasilii Griaznoi, a servitor captured by the Crimean Tatars. As a group, then, Ivan's letters are unique, combining qualities that come together nowhere else in Muscovite literature.[58]

Men and women of our own day know the imperial style of Ivan IV's time primarily through buildings. Drawing on the popular tradition in wooden architecture, the builders of the mid-sixteenth century created a series of arresting churches which have nothing whatsoever in common with the great cathedrals of the Moscow Kremlin. The first, and most beautiful, of these brick structures is the Church of the Ascension, built in 1532 at Kolomenskoe, an imperial summer residence south-east of the capital. The building's architectural form perfectly reflects the name of the church feast for which it is named, for its vertical lines draw the eye of the viewer upward towards heaven. On a bluff above the Moskva river, the builders erected a high octagonal structure of brick topped with a steep 'tent-shaped' roof of the type frequently encountered in wooden churches and fortifications. The building's decoration is as simple and effective as its basic structure is dramatic. Graceful lines of small white stones lighten the appearance of the 'tent' and rectangular columns and *kokoshniki*, purely decorative gables which supposedly resemble the head-dresses of peasant women, break the surface of the vertical outer walls of the octagon. Symmetrical stairs and porches lead into the sanctuary. The interior of the Church of the Ascension is very small and extremely high, rather like a sanctified elevator shaft. Evidently the priorities of its builders were clear. A visually stunning exterior was their primary consideration: the practicality of the church as a place of worship was a comparatively minor matter.

The new tendency in church architecture reached its apogee in the Cathedral of St Basil the Blessed on Red Square in Moscow. This extraordinary building often strikes foreigners as the epitome of 'rude and barbarous' Muscovy. Yet, it is absolutely unique. On first seeing it, the visitor is stunned by its exuberance and vitality. Ivan IV's government intended the church to be a central part of the celebration of the conquest of Kazan. Originally dedicated to the feast of the Veil, the day on which the Tatar capital fell, the building was to consist of eight separate sanctuaries, one for each of the Russian victories in the campaign.

In reality, the building combines nine separate churches. In the centre is a high tent-shaped structure, a more elaborately decorated equivalent of the Kolomenskoe church. Around it are eight smaller octagonal units of varying sizes. Each has its own prominent onion-shaped cupola. Throughout the entire structure, the architects used popular decorative devices – porches, stairways, kokoshniki, faceted brickwork and brightly coloured tile – all in inspired excess. As a place of worship, St Basil's surely had its limitations. The view across Red Square fully justifies the builders' efforts, however, and, in recognition of that fact, the Muscovite church made it the backdrop for important festivities, particularly the great Palm Sunday procession which traditionally began at its doors.[59]

Icon painters joined in celebrating the Orthodox tsardom and its victory over Kazan. Many of the most interesting icons of the mid-sixteenth century take the monumentalism and the didactic element in Dionysius's paintings to extremes. Painters of the time often created complex compositions illustrating theological doctrines or devotional texts. The artists of Ivan IV's time were undoubtedly skilled craftsmen: their best work displays fine drawing, a good sense of composition, and rich, although rather dark, colouring. At the same time, their icons, by their nature, lack the emotional appeal of their predecessors. Their work can be appreciated in two ways: either the viewer can take in each icon at a glance as a single decorative composition or, one by one, study and decipher the individual symbols that make up the whole.[60]

The best example of the new type of icon is the *Church Militant*, the precise counterpart of the Cathedral of St Basil. In this anonymous work, the warrior Archangel Michael and Ivan IV lead the victorious Christian army toward the heavenly city or Moscow over which presides the Mother of God. Behind the three columns of troops burns Sodom or Kazan. In the centre of the main body of warriors rides a disproportionately large figure, representing Vladimir Monomakh, and other Russian warrior-saints of earlier generations can be seen among their ranks. Although the icon is extremely detailed, its basic composition is clear and dramatic. It would be hard to imagine a more powerful statement that, in conquering Kazan, Orthodox Muscovy had carried out its divinely ordained historical mission.[61]

The new theological and political icons shocked some of the faithful. No less a man than Ivan Viskovatyi denounced a number of them as heretical. While political rivalries may have influenced Viskovatyi's decision to make his doubts public, he concentrated his fire on the questionable theological implications of works such as the *Four-Part Icon* in the Annunciation Cathedral in the Kremlin. For one thing, he objected to the very idea of an icon illustrating the Creed since, in his view, it was impossible to portray God the Father. He also criticized more specific details, for example the representation of Christ clothed in armour sitting on a cross to symbolize his victory over death.[62] In many respects, Viskovatyi was right, for the official court art of the mid-sixteenth century violated the traditional canons of Eastern Orthodox iconography in a variety of ways, not least by using sacred symbols for blatantly political purposes and portraying living contemporaries alongside the usual holy figures. Nevertheless, led by Macarius, the leaders of the church vigorously defended the new works of art which they had commissioned.[63] An ecclesiastical council which met in 1554 condemned Viskovatyi's criticisms: he recanted and continued to hold high office for many years thereafter.

In the reign of Ivan IV, then, the rulers of Muscovy completed the process of creating an intellectual and artistic system, controlled and defended by the power of the church and the state. Built upon the achievements of previous generations of writers and artists, this cultural edifice was imposing in its size and in the thickness of its battlements. It was also airless and stifling. Later generations of painters or poets could find renewing springs of creativity only by adopting Central or Western European themes, styles and genres or by drawing on the Russian popular tradition as Ivan IV's architects had already done.

At the same time, the solidity and undisputed Orthodoxy of the official culture of Ivan IV's time were irresistibly attractive to men and women living in later times of turmoil. During the cultural crises of the seventeenth century and later, disillusioned conservatives like the Old Believers looked back nostalgically to the 'good old days' of Ivan IV and, in their own communities, did their best to preserve the literary and artistic traditions of the world they had lost. As long as such conservative groups exist – and they are alive today – the cultural attainments of Muscovy will remain a living reality.

REFERENCES AND NOTES

1. See, for example, Likhachev, *Razvitie*, pp. 44–9 on the Kievan period.
2. Florovsky, 'Problem'.

3. For interpretative surveys of medieval Russian literature, see Fennell and Stokes, *Early Russian Literature* and the works of D. S. Likhachev.
4. See *Istoriia russkogo iskusstva*, vol. 1, pp. 128–32.
5. Karger, *Novgorod*, pp. 82–93, 226–33.
6. Voronin, *Zodchestvo*, vol. 1, pp. 149–86; *Vladimir*, pp. 37–66.
7. Ibid., pp. 67–86.
8. Ibid., pp. 129–39; Voronin, *Zodchestvo*, vol. 1, pp. 262–300.
9. Onasch, *Ikonenmalerei*, pp. 151–2.
10. See Onasch, *Icons*, plates 1 and 15 and pp. 341–2, 350–1.
11. Likhachev, *Chelovek*, pp. 25–62.
12. *Istoriia russkoi literatury*, pp. 64–83.
13. *Povest*, pp. 90–4; *Russian Primary Chronicle*, pp. 126–30.
14. Ibid., pp. 187–91; *Povest*, pp. 170–5.
15. Voronin, *Zodchestvo*, vol. 2, pp. 130–9; Rybakov, *Remeslo*, pp. 525–38.
16. Thompson, *Novgorod*, pp. 55–63.
17. Karger, *Novgorod*, pp. 163–84.
18. See *Pskov*.
19. Lazarev, *Feofan Grek*, pp. 5–45.
20. *Novgorod Icons*, plates 76 and 198; Onasch, *Icons*, p. 358.
21. For example, Onasch, *Icons*, plate 62 and p. 372.
22. *Novgorodskaia pervaia letopis*, pp. 409–10.
23. *Novgorod Icons*, plate 123; Onasch, *Icons*, pp. 364–5.
24. *Khrestomatiia*, pp. 190–9; *Pamiatniki literatury. XIV-seredina XV veka*, pp. 256–429; in English, Zenkovsky, *Medieval Russia's Epics*, pp. 259–90. The surviving version of the *Life* was heavily edited by a later writer, perhaps Pakhomius the Serb (Fennell and Stokes, *Early Russian Literature*, p. 136).
25. *The Tale of the Life and Death of Grand Prince Dmitrii Ivanovich*, a hagiographic biography of Dmitrii Donskoi also exhibits the abstractness and emotionalism characteristic of the 'weaving of words' school (Fennell and Stokes, *Early Russian Literature*, pp. 122–34).
26. Bçrtnes, 'Function'.
27. *Istoriia russkoi literatury*, pp. 217–20; Likhachev, *Chelovek*, pp. 72–92; *Razvitie*, pp. 75–126.
28. Lazarev, *Andrei Rublev*, pp. 67–9.
29. Ibid., plate XII and pp. 32–3; Onasch, *Icons*, plates 94 and 95 and p. 385.
30. Lazarev, *Andrei Rublev*, pp. 134–7; compare Onasch, *Icons*, p. 386.
31. Demina, 'Troitsa', pp. 35–557.
32. See, for example, Fennell's comments on Pakhomius the Serb in *Early Russian Literature*, pp. 136–8.
33. *Istoriia russkoi literatury*, pp. 231–41; *Slovo*, pp. 344–84; Salmina, 'Eshche raz o datirovke'; Grekov, *Evropa*, pp. 384–418.
34. Fennell and Stokes, *Early Russian Literature*, pp. 80–107.
35. *Povesti*, pp. 9–17, 211–19; Zenkovsky, *Medieval Russia's Epics*, pp. 212–23.
36. *Povesti*, pp. 29–76, 227–77.
37. See Likhachev, *Kultura*, pp. 89–93.
38. *Pamiatniki literatury. Vtoraia polovina XV veka*, pp. 216–67, 554–65.
39. Skripil, "Istoriia", pp. 177–82; Lure, *Ideologicheskaia borba*, pp. 395–403.
40. Lure, *Obshcherusskie letopisi*, pp. 160, 166–7, 248–54.
41. *PSRL* 26:230–42, **27**:129–36; *Pamiatniki literatury. Vtoraia polovina XV veka*, pp. 376–401.

42. Ibid., pp. 514–21; Lure, *Obshcherusskie letopisi*, pp. 244–7.
43. Tolstaia, *Uspenskii sobor*, p. 28.
44. See Alef, 'Adoption'.
45. Mneva, *Iskusstvo*, pp. 13–29.
46. Tolstaia, *Uspenskii sobor*, pp. 5–32.
47. *Pervaia rospis*.
48. Lure, *Ideologicheskaia borba*, pp. 266–84.
49. See Zimin, *Rossiia*, pp. 323–63.
50. Kloss, *Nikonovskii svod*, pp. 88–95.
51. Admirably reproduced in *Freski*. See also Lazarev, *Old Russian Murals*, pp 193–212.
52. For a good sample, see Alpatov, *Drevnerusskaia ikonopis*, plates 150–65.
53. Onasch, *Icons*, p. 389.
54. Lazarev, *Moskovskaia shkola*, pp. 36–49; Popov, *Zhivopis*, pp. 73–120.
55. See Miller, 'Viskovatyi affair' and Andreyev, 'Metropolit Makarii' and 'O 'dele diaka Viskovatago''.
56. See Podobedova, *Moskovskaia shkola*.
57. *Istoriia russkoi literatury*, pp. 300–27.
58. *Perepiska* and *Poslaniia Ivana Groznogo*, esp. pp. 139–94; Fennell and Stokes, *Early Russian Literature*, pp. 182–90. For an English translation of the 'correspondence' of Ivan IV and Prince Kurbskii, see *Correspondence*.
59. Mneva, *Iskusstvo*, pp. 86–95.
60. Podobedova, *Moskovskaia shkola*, p. 93.
61. Ibid., pp. 22–7.
62. Ibid., pp. 40–58; Miller, 'Viskovatyi affair', pp. 306–7, 315; Andreyev, 'O 'dele diaka Viskovatago''.
63. Miller, 'Viskovatyi affair', pp. 318–20.

CHAPTER EIGHT

The Time Of Troubles

After the death of Ivan IV, Muscovy underwent a devastating crisis. In the years between 1584 and 1613, the society suffered a complete political, social, institutional and moral collapse. In the sixteenth and seventeenth centuries, serious political and social upheavals took place in many countries of Europe. Few, however, experienced the horrors that Muscovy lived through during the Time of Troubles. Many of the resources so carefully hoarded in the past disappeared: desperate temporary governments and their greedy officials emptied the royal treasury, many of the tsars' military servitors abandoned their posts and entire regions went their own way, oblivious of Moscow's leadership. At the lowest depths, the tsars' government had virtually ceased to function, society was in chaos, foreign invaders and native brigands stalked the land, and desperate men and women fed on one another – figuratively and sometimes literally. Yet ultimately, the administrative habits, modes of political behaviour and convictions that Orthodox Russia had a unique mission in the world – all developed in the process of nation-building – saved the community from annihilation. Against all odds, Muscovite society found strength to restore order and rebuild the monarchy along the lines established in the three previous centuries of development.

Any writer who attempts to describe the Time of Troubles must stand on the shoulders of a giant. In a magnificent book, first published in 1899, S. F. Platonov analysed the period with a mastery that has never been equalled. Although some of his judgements, particularly his treatment of the reign of Ivan IV, have not passed the test of time, his general interpretation of the interlocking crises that made up the Troubles still holds historians – both Soviet and foreign – in its thrall.[1] This chapter will be still one more tribute to his achievement. At the same time, Platonov has worthy successors, above all R. G. Skrynnikov, whose continuing work on the origins and course of the Time of Troubles adds many valuable details and nuances to his basic scheme.[2]

On the death of Ivan IV in 1584, the crown passed to his son, Fedor. As contemporaries were well aware, his accession posed more problems than it solved. The new tsar displayed the saintly qualities of gentleness and piety, but none of the strength of body or will needed to rule. He may well have been mentally retarded. Clearly, others would rule in his name. Moreover, given his weak health, there was a good chance that Muscovy would soon face a crisis over the succession to his throne.[3]

The new regime's first concern was to establish its legitimacy in the eyes of the populace. In his will, Ivan IV designated several prominent courtiers as his executors. Under their leadership, the government summoned a meeting of the zemskii sobor to give its assent to Fedor's accession and arranged his coronation.

With Fedor safely on the throne, the most powerful men and clans at court faced the crucial political question of the day – who would really rule in his name. Several contending clans appeared in the arena, each with its own weapons. The Shuiskiis, a distinguished princely family, had preserved their lives and lands through the storms of the preceding reign. The Romanovs, Fedor's mother's kin, had not only family ties with the ruling dynasty, but also many years of leadership under Ivan IV. Late in his life, however, they fell into disfavour and, at the time of the new tsar's accession, were only beginning a struggle to recoup their lost position. From the outset, however, Boris Godunov held the strongest hand. A man of solid, but undistinguished lineage, Godunov had risen through the oprichnina until he became one of Ivan IV's closest confidants and an executor of his will. Even more importantly for his future, his sister, Irina, had earlier married the future Tsar Fedor. In the first weeks of his brother-in-law's reign, Boris received the title of koniushii (master of the horse), symbolizing his pre-eminence at court.

With the tacit support of the Romanovs, Godunov slowly consolidated his power. In 1584, he made use of popular unrest to disgrace B. Ia. Belskii, one of Ivan IV's parvenu favourites. Two years later, another uprising in Moscow struck at Godunov's weak point, his dependence on his sister's marriage to the tsar. In this episode, the demonstrators demanded that, for the welfare of the realm, Fedor divorce Irina, by whom he had no children, and remarry. Moving quickly, Godunov had several of the protesters executed early in 1587. Moreover, interpreting the incident as an attempt by the Shuiskiis to oust him, he arrested the leaders of the clan.

In 1588, Godunov launched a more general purge of his enemies. He reopened the case against the Shuiskiis, whom he had recently pardoned, and rearrested their leaders, two of whom soon died mysteriously. Many other powerful or prominent figures joined them in disgrace – former oprichniki; the Nagois, Ivan IV's last in-laws; the former 'tsar', Semen Bekbulatovich; and several distinguished princely and non-titled clans. Just as a new oprichnina seemed imminent, however, Godunov recognized that he had won the struggle for power and relaxed the pressure on his potential rivals at court. For the rest of his royal master's reign, he ruled Muscovy unchallenged.

In the opinion of recent scholars, Godunov was a remarkably intelligent and resourceful leader, drawing small but significant triumphs from unpromising circumstances. On the domestic scene, his government had to deal with the severe economic and social crisis which began in the last years of Ivan IV's reign. High taxes and a succession of natural disasters forced many peasants into slavery or into migration from their ancestral homes to the frontiers of the state. Under the circumstances, many lesser nobles, who depended on their labour, also found conditions intolerable and abandoned their estates. From the government's point of view, these developments were an unmitigated disaster. Apart from the threat to social order, the royal fisc suffered, for officials could not collect taxes from peasants who had disappeared. As for the lesser nobles, the royal army depended on them to provide the bulk of its cavalry. Their survival was essential to the safety of the realm.

Godunov's regime responded to these problems in a variety of ways. It lowered the pressure of taxation on the estates of the lesser nobles by granting exemption to the nobles' own portion of the estate. In addition, to help landlords and the royal treasury, the government continued to forbid peasants – and urban taxpayers, for that matter – to leave their registered places of residence. Moreover, the decree of 1597 gave the hard-pressed nobles the right to reclaim any of their peasants who had fled from their estates in the preceding five years. Finally, the government built up the depleted ranks of the tsar's military entourage by recruiting new members into the lower echelons of the court and attempting to find them estates in the regions around Moscow. In the end, however, such measures failed to save Muscovy from even worse social and economic dislocation. The fault was not Godunov's: no sixteenth-century European government could have solved the problems that eventually destroyed his regime.

Tsar Fedor's government also faced acute difficulties on the international scene. The Livonian War had left the country exhausted and on the defensive. As always, moreover, Muscovy ran the risk of simultaneous warfare on two fronts – in the west, against Poland and Sweden and, in the south, against the Crimean Tatars. The latter struck first. In the early years of Fedor's reign, Crimean raiding parties annually invaded the southern regions of Muscovy. Their activity reached its climax in 1591 when Muscovite forces defeated Khan Kazy-Girey and his troops in a major battle just south of Moscow. Two years later, Godunov's government made a truce with the Crimea and, for the moment, raids ceased.

In his dealings with the powers of Western and Central Europe, Godunov's administration did a masterful job of hiding Muscovy's weaknesses and exploiting her few diplomatic advantages. For one thing, the regent continued to cultivate good relations with England and encourage trade between the two countries through the White Sea. In his dealings with Queen Elizabeth, Godunov protected Muscovite interests more tenaciously than had Ivan IV in his more desperate moments. Even so, conflict erupted within the government over the country's basic diplomatic orientation: in 1588, Boris ousted his 'foreign minister', the chancery official Andrei Shchelkalov, because the latter opposed ties with England, preferring a *rapprochement* with her most determined enemies, the Habsburgs.

Godunov also used Poland's domestic problems to gain breathing room for Muscovy. In 1586, the Polish throne became vacant once again when Stefan Bathory died. Seizing the opportunity, the Moscovite government offered Tsar Fedor as a candidate and proposed a plan for the union of the two realms under his sceptre. Fedor stood no real chance of becoming king of Poland, but his candidacy exacerbated the political struggles within the commonwealth. In the end, the electors chose Sigismund Vasa, heir to the throne of Sweden. His accession raised the harrowing spectre of a dynastic union of Muscovy's main enemies. In the late 1580s and early 1590s, however, the Polish government was content to give Sweden its tacit support in the latter's struggle with Muscovy. In the long run, moreover, Muscovy's western neighbours became the bitterest of enemies.

Conflict between Sweden and the Muscovite state was unavoidable. Neither was satisfied with the truce that ended their share of the Livonian War. The Muscovite government smarted under the loss of most of its territory along the Gulf of Finland. For its part, the regime of John III aspired to control Muscovy's export trade with Western Europe. After the Livonian War, however, the Muscovites diverted much of their export trade to the White Sea ports or to Pskov and thence to Polish-held cities such as Riga.[4]

War between the two powers broke out in 1590 and lasted, with interruptions, for five years. On the whole, the Muscovite army fought well. In the first stage of the war, Russian forces recaptured the coast of the Gulf of Finland up to Narva and later made significant advances in Karelia. Narva itself remained in Swedish hands. The peace settlement – the Truce of Teusina or Tiavzino of 1595 – was an elaborate compromise of the two powers' interests. Muscovy retained the territory which her army had captured. For her part, Sweden received guarantees that Russia's exports would flow through her ports and that her merchants would have the right to trade free of duty throughout Muscovy. In practice, of course, nothing guaranteed that Muscovite traders would not continue to avoid Swedish territory altogether when shipping their goods to the West.[5]

Under Godunov's leadership, Muscovy made far more important gains in the south and east. In the late 1580s and 1590s, his government founded new military outposts in the valleys of the Volga, Don and Donets rivers. One even appeared on the Terek river on the northern fringe of the Caucasus. The new forts served two purposes: they strengthened the country's defences against Crimean raids and gave the tsar's government far greater control than before over the restless warrior bands of Cossacks.

In the 1580s and 1590s, moreover, Muscovite power expanded across the Urals into Siberia. At first, Russia's Siberian adventure had very little to do with the government in Moscow. In the latter half of the sixteenth century, the Stroganov family of merchants controlled the north-eastern corner of European Russia as its private preserve. Moving outward from their headquarters at Sol Vychegodsk in the northern Dvina valley, the Stroganovs and their agents made a fortune manufacturing salt and collecting furs from a vast region of forest and tundra stretching up to the Urals and beyond. As their ambitions grew and their territory expanded, they increasingly clashed with the rulers and people of the khanate of Siberia, the small and loosely governed Tatar state centred in the basin of the Ob river.

In order to fight their private wars with the Siberian Tatars, the Stroganovs needed their own army. At the end of the Livonian War, they recruited the Cossack leader, Ermak, and his force of about 1,500 men to defend their territory. Popular tradition describes Ermak as an imposing and energetic warrior and credits his band with spectacular feats of brigandage. On a more respectable note, he and his men fought in the tsar's army against the Poles in the closing stages of the Livonian conflict. Before long, the Stroganovs' new employees went on the attack. In the autumn of 1582, they descended the river network of western Siberia and launched a surprise attack on the heart of the khanate. Taking the old khan, Kuchum, by surprise, Ermak's men defeated his troops in battle, captured his capital and drove him into exile.

At that juncture, Ermak turned to the government of Ivan IV for reinforcements and assistance in organizing the administration of the conquered territory. Help arrived too late. Kuchum rallied his followers, killed Ermak in a sudden attack and drove the surviving Cossacks out of his domain.[6]

Once involved in Siberia's affairs, the Muscovite government doggedly worked to annex the area. Exploiting domestic conflicts within the restored khanate, Godunov's regime sent regular troops into the area to make the Russian presence permanent. One after another, his agents built forts in strategic locations, particularly at the confluence of important rivers. From these log stockades, small Muscovite garrisons kept control of the surrounding country and collected tribute from the native peoples. By 1600, thanks to Godunov's efforts, western Siberia rested firmly in Moscow's hands and the way lay open to the shores of the Pacific.

As he worked, with considerable success, to restore the fortunes of the Muscovite state, Boris Godunov occupied a tenuous political position. His claim to leadership rested, above all, on the fact that he was the brother-in-law of an ailing monarch. Fedor's death, especially if he had no heir, would gravely threaten the foundation of his power.

On the horizon, Godunov faced a more remote menace in the person of Fedor's young half-brother, Dmitrii. After the death of Ivan IV, the new government created an appanage for the boy at Uglich. There he and his mother's kin, the Nagois, lived in comfortable exile under the watchful eye of the chancery official, M. I. Bitiagovskii. The position of the Nagois contained elements of promise and of menace. On one hand, as long as Fedor remained childless, Dmitrii was his most likely successor. On the other, his claim to the throne was open to challenge on canonical grounds since, as the son of a seventh marriage, he was technically illegitimate. Moreover, he and his kin lived in an isolated and vulnerable position away from the court. In the late 1580s, rumours of threats on Dmitrii's life were already in circulation.

Then, on 15 May 1591, tragedy struck. While playing with his friends, Dmitrii died of a stab wound in the neck. His distraught mother and her kinsmen immediately charged that agents of Boris Godunov had murdered the boy. In response to their accusations, a crowd attacked the headquarters of the royal administration in Uglich and lynched Bitiagovskii and several others.

In response to these bloody incidents, Godunov appointed a commission of inquiry. Under the leadership of Prince V. I. Shuiskii, the investigators visited the scene of the tragedy and carefully questioned the witnesses. Their verdict cleared Boris of any wrongdoing. Dmitrii, they concluded, had epilepsy and, while playing a game with knives, had suffered a seizure and accidentally stabbed himself. With that, the government closed the case, exiled the Nagois, now deprived of their ties to the throne, and severely punished the people of Uglich who had taken part in the uprising.

Before long, Dmitrii's death came to haunt Boris Godunov and captured the imaginations of generations of Russian writers. In the English-speaking world, we know the story best from Mussorgskii's opera, *Boris Godunov*. According to this familiar version, Godunov ordered the murder of the young prince in order to clear his own path to the throne. The crime, the one mortal sin of an otherwise humane ruler, had profoundly tragic consequences, for it destroyed Godunov's physical and mental health and political credibility and brought retribution not only on the murderer, but on Russian society as a whole.

The claim that Godunov had Dmitrii murdered has an ancient and honourable history. It can be traced back to rumours circulating immediately after the young prince's death and soon became a central leitmotif in the historical compositions about the Time of Troubles written in the first decades of the seventeenth century. Why were contemporaries and people of succeeding generations determined to disregard the report of the investigating commission, to believe that Dmitrii's death was a political assassination? First of all, a number of people, above all the Nagois, had a vested interest in the theory that Dmitrii had been murdered. After all, it was Boris Godunov, the presumed murderer, who had appointed the commissioners and, in later times, when it suited his purposes, their spokesman, Shuiskii, renounced the verdict as a fraud. Second – and more significantly – the later writers who struggled to explain the horrors of the Time of Troubles had ideological reasons for believing in the murder. Like other medieval Christian writers, they believed that God allowed his people to suffer in punishment for their sins. But for what sins? From the vantage point of 1610 or 1630, the answer was clear – for Godunov's murder of Dmitrii and his subjects' silent acquiescence in the crime. For that, Boris was overthrown by a pretender who called himself Dmitrii, and the people suffered the horrors of famine and civil war.

Rejecting theological or Shakespearian explanations of Dmitrii's death, historians of recent times, beginning with Platonov, have reaffirmed Godunov's innocence. First, they argue, the investigating commission carried out its mandate thoroughly and intelligently. Moreover, its verdict fits the circumstances of 1591 better than any other explanation. At that time,

Godunov could hardly have foreseen that Dmitrii might stand between him and the crown. For one thing, it was still possible that Tsar Fedor might beget an heir; his wife bore him a daughter in 1592. In addition, Dmitrii's doubtful legitimacy might bar his way to the throne. Finally, were Fedor to die without an heir, other prominent courtiers could present better claims than Godunov to succeed him. In short, in 1591, Boris Godunov had no motive for murdering Dmitrii.[7]

On 6 January 1598, Tsar Fedor died, leaving neither an heir nor a will. With him ended the dynasty which had ruled Moscow uninterruptedly since its emergence from obscurity. For a century and a half, the crown had passed without question or struggle from father to son. Now no one had a clear right to be tsar and Muscovite society had no rules or traditions for selecting one.

At the time of his brother-in-law's death, Boris Godunov held the reins of power. Even so, gaining the throne was no easy matter. Several other courtiers – above all, Fedor Nikitich Romanov – could make more convincing genealogical claims to rule. As a result, as Skrynnikov's detailed studies show, frantic political manoeuvring took place in the early months of 1598. For example, Boris and his allies considered crowning his sister, Irina, as ruler, since she enjoyed the prestige that came from years as the tsar's consort. In the end, however, following the custom of well-born widows, she took the veil.

Energetically organizing support for his candidacy, Godunov defeated his rivals. With the help of his ally, Patriarch Job, he hastily summoned a series of assemblies which urged him to take the throne. Then carefully arranged demonstrations overcame the reluctance of the Boyar Council whose members, in any case, failed to agree on an alternative candidate. The Crimean menace also served Boris well. In the early summer of 1598, claiming that Muscovy faced an invasion from the south, Godunov mobilized a large army at Serpukhov. By so doing, he demonstrated his leadership before thousands of lesser nobles and gained their tacit support for his candidacy. By the time he returned to Moscow, the struggle for power was over. Amid lavish ceremonies, Boris was crowned tsar on 3 September.[8]

Godunov's accession marks the beginning of Muscovy's agony. Because he was not from the old dynasty and had gained the throne by means that were, at best, questionable, he never succeeded in fully establishing his right to demand his subjects' obedience and loyalty. These doubts about his legitimacy opened a Pandora's box of political, social and diplomatic problems.

According to Platonov's masterful analysis of the Time of Troubles, Muscovite society faced three profound crises – the dynastic, the social and the national – which arose one after the other and, in the end, became inextricably intertwined. First, Boris Godunov and the regimes which succeeded him failed to establish their legitimacy. Men and women with grievances could always justify rebellion against the government: many joined movements to find and enthrone the true tsar as opposed to the usurper who, in their view, sat on the throne in Moscow. Second, at the turn of the sixteenth and seventeenth centuries, embittered men and women abounded in Muscovy. As political constraints loosened, the oppressed and dispossessed of society rose in revolt or simply took to the roads to live as best they could outside of the government's control. Again and again, bands of Cossack warriors, restless and increasingly fearful of losing their treasured freedom of action, served as catalysts for the rebellions of others. Finally, when the government in Moscow lost control over its subjects, the country's traditional enemies took advantage of their opportunity. Before long, Polish and Swedish armies occupied salients of Muscovite territory and meddled in the political struggles of the country as a whole. In the end, it required the mobilization of all of the nation's remaining resources to restore the monarchy in 1613 and begin to rebuild the shattered society.

After nearly a century, this general pattern still dominates historians' thinking about the Time of Troubles. At the same time, its neatness and clarity are a little misleading. As Platonov would surely have admitted, Muscovy faced all three problems – at least potentially – throughout the years after the extinction of the old dynasty. In particular, the government's difficulty in establishing its legitimacy and social unrest and rebellion remained constants from 1598 to 1613 and beyond.

In his analysis of the Time of Troubles, Platonov also dissected the Muscovite state along geographical lines.[9] At the end of the sixteenth century, he argued, the most important regions of the country had distinct local traditions and social structures. Thus, the crises of the Troubles affected different parts of Muscovy in different ways. Moreover, as the authority of the central government declined to the vanishing point, the leaders of local society had to take their fate into their own hands. Several of the regions of Muscovy virtually became independent actors in the drama.

According to Platonov's analysis, the central core of the Muscovite state encompassed a huge area stretching from Vologda and Beloozero in the north to Kolomna in the south, and from the watershed between Novgorod and Tver in the west to Nizhnii-Novgorod in the east. In historical terms, the region consisted of the principalities of north-east Russia which came under Moscow's control over the course of the fourteenth and fifteenth centuries.

When the Time of Troubles began, the central region had a comparatively highly developed social and economic structure. By that time, most land which peasants farmed had come under the control of outsiders to the village. In many areas, monasteries owned the largest proportion of the cultivated land. Laymen – boyars and lesser nobles – also controlled a great deal of land in the centre. That was where the great nobles' ancestral estates were located. Moreover, over the years, the government had granted many pomeste estates to its servitors, both great and small. By the end of the sixteenth century, laymen probably held more land on conditional tenure than in outright ownership. At that time, landlords of all types had to contend with increasingly restless peasants, many of whom moved from one master to another or fled from the region altogether.

The cities and towns of the area served a wide variety of functions – as centres of trade and artisan production, as military strongpoints and as administrative centres. Their populations were correspondingly diverse. Apart from ordinary traders, journeymen and labourers, their inhabitants included garrison troops, clergymen and the employees of monasteries, and peasants temporarily in town, all of whom were, in some sense, exempt from regular taxes. The precise combination of elements, of course, varied from one town to another: in the north, cities like Vologda and Iaroslavl were primarily trading centres while southern towns like Kolomna and Mozhaisk were, first and foremost, military outposts. Moscow, the capital, towered over the entire region and its population included every kind of person who could be found in the other towns. In addition, it housed the court and the central bureaucracy whose staffs, with their dependants, numbered in the thousands.

The north-west of Muscovy presents a very different picture. The commercial cities of Novgorod and Pskov – the second and third largest urban centres of the realm – completely dominated its economy. Despite the ravages of the oprichnina and the Livonian War, both remained important trading centres through which goods from the Russian interior passed on to the markets of Europe. With one or two exceptions, the other towns of the area were small and weak.

On the eve of the Time of Troubles, the rural areas of the north-west suffered from numerous problems. To begin with, except for some districts near Pskov, the entire region has poor soil and an inhospitable climate. Given its strategic location, however, the Muscovite government had distributed many small estates to loyal servitors who acted as frontier troops and an occupation force in the territory of the former republics. In the late sixteenth century, these petty landlords had a particularly hard time making ends meet: peasant flight reached epidemic proportions in the old Novgorodian lands and, as a result, some minor nobles also had to flee or hide out to escape their obligations to the state.

The disastrous conditions in the north-west present a sharp contrast to the peace and prosperity of the far north. Once part of the republic of Novgorod, the belt of northern forest and coastline that stretched from Finland to the Urals thrived in the latter half of the sixteenth century. For one thing, the north had a unique and vigorous society. Most of the sparse population consisted of free peasants and fishermen who, by and large, managed their own affairs. The great northern monasteries controlled large tracts of inhabited land, but virtually no nobles owned estates in this remote and infertile area.

In the time of Ivan IV, the north enjoyed an economic boom that continued unabated until the end of the century. Apart from subsistence agriculture, the inhabitants engaged in the fur trade, fishing and the manufacture of salt. In addition, the region profited from Muscovy's trade with England. Because they could not use the Baltic route, the English traders shipped their goods through Muscovy's ports on the White Sea, using the northern Dvina river, the north's main artery, as their link with the centre of the country. As a result, towns such as Kholmogory and Velikii Ustiug, although small, enjoyed unequalled prosperity.

The regions to the south and east of the centre also had their own distinct characteristics. From time immemorial, the towns south of Moscow had guarded the heart of the country against invaders from the steppe, above all, the Crimean Tatars. Over the course of the sixteenth century, the Muscovite government had extended its defence lines further and further to the south. Its agents founded and garrisoned new fortresses in strategic locations. As soon as these new forts provided a minimum of security, settlers began arriving to take advantage of the rich soil and other natural advantages of the area. Many of them were fugitive peasants from the central and north-western regions of the country.

The characteristics of southern society varied from north to south. In the areas close to Moscow which had long been settled, the social and economic structure resembled that of the centre itself. Around Riazan, for example, noble servitors of the tsar owned much of the cultivated land and some of their estates were of considerable size. Although historically military garrisons, the towns contained a sizeable population of artisans as well as soldiers of many types. Yet, even though, by the end of the sixteenth century, the older northerly section of the southern defence perimeter was similar, in many ways, to the central region of Muscovy, its people retained their combative frontier spirit.

The further one went into the steppe or 'Field', as contemporaries called it, the more clearly it became a military frontier zone. The only noble estates in the countryside were the small pomestes of military servitors. The population of the small towns consisted almost entirely of musketeers, artillerymen and other soldiers of the garrison with their families. Many of the people of the Field – including a number of the soldiers – had originally settled in the area to escape the control of the government or the landlords. They resented the monarchy's attempts to bring their new homeland under tighter control. A particular source of bitterness was the *desiatinnaia pashnia*, the system under which lesser military servitors had to farm certain areas for the government. The resulting crops went directly into the tsar's granaries from which it was most often shipped to newly founded military outposts whose garrisons had not begun to feed themselves.

The lower Volga presents an interesting variation on the southern theme. Muscovy acquired this rich territory when it conquered the khanate of Kazan. Thus the region already had a substantial population of Tatars and other nationalities, most of them Moslem, when Russian settlers began to move in. Rich soil and remoteness from the centres of authority made the area an attractive refuge for fugitives from other parts of Muscovy. In many respects, the Volga valley resembled the Field: all of the cities and towns were primarily strongholds for occupying Russian garrisons. At the same time, the region was beginning to take on some of the features of the centre. In the latter half of the sixteenth century, the Muscovite government granted a number of estates to Russian nobles and gave land and privileges to several Eastern Orthodox monasteries.

Beyond the southern frontiers of Muscovy lay the 'Wild Field'. This area of grassland with occasional patches of forest had no farming population. From the middle of the fifteenth century, it was the home of the Cossacks, the bands of Tatar and Slavic warriors who lived by fishing, herding, banditry, and military service to the neighbouring states. There was a large concentration of Cossacks in the valley of the Don, and smaller groups lived scattered across the steppe. The largest single Cossack community, the Zaporozhian Host, was located across the border in Lithuanian territory in the lower Dniepr valley. At the end of the sixteenth century, the Cossacks along Muscovy's frontiers remained fiercely independent of all outside authorities. They lived and fought in bands under the leadership of elected military commanders. Some of these small armies, like Ermak's, accepted service as special units of the Muscovite army, or hired themselves out to private individuals and families.[10]

To the surrounding states, the Cossacks presented the threat of continual unrest. Thus, as it extended its defence lines southward, the Muscovite government attempted to bring them under its control. Some of the fortresses founded at the very end of the sixteenth century served specifically as Moscow's watchtowers in the Cossack lands. For their part, the Cossacks treasured their untrammelled style of life and looked askance at all attempts to bring them under control. The fact that many of them were runaways from the centre of Muscovy served only to increase their suspiciousness.

Thus, at the turn of the sixteenth and seventeenth centuries, the Muscovite state showed clear symptoms of social and political dislocation. The old centres of population – the centre and, above all, Novgorod – were losing their primary economic resource, peasants. Whether they simply hid from the tax-collector or fled to the wild frontier, the fugitives played havoc with governmental administration and ruined the economic prospects for their landlords. The southern and eastern frontier areas presented a different problem. With abundant natural resources and rapidly growing populations they offered the promise of economic prosperity. At the same time, the people who settled these areas were notoriously difficult to govern. Many of them had fled from the demands of the royal fisc and their landlords and had no intention of submitting again without a struggle. Only the north remained a haven of prosperity, remote and peaceful, on the eve of the storm.

Such was the realm that Boris Godunov attempted to rule. As his first order of business, the new tsar strengthened his hand by attacking his enemies within the court. In particular, in 1600, he arrested his chief rivals, the Romanovs, accusing them of plotting to assassinate him. After questioning under torture, the government forced the head of the clan, Fedor Nikitich, to enter a monastery and sent his younger brothers into exile where they soon died.[11]

Once secure on the throne, Boris displayed the same political skill that he had shown as regent for Fedor. In foreign affairs, he worked hard to build good relations alike with Muscovy's traditional allies and enemies. In order to increase his prestige as ruler, he attempted to arrange a foreign marriage for his daughter. In 1602, the bridegroom designate, Prince Hans of Denmark, came to Moscow. The prince's Lutheran faith immediately posed serious problems and, to make matters far worse, he suddenly took ill and died.

His demise was the least of Russia's problems. At the beginning of the seventeenth century, Europe experienced a period of unusually cold weather. In Russia, where agriculture was especially vulnerable to slight changes of weather, the consequences were disastrous. A cold and rainy summer in 1601 stunted crops and early frost killed them. As though this were not enough, unseasonable frosts destroyed the crops in 1602 as well. The twin catastrophes reduced millions of Russian peasants to starvation. By the end of 1602, they had eaten up their grain including seed for future sowing. To buy food on the market was out of the question, since supplies were limited and prices very high. There was nothing left but to die quietly at home or take to the roads in a desperate search for relief.

Godunov's government took energetic measures to meet the emergency. Its agents distributed money from the treasury and sold grain from its storehouses. Such efforts could do little to stem the tide of misery, however, and may have caused considerable harm, since rumours of help drew thousands of homeless and starving people into Moscow where many died. Godunov's regime also took concrete legal steps to ease the hardships of the peasantry and lesser nobility. In 1601, as the crisis was beginning, a decree temporarily restored the peasants' freedom to leave their lords in the St George's Day period. This return to the conditions of old lasted only one year. At about the same time, other legislation forbade the managers of large estates – both ecclesiastical and lay – to lure away peasants from the estates of the lesser nobility.

These well-intentioned measures did little to stem the rising tide of social discontent. Fugitive peasants roamed the countryside and many former slaves joined their ranks. At the end of the sixteenth century, most slaves were household servants and retainers of the nobility. Many, dissatisfied with their lot, took advantage of deteriorating social conditions to escape bondage. In the years of famine, moreover, lords, who could no longer feed their slaves, cast them out to fend for themselves. These explosive materials burst into flame in 1603. Brushfires of rebellion surrounded Moscow. In a number of districts in the heart of the country, fugitive peasants and slaves rose in revolt under the leadership of an obscure bandit nicknamed Khlopka. Godunov's regime responded decisively. A regular army marched out against the rebels and routed them in a pitched battle near the capital. At about the same time, the government attempted to defuse social tensions by inviting homeless slaves to appear at the Bondage Chancery in Moscow to register their new status as free men. For the moment, the danger passed.[12]

A far greater menace loomed in the south. In August 1604, a man claiming to be Ivan IV's son, Dmitrii, invaded south-west Muscovy with a small army of Russian and Polish supporters. For months, the pretender had lived in the frontier region of Poland mobilizing support on both sides of the border. Among other things, he and his sponsors sent manifestos or 'seductive letters' into Muscovite territory. There the restless population of the southern frontier enthusiastically received the message that he was the true tsar. Even before the pretender crossed the border, armed bands of Cossacks and military servitors mobilized in his name. Godunov's government faced the gravest menace imaginable.

In order to meet the threat, Tsar Boris attempted to unmask the leader of the revolt. Beginning in 1603, his government issued pronouncements that the so-called Dmitrii was, in reality, Grishka Otrepev, a defrocked monk who had run away from the Chudov Monastery in Moscow. Some of Boris's contemporaries accepted his explanation while others, like the well-informed French mercenary, Jacques Margeret, firmly believed that Dmitrii was precisely who he claimed to be – the youngest son of Ivan IV, miraculously rescued from Boris's attempt to assassinate him.[13] Most recent Russian scholars of the problem agree with Godunov's claims and plausibly argue that Otrepev appeared on the scene as an agent of the Romanovs with whom he and his family had connections. He seems to have taken monastic vows at precisely the time when Godunov purged the Romanovs and his campaign for the throne may well have begun as one of their desperate attempts to regain power. If so, their intrigue ultimately achieved its objective, although probably not in the way that they planned.[14] At the same time, there are many inconsistencies and loose ends in all of the theories concerning 'Dmitrii's' origins. Moreover, as Philip Barbour pointed out in his biography, whoever 'Dmitrii' may have been, his conduct shows that he was no mere charlatan: he truly believed that he was Dmitrii Ivanovich, the rightful tsar.[15]

With the appearance of the False Dmitrii, the phenomenon of pretendership in Russia at once began and reached its zenith. None of the numerous later pretenders ever succeeded in seizing power. The reasons why pretendership became a prominent feature of the Russian political landscape are clear. The oppressed elements in Muscovite society needed to express their grievances and try to better their lot. At the same time, they had no ideology or alternative vision of the political and social order with which to legitimize their rejection of the government and society of their day. Like their social betters, they accepted hereditary monarchy as the only legitimate form of rule. Thus rebellion was morally defensible only in the name of a truly legitimate tsar who had been displaced by the usurper currently occupying the throne.

Pretendership was therefore likely to occur when two conditions coincided – when economic conditions were bad and social tensions high, and when one could reasonably question the ruling tsar's right to the throne. Boris Godunov's government faced both problems in a most dramatic form. Understandably, then, rumours that the Tsarevich Dmitrii was still alive began to circulate within two years of Godunov's coronation. The False Dmitrii appeared, as it were, by popular demand.

The men and women who followed him should not be seen as naïve. Some of those who believed in him – or professed to – were among the most worldly-wise and cynical people of the day. Moreover, the pretender, a man of noble origin and good breeding, played his role convincingly: many of his followers undoubtedly believed the truth of his claims. The later pretenders of the Time of Troubles were not nearly as plausible. Yet it would be a mistake to see their followers merely as misguided innocents. As Daniel Field has reminded us, peasant and Cossack rebels manipulated the prevailing ideology in order to improve their lot. Understandably, pretendership as a form of social protest lasted, in Russia, well into the nineteenth century![16]

Once the False Dmitrii crossed into Muscovy, his rebellion quickly gained momentum. The military servitors, Cossacks and peasants of the southern frontier enthusiastically rallied to his banner. While the pretender's army moved slowly north-eastward, town after town in the south declared its allegiance to him. For his part, Boris Godunov waited to discern the False Dmitrii's plans before sending his troops into the field. Once committed to the fray, regular Muscovite units easily defeated the rebel force and blocked its path to Moscow. At the same time, operating cautiously in hostile territory, Godunov's commanders missed their chance to take the pretender prisoner and crush his movement once and for all. The False Dmitrii escaped southward and shut himself up in the fortress of Putivl. Yet even while on the defensive, his movement continued to swell since the garrisons of still more towns recognized him as the rightful tsar.

On 13 April 1605, the situation changed completely: Boris Godunov suddenly died, leaving as his heir his sixteen-year-old son, Fedor. Resistance to the pretender's revolt quickly collapsed. Many of the men in the royal army, facing the rebels at Kromy, refused to swear allegiance to Fedor Godunov. Even more devastating, their most important generals – P. F. Basmanov and the Golitsyns – went over to the False Dmitrii with their troops. With that, the rebellion became a triumphal procession northward towards Moscow. As the pretender advanced at a leisurely pace, issuing manifestos to his subjects, he sent spokesmen ahead to win over the people of the capital. Their appearance in the city set off a *coup d'état* against the Godunovs. Conspirators, led by Vasilii Golitsyn, forcibly deposed Patriarch Job and murdered Fedor and his mother. After receiving the homage of Muscovites of all ranks on the outskirts of the capital, the False Dmitrii entered the city as a conquering hero.

His accession changed the fortunes of a number of leading noble clans. The Romanovs emerged from the obscurity to which Godunov had consigned them. The new regime promoted the leader of the family, Filaret – formerly Fedor Nikitich – a churchman against his will, to the influential position of metropolitan of Rostov. Moreover, the pretender gave the Nagois, his supposed kinsmen, prominent positions at his court. Ivan IV's widow, Maria Nagaia, now the nun Martha, accepted her 'son's' invitation to leave the convent and live near him. Whether they believed the pretender's claims or not, the Nagois had every reason to take advantage of his generosity. Other prominent courtiers did not fare so well. The Shuiskiis immediately fell into disfavour: their leader, Prince Vasilii, was condemned to death and received clemency at the place of execution. With some justification, historians have often castigated Vasilii Shuiskii as a grasping and unprincipled intriguer. At the same time, he was in a very difficult position. As head of the commission that investigated the death of the real Dmitrii, his testimony on the truth of the False Dmitrii's claims carried special authority. Twice, within a short period in 1605, he appeared before crowds of Muscovites to explain what had happened fourteen years earlier. On the first occasion, when Godunov's regime still seemed secure, he insisted that the real Dmitrii had died: when the pretender's victory was assured, however, he claimed the exact opposite – that Ivan IV's son had escaped death. It is a measure of the False Dmitrii's generosity of spirit – and naïvety – that, within months, he pardoned so dangerous a witness and allowed him to return to Moscow.

Despite his charm and magnanimity, the pretender quickly disillusioned many of his supporters. From the very beginning, there were signs of danger to come; for one thing, the False Dmitrii was no ordinary Muscovite. While in Poland, he had secretly become a Roman Catholic and, when he arrived in Moscow, his suite included a Polish bodyguard, his Protestant private secretary and Jesuit priests. Rumours about the new ruler's unconventional ways soon began to circulate: 'Dmitrii', it was claimed, did not attend the Divine Liturgy regularly, did not fast strictly, and behaved indecently with women. With time, the arrival of more and more Polish supporters and the False Dmitrii's increasingly obvious ties with the Church of Rome fed further fuel to Muscovite suspiciousness and resentment. The pretender's tactlessness reached its peak in his marriage to Marina Mniszech, daughter of one of the powerful magnates of Poland's eastern frontier who had given him shelter while he was in exile. The bride journeyed to Moscow with her father and a large retinue and, on 8 May 1606, was crowned tsaritsa and married 'Dmitrii' in Eastern Orthodox rites. Many features of the celebration offended Muscovite sensibilities: to mention only two, the bride and groom neglected to make their communion and, after the ceremony, their Polish followers strenuously celebrated their triumph for several days, all the while showing their contempt for the natives.

As bitterness grew, Vasilii Shuiskii and other boyars determined to take advantage of the situation. These aristocrats firmly believed that, on genealogical grounds, several of them had far better claims to the throne than the previous tsar, Boris Godunov, to say nothing of the pretender. The conspirators moved forces of their retainers into the city and, early on 17 May 1606, they struck. Aroused by the ringing of the alarm bell, the people of Moscow took to the streets. In the confusion, Shuiskii and his confederates broke into the Kremlin where they lynched the pretender and P. F. Basmanov, Godunov's former general who had become the False Dmitrii's most important Muscovite adviser and favourite. Having accomplished their objective, the chief conspirators began to act as leaders of a new government, going out into the city to restore order. Once aroused, however, popular fury could not be quelled quickly. For two days, mobs surged through Moscow lynching any Poles they could find. As many as 2,000 people may have perished at their hands.

Out of the bloody coup, Vasilii Shuiskii emerged as the new ruler. Two days after the False Dmitrii's assassination, a crowd of his supporters proclaimed him tsar. Seizing the throne was much easier than governing, however. First, it was necessary to exorcize the ghost of Dmitrii. Many Muscovites believed in the pretender and the confusing circumstances surrounding his death provided some grounds for believing that he was still alive. The frequent changes in Shuiskii's recent public testimony about Dmitrii's fate left the new ruler with little credibility. Therefore he had to take extraordinary measures to convince his subjects that Ivan IV's son had indeed died many years before. Shuiskii sent a commission to Uglich to dig up the boy's body and bring it to Moscow for reburial with full honours. The government duly reported that Dmitrii's remains had not decayed and had worked miraculous cures. Having marshalled such clear evidence of his sanctity, the new regime saw to it that Dmitrii was canonized. As for the pretender, Shuiskii's government issued formal proclamations explaining who he really was, how he had planned to hand Muscovy over to the Poles, and how he had been overthrown.

Second, Shuiskii's regime had trouble establishing its legitimacy, both dynastically and socially. In spite of his princely lineage, the new tsar was as vulnerable as Boris Godunov to charges that he had no right to the throne since, in the popular mind, only a member of the old dynasty could rightfully rule. Moreover, many of his subjects saw his government as the plaything of the aristocratic clans which dominated the royal court. The disgruntled and dispossessed of society had no hope that Shuiskii would redress their grievances. Even the new ruler's most conciliatory gestures seemed to be directed towards a very small élite. At the time of his accession, Shuiskii publicly promised his subjects not to execute or exile any of them without due process of law. In effect, he obligated himself not to use the arbitrary methods of Ivan IV or Godunov in dealing with his enemies within the aristocracy. Such reassuring statements, however, failed to unite even the great clans of the court around his throne. The Romanovs quickly fell out with him, for example, probably because he did not appoint Filaret to the vacant office of patriarch.

Finally, by 1606, social unrest had become endemic. Once mobilized behind the first False Dmitrii, the lesser nobles, minor military servitors, Cossacks and peasants of the southern frontier continued to resist the authority of the government in Moscow. Moreover, within the capital itself, the poorer inhabitants, now used to expressing their grievances, frequently took to the streets. Only the wealthiest nobles and the most prosperous and stable regions of the country – above all, the north – accepted the authority of Shuiskii's regime and did so, not so much because they had confidence in him, as because his government appeared the least of evils.

Thus, from the moment of his accession, Shuiskii faced endemic rebellion against his rule. The garrison towns of the south refused to recognize him as tsar and became the centres of a rapidly spreading revolt. In many ways, the new movement represented a direct continuation of the campaign to enthrone the first False Dmitrii. The same people and regions took the leading parts. Once again, moreover, the rebels united around the banner of Dmitrii, son of Ivan IV. Rumours that the first pretender had escaped death during Shuiskii's *coup d'état* circulated widely, giving hope to his former followers. This time, however, no pretender appeared to impersonate Dmitrii. Instead, commanders of the most varied origins – first, Prince Grigorii Shakhovskoi, the royal administration's governor in Putivl, then Ivan Bolotnikov, a former slave – led the revolt.

By all accounts, Bolotnikov was a remarkable leader. As a youth, he had run away from servitude in an aristocratic household to join the Cossacks. After some years as a free warrior, he was taken prisoner and became a galley slave in the Ottoman navy. Freed during a battle at sea, he appeared in the eastern marches of Poland just as the new rebellion began. The toughness and resourcefulness that years of adventure and suffering had honed made Bolotnikov the ideal leader of such a movement. As soon as he assumed command, the rebels became a powerful force.

With Bolotnikov at their head, the rebels marched northward towards Moscow. Once again, the royal army, mustered at Kromy, melted away before them. Moreover, the momentum of their success brought more and more recruits into their ranks. The minor nobles and other servitors of the regions through which they passed joined them. Indeed, whole private armies – a large contingent of nobles from Riazan under the leadership of Prokopii Liapunov and Istoma Pashkov's heterogeneous force – lent their support. As the movement swelled, Shuiskii's government experienced understandable panic. Fortunately, at the last minute, the tsar had the good sense to appoint his gifted nephew, Prince M. V. Skopin-Shuiskii, commander of his forces. Although unable to stop the rebels' advance, Skopin at least succeeded in bringing order into the government's defences and preventing the fall of Moscow itself. In mid-October 1606, the Bolotnikov revolt had reached its zenith. From their headquarters in the nearby royal summer residence of Kolomenskoe, its leaders held the capital under siege.

Just when the rebels neared complete victory, the social divisions within their ranks took their toll. Bolotnikov's followers were a remarkably motley lot – nobles, soldiers, Cossacks and fugitive slaves and serfs. Indeed, even though the revolt is often labelled a 'peasant uprising', peasants contributed comparatively little to the movement. If anything, Bolotnikov's supporters consisted primarily of disgruntled royal servitors and the rootless and dispossessed of Muscovite society.[17]

All that united such disparate individuals and groups was hostility towards Shuiskii's government. As far as their social attitudes and goals were concerned, they had nothing at all in common. A number of the noblemen who joined the movement – Shakhovskoi and the Riazan contingent, for example – were well-off and conservative men who had their own scores to settle with the new government. Many of their fellow rebels, however, wanted to turn the world upside-down. Bolotnikov's manifestos to the people of Moscow apparently reflected their views. If we can believe the accusations of Shuiskii's government, the rebel proclamations urged slaves to murder their masters and take their wives and lands while the poor were to kill the merchants and expropriate their goods. While these appeals seem to have struck a chord among the poorer people of Moscow, they frightened Bolotnikov's more conservative supporters.

Thus, on the eve of victory, the rebels' forces began to disintegrate. In November, Liapunov led the Riazan nobles over to the government's side and, soon after, Pashkov's warriors followed suit. Buoyed by these desertions, Skopin-Shuiskii beat back rebel attempts to close off Moscow from the north. Then, in December, the government's army moved directly against Bolotnikov's headquarters. Skopin won a smashing victory just outside the capital and drove the remnants of the shattered rebel forces southward. Moscow was saved.

Although now on the defensive, the rebels remained a threat. Bolotnikov's men barricaded themselves in Kaluga and fought off government forces with desperate courage and considerable ingenuity. On one occasion, for example, the defenders destroyed a wooden tower with which the besiegers hoped to set the town on fire by tunnelling under it from within the fortress and blowing it up. Bravery was not enough to hold off superior government forces indefinitely, however.

Just when the defenders of Kaluga became desperate, Bolotnikov received help from an unexpected quarter. The Cossack communities threw up another pretender, this one calling himself the Tsarevich Peter, son of the late Tsar Fedor. The fact that no such prince had ever existed in no way inhibited the imposter or the warriors who quickly gathered around him. 'Peter' and his band moved across the southern borderlands, looting and murdering nobles and officials as they went. Hearing of his campaign, Prince Shakhovskoi, still Bolotnikov's ally, convinced the new pretender to join their cause. The two gathered a large force and moved their headquarters to Tula, from which they launched a series of expeditions to rescue Bolotnikov from the encircling government forces. In May 1607, a rebel army, commanded by another aggrieved aristocrat, Prince Andrei Teliatevskii, defeated the tsar's army and raised the siege of Kaluga. Bolotnikov and his men joined their compatriots in Tula.

Victory gave the rebels only a momentary reprieve. Under Skopin-Shuiskii's command, the government's troops continued their unrelenting advance southward. In bitter fighting, they drove Bolotnikov's forces back inside Tula and laid siege to the fortress. This time there was no escape. Rumours – correct as it turned out – that a new False Dmitrii had appeared on Polish territory only increased the tsar's determination to destroy Bolotnikov's forces quickly and completely. In October 1607, the defenders of Tula surrendered. The victors took the leaders of the rebellion – the False Peter, Bolotnikov, Shakhovskoi and the others – back to Moscow.

In dealing with the captured rebels, the government showed its acute awareness of social hierarchy. The pretender was publicly hanged. With the others, the government proceeded more circumspectly: its agents killed

Bolotnikov on his way to exile. The rebel aristocrats suffered nothing worse than exile from the court. In dealing with the rank-and-file rebels, however, Shuiskii's government showed no such delicacy: many were executed and others handed over to nobles as slaves. In addition, the royal army conducted punitive expeditions in the southern districts which had supported the revolt. The tsar's triumph seemed complete.

During Shuiskii's victorious campaign against the rebels, his government attacked social disorder on the legal plane as well. Decrees of March 1607 further regulated the relations between peasants and slaves and their lords. Explicitly reversing Boris Godunov's policies, Shuiskii's regime rescinded the peasants' right to leave the landlords' estates on which they were registered. Landlords had the right to find and repatriate any peasants who had fled, in defiance of the law, in the previous fifteen years, that is, since the compilation of the cadastres of 1592–93. Any landlord who received fugitive peasants had to pay damages to their legal owner and a fine to the government. Moreover, the legislation made local officials responsible for checking the identity of newcomers to their district: any fugitive peasants whom they discovered were to be returned to their lords. As for slaves, their owners were to register them formally with the government from the very first day of their servitude.[18]

The primary intent of Shuiskii's social legislation seems clear enough – to restore social order. Another of its objectives was to improve the government's record-keeping. At a time when society was drifting into chaos, Shuiskii's administration was trying desperately just to keep track of his subjects. The social implications of the decrees of 1607 were strictly conservative: Shuiskii's government clearly attempted to meet the needs of the landlords at the expense of the peasants. What the legislation meant in practice is another matter. At the best of times, Shuiskii's effective authority extended only to the more stable and conservative parts of Muscovy. The regions to which fugitive peasants and slaves fled were never under his control. At worst, he ruled little more than the capital itself. Thus his legislation on peasants and slaves had virtually no impact on society.[19]

Throughout his short reign, Vasilii Shuiskii's fortunes swung, like a pendulum, between triumph and defeat. A new crisis quickly followed each apparent victory. Even before the royal army captured Tula, a new pretender had appeared in eastern Poland. The second False Dmitrii is a far more shadowy figure than his predecessor. Apparently by origin a Muscovite, he quickly attracted the support of Polish noble adventurers eager to avenge their compatriots slain in the massacre that followed the overthrow of the first pretender. Once his forces had crossed into Muscovite territory, the new 'Dmitrii' attracted the support of the elements in society, particularly the Cossacks, who had joined the previous uprisings. The Cossack chief, Zarutskii, and the Polish adventurer, Lisowski, agreed to contribute their private armies to the cause. Early in 1608, after several months of mobilizing, the pretender's forces moved northward along the familiar routes towards the capital. In the face of the new threat, Shuiskii's government displayed remarkable passivity and, when columns of rebels converged on Moscow from several directions, the royal army could do little to stop them. After failing to storm the city, the pretender and his advisers set up shop in Tushino, a village only a few kilometres north of the Kremlin.

Muscovy now had two governments, both of doubtful legitimacy. The False Dmitrii's forces fanned out across northern and central Russia, taking control of much of the realm in his name. At the same time, the Shuiskii regime managed to maintain the support of the volatile Riazan nobility and kept the road between that region and the capital open.

Under the circumstances, Muscovites of all social ranks faced difficult choices. Which government should they obey? Casting moral scruples aside, many carefully calculated where their best advantage lay. In contemporaries' words, a number of prominent nobles became 'migratory birds', flitting back and forth between Moscow and Tushino. The competing regimes vied for their support with land grants and other rewards. Most prominent of the migrants was Filaret Romanov, then metropolitan of Rostov. Probably not by accident, this ambitious enemy of the Shuiskiis fell into the pretender's hands. The False Dmitrii accorded him great honour and promoted him to the office of patriarch.

As the pretender consolidated his position, Shuiskii cast about desperately for support. For one thing, he called on the commanders of the border fortresses to send him reinforcements. He turned as well to the country's traditional enemies, Poland and Sweden. In 1608, he made a treaty with Sigismund III, obliging the king to withdraw his subjects from the pretender's forces. The agreement was worth less than the parchment on which it was written. Negotiations with Sweden were much more fruitful. The new king, Charles IX, was eager to counter the influence of his nephew, Sigismund, and had, for some time, held out to Shuiskii an offer of his services. Accordingly, Skopin-Shuiskii, the tsar's nephew, proceeded to Novgorod to arrange for Swedish troops to join the royal army.

The heavy-handedness of the Tushino government provided Shuiskii with unexpected allies. In order to finance his court and reward his supporters, the pretender turned to the one remaining peaceful and prosperous region of Muscovy – the north. His agents began to collect heavy taxes there and interfere in the operation of institutions of local government. An explosion of resistance ensued. At first unwilling to commit themselves to either camp, the leading citizens of the north came to the conclusion that, for all his faults, Shuiskii represented the lesser evil. With Vologda as their headquarters, they organized militia bands in the upper Volga and Dvina valleys and the regions between. Fighting at first against heavy odds, the northern guerrillas gradually won the upper hand and, by early 1609, expelled the Tushino forces from their land.

The defeat of their adversary emboldened Shuiskii's forces. With a revitalized Russian army and Swedish troops, Skopin advanced from Novgorod towards Moscow. Once he reached the Volga, the northern militia and reinforcements from other parts of the realm joined him. Having achieved overwhelming superiority in the field, Skopin systematically beat back the pretender's forces until, in the face of overwhelming odds and increasing dissension among his followers, the False Dmitrii abandoned his Tushino headquarters and withdrew southward.

Once again, Shuiskii saved his throne. This time, however, he paid an exorbitant price – direct foreign intervention in Muscovy's affairs. The presence of Swedish troops in Skopin's army gave King Sigismund a pretext for action. Late in 1609, the Polish army invaded Muscovite territory and advanced on Smolensk. From there, the king sent appeals to his subjects in Tushino to come and fight under the royal banner. For the most part, the pretender's Polish supporters refused to obey the summons. Oddly enough, Sigismund had better luck with the powerful Muscovite nobles who served in Tushino, particularly the Romanovs and their kinsmen. As the False Dmitrii's fortunes waned, these 'migratory birds' who had finally alighted on the losing side could not make their peace with Shuiskii. Instead, in February 1610, they made a treaty with the king agreeing to accept his son, Wladyslaw, as tsar on condition that he convert to Eastern Orthodoxy and respect Muscovite political traditions and the leading families of the realm.

For the moment, however, Shuiskii's position appeared secure. Even Filaret, the architect of the Polish candidacy for the throne, fell into his hands. Then disaster struck. In April 1610, the regime's one effective and popular leader, Skopin-Shuiskii, suddenly died in the prime of life. Cynical after decades of almost uninterrupted misfortune, many contemporaries jumped to the conclusion that jealous relatives had poisoned him. Whatever their truth, the rumours had devastating consequences. The Riazan nobles, headstrong as ever, deserted Shuiskii en masse. As the royal army disintegrated, the government's enemies reasserted themselves. Polish troops under Hetman Zolkiewski marched towards Moscow and the False Dmitrii came out of hibernation. When Shuiskii's army advanced to meet the Poles, Zolkiewski soundly defeated it at Klushino. Tsar Vasilii's days were numbered.

The end came quickly. As the second False Dmitrii approached Moscow, Shuiskii's enemies within the city went into action. Two distinct groups of conspirators – the Liapunovs, leaders of the Riazan nobles, and the Romanovs and their kin – exploited popular agitation. On 17 July 1610, under their leadership, a crowd of Muscovites demanded Shuiskii's abdication, seized the Kremlin and arrested him. To prevent his return to power, the deposed tsar was quickly tonsured a monk. Canonical regulations accomplished what earlier rulers could not: at last, Shuiskii, the quintessential survivor, disappeared from the political scene.

With his fall, the disintegration of the Muscovite state and society reached its culmination. No tsar sat on the throne and, even within the ranks of the court aristocracy, there was no agreement on a candidate to fill the void. The central administration had no control over most areas of the country. Individually, Muscovites of all ranks fought desperately for survival. The most powerful aristocrats sought security and political advantage wherever they could, while thousands of former peasants and slaves roamed the countryside living from hand to mouth and, in many instances, preying upon their more fortunate fellow citizens. And, to complete the picture, Swedish troops threatened Novgorod and the forces of Sigismund III, advancing from besieged Smolensk, approached Moscow itself.

In these difficult circumstances, the people of Muscovy clung desperately to their conventional beliefs and ideals. In practical terms, Muscovy in 1610 seemed to be a reformer's or revolutionary's dream. The tsars' government had collapsed and social bonds had come unravelled: Cossacks, peasants and townspeople gave vent to their rage against the established order and its leaders. Yet, deeply entrenched habits of thought could not be broken. The polemical tracts and political demands of the period reveal no new visions of a just society and no plans for the reform or renewal of the state. In the sources of the time, for example, we find no sign that the nobles aspired to win corporate rights and decisive political power on the Polish model. Of republican thinking, there is, of course, not a trace. Instead, for noble and peasant alike, monarchy, as it had existed under Ivan III or Ivan IV, remained the only form of government imaginable. The problem was to find the right tsar, for each group in society yearned for a monarch who would restore order and rule justly.[20] Order and justice, however, meant very different things to aristocrats, peasants and Cossacks.

Even in its hour of greatest need, Muscovite society had untapped resources. The very process of disintegration produced new leaders and unleashed new social forces. First, the military servitors and Cossacks of the south and, later, the people of the north learned to fend for themselves. Moreover, although they differed on many issues, the leaders of provincial society shared much – bitter antipathy towards the foreign invaders of their country and a fierce loyalty to Eastern Orthodoxy. Whether pious or not, most Muscovites wanted no truck with Roman Catholicism. And, as elsewhere in seventeenth-century Europe, confessional allegiance, more than any other, shaped men's choices.

After the overthrow of Vasilii Shuiskii, a group of seven boyars assumed the leadership of the government. With Hetman Zolkiewski approaching Moscow from the west and the second False Dmitrii advancing from the south, its members looked for a way out of their dangerous predicament. The aristocrats who had served the pretender in Tushino had already tried one solution – offering the throne to Prince Wladyslaw of Poland. Now, in mid-1610, the boyar government returned to this scheme as the best of several undesirable alternatives. While the thought of a foreign and Roman Catholic tsar had little appeal, Wladyslaw's candidacy at least offered the prospect of Polish military aid in restoring order within Muscovy. Certainly the other obvious possibilities seemed even less desirable. Shuiskii's reign had demonstrated the dangers of elevating a native aristocrat to the throne. To the conservative men in the Kremlin, the False Dmitrii represented the forces of rebellion and disorder and indeed, by this time, his following consisted almost entirely of Cossacks and foreign adventurers.

Thus, with the approval of a hastily convened zemskii sobor, the boyars decided to offer Wladyslaw the crown. They admitted Zolkiewski and his troops to the city and began to negotiate the conditions under which the prince would take the throne. Zolkiewski gave the Muscovite leaders precisely what they wanted. He agreed that Wladyslaw would convert to Eastern Orthodoxy and respect traditional Muscovite institutions and social arrangements. Moreover, the Hetman used his army to prevent rebellion within Moscow and drive the pretender's forces away from the capital. All the same, Zolkiewski was neither altruistic nor a fool. He carefully guarded Poland's interests, making sure that, as the king's representative, he had the decisive voice in Muscovite affairs. When the boyars sent a delegation to Smolensk to complete the negotiations for Wladyslaw's accession, the Hetman saw to it that it included the most powerful political figures in Moscow – Filaret Romanov and Vasilii Golitsyn – and even the deposed tsar, Vasilii Shuiskii.

The boyars' hopes for Prince Wladyslaw quickly proved illusory. The royal father, Sigismund III, was the main stumbling-block. Apparently the king had no intention of letting his son become tsar. Instead, he wanted to rule Muscovy himself and use his power to bring her into the Roman Catholic fold. His attitude destroyed any hope of an agreement. Realizing the foolishness of Sigismund's policy, Zolkiewski left Moscow. In his place, the king appointed Alexander Gosiewski who, with the help of Russian renegades, began to rule Moscow as a military dictator. At that point, the members of the 'great embassy' found themselves in a completely untenable position. They had come to the king's camp to arrange Wladyslaw's accession, not Sigismund's, and quite legitimately refused to submit to the latter's demands. When negotiations collapsed, the king arrested them and sent them off to Poland where they were to remain prisoners for years.

At this moment of confusion, Muscovite society found a leader in an unexpected quarter. Patriarch Hermogen outspokenly urged his flock not to accept a Roman Catholic as their ruler. A man of limited gifts and vision, Hermogen had, until this time, shown no inclination to take the initiative in political matters. Sigismund's pretensions to the throne, however, convinced him that the fate of Russian Orthodoxy and the Muscovite tsardom was at stake. Once he began to speak out late in 1610, his pronouncements became the rallying cry of opposition to the king and the Polish presence in Moscow.

Hermogen's message struck a responsive chord in the hearts of many Muscovites of the most varied social origins and political affiliations. Moreover, the civil war between competing native factions temporarily ended when the second False Dmitrii was murdered and his forces melted away. Muscovites could now unite against the Polish occupation.

Early in 1611, the leaders of provincial society responded to the patriarch's appeals for action. First to answer the call were the Riazan nobles under Prokopii Liapunov. Long accustomed to taking political and military initiative, the Riazanians provided the core of the national force. The people of Nizhnii Novgorod and other provincial cities quickly followed suit. In order to build up a powerful army, Liapunov systematically recruited the Cossack detachments and private armies which had served the various pretenders of the past. In particular, the well-known warlords, Hetman Zarutskii and Prince Dmitrii Trubetskoi, agreed to join the cause.

Soon Liapunov's motley troops advanced on Moscow. The Polish garrison took measures to defend its position. Gosiewski arrested Patriarch Hermogen who later died in confinement, a martyr for the faith and the national cause. Moreover, he and his men strengthened Moscow's fortifications. The Polish administration controlled a sullen and ruined city, however: its soldiers had to beat down a popular rebellion and, in doing so, touched off a disastrous fire.

By the beginning of the summer of 1611, the national movement stood on the verge of victory. Its men occupied the charred outskirts of Moscow besieging the Polish garrison trapped in the inner fortifications. Moreover, Liapunov and his colleagues acted as leaders of a national government. Speaking in the name of 'the whole land', they began to administer the regions under their control.

Before long, however, social tensions destroyed the movement's fragile unity. Like Bolotnikov's levies before them, Liapunov's forces were made up of disparate elements united only by common hatred of the enemy. Other than that, the provincial nobles and townsmen in their ranks had nothing in common with their Cossack comrades in arms. At first, Liapunov was inclined to make his peace with the rebellious elements of society, promising freedom to all Cossacks and fugitives who joined the cause. As a consequence, Cossacks and runaway serfs and slaves streamed into his camp. As tensions between the more conservative and more radical of his followers mounted, however, Liapunov decided that he must, at all costs, bring order to his movement. At the end of June 1611, he called an assembly which set up a temporary government and established norms for society.

The resulting agreement reflected the values of the national movement's more conservative leaders. Under its terms, sovereignty resided in the council of the army and its commanders exercised day-to-day leadership. Some of their policies pointed to a significant change in the economic and social balance of forces within the Muscovite nobility. The agreement stipulated, for example, that the estates of boyars who had sided with the Polish occupation be confiscated and distributed to needy members of the provincial nobility in the national force, particularly refugees from the western frontier districts ruined by the Polish invasion.[21] In other respects, the 'constitution' meant a return to the established practices of the Muscovite state. The movement's leaders took steps to re-establish the central bureaucratic chanceries. Moreover, they made a sharp distinction between long-established Cossacks and the fugitive peasants and slaves who had recently joined their ranks. The former could maintain their special status and choose to receive either a small service estate or a salary as a reward for serving the national cause. Fugitive peasants and slaves, however, were to be returned to their lords.

The attempt to discipline the Cossacks and take away their liberties provoked a swift and violent reaction. On 22 July 1611, Cossacks murdered

Liapunov. With that, the noble contingents in the national force melted away. Only the Cossacks remained in the field and they had no programme except to maintain their freedom and live off the land. Hetman Zarutskii had even found a new pretender, the so-called 'Baby Brigand', the infant son of Marina Mniszek and her most recent consort, the second False Dmitrii. The first attempt to restore Muscovy's fortunes had come to a sad end.

The news from other fronts was equally disastrous. After a long siege, Smolensk finally fell to Sigismund III's troops on 3 June. Then, on 16 July, the Swedish army captured Novgorod.

All was not lost, however. Enmity towards the Poles and devotion to Orthodoxy remained intense. Moreover, the social and regional forces that had supported the first national movement were still intact, waiting to be mustered. The surviving participants of the first attempt now had the wisdom born of bitter experience. They would not make the same mistakes again.

Even though in confinement in occupied Moscow, Patriarch Hermogen again provided the spark that set other men on fire. In a smuggled message, he urged the people of Nizhnii-Novgorod to turn their backs on the Cossacks and their new pretender and work for the revival of the nation. In a mood of repentance and expectation, his flock quickly responded.

Out of Muscovy's desperate situation emerged dynamic new leaders. In Nizhnii-Novgorod, Kuzma Minin, a local trader, began to organize a new national movement. An impassioned orator and efficient organizer, Minin convinced his fellow citizens to raise money for an army 'for the cleansing of the Muscovite state'. As commander of the force, he chose Prince Dmitrii Pozharskii who lived on his nearby estate, recuperating from wounds suffered while serving under Liapunov in the first national force. Minin and Pozharskii soon gathered a detachment of noble cavalrymen composed primarily of refugees from the districts around Smolensk.

The national movement gathered strength like an avalanche. By the beginning of 1612, all of the major towns in the Volga valley had joined the cause. Nobles from Riazan and other districts – and even some Cossack detachments – flocked to Pozharskii's banner.

The more prosperous and conservative members of society – nobles, ranging from aristocrats to provincial servitors, and merchants and traders – set the tone for the new movement. They had two goals, to free the country from the Poles and to restore social order. The latter objective made them irreconcilable enemies of the Cossack bands, particularly those now operating in the name of the 'Baby Brigand'. The political programme of the leaders of the coalition was equally conventional. Rejecting both Sigismund III and the latest pretender, they wanted to choose a new tsar, who would preside over a restored tsardom. In the meantime, they themselves would act as the nation's leaders.

Minin and Pozharskii proceeded very cautiously. They were well aware that, if their movement was not well organized, it could easily disintegrate as had its predecessor. At the same time, they were prepared to take decisive action when the need arose. Seeing the national movement as the chief threat to his fortunes, Hetman Zarutskii marched from his headquarters outside Moscow northward towards Iaroslavl, the pivotal city that commanded the upper Volga valley and connected it with the far north. His action provoked a determined response: Pozharskii quickly moved up the Volga and beat back Zarutskii's advancing forces.

Thus Iaroslavl became the new headquarters of the movement and the seat of a provisional government. Pozharskii and the council of leaders of the national movement began to build a bureaucratic administration along traditional lines. Moreover, they worked to reconstruct the social and political hierarchy of sixteenth-century Muscovy. They welcomed any representatives of the great aristocratic clans of the court who were willing to join their ranks. In addition, they brought together as much of the ecclesiastical hierarchy as they could and summoned representatives from the towns of the realm to form a kind of zemskii sobor.

While they built their political base, Pozharskii and his colleagues strengthened their military position. Their troops cleared the north of Cossacks. In addition, they bought the neutrality of the Swedish army in Novgorod with a promise to promote the candidacy of Prince Karl Philipp, brother of King Gustavus II Adolphus, as tsar. In practice, their commitment meant next to nothing, however, since the Swedish prince was most unlikely to convert to Eastern Orthodoxy or take up residence in Novgorod, two essential conditions of the agreement.[22] Before the leaders of the national movement could arrange the election of a new tsar, however, circumstances forced their hand. A Polish army under Hetman Chodkiewicz marched eastward to relieve their countrymen trapped in Moscow. Pozharskii quickly advanced to intercept them before they reached the capital.

The arrival of the national forces before Moscow raised a perennial problem once again. How were the leaders of the conservative elements in society to deal with the Cossacks? In one sense, the Cossacks were giving yeoman service to the cause of national revival by besieging the Polish garrison of the city. At the same time, as Liapunov's bitter experience had shown, they could not be trusted because they had a vested interest in maintaining the prevailing condition of anarchy. The Cossacks were just as uncertain how to deal with the leaders of the national movement. Pozharskii's advance on Moscow threw them into confusion. Some joined the national army: in October 1612, their leader, Prince Trubetskoi, made a formal alliance with Minin and Pozharskii. The latter made sure, however, that the conservative elements in the national movement dominated the coalition. Other Cossacks, led by Hetman Zarutskii, rejected any compromise and retreated to the south.

Alliance with the Cossacks brought the desired results in the field. The strengthened national forces drove off Chodkiewicz's advancing army. The position of the Polish garrison of Moscow was now hopeless. Overcoming bitter resistance, Pozharskii's men captured most of central Moscow on 22 October 1612. Four days later, the defenders of the Kremlin surrendered. At last Muscovy's capital was again in Russian hands.

From past experience, the leaders of the national revival knew that military victory meant nothing without a political solution. Only an effective government of unquestionable legitimacy could restore a shattered society. Clearly, a first step in achieving that goal was the election of a new tsar. The search for a ruler was a matter of the greatest urgency, for, if the new monarch were not chosen quickly, the national forces might well fall apart in suicidal internecine strife.

Soon after the capture of Moscow, Minin, Pozharskii and Trubetskoi wrote to the districts of the realm, urging them to select representatives to choose a tsar. The nation responded enthusiastically. In January 1613, delegates to the zemskii sobor began arriving from all corners of Muscovy. They represented all major groups of free men – nobles, clergymen, townspeople and peasants. Precisely how many of them there were is not clear: the protocols of the assembly record 277 names and as many as 500 men may have taken part.

The delegates' task was as complicated as it was important. In the preceding years, factions of Muscovites had offered the crown to two foreign princes. In spite of the bitter after-taste left by the candidacies of Wladyslaw and Karl Philipp, however, a few prominent leaders could still see the advantages of recruiting a ruler from abroad. Choosing a foreigner as tsar would at least avoid enthroning one native aristocratic clan at the expense of its rivals. Most influential Muscovites apparently did not share this sentiment. The latest pretender, the 'Baby Brigand', attracted even less support.

After reaching a consensus that the new tsar should be a native Muscovite, the zemskii sobor faced a difficult decision. Whom were they to choose? First of all, the heads of three of the most powerful aristocratic clans – the Romanovs, Golitsyns and Shuiskiis – were absent from the scene, prisoners in Poland. Second, a number of prominent courtiers had fallen into general disfavour by collaborating too long with the Polish occupation. Finally, many people did not regard Pozharskii and Trubetskoi, the noble leaders of the provisional government, as suitable candidates for the throne because their families were not distinguished enough. Under these circumstances, the process of selecting a tsar consumed several weeks of discussion, negotiation and intrigue.[23]

Ultimately, on 7 February 1613, the assembly chose Michael, the teenage son of Filaret Romanov. Then, exactly two weeks later, another session, attended by a number of leading aristocrats who had been called back to the capital for this purpose, confirmed the choice. On the surface, Michael, an inexperienced young man of limited gifts, appeared to have little claim to the throne. From beginning to end of the selection process, the Cossacks, now the main component of the Moscow garrison, championed him.[24] They were favourably disposed to the Romanovs because of Filaret's service in the court of the second False Dmitrii in Tushino and perhaps, as well, because of the family's suspected connections with the first pretender. In addition, the Romanovs' family ties with the former ruling dynasty carried weight with all factions, for, thanks to the marriage of Ivan IV and Anastasia Romanova, Filaret was the first cousin of Tsar Fedor, the last indisputably legitimate ruler of Muscovy. Moreover, Michael's very youth and insignificance stood him in good stead: as an individual he threatened no one.

Even after Michael's election, the leaders of the provisional government could not relax. Until the new monarch was crowned, he was not really tsar. Arranging the coronation, however, proved to be a delicate undertaking. At the beginning of 1613, Michael lived in Kostroma under the protection of his mother, a nun in a local convent. After years of suffering, Sister Martha was reluctant to let her son leave her and journey across a ruined country to an uncertain fate. For their part, the leaders of the government in Moscow could tolerate no delay for fear that their uneasy coalition might yet break apart. At last, in response to repeated entreaties, Michael came to the capital and was crowned tsar on 21 July 1613. Muscovy's time of tribulation had ended at last.

The conservative forces in society, the nobles and townspeople, had found in themselves the strength to defeat the invading foreigners and restore the monarchy. In the process, they triumphed as well over the Cossacks and the fugitives and dispossessed who followed them. In geographical and social terms, the more stable regions of the realm – the north, the centre, and the Volga valley – won out over the restless southern frontier.

Thus the rule of the Romanovs began on a cautious, conservative note. The new regime faced a sea of problems, not least the immediate consequences of recent struggles. The first item of business was the restoration of law and order. As Michael's government rebuilt its army, its commanders concentrated on destroying the Cossack bands which still plagued the central regions of the country. With the pretender in tow, Zarutskii and his men retreated southward until they were finally trapped and destroyed at Astrakhan in 1614. Dealing with international complications came next. The Peace of Stolbovo ended Swedish intervention in 1617 and, in the following year, the Truce of Deulino gave Muscovy and Poland a respite from conflict. Under the terms of the latter agreement, however, the Poles retained Smolensk and refused to accept the legitimacy of the new government in Moscow: it was a clear warning of warfare to come. By the time that Filaret Romanov returned to Moscow from captivity, under the terms of the truce, his son's government had firm control of a country on the road to recovery.

Patterns of thought and behaviour, forged in the preceding centuries, and the struggles and sacrifices of its people had saved Muscovy. Nevertheless, the new government of the Romanovs faced an imposing challenge – to reassemble the resources of society which had been dissipated during the recent Troubles. Its leaders worked hard – and with remarkable success – to rebuild the central bureaucratic administration, muster the army and bring order and stability to society. Soon, the traces of recent unrest disappeared from the surface of national life. Muscovites of all classes, however, retained potent memories of the Time of Troubles and drew their own, often conflicting, conclusions from recent experiences. Muscovy would never be quite the same again.

REFERENCES AND NOTES

1. In English, Platonov, *Time of Troubles*.
2. Skrynnikov, *Rossiia nakanune 'smutnogo vremeni'*, *Sotsialno-politicheskaia borba* and *Minin i Pozharskii*.
3. Unless otherwise noted, the discussion of Fedor's reign is based on Platonov, *Ocherki* and Skrynnikov, *Rossiia nakanune 'smutnogo vremeni'*.
4. Attman, *Struggle*, pp. 119–23.
5. Ibid., pp. 140–5.
6. Skrynnikov, *Sibirskaia ekspeditsiia*; Longworth, *Cossacks*, pp. 47–65. For a lavishly illustrated English edition of many of the sources on the campaign, see *Yermak's Campaign*.
7. See Skrynnikov, *Rossiia nakanune 'smutnogo vremeni'*, Ch. 7; Vernadsky, 'Death'.
8. Skrynnikov, 'Boris Godunov's struggle'.
9. Platonov, *Ocherki*, pp. 1–114.
10. Stökl, *Entstehung*; Longworth, *Cossacks*, pp. 11–46.
11. Skrynnikov, *Boris Godunov*, pp. 131–6.
12. Koretskii, *Formirovanie*, pp. 222–35.
13. Margeret, *Russian Empire*.
14. Platonov, *Time of Troubles*, pp. 64–9; Skrynnikov, *Boris Godunov*, pp. 155–75.
15. See Barbour, *Dimitry*.
16. Chistov, *Russkie legendy*, pp. 24–66; Longworth, 'Pretender phenomenon'; Field, *Rebels*.
17. See Avrich, *Russian Rebels*, pp. 17–47.
18. *Muscovite Society*, pp. 137–41.
19. Koretskii, *Formirovanie*, pp. 312–33; Hellie, *Enserfment*, pp. 108–9.
20. See Rowland, 'Muscovite political attitudes'.
21. Skrynnikov, *Minin i Pozharskii*, pp. 206–7.
22. Ibid., pp. 250–5.
23. Ibid, pp. 307–13.
24. Both Platonov, *Time of Troubles*, pp. 159–62 and Skrynnikov, *Minin i Pozharskii*, pp. 309–13 stress this point.

Looking ahead: the seventeenth century

The legacy of the Time of Troubles was complex and ambiguous. In many ways, Muscovite society recovered quickly from the crisis. By the end of the 1620s, the population of the central core of the country had returned to the level of the last normal years of the sixteenth century – hardly the most prosperous of times – and continued to grow steadily for the rest of the century.[1]

The established forms of political and social order were restored just as quickly. After the national movement resurrected the autocracy in 1613, its leaders worked quickly to rebuild the foundations of its power, the army and the administrative chanceries, and used them to renew the flow of revenue into its treasury and men into its service. The new regime also dealt directly with the tangled legacy of the Troubles. Sorting out contradictory grants made by successive governments during the Time of Troubles, its officials systematically settled claims to disputed estates. Its criteria for awarding land to particular claimants make its social philosophy clear: the government accepted as authentic the charters of the conservative regimes of Boris Godunov and Vasilii Shuiskii while rejecting those of the various pretenders. In the same spirit, the government returned many fugitive peasants to their lawful lords.

In other respects, the memories of the Troubles remained vivid for generations. Even though the new government of the Romanovs succeeded in establishing its authority, rumours casting doubt on its legitimacy periodically came to the surface and new pretenders popped up from time to time. Moreover, social unrest remained a central fact of Muscovite life. Through most of the seventeenth century, the government's control over the Cossacks and other inhabitants of the southern frontier regions was tenuous at best. In addition, in all parts of the country, there remained significant numbers of 'free, wandering people' who fitted none of the respectable, established niches of society – noble, townsman, peasant or churchman.

In his imaginative study of the origins of the church schism of the seventeenth century, Pierre Pascal has described the psychological scars left by the Troubles. Judging by the books they read and the polemics they conducted, articulate seventeenth-century Muscovites were nervous and frightened. The one authentically Eastern Orthodox tsardom had nearly disappeared under the assaults of heretics from abroad and enemies from within. Thus, many believed, it behoved true Orthodox Muscovites to fight to the death, if need be, to preserve the purity of their faith. The stakes made the struggle worth while, for if they failed and the last truly Christian kingdom, Muscovy, also fell prey to heresy, its fall from grace would initiate the Apocalypse.[2]

From these contrasting materials, the history of seventeenth-century Muscovy is woven. At most times, the restored autocracy seemed to be in control of the people and resources of its vast domains. Periodically, however, popular revolts shook it to its core and convulsed society. Within the church, the very zeal of pious men and women to guard and strengthen Russian Orthodoxy led to a profound split in the ranks of the faithful.

Let us examine some of the central themes of seventeenth-century history in slightly greater detail. The shape of the Romanov tsardom reflected the fear of chaos and the longing for order from which it had emerged. As men, the early Romanov tsars were an unimpressive lot. None of them showed the fierce determination and will to power of Patriarch Filaret, the clan's leader who ruled in the name of his son, Michael. The latter's successor, Alexis, was, in many respects, an attractive figure, both a man of genuine piety and a patron of learning and the arts. At the same time, he left the conduct of the affairs of state to a succession of chief ministers, favourites and in-laws, much as his father had done. Yet, the royal office remained strong. In lavish, brilliantly costumed ceremonies, the tsars of the house of Romanov presided over the state and shepherded the church, symbolizing, in their public personalities, the divine origin of their prerogatives.

Whether or not they governed from day to day, moreover, they faced no principled challenge to their rule. Neither the fractious nobles who criticized their officials nor the rebellious townsmen and peasants who lynched them could imagine an alternative to the Romanovs' autocracy. Only among the most privileged of aristocrats in the late 1670s and early 1680s do we see visions of alternative modes of governing and they are faint indeed.

At the same time, as Hans-Joachim Torke reminds us, behind the façade of absolute power, the rulers of seventeenth-century Russia regularly consulted with their more powerful subjects, particularly the provincial nobles and the merchants, and mobilized their talents and initiative for the good of the realm. The local judicial and fiscal officials, created under Ivan IV, continued to function well into the new century. Until mid-century, moreover, the Romanov regime went on using the zemskii sobor to gain its leading subjects' assent to its policies. On occasion, consultation was transformed into blunt pressure from below. In their campaign of petitions and as delegates to the sobor of 1648, spokesmen for the provincial nobility made clear that nothing less than the full legal enserfment of the peasantry would satisfy them. Consultation with 'society' took place less frequently in the second half of the century, but some traces of earlier practices survived until Peter the Great's reforms created an 'autocratic absolutism' of an outwardly European type.[3]

Like its counterparts elsewhere in Europe, the government of the first Romanovs devoted most of its efforts to waging war. The ancient rivalry with Poland remained the touchstone of Muscovite foreign policy in the seventeenth century. The legacy of the Time of Troubles made war inevitable. As far as both parties were concerned, the Truce of Deulino merely provided time to rest before the next round of fighting, for the Poles made clear that they regarded Prince Wladyslaw, not Michael, as the legitimate tsar. In the end, Muscovy made the first move, an unsuccessful attack on Polish-occupied Smolensk between 1632 and 1634.

In spite of this initial defeat, the Romanov regime quietly brought more and more territory under its control. One by one, its agents established forts at pivotal locations in Siberia until the chain stretched all the way to the shores of the Pacific. Within Europe, a similar process steadily moved the boundary of the territories under Moscow's effective control southward through the rich lands of the steppe towards the Black Sea. Expansion to the south inevitably brought conflict with the Ottoman Empire and the Crimea – war with the former from 1676 to 1681 and two botched attempts to capture the latter in the 1680s.

Muscovy's drive to the south coincided with a wave of local patriotism in the Ukraine. Although part of the Polish kingdom, the area was East Slavic in language and Orthodox in faith, and had a political tradition and style of life shaped primarily by the Cossacks of the Zaporozhian Host. Beginning in the late sixteenth century, local leaders regularly rebelled against the authority of the king. The greatest of the revolts, under the banner of Bogdan Khmelnitskii, the most powerful of all Cossack warlords, momentarily threatened the very existence of the Polish monarchy and led, in the end, to major changes in the area. In 1654, hard-pressed by the revitalized Polish army, Khmelnitskii accepted the suzerainty of Tsar Alexis. Thus, with virtually no effort, Muscovy acquired a rich, culturally sophisticated and politically fractious land.

The tsardom soon paid a high price for its new acquisition. War with Poland immediately broke out and lasted thirteen years until 1667. At first, the tsar's armies were everywhere victorious, not so much thanks to their own valour as because Poland simultaneously fought against Sweden, probably the greatest military power on the continent. For a time, the Swedish army marched back and forth, ravaging the heartland of Poland virtually unopposed. Once Poland and Sweden made peace, however, Muscovite troops found the going considerably more difficult. The Polish army gradually retook some of the territory which it had earlier lost. Even so, Muscovy held on to enough of its conquests to dictate a favourable peace, recognizing its right to Smolensk and the eastern Ukraine.

As elsewhere in Europe, war forced the tsar's government, however reluctantly, to join the 'military revolution'. Beginning with the preparations for the attack on Smolensk, its leaders recruited foreign mercenaries to organize 'new-style' infantry and cavalry units equipped with the latest firearms. Reforming the army proved to be a complicated business. By the latter stages of the Thirteen Years War with Poland, modern European-style units formed the core of the Muscovite army and the old-fashioned levies of noble cavalrymen had lost much of their significance.

All over Europe, governments and their people paid a high price for the 'military revolution'. As the Romanovs worked to rebuild their army, they looked for more efficient ways of mobilizing the financial and human resources of their realm. Their agents took measures to keep track of all of their subjects and to see to it that they met their obligations to the state.

That, in turn, meant a rapid growth in the central bureaucratic chanceries. After the Time of Troubles, Michael's government quickly reconstructed the sixteenth-century chancery system built around offices with vitally important and clearly defined functions – the Foreign Office, the Razriad and the Pomestnyi Prikaz. Then, over the course of the century, the number of chanceries rose until it reached more than 60 with more than 3,000 employees. Many of the new offices had specific new tasks – to administer Siberia, the Ukraine or the occupied parts of Lithuania, for example.

At the height of its development, as historians have frequently observed, the seventeenth-century bureaucracy had a ramshackle appearance. A large number of the chanceries simultaneously performed a wide variety of functions – collecting specific revenues, discharging administrative duties and settling judicial cases. Without question, then, the Muscovite central administration had little resemblance to Max Weber's ideal type of a bureaucracy. At the same time, as Borivoj Plavsic has recently argued, it is easy to judge it too harshly. In spite of the obvious overlapping of its branches and the notorious venality of some of its employees, the Muscovite bureaucracy performed its rudimentary tasks – keeping order, collecting taxes and recruiting and supporting warriors – remarkably well. Beginning as apprentices, the clerks and scribes perfected exacting routines of paperwork within a clearly organized institutional structure. Those who, over the years, rose to the top of their profession appear to have been men of genuine talent and dedication.[4] Finally, the clearest sign of the central position of the bureaucracy in seventeenth-century Muscovite life is the increasing frequency with which men from the traditional military nobility took positions as heads of chanceries. They, of all men, knew where power lay!

During the seventeenth century, the bureaucratic impulse spread throughout Muscovite life. The central administration and its agents in the provinces took it upon themselves to regulate more and more features of people's lives and their power reached into the most distant corners of the realm. By the end of the century, the bureaucracy was steadily undercutting the traditional autonomy of the Cossack hosts in the south and the peasant communes of the north. No enemy of the government could find a steppe or forest remote enough to hide him from its tentacles.

Not even the church escaped bureaucratization. Particularly under the autocratic leadership of Nikon, the patriarch and his officials controlled the destiny of the whole Orthodox Church. Increasingly it became the role of bishops, abbots and priests not to lead the flock, but to obey its supreme pastor.

In the seventeenth century, Muscovite society underwent significant changes. To begin at the top, the court aristocracy – the network of powerful clans surrounding the tsar's throne – evolved into a larger and more open ruling élite. After the Time of Troubles, the government of Michael Romanov carefully reconstructed the court of the late sixteenth century, restoring almost all of its surviving members and their families to high rank. Once again, the monarch and his advisers, often close relatives by birth or marriage, ruled with the cooperation of the leading aristocratic families. In another sense, however, Michael's accession created an anomalous situation; the new ruling dynasty had long been a part of the political machinery of the court and had long-standing family ties to other aristocratic clans.

In part for this reason, the great families of the court prospered in the seventeenth century. As before, their members enjoyed a monopoly of the highest military commands and served as advisers and ministers to a succession of weak or indifferent rulers. While still expected to serve the monarch, the high nobles of Muscovy worked in far more comfortable conditions than their sixteenth-century forefathers. Many of them enjoyed periods of rest at court between assignments in the field and a number, particularly in the latter decades of the century, became courtiers much like their counterparts in Versailles. More significant still was the aristocracy's success in taking advantage of the increasing bureaucratization of society. More and more as the century passed, royal favourites and other noble courtiers became heads of administrative chanceries, thus gaining access to increased income and opportunities for patronage. Finally, thanks to the generosity of their kinsmen on the throne, the great aristocratic clans accrued unheard-of wealth. The richest families like the Sheremetevs and Golitsyns owned thousands of hectares, scattered across Russia, farmed by thousands of serfs. The seventeenth century was indeed a good time to be an aristocrat.

The demands of warfare and the growing importance of the bureaucracy forced the court aristocracy to share its privileges with increasing numbers of social upstarts. Over the course of the century, the tsars, especially Alexis, promoted successful officials and commanders to high rank and positions of great power. Moreover, by the choice of their brides, the tsars of the house of Romanov brought new blood into the inner circle, for to avoid exacerbating the rivalries of the well-established aristocratic clans, they married the daughters of comparatively obscure nobles. Once ensconced in the palace, however, the new royal in-laws brought their equally obscure relatives to court in their train and claimed the prizes for their good fortune – rank, offices and lands. In the long run, a number of the parvenus of the seventeenth century succeeded in winning the grudging acceptance of the older families of the court, thereby becoming integral parts of the evolving Russian aristocracy.[5]

The requirements of the state and the power of the ruling élite shaped the lives of the rest of the population. In the Law Code of 1649, the Muscovite government completed the creation of a caste society. The statute reiterated that peasants could not leave their registered place of residence and stipulated that those who fled in defiance of the law could be reclaimed by their lords without any time limit. The code also tied the taxpaying townsmen to their places of residence in perpetuity. In this area, the interests of the royal administration and the nobility coincided almost completely. Prohibiting all taxpayers from moving made the job of the fisc much easier and improved the prospects for preserving social order. The nobles, particularly the poorer ones, depended on the peasants to farm their estates and thus maintain them in royal service.

Thus, in 1649, at the end of a long process, serfdom came to Russia. Thereafter, the majority of peasants were tied to the lord's manor and thus, by extension, to his person. Over the course of time, the peasants' status, legally and practically, declined until they became chattels to be bought, sold and exploited at their lord's whim. They had only two ways to escape their fate. The first – illegal flight – became increasingly difficult as the government steadily improved its machinery for identifying and repatriating fugitives. The second – joining one of the Cossack-inspired revolts such as the Razin uprising of 1670–71 – offered even less hope. The government invariably drowned such rebellions in blood.

In the spheres of religion and culture, Muscovy underwent jarring changes during the seventeenth century. As we have noted, the Time of Troubles drove the nation back upon its religious traditions. From Patriarch Filaret to the humblest monks and peasants, men and women prepared to defend Russian Orthodoxy to the death if need be.

At the same time, man does not live by zeal alone. Just as in earlier times, Muscovite society remained open to influences from abroad. The tsar's court and the religious foundations under its patronage, in particular, used foreign techniques and artistic styles to suit their purposes. First in time came a wave of importations from Safavid Persia, particularly in the decorative arts.[6] Then followed streams of influence from the Ukraine and north-western Europe. Each of the two areas had something special to offer. The military revolution brought to Russia hundreds of mercenaries, most often Protestants from northern Europe. Along with their military skills, they brought an entire style of life which found its most dramatic expression in the enclosed communities in which the Muscovite authorities required them to live. The 'German Quarter' on the outskirts of Moscow was a rough-and-tumble parody of a real Dutch or German town and served as a magnet for rebellious Russian youth like the future Peter I. More conservative Muscovites were far more selective in their borrowing of European customs; yet even the pious Tsar Alexis, at the end of his reign, maintained a court theatre for the performance of plays written in the staid baroque manner.

Influences from the Ukraine touched the life of the mind and spirit. There, largely in response to pressure from a revived and expansionist Roman

Catholicism, the Eastern Orthodox community had founded schools, imitating those of their enemies, to train themselves to defend their faith. In the middle of the seventeenth century, Tsar Alexis and a handful of advisers at court and in the church realized that Muscovite Orthodoxy had need of the linguistic and cultural skills of the Ukrainian scholars. Under their patronage, Ukrainians began to settle in Muscovy in order to teach foreign languages and rhetoric and to help with the editing and translation of ecclesiastical texts. Before long, Alexis had entrusted the education of his children to the most celebrated of the immigrants, Simeon Polotskii, and made him court poet and arbiter of the Muscovite literary scene.

Cultural innovation ran counter to the militant conservatism of Muscovite society. For the most part, the influences from abroad touched a very small circle within the social and cultural élite of the realm. The church reforms of the mid-seventeenth century were an entirely different matter. Changing the life of every Muscovite believer, they threw the entire society into turmoil.

The trouble began with a campaign, led by Tsar Alexis and a group of zealous clergymen, to purify the celebration of the liturgy and raise the moral tone of parish life. Before long, in 1652, Nikon, the new patriarch, turned the drive for reform into different channels. At the centre of Nikon's ministry was his determination to preserve the integrity of the Orthodox Church from the encroachments of the secular world, particularly the state. In order to do so, he adopted a two-pronged strategy. First, he decided to bring Russian liturgical practices into uniformity with the rest of the Eastern Orthodox world, taking contemporary Greek usage as his model. Then, adapting the papalist theory of the Middle Ages, he transformed himself into an autocratic monarch within the church. The combination was too much for many pious clergy and laymen to swallow. The moment that Nikon changed the manner of crossing oneself and other liturgical details, a storm of protest erupted. Then, when he used his arbitrary power to stifle all criticism, the dispute spilled over into the town squares and forest clearings of Muscovy.

Tsar Alexis's government found itself in a very awkward position. With the welfare of the church at heart and friends in both camps, the monarch and his lay advisers tried desperately to find a compromise. When conciliation failed, they took decisive steps to deal with both parties; in the name of religious uniformity, the government adopted Nikon's reforms, but deposed the patriarch himself. By so doing, however, the regime transformed a protest against liturgical reform into a banner for revolt against the social and political order. By the 1680s, the church and society were irrevocably split. In its desperate campaign to keep control of the realm, the government hunted down its opponents and sent the most outspoken of them to the stake. The opposition responded with the most dramatic form of protest imaginable – mass self-immolation. The Muscovite period of Russian history literally ended in flames.

In the first decades of the eighteenth century, Peter I completed the construction of Russian absolutism by adopting European institutional forms and cultural tastes and values. By that time, many features of Muscovite life had taken root – strong governmental authority, the absence of legal corporations and corporate rights, the requirement that all Russians contribute to the defence of the nation and, if necessary, sacrifice their own well-being to the cause. The Muscovite inheritance would continue to shape Russia's historical development for centuries to come.

REFERENCES AND NOTES

1. Gote, *Zamoskovnyi krai*, pp. 156–68.
2. See Pascal, *Avvakum*.
3. See Torke, *Staatsbedingte Gesellschaft* and 'Staat'.
4. Plavsic, 'Seventeenth-century chanceries'.
5. See Crummey, *Aristocrats*.
6. Keenan, 'Royal Russian behavior', p. 9.

Select bibliography

Alef, Gustave, 'The adoption of the Muscovite two-headed eagle: a discordant view', *Speculum* **41**(1966):1–21.

Alef, Gustave, 'Aristocratic politics and royal policy in Muscovy in the late fifteenth and early sixteenth centuries', *FzGO* **27**(1980):77–109.

Alef, Gustave, 'The crisis of the Muscovite aristocracy: a factor in the growth of monarchical power', *FzOG* **15**(1970):15–58.

Alef, Gustave, 'Das Erlöschen des Abzugrechts der Moskauer Bojaren', *FzOG* **10**(1965):7–74.

Alef, Gustave, 'A history of the Muscovite civil war: the reign of Vasilii II (1425–1462)', Ph.D. dissertation, Princeton University, 1956.

Alef, Gustave, 'Muscovite military reforms in the second half of the fifteenth century', *FzOG* **18**(1973):73–108.

Alef, Gustave, 'Muscovy and the Council of Florence', *Slavic Review* **20**(1961):389–401.

Alef, Gustave, 'The political significance of the inscriptions on Muscovite coinage in the reign of Vasilii II', *Speculum* **34**(1959):1–19.

Alef, Gustave, 'Reflections on the Boyar Duma in the reign of Ivan III', *Slavonic and East European Review* **45**(1967):76–123.

Alef, Gustave, *Rulers and Nobles in Fifteenth-century Muscovy*. London, 1983.

Alekseev, Iu. G., *Agrarnaia i sotsialnaia istoriia severo-vostochnoi Rusi XV–XVI vv. Pereiaslavskii uezd*. Moscow–Leningrad, 1966.

Alpatov, M. V., *Drevnerusskaia ikonopis*. Moscow, 1974.

Alshits, D. N., 'Ivan Groznyi i pripiski k litsevym svodam ego vremeni', *Istoricheskie zapiski* **23**(1947):251–91.

Ammann, A. M., *Abriss der ostslavischen Kirchengeschichte*. Vienna, 1950.

Andreyev, N., 'Filofey and his epistle to Ivan Vasilyevich', *Slavonic and East European Review* **38**(1959):1–31.

Andreyev, N., 'Interpolations in the 16th-century Muscovite chronicles', *Slavonic and East European Review* **35**(1956):95–115.

Andreyev, N., 'Metropolit Makarii, kak deiatel religioznago iskusstva', *Seminarium Kondakovianum* **7**(1935):227–44.

Andreyev, N., 'O "dele diaka Viskovatago"', *Seminarium Kondakovianum*

5(1932):191–242.

Attman, Artur, *The Struggle for Baltic Markets. Powers in Conflict, 1558–1618*. Göteborg, 1979.

Avrich, Paul, *Russian Rebels, 1600–1800*. New York, 1972.

Barbour, Philip L., *Dimitry*. Boston, 1966.

Baron, Samuel H., 'Ivan the Terrible, Giles Fletcher, and the Muscovite merchantry: a reconsideration', *Slavonic and East European Review* 56(1978):563–85.

Baron, Samuel H., 'The Muscovy Company, the Muscovite merchants and the problem of reciprocity in Russian foreign trade', *FzOG* 27(1979):133–55.

Baron, Samuel H., 'The town in "feudal" Russia', *Slavic Review* 18(1969):116–22.

Bazilevich, K. V., *Vneshnaia politika russkogo tsentralizovannogo gosudarstva: vtoraia polovina XV veka*. Moscow, 1952.

Berg, L. S., *Die geographischen Zonen der Sowjetunion*, vol. 1. Leipzig, 1958.

Bernadskii, V. N., *Novgorod i novgorodskaia zemlia v XV veke*. Moscow–Leningrad, 1961.

Birnbaum, Henrik, *Lord Novgorod the Great: Essays in the History and Culture of a Medieval City-State*, part 1. Columbus, Ohio, 1981.

Birnbaum, Henrik,. 'Lord Novgorod the Great: its place in medieval culture', *Viator* 8(1977):215–54.

Blum, Jerome, *Lord and Peasant in Russia from the Ninth to the Nineteenth Century*. Princeton, 1961.

Borisov, A. A., *Klimaty SSSR*. Moscow, 1959.

Børtnes, Jostein, 'The function of word-weaving in the structure of Epiphanius's *Life of Saint Stephen, Bishop of Perm*'. In *Medieval Russian Culture*, eds. Henrik Birnbaum and Michael S. Flier. (*California Slavic Studies*, vol. 12). Berkeley and Los Angeles, 1984, pp. 311–42.

Brown, Peter Bowman, 'Early modern Russian bureaucracy: the evolution of the chancellery system from Ivan III to Peter the Great, 1478–1717', Ph.D. dissertation, University of Chicago, 1978.

Budovnits, I. U., *Monastyri na Rusi i borba s nimi krestian v XIV–XVI vekakh*. Moscow, 1966.

Bushkovitch, Paul, 'The limits of hesychasm: some notes on monastic spirituality in Russia, 1350–1500', forthcoming in *FzOG*.

Bushkovitch, Paul, *The Merchants of Moscow, 1580–1650*. Cambridge, 1980.

Cherepnin, L. V., *Obrazovanie russkogo tsentralizovannogo gosudarstva v XIV–XV vekakh*. Moscow, 1960.

Cherepnin, L. V., *Russkie feodalnye arkhivy XIV–XV vekov*, 2 vols. Moscow–Leningrad, 1948–51.

Cherepnin L. V., *Zemskie sobory russkogo gosudarstva v XVI–XVII vv*. Moscow, 1978.

Cherniavsky, Michael, 'Ivan the Terrible as Renaissance prince', *Slavic Review* 27(1968):195–211.

Cherniavsky, Michael, 'Khan or Basileus; an aspect of Russian medieval political theory', *Journal of the History of Ideas* **20**(1959):459–76. Reprinted in *Structure*, pp. 65–79.

Cherniavsky, Michael, 'The reception of the Council of Florence in Moscow', *Church History* **24**(1955):347–59.

Chernov, A. V., *Vooruzhenye sily Russkogo gosudarstva v XV–XVII vv.* Moscow, 1954.

Chistov, K. V., *Russkie narodnye sotsialno–utopicheskie legendy XVII–XIX vv.* Moscow, 1967.

Confino, Michael, *Systèmes agraires et progrès agricole. L'assolement triennal en Russie aux XVIIIe–XIXe siècles.* Paris and The Hague, 1969.

The Correspondence between Prince A. M. Kurbsky and Tsar Ivan IV of Russia, 1564–1579, ed. J. L. I. Fennell. Cambridge, 1963.

The Council of 1503: Source Studies and Questions of Ecclesiastical Landowning in Sixteenth-century Muscovy, eds. Edward L. Keenan and Donald G. Ostrowski. Cambridge, Mass., 1977.

Crummey, Robert O., *Aristocrats and Servitors: the Boyar Elite in Russia, 1613–1689*. Princeton, 1983.

Crummey, Robert O., 'Court spectacles in seventeenth-century Russia: illusion and reality'. In *Essays in Honor of A. A. Zimin*. Columbus, Ohio, 1983, pp. 130–58.

Crummey, Robert O., 'Crown and boiars under Fedor Ivanovich and Michael Romanov', *Canadian/American Slavic Studies* **6**(1972):549–74.

Crummey, Robert O., 'Ivan the Terrible'. In *Windows on the Russian Past*, eds. Samuel H. Baron and Nancy W. Heer. Columbus, Ohio, 1977, pp. 57–74.

Crummey, Robert O., 'Reflections on mestnichestvo in the 17th century', *FzOG* **27**(1980):269–81.

Dejevsky, N. J., 'Novgorod: the origin of a Russian town'. In *European Towns: their Archaeology and Early History*, ed. M. W. Barley. London, 1977, pp. 391–403.

Demina, N. D., *'Troitsa' Andreia Rubleva*. Moscow, 1963.

Dewey, Horace W., 'The decline of the Muscovite *namestnik*', *Oxford Slavonic Papers* **12**(1965):21–39.

Dewey, Horace W., 'The 1550 *Sudebnik* as an instrument of reform', *JfGO* **10**(1962):161–80.

Dewey, Horace, W., 'Immunities in Old Russia', *Slavic Review* **33**(1964):643–59.

Dewey, Horace W., 'The White Lake Charter: a medieval Russian administrative statute', *Speculum* **32**(1958):74–83.

Donnert, Erich, *Russland an der Schwelle der Neuzeit*. Berlin, 1972.

Ekzempliarskii, A. V., *Velikie i udelnye kniazia severnoi Rusi v tatarskii period s 1238 po 1550 g.*, 2 vols. St Petersburg, 1889–91.

Esper, Thomas, 'Russia and the Baltic, 1494–1558', *Slavic Review* **25**(1966):458–74.

Fedotov, G. P., *The Russian Religious Mind*, vol. 2, ed. John Meyendorff. Cambridge, Mass., 1966.

Fedotov, G. P., *Sviatye drevnei Rusi (X – XVII st.)*. Paris, 1931.

Fedotov, G. P. ed., *A Treasury of Russian Spirituality*. New York, 1965.

Fennell, J. L. I., *The Crisis of Medieval Russia, 1200 – 1304*. London and New York, 1983.

Fennell, J. L. I., *The Emergence of Moscow, 1304 – 1359*. Berkeley and Los Angeles, 1968.

Fennell, J. L. I., *Ivan the Great of Moscow*. London, 1963.

Fennell, J. L. I., 'The Tver uprising of 1327: a study of the sources', *JfGO* **15**(1967):161 – 79.

Fennell, J. L. I. and Stokes, A., *Early Russian Literature*. London, Berkeley and Los Angeles, 1974.

Field, Daniel, *Rebels in the Name of the Tsar*. Boston, 1976.

Fisher, Alan, 'Muscovy and the Black Sea slave trade', *Canadian – American Slavic Studies* **6**(1972):575 – 94.

Floria, B. N., *Russko-polskie otnosheniia i baltiiskii vopros v kontse XVI – nachale XVII v.* Moscow, 1973.

Florovsky, Georges, 'The problem of Old Russian culture', *Slavic Review* **21**(1962):1 – 15. Reprinted in *Structure*, pp. 126 – 39.

Freski Ferapontova monastyria, text by I. E. Danilova. London, 1966.

Gill, Joseph, *The Council of Florence*. Cambridge, 1959.

Goehrke, Carsten, 'Einwohnerzahl und Bevölkerungsdichte altrussischer Städte – Methodische Möglichkeiten und vorläufige Ergebnisse', *FzOG* **18**(1973):25 – 53.

Goehrke, Carsten, 'Geographische Grundlagen der russischen Geschichte', *JfGO* **18**(1970):161 – 204.

Goehrke, Carsten, 'Die geographischen Gegebenheiten Russlands in ihrem historischen Beziehungsgeflecht', *Handbuch der Geschichte Russlands*, vol. 1(1976), pp. 8 – 72.

Goehrke, Carsten, 'Die Witwe im alten Russland', unpublished paper presented at the Fifth International Congress on the History of Muscovy, Klagenfurt, Aug. 1984.

Goehrke, Carsten, *Die Wüstungen in der Moskauer Rus*. Wiesbaden, 1968.

Goehrke, Carsten, 'Zur Problem von Bevölkerungsziffer und Bevölkerungsdichte des Moskauer Reiches im 16. Jahrhundert', *FzOG* **24**(1978):65 – 85.

Goldberg, A. L., 'Tri "poslaniia Filofeia"', *TODRL* **29**(1974):68 – 97.

Golubinskii, E. E., *Istoriia russkoi tserkvi*, 2 vols. Moscow, 1900 – 11.

Gorskii, A. D., *Ocherki ekonomicheskogo polozheniia krestian severo-vostochnoi Rusi XIV – XV vv*. Moscow, 1960.

Gote, Iu. V., *Zamoskovnyi krai v XVII veke*. Moscow, 1937.

Grekov, B. D., *Novgorodskii dom Sviatoi Sofii*, part I. St Petersburg, 1914.

Grekov, B. D. and Iakubovskii, A. Iu., *Zolotaia orda i ee padenie*. Moscow – Leningrad, 1950.

Grekov, I. B., *Vostochnaia Evropa i upadok Zolotoi Ordy*. Moscow, 1975.

Grobovsky, Antony N., *The 'Chosen Council' of Ivan IV: a Reinterpretation*. Brooklyn, 1969.

Halperin, Charles J., *Russia and the Golden Horde: the Mongol Impact on Medieval Russian History*. Bloomington, Ind., 1985.

Halperin, Charles J., 'The Russian land and the Russian tsar: the emergence of Muscovite ideology, 1380–1408', *FzOG* **23**(1976):7–103.

Haney, Jack V., *From Italy to Muscovy: the Life and Works of Maxim the Greek*. Munich, 1973.

Hellie, Richard, *Enserfment and Military Change in Muscovy*. Chicago, 1971.

Hellie, Richard, 'The foundations of Russian capitalism', *Slavic Review* **26**(1967):148–54.

Hellie, Richard, *Slavery in Russia, 1450–1725*. Chicago, 1982.

Herberstein, Sigismund Freiherr von, *Notes upon Russia*, transl. R. H. Major, 2 vols. London, 1851–52.

Ianin, V. L., *Novgorodskie posadniki*. Moscow, 1962.

Istoriia russkogo iskusstva, 13 vols. Moscow, 1953–1969.

Istoriia russkoi literatury X–XVII vekov, ed. D. S. Likhachev. Moscow, 1980.

Jablonowski, H., *Westrussland zwischen Wilna und Moskau*. Leiden, 1961.

Joseph of Volokolamsk, *Prosvetitel*. Kazan, 1903.

Kämpfer, Frank, 'Beobachtungen zu den Sendschreiben Filofejs', *JfGO* **18**(1970):1–46.

Kahan, Arcadius, 'Natural calamities and their effect upon food supply in Russia (an introduction to a catalogue)', *JfGO* **16**(1968):353–77.

Kappeler, Andreas, *Ivan Groznyj im Spiegel der ausländischen Druckschriften seiner Zeit (Geist und Werk der Zeiten, no. 33)*. Berne and Frankfurt-on-Main, 1972.

Kappeler, Andreas, *Russlands erste Nationalitäten*. Cologne and Vienna, 1982.

Kargalov, V. V., *Vneshnepoliticheskie faktory razvitiia feodalnoi Rusi. Feodalnaia Rus i kochevniki*. Moscow, 1967.

Karger, M. K., *Novgorod the Great*. Moscow, 1973.

Kartashev, A. V., *Ocherki po istorii russkoi tserkvi*, 2 vols. Paris, 1959.

Kashtanov, S. M., *Sotsialno-politicheskaia istoriia Rossii kontsa XV–pervoi poloviny XVI v*. Moscow, 1967.

Kazakova, N. A., *Ocherki po istorii russkoi obshchestvennoi mysli. Pervaia tret XVI veka*. Leningrad, 1970.

Kazakova, N. A., *Russko-livonskie i russko-ganzeiskie otnosheniia*. Leningrad, 1975.

Kazakova, N. A., *Vassian Patrikeev i ego sochineniia*. Moscow–Leningrad, 1960.

Kazakova, N. A. and Lure, Ia. S., *Antifeodalnye ereticheskie dvizheniia na Rusi, XIV–nachala XVI veka*. Moscow–Leningrad, 1955.

Keenan, Edward L., 'The *Jarlyk* of Axmed-Xan to Ivan III: a new reading', *International Journal of Slavic Linguistics and Poetics* **12**(1969):33–47.

Keenan, Edward L., *The Kurbskii-Groznyi Apocrypha*. Cambridge, 1971.

Keenan, Edward L., 'Muscovy and Kazan: some introductory remarks on the patterns of steppe diplomacy', *Slavic Review* **26**(1967):548–58.

Keenan, Edward. L., 'Muscovy and Kazan, 1445–1552: a study in steppe politics', Ph.D. dissertation, Harvard University, 1965.

Keenan, Edward L., Review of N. E. Nosov, *Stanovlenie soslovno-predstavitelnykh uchrezhdenii v Rossii*. In *Kritika* 7(1970–71):67–96.

Keenan, Edward. L., 'Royal Russian behavior, style and self-image'. In *Ethnic Russia in the USSR*, ed. Edward Allworth. New York, 1980, pp. 3–16.

Keenan, Edward L., 'Vita. Ivan Vasilevich, Terrible Tsar: 1530– 1584'. *Harvard Magazine* 80, no. 3(1978):48–9.

Khoroshkevich, A. L., *Russkoe gosudarstvo v sisteme mezhdunarodnykh otnoshenii*. Moscow, 1980.

Khoroshkevich, A. L., *Torgovlia Velikogo Novgoroda s Pribaltikoi i Zapadnoi Evropy v XIV–XV vekakh*. Moscow, 1963.

Khrestomatiia po drevnei russkoi literature XI–XVII vekov, ed. N. K. Gudzii. Moscow, 1952.

Khudozhestvennye pamiatniki Moskovskogo Kremlia. Moscow, 1956.

Kleimola, A. M., 'The changing face of the Muscovite aristocracy. The 16th century: sources of weakness', *JfGO* 25(1977):481–93.

Kleimola, A. M., 'Military service and elite status in Muscovy in the second quarter of the sixteenth century', *Russian History* 7(1980):47–64.

Kleimola, A. M., 'Status, place, and politics: the rise of mestnichestvo during the *Boiarskoe Pravlenie*', *FzOG* 27(1980):195–214.

Klibanov, A. I., *Reformatsionnye dvizheniia v Rossii v XIV–pervoi polovine XVI vv.* Moscow, 1960.

Kliuchevskii, V. O., *Sochineniia*, 8 vols. Moscow, 1956–59.

Kloss, B. M., *Nikonovskii svod i russkie letopisi XVI–XVII vekov*. Moscow, 1980.

Knackstedt, Wolfgang, *Moskau. Studien zur Geschichte einer mittelalterlichen Stadt*. Wiesbaden, 1975.

Kobrin, V. B., 'Sostav oprichnogo dvora Ivana Groznogo'. In *Arkheograficheskii ezhegodnik za 1959 god*. Moscow, 1960, pp. 16–91.

Kochin, G. E., *Selskoe khoziaistvo na Rusi kontsa XIII– nachala XVI v.* Moscow–Leningrad, 1965.

Kollmann, Jack Edward, Jr, 'The Moscow Stoglav ('Hundred Chapters') Church Council of 1551', Ph.D. dissertation, University of Michigan, 1978.

Kollmann, Jack Edward, Jr, 'The *Stoglav* Council and parish priests', *Russian History* 7(1980):65–91.

Kopanev, A. I., *Istoriia zemlevladeniia Belozerskogo kraia XV–XVI vv.* Moscow, 1951.

Kopanev, A. I., *Krestianstvo Russkogo Severa v XVI v.* Leningrad, 1978.

Kopanev, A. I., 'Naselenie Russkogo gosudarstva v XVI v', *Istoricheskie zapiski* 64(1959):233–54.

Kopanev, A. I., 'O "kupliakh" Ivana Kality', *Istoricheskie zapiski* 20(1946):24–37.

Koretskii, V. I., *Formirovanie krepostnogo prava i pervaia krestianskaia voina v Rossii*. Moscow, 1975.

Koretskii, V. I., *Zakreposhchenie krestian i klassovaia borba v Rossii*. Moscow, 1970.

Koroliuk, V. D., *Livonskaia voina*. Moscow, 1954.

Kuchkin, V. A., 'Nizhnii Novgorod i Nizhegorodskoe kniazhestvo'. In *Polsha i Rus*. Moscow, 1974, pp. 234–60.

Kuchkin, V. A. and Floria, B. N., 'O dokonchanii Dmitriia Shemiaki s nizhegorodsko-suzdalskimi kniaziami'. In *Aktovoe istochnikovedenie*. Moscow, 1979, pp. 191–217.

Kuzmin, A. G., *Riazanskoe letopisanie*. Moscow, 1965.

Labunka, Miroslav, 'The legend of the Novgorodian White Cowl: the study of its "Prologue" and "Epilogue" ', Ph.D. dissertation, Columbia University, 1978.

Langer, Lawrence N., 'The Black Death in Russia: its effects upon urban labor', *Russian History* 2(1975):53–67.

Langer, Lawrence N., 'The medieval Russian town'. In *The City in Russian History*, ed. Michael F. Hamm. Lexington, Ky., 1976, p. 11–33.

Langer, Lawrence N., 'Plague and the Russian countryside: monastic estates in the late fourteenth and fifteenth centuries', *Canadian/American Slavic Studies* 10(1976):351–68.

Lazarev, V. N., *Andrei Rublev i ego shkola*. Moscow, 1966.

Lazarev, V. N., *Feofan Grek i ego shkola*. Moscow, 1961.

Lazarev, V. N., *Moskovskaia shkola ikonopisi*. Moscow, 1971.

Lazarev, V. N., *Old Russian Murals and Mosaics*. London, 1966.

Levy, Sandra, 'Women and the control of property in sixteenth-century Muscovy', *Russian History* 10(1983):201–12.

Likhachev, D. S., *Chelovek v literature drevnei Rusi*. Moscow, 1970.

Likhachev, D. S., *Kultura Rusi vremeni Andreia Rubleva i Epifaniia Premudrogo (konets XIV–nachalo XV v.)*. Moscow–Leningrad, 1962.

Likhachev, D. S., *Razvitie russkoi literatury X–XVII vekov*. Leningrad, 1973.

Likhachev, D. S. and Panchenko, A. M., 'Smekhovoi mir' drevnei Rusi. Leningrad, 1976.

Lilienfeld, F. von, 'Die "Häresie" des Fedor Kuricyn', *FzOG* 24(1978):37–64.

Lilienfeld, F. von, *Nil Sorskij und seine Schriften*. Berlin, 1963.

Longworth, Philip, *The Cossacks*. London, 1969.

Longworth, Philip, 'The pretender phenomenon in eighteenth-century Russia', *Past & Present* 66(1975):61–83.

Lure, Ia. S., *Ideologicheskaia borba v russkoi publitsistike kontsa XV–nachala XVI veka*. Moscow–Leningrad, 1960.

Lure, Ia. S., *Obshcherusskie letopisi XIV–XV vv.* Leningrad, 1976.

Luria, Jakov S., 'The ideological movements of the late fifteenth century'. In *Medieval Russian Culture*, eds. Henrik Birnbaum and Michael S. Flier. Berkeley and Los Angeles, 1984, pp. 150–71.

Lyashchenko, P. I., *History of the National Economy of Russia*. New York, 1949.

Lydolph, Paul, *Geography of the U.S.S.R.* 3rd edn. New York, 1977.

McGeehon, M. B., 'The problem of secularization in sixteenth-century Muscovy'. In *The Council of 1503*, pp. 164–88.

Makarii, Metropolitan of Moscow, *Istoriia russkoi tserkvi*, 12 vols. St Petersburg, 1877–91.

Makovskii, D. P., *Pervaia krestianskaia voina v Rossii.* Smolensk, 1967.

Makovskii, D. P., *Razvitie tovarno-denezhnykh otnoshenii v selskom khoziaistve Russkogo gosudarstva v XVI veke.* Smolensk, 1963.

Margeret, Jacques, *The Russian Empire and Grand Duchy of Muscovy*, ed. Chester S. L. Dunning. Pittsburgh, 1983.

Martin, Janet, 'The land of darkness and the Golden Horde: the fur trade under the Mongols, XIII–XIV Centuries', *Cahiers du monde russe et soviétique* **19**(1978):401–21.

Martin, Janet, 'Les *uškujniki* de Novgorod: marchands ou pirates?', *Cahiers du monde russe et soviétique* **16**(1975):5–18.

Massa, Isaac, *A Short History of the Beginnings and Origins of These Present Wars in Moscow under the Reign of Various Sovereigns down to the Year 1610*, ed. G. Edward Orchard. Toronto, 1982.

Meyendorff, John, *Byzantium and the Rise of Russia.* Cambridge, 1981.

Miller, David B., 'The Coronation of Ivan IV of Moscow', *JfGO* **15**(1967):559–74.

Miller, David B., 'The Velikie Minei Chetii and the Stepennaia Kniga of Metropolitan Makarii and the origins of Russian national consciousness', *FzOG* **26**(1979):263–382.

Miller, David B., 'The Viskovatyi affair of 1553–54: official art, the emergence of autocracy, and the disintegration of medieval Russian culture', *Russian History* **8**(1981):293–332.

Mneva, N. E., *Iskusstvo Moskovskoi Rusi. Vtoraia polovina XV–XVII vv.* Moscow, 1965.

Muscovite Judicial Texts: 1488–1556 (Michigan Slavic Materials, no. 7), ed. H. W. Dewey. University of Michigan, Ann Arbor, 1966.

Muscovite Society, ed. Richard Hellie. Chicago, 1967.

Nasonov, A. N., *Mongoly i Rus.* Moscow–Leningrad, 1940.

Nolde, B. E., *La formation de l'Empire russe*, 2 vols. Paris, 1952–53.

Noonan, Thomas S., 'Medieval Russia, the Mongols, and the West: Novgorod's relations with the Baltic, 1100–1350', *Medieval Studies* **37**(1975):316–39.

Nosov, N. E., *Stanovlenie soslovno-predstavitelnykh uchrezhdenii v Rossii.* Leningrad, 1969.

Novgorod Icons, 12th–17th Century. Oxford and Leningrad, 1980.

Novgorodskaia pervaia letopis starshego i mladshego izvodov. Moscow–Leningrad, 1950.

Novoselskii, A. A., 'Rospis krestianskikh dvorov, nakhodivshikhsia vo vladenii vysshego dukhovenstva, monastyrei i dumnykh liudei po perepisnym knigam 1678 g.', *Istoricheskii arkhiv* **4**(1949):88–149.

Obolensky, Dimitri, *The Byzantine Commonwealth. Eastern Europe, 500–1453.* London, 1971.

Obolensky, Dimitri, 'A *Philorhomaios Anthropos*: Metropolitan Cyprian of Kiev and all Russia (1375–1406)', *Dumbarton Oaks Papers* **32**(1978):77–98.

Obolensky, Dimitri, 'Popular religion in medieval Russia'. In *Russia and Orthodoxy. Essays in Honor of Georges Florovsky*, ed. Andrew Blane, vol.

2, *The Religious World of Russian Culture*. The Hague, 1975, pp. 43–54.

Ocherki istorii SSSR. Period feodalizma. IX–XV vv., Part 2. Moscow, 1953.

Ocherki istorii SSSR. Period feodalizma. Konets XV v.–nachalo XVII v. Moscow, 1955.

Ocherki russkoi kultury XIII–XV vekov, 2 vols. Moscow, 1969–70.

Onasch, Konrad, *Icons*. London, 1963.

Onasch, Konrad, *Die Ikonenmalerei*. Leipzig, 1968.

Ostrowski, Donald G., 'Church polemics and monastic land acquisition in sixteenth-century Muscovy', *Slavonic and East European Review* **64**(1986):357–79.

Ostrowski, Donald G., 'A "Fontological" investigation of the Muscovite Church Council of 1503', Ph.D. dissertation, Pennsylvania State University, 1977.

Palitsyn, Avramii, *Skazanie Avramiia Palitsyna*, eds. O. A. Derzhavina and E. V. Kolosova. Moscow–Leningrad, 1955.

Pamiatniki literatury drevnei Rusi. XIV–seredina XV veka. Moscow, 1981.

Pamiatniki literatury drevnei Rusi. Vtoraia polovina XV veka. Moscow, 1982.

Pascal, Pierre, *Avvakum et les débuts du raskol*. Paris and The Hague, 1963.

Pashuto, V. T., *Obrazovanie litovskogo gosudarstva*. Moscow, 1959.

Perepiska Ivana Groznogo s Andreem Kurbskim, eds Ia. S. Lure and Iu. D. Rykov. Leningrad, 1979.

Pervaia rospis Uspenskogo Sobora, ed. O. V. Zonova. Leningrad, 1971.

Petrej, Peter, *Reliatsiia Petra Petreia o Rossii nachala XVII v.*, ed. Iu. A. Limonov. Moscow, 1976.

Philipp, Werner, 'Die gedankliche Begründung der Moskauer Autokratie bei ihrer Entstehung (1458–1522)', *FzOG* **15**(1970):59–118.

Philipp, Werner, 'Die religiöse Begründung der altrussischen Hauptstadt', *FzOG* **33**(1983):227–38.

Pierling, P., *La Russie et le Saint-Siège. Études diplomatiques*, 3 vols. Paris, 1896–1901.

Platonov, S. F., *Ocherki po istorii Smuty v moskovskom gosudarstve XVI–XVII vv.* St Petersburg, 1910.

Platonov, S. F., *The Time of Troubles*, transl. John T. Alexander. Lawrence, Kans., 1970.

Plavsic, Borivoj, 'Seventeenth-century chanceries and their staffs'. In *Russian Officialdom*, eds. Walter M. Pintner and Don K. Rowney. Chapel Hill, NC, 1980, pp. 19–45.

Podobedova, O. I., *Moskovskaia shkola zhivopisi pri Ivane IV*. Moscow, 1972.

Popov, G. V., *Zhivopis i miniatiura Moskvy serediny XV–nachala XVI veka*. Moscow, 1975.

Poslaniia Iosifa Volotskogo, eds. A. A. Zimin and Ia. S. Lure. Moscow–Leningrad, 1959.

Poslaniia Ivana Groznogo, eds D. S. Likhachev and Ia. S. Lure. Moscow–Leningrad, 1951.

Possevino, Antonio, *The Moscovia of Antonio Possevino*, ed. Hugh F. Graham. Pittsburgh, 1977.

Povest vremennykh let, eds. D. S. Likhachev and B. A. Romanov, Part I. Moscow-Leningrad, 1950.

Povesti o Kulikovskoi bitve, eds. M. N. Tikhomirov, V. F. Rzhiga and L. A. Dmitriev. Moscow, 1959.

Presniakov, A. E., *The Formation of the Great Russian State*. Chicago, 1970.

Presniakov, A E., *The Tsardom of Muscovy*. Gulf Breeze, Fl., 1978.

Priselkov, M. D., *Istoriia russkogo letopisaniia XI – XV vv*. Leningrad, 1940.

Pritsak, Omeljan, 'Moscow, the Golden Horde, and the Kazan khanate from a polycultural point of view', *Slavic Review* **26**(1967):577 – 83.

Prokhorov, G. M., 'Isikhazm i obshchestvennaia mysl v Vostochnoi Evrope v XIV v.', *TODRL* **23**(1968):86 – 108.

Pronshtein, A. P., *Velikii Novgorod v XVI veke*. Kharkov, 1957.

Pskov. Art Treasures and Architectural Monuments. 12th – 17th Centuries, ed. S. Yamshchikov. Leningrad, 1978.

Pskovskie letopisi, ed. A. N. Nasonov, 2 vols. Moscow – Leningrad, 1941 – Moscow, 1955.

Raba, Joel, 'Novgorod in the fifteenth century: a re-examination', *Canadian Slavic Studies* **1**(1967):348-64.

Rossing, Niels and Rønne, Birgit, *Apocryphal – not Apocryphal?* Copenhagen, 1980.

Roublev, Michel, 'Le tribut aux Mongoles d'après les testaments et accords des princes russes', *Cahiers du monde russe et soviétique* **7**(1966):487 – 530. In English, 'The Mongol tribute according to the wills and testaments of the Russian princes'. In *Structure*, pp. 29 – 64.

Rowland, Daniel, 'Muscovite political attitudes as reflected in early seventeenth-century tales about the Time of Troubles', Ph.D. dissertation, Yale University, 1976.

Rowland, Daniel, 'The problem of advice in Muscovite tales about the Time of Troubles', *Russian History* **6**(1979):259 – 83.

Rozhdestvenskii, S. V., *Sluzhiloe zemlevladenie v moskovskom gosudarstve XVI veka*. St Petersburg, 1897.

Rozhkov, N. A., *Selskoe khoziaistvo Moskovskoi Rusi v XVI veke*. Moscow, 1899.

Rozov, N. N., *Kniga v Rossii v XV veke*. Leningrad, 1981.

Rude & Barbarous Kingdom, eds. Lloyd E. Berry and Robert O. Crummey. Madison, Wis., 1958.

The Russian Primary Chronicle, eds. Samuel Hazzard Cross and Olgerd P. Sherbowitz-Wetzor. Cambridge, Mass., 1953.

Rüss, Hartmut, *Adel und Adelsoppositionen im Moskauer Staat*. Wiesbaden, 1975.

Rüss, Hartmut, 'Der Kampf um das Moskauer Tysjackij-Amt im 14. Jahrhundert', *JfGO* **22**(1974):481 – 93.

Rybakov, B. A., *Remeslo drevnei Rusi*. Moscow – Leningrad, 1948.

Sadikov, P. A., *Ocherki po istorii oprichniny*. Moscow – Leningrad, 1950.

Safargaliev, M. G., *Raspad Zolotoi Ordy*. Saransk, 1960.

Sakharov, A. M., *Goroda severo-vostochnoi Rusi XIV – XV vekov*. Moscow,

1959.

Sakharov, A. M., *Obrazovanie i razvitie rossiiskogo gosudarstva v XIV–XVII vv.* Moscow, 1969.

Salmina, M. A., 'Eshche raz o datirovke "Letopisnoi povesti" o Kulikovskoi bitve', *TODRL* 32(1977):3–39.

Salmina, M. A., 'K voprosu o datirovke "Skazaniia o Mamaevom poboishche" ', *TODRL* 29(1974):98–124.

Schaeder, Hildegard, *Moskau das dritte Rom.* Darmstadt, 1957.

Ševčenko, Ihor, 'A neglected Byzantine source of Muscovite political ideology', *Harvard Slavic Studies* 2(1954):141–79. Reprinted in *Structure*, pp. 80–107.

Shapiro, A. L., *Problemy sotsialno-ekonomicheskoi istorii Rusi XIV–XVI vv.* Leningrad, 1977.

Shapiro, A. L. et al., *Agrarnaia istoriia severo–zapada Rossii: vtoraia polovina XV–nachalo XVI v.* Leningrad, 1971.

Shapiro, A. L. et al., *Agrarnaia istoriia severo-zapada Rossii XVI veka.* Leningrad, 1974.

Shields Kollmann, Nancy, 'The Boyar clan and court politics. The founding of the Muscovite political system', *Cahiers du monde russe et soviétique* 23(1982):5–31.

Shields Kollmann, Nancy, 'Kinship and politics: the origin and evolution of the Muscovite boyar elite in the fifteenth century', Ph.D. dissertation, Harvard University, 1980.

Shields Kollmann, Nancy, 'The seclusion of elite Muscovite women', *Russian History* 10(1983):170–87.

Shmidt, S. O., *Stanovlenie rossiiskogo samoderzhavstva.* Moscow, 1973.

Sinitsyna, N. V., 'Eticheskii i sotsialnyi aspekty nestiazhatelskikh vozzrenii Maksima Greka'. In *Obshchestvo i gosudarstvo feodalnoi Rossii.* Moscow, 1975, pp. 159–70.

Sinitsyna, S. O., *Maksim Grek v Rossii.* Moscow, 1977.

Skripil, M. O., ' "Istoriia" o vziatii Tsargrada turkami Nestora Iskandera', *TODRL* 10(1954):166–84.

Skrynnikov, R. G., *Boris Godunov.* Moscow, 1978.

Skrynnikov, R. G., 'Boris Godunov's Struggle for the Throne', *Canadian/American Slavic Studies* 11(1977):325–53.

Skrynnikov, R. G., *Ivan Groznyi.* Moscow, 1975.

Skrynnikov, R. G., *Minin i Pozharskii.* Moscow, 1981.

Skrynnikov, R. G., *Nachalo oprichniny.* Leningrad, 1966.

Skrynnikov, R. G., *Oprichnyi terror.* Leningrad, 1969.

Skrynnikov, R. G., *Perepiska Groznogo i Kurbskogo. Paradoksy Edvarda Kinana.* Leningrad, 1973.

Skrynnikov, R. G., *Rossiia nakanune 'smutnogo vremeni'.* Moscow, 1981.

Skrynnikov, R. G., *Rossiia posle oprichniny.* Leningrad, 1975.

Skrynnikov, R. G., *Sibirskaia ekspeditsiia Ermaka.* Novosibirsk, 1982.

Skrynnikov, R. G., *Sotsialno-politicheskaia borba v Russkom gosudarstve v nachale XVII veka.* Leningrad, 1985.

Slicher van Bath, B. H., *The Agrarian History of Western Europe. A.D. 500–1850*. London, 1963.

Slovo o polku Igoreve i pamiatniki Kulikovskogo tsikla. Moscow–Leningrad, 1966.

Smirnov, I. I., *Ocherki politicheskoi istorii Russkogo gosudarstva 30–50kh godov XVI veka*. Moscow–Leningrad, 1958.

Smith, R. E. F., *Peasant Farming in Muscovy*. Cambridge, 1977.

Smith, R. E. F. ed., *The Enserfment of the Russian Peasantry*. Cambridge, 1968.

Smith, R. E. F. and Christian, David, *Bread and Salt. A Social and Economic History of Food and Drink in Russia*. Cambridge, 1984.

Smolitsch, Igor, *Russisches Mönchtum. Entstehung, Entwicklung und Wesen, 988–1917*. Würzburg, 1953.

Spuler, Bertold, *Die Goldene Horde. Die Mongolen in Russland, 1223–1502*. Wiesbaden, 1965.

Stoglav, ed. D. E. Kozhanchikov. St Petersburg, 1863.

Stökl, Günter, *Die Entstehung des Kosakentums*. Munich, 1953.

Strémooukhoff, Dimitri, 'Moscow the Third Rome: sources of the doctrine', *Speculum* **28**(1953):84–101. Reprinted in *Structure*, pp. 108–25.

Syroechkovskii, V. E., *Gosti-surozhane*. Moscow–Leningrad, 1935.

Szeftel, Marc, 'The title of the Muscovite monarch up to the end of the seventeenth century', *Canadian/American Slavic Studies* **13**(1979):59–81.

The Testaments of the Grand Princes of Moscow, ed. Robert Craig Howes. Ithaca, NY, 1967.

Thompson, M. W., *Novgorod the Great*. London, 1967.

Tikhomirov, M. N., *Drevniaia Moskva (XII–XV vv.)*. Moscow, 1947.

Tikhomirov, M. N., *Rossiia v XVI stoletii*. Moscow, 1962.

Timofeev, Ivan, *Vremennik Ivana Timofeeva*, ed. O. A. Derzhavina. Moscow–Leningrad, 1951.

Tolstaia, T. V., *Uspenskii sobor Moskovskogo Kremlia*. Moscow, 1979.

Torke, Hans-Joachim, *Die staatsbedingte Gesellschaft im Moskauer Reich*. Leiden, 1974.

Torke, Hans-Joachim, 'Staat und Gesellschaft in Russland im 17. Jahrhundert als Problem der europäischen Geschichte', *Handbuch der Geschichte Russlands*, vol. 2(1982), pp. 200–12.

Uspenskii sobor Moskovskogo Kremlia. Moscow, 1971.

Vernadsky, George, 'The death of the Tsarevich Dimitry: a reconsideration of the case', *Oxford Slavonic Papers* **5**(1954):1–19.

Vernadsky, George, *Kievan Russia*. New Haven, Conn., 1948.

Vernadsky, George, *The Mongols and Russia*. New Haven, Conn., 1953.

Vernadsky, George, *Russia at the Dawn of the Modern Age*. New Haven, Conn., 1959.

Veselovskii, S. B, *Feodalnoe zemlevladenie v severo-vostochnoi Rusi*, vol. 1. Moscow–Leningrad, 1947.

Veselovskii, S. B., *Issledovaniia po istorii klassa sluzhilykh zemlevladeltsev*. Moscow, 1969.

Veselovskii, S. B., *Issledovaniia po istorii oprichniny*. Moscow, 1963.

Veselovskii, S. B., 'Monastyrskoe zemlevladenie v Moskovskoi Rusi vo vtoroi polovine XVI v.,' *Istoricheskie zapiski* **10**(1941):95–116.

Vodoff, W., 'A propos des "achats" (*Kupli*) d'Ivan Ier de Moscou', *Journal des Savants* (1974):95–127.

Vodoff, W., 'La place du Grand-Prince de Tver dans les structures politiques russes de la fin du XIVe et du XVe siècle', *FzOG* **27**(1980):32–63.

Voronin, N. N., *Vladimir. Bogoliubovo. Suzdal. Iurev-Polskoi*. Moscow, 1967.

Voronin, N. N., *Zodchestvo severo-vostochnoi Rusi XII–XV vekov*, 2 vols. Moscow, 1961–62.

Voyce, Arthur, *The Art and Architecture of Medieval Russia*. Norman, Okla., 1967.

Vzdornov, G. I., *Iskusstvo knigi v drevnei Rusi. Rukopisnaia kniga severo-vostochnoi Rusi XII–nachala XV vekov*. Moscow, 1980.

Willan, T. S., *The Early History of the Russia Company, 1553–1603*. Manchester, 1956.

Yermak's Campaign in Siberia, ed. Terence Armstrong. London, 1975.

Zabelin, I., *Domashnii byt russkikh tsarei v XVI i XVII st*. Moscow, 1895.

Zenkovsky, Serge, ed. *Medieval Russia's Epics, Chronicles and Tales*. New York, 1974.

Zernack, Klaus, *Die burgstädtischen Volksversammlungen bei den Ost–und Westslawen. Studien zur verfassungsgeschichtlichen Bedeutung des Veče*. Wiesbaden, 1967.

Zguta, Russell, 'Monastic medicine in Kievan Rus and early Muscovy'. In *Medieval Russian Culture*, eds. Henrik Birnbaum and Michael S. Flier (*California Slavic Studies*, vol. 12). Berkeley and Los Angeles, 1984, pp. 54–70.

Zguta, Russell, *Russian Minstrels. A History of the Skomorokhi*. Philadelphia, 1978.

Zimin, A. A., 'Diacheskii apparat v Rossii vtoroi poloviny XV–pervoi treti XVI v.', *Istoricheskie zapiski* **87**(1971):219–86.

Zimin, A. A., *I. S. Peresvetov i ego sovremenniki*. Moscow, 1958.

Zimin, A. A., *Krupnaia feodalnaia votchina*. Moscow, 1977.

Zimin, A. A., *Oprichnina Ivana Groznogo*. Moscow, 1964.

Zimin, A. A., *Reformy Ivana Groznogo*. Moscow, 1960.

Zimin, A. A., *Rossiia na poroge novogo vremeni*. Moscow, 1972.

Maps

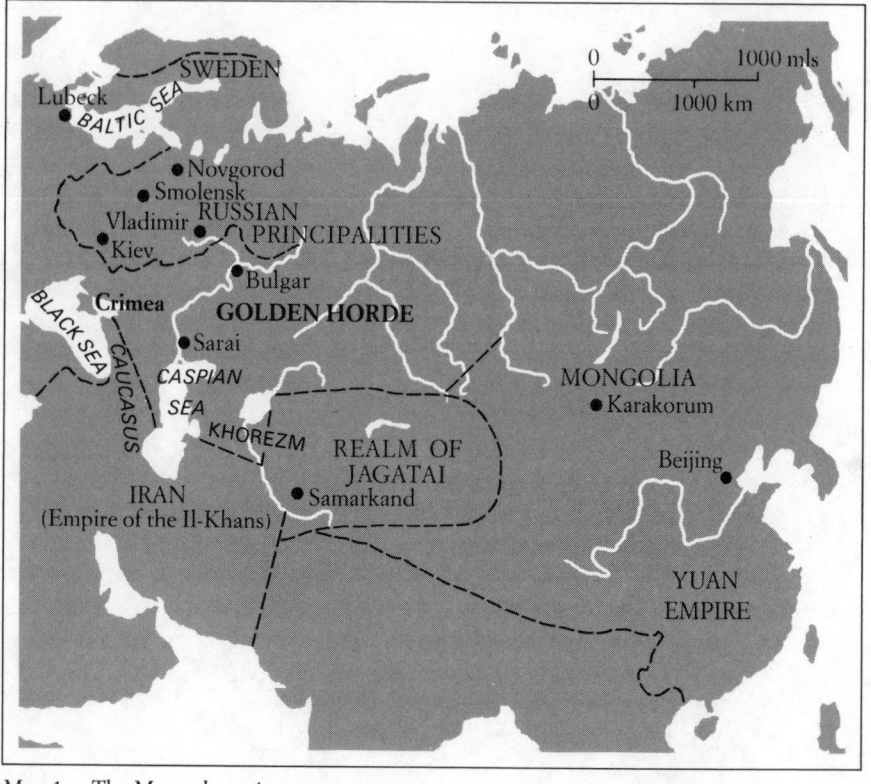

Map 1. The Mongol empire.

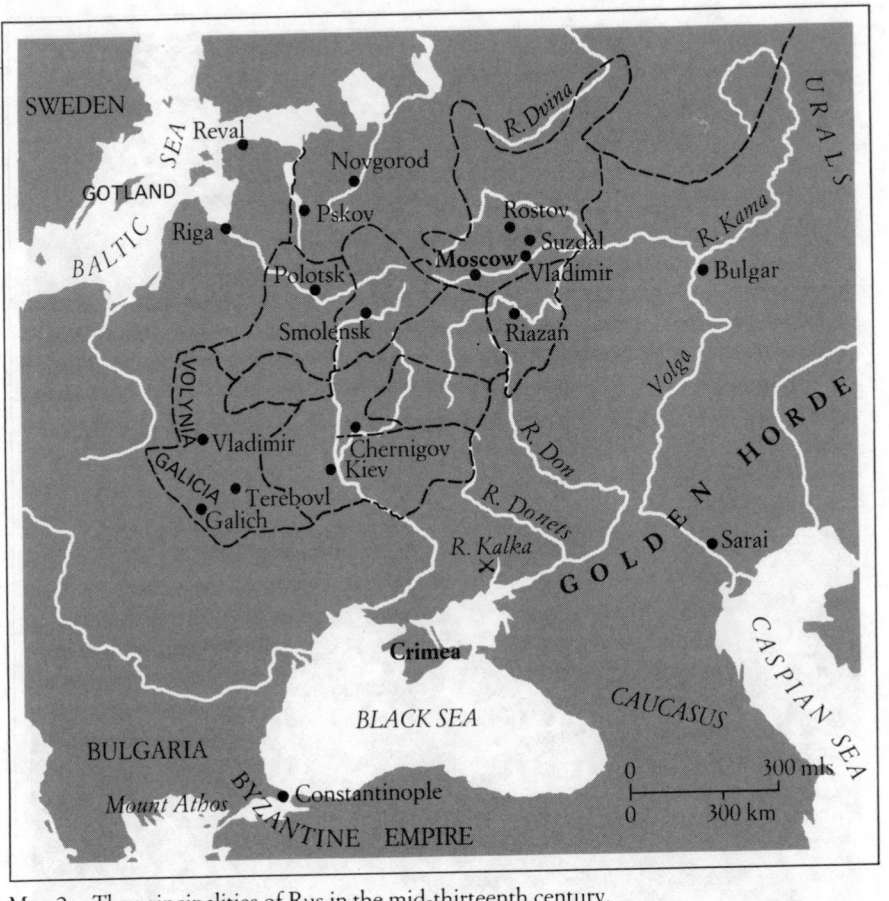

Map 2. The principalities of Rus in the mid-thirteenth century.

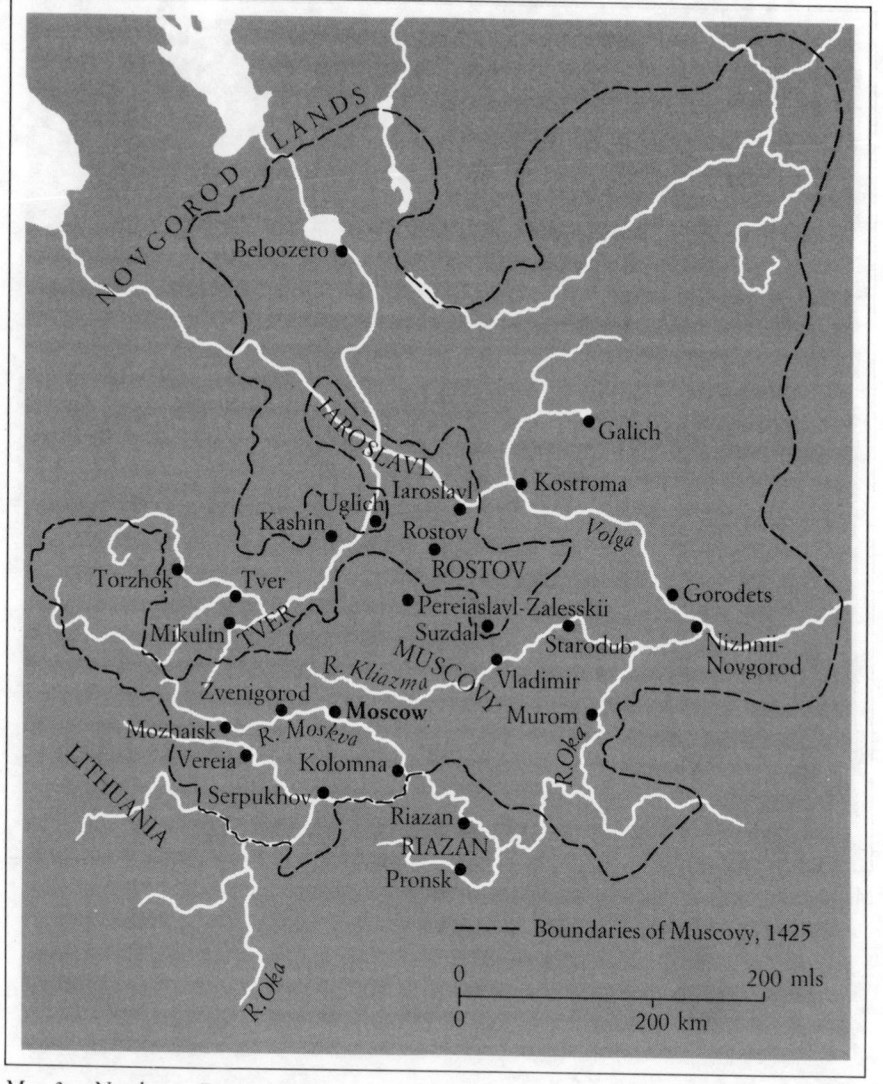

Map 3.   North-east Russia, 1425.

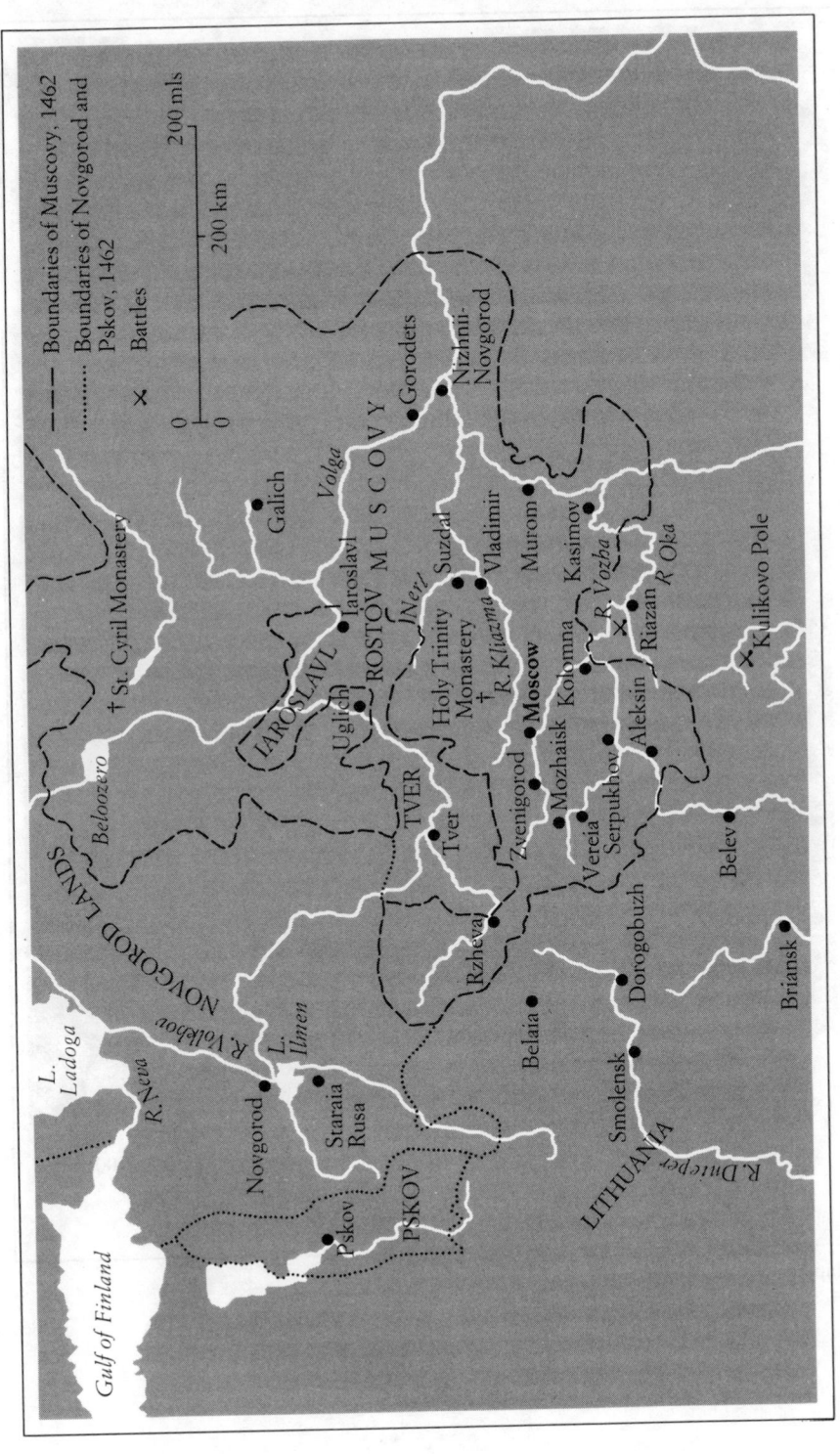

Map 4.   North-east Russia, 1462.

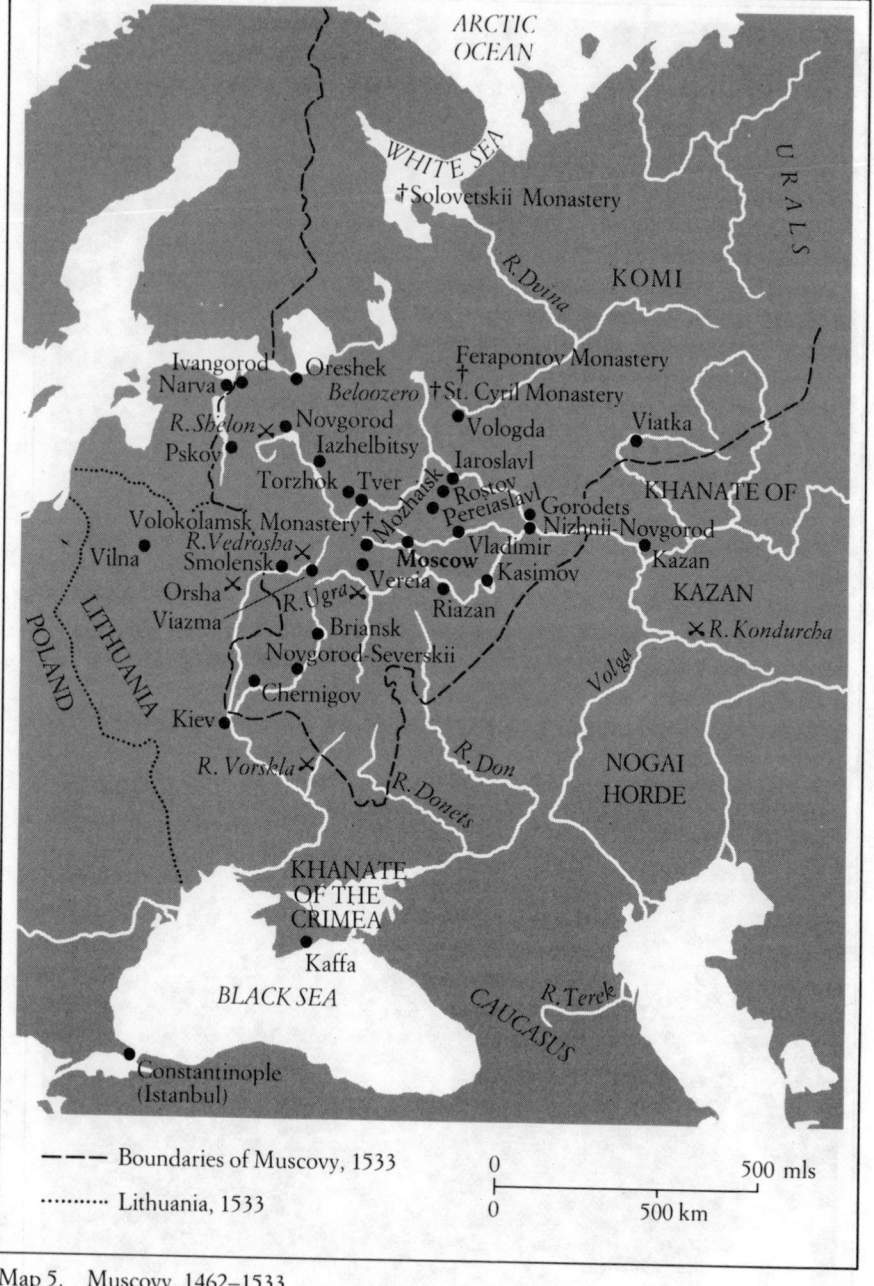

ARCTIC OCEAN

WHITE SEA

† Solovetskii Monastery

R. Dvina

KOMI

URALS

Ivangorod
Narva
Oreshek
Beloozero
Ferapontov Monastery
† St. Cyril Monastery

R. Shelon ✕
Novgorod
Iazhelbitsy
Vologda
Viatka

Pskov
Torzhok
Tver
Mozhaisk
Iaroslavl
Rostov
Pereiaslavl
Gorodets
KHANATE OF

Volokolamsk Monastery
Nizhnii-Novgorod

Vilna
R. Vedrosha ✕
Smolensk
Moscow
Vladimir
Kasimov
Kazan
KAZAN

Orsha ✕
R. Ugra ✕
Vereia
Viazma
Riazan
✕ *R. Kondurcha*

POLAND

LITHUANIA

Briansk
Novgorod-Severskii

Volga

Chernigov

NOGAI
HORDE

Kiev

R. Vorskla ✕
R. Don

R. Donets

KHANATE
OF THE
CRIMEA

Kaffa

BLACK SEA
CAUCASUS
R. Terek

Constantinople
(Istanbul)

– – – Boundaries of Muscovy, 1533

· · · · · · · · Lithuania, 1533

| 0 | | 500 mls |

| 0 | | 500 km |

Map 5.   Muscovy, 1462–1533.

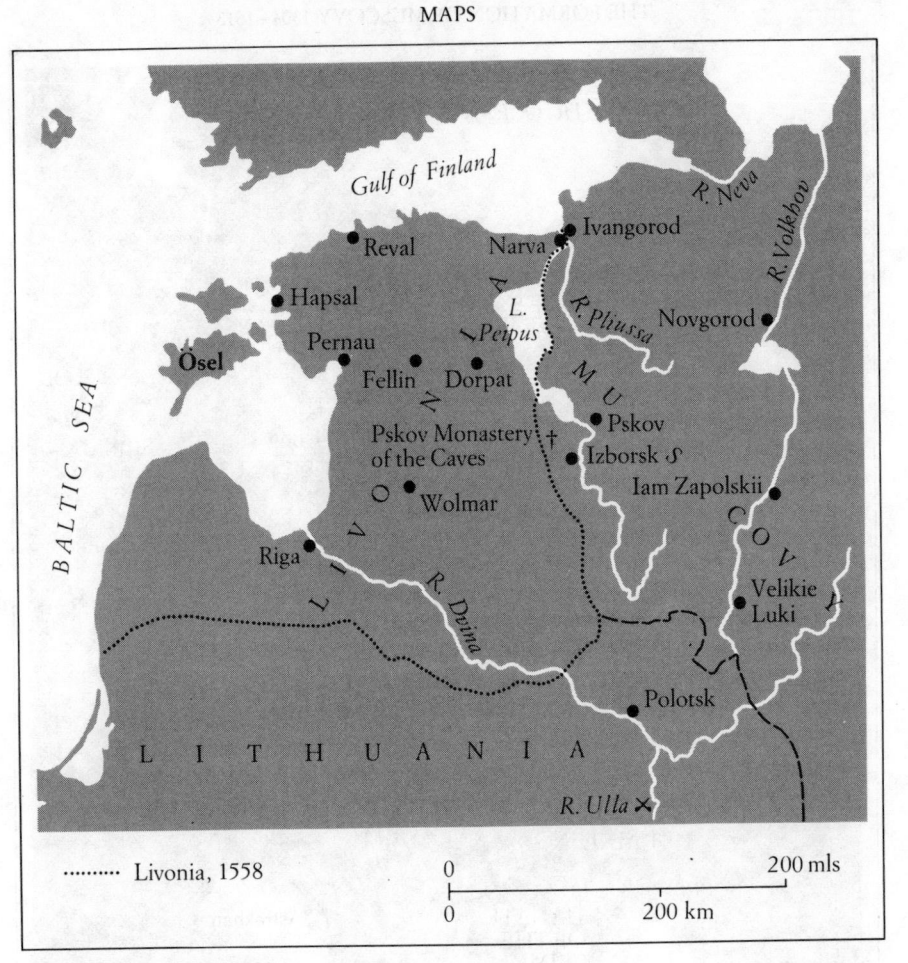

Map 6. Livonia, 1558–83

ARCTIC OCEAN

WHITE SEA

† Solovetskii Monastery

● Kholmogory

KHANATE OF

R. Devina

Sibir ●

SIBERIA

● Sol Vychegodsk

St.Cyril
Monastery
Stolbovo ●

Vologda

Ustiug Velikii

BALTIC SEA

Reval ●

Volkhov

Beloozero ●

Romanov

Novgorod ●

Yaroslavl

● Kostroma

Uglich

Aleksandrova Sloboda

Pskov ●

Tushino

Rostov

KHANATE OF

Riga ●

Tver

Nizhnii-Novgorod

Staritsa ●

Deulino

× Kazan

Klushino ×

Moscow

Sviiazhsk ×

KAZAN

Mozhaisk

● Kolomna

Smolensk ●

Viazma

● Riazan

Kaluga ●

Molodi

Tula

Serpukhov

POLAND -

Volga

LITHUANIA

● Kromy

Kiev ●

● Putivl

R. Don

KHANATE OF

UKRAINE

R. Donets

ASTRAKHAN

Zaporozhian Host ●

KHANATE
OF THE
CRIMEA

Astrakhan ■

BLACK SEA

– – – Boundaries of Muscovy, 1598

0   500 mls

0   500 km

Map 7.   Muscovy, 1533–1613.

Index

his priestly calling altogether. In practice, these rigid regulations proved very difficult to enforce.

Another problem was the low level of education of the clergy. Muscovite society before the seventeenth century had no formal system of education. Men learned to read and write by taking individual instruction from literate priests or attending informal classes in their homes. Many future clergymen never did so: the leaders of the Muscovite hierarchy and foreign visitors alike complained that many priests could not read at all and that others were barely literate.

Not all priests lived in material and cultural poverty. Those who served in cathedrals and large, well-endowed urban parishes were probably adequately prepared for their duties; they most likely received a comfortable income, and might well rub shoulders with the leaders of lay society.

The web of village life, however, held most priests fast. The vast majority of them lived and thought like their parishioners. In Muscovite society, the priesthood was virtually a hereditary occupation passed, like any other trade, from father to son. In this case, a boy usually began by assisting his father with the liturgy, then passed upward through the ranks until he was ready for the bishop to ordain him a priest. As often as not, with the support of his old neighbours, he would return to serve in his native village. There he worked the land like everyone else and, if contemporary sources can be believed, was not above a good drinking bout now and again. For such a man, the aspirations of the hierarchy must have seemed the wildest of dreams. He would have every reason not to press his flock too hard, to 'look through his fingers' at their lapses from grace.[7]

In the eyes of the church's leaders, parish life left much to be desired. The spiritual life of ordinary Russians was a complex tapestry woven both from the official teachings and worship of Eastern Orthodoxy and from popular rituals and beliefs, some drawn from pre-Christian nature cults. In this respect, Russian popular religion resembled the systems of belief of other peasant societies. Such a notion would bring little comfort to the fathers of the church who did their futile best to stamp out the survivals of pre-Christian cults and purify village life. The Stoglav Council of 1551 explicitly condemned the custom of gathering at night at Midsummer and other times of the year for 'devilish songs, dancing and jumping about' leading to sexual excesses and an orgiastic plunge into a river. Such immoral goings-on were not to be tolerated![8]

Other practices of their flock caused the church's leaders much less concern. Pre-Christian deities underwent conversion and comfortably joined the ranks of Christian saints. Judging by the number of icons depicting them, the prophet Elijah enjoyed widespread veneration as the maker of thunder and St Blaise as the patron of cattle.[9]

The authorities reacted ambiguously to certain features of popular culture. The wandering folk minstrels or *skomorokhi*, whose tradition antedated the conversion to Christianity, delighted audiences with their irreverent and bawdy performances. It was precisely these qualities, of course, that led church and state to condemn them. At the same time, in the sixteenth century, the government of Muscovy attempted to channel their activities, extending toleration to those skomorokhi who settled down to live like honourable tradesmen. Ivan IV even employed some as court entertainers. Only in the middle of the seventeenth century did the ecclesiastical establishment and the tsar combine to stamp them out.[10]

In the centuries following the Mongol conquest, the most significant development in the life of the Russian Church was the remarkable revival and flowering of monasticism. Monasteries of a cenobitic or communal type had played a central role in the institutional and spiritual life of Kievan Rus. By the time of the Mongol conquest, the initial wave of enthusiasm for the monastic life seemed to have waned somewhat. In the fourteenth, fifteenth and sixteenth centuries, however, the impulse to withdraw from the secular world and live only to serve God revived and spread with unprecedented vigour. According to one estimate, men and women of faith founded about 250 cenobitic monasteries and convents in Muscovy in these centuries, many in remote corners of the realm.[11]

St Sergius of Radonezh was both the catalyst and epitome of the monastic revival. As his hagiographic 'Life' portrays him, he felt a special calling from God while still in his mother's womb! His childhood led directly to the central decision of his life – the commitment to serve God as a monk. In the late 1320s while he was in his teens, he and his older brother became hermits in a tract of dense forest north of Moscow. They devoted themselves to rigorous self-discipline and prayer, providing for their material needs entirely by their own efforts. It was no easy life: Sergius's brother soon gave up the lonely struggle. The saint, now completely alone except for visits from a sympathetic priest, held out in the face of hunger, cold and isolation.

In time, Sergius's growing reputation for sanctity drew disciples to him. They settled in huts near his, joined him in worship in his chapel, and accepted him as their spiritual director. In this manner, the group around Sergius formed an idiorrhythmic community in which the individual members maintained their own style of life and kept their own property, uniting only for common devotions. As time passed, this comparatively loose form of organization, frequently encountered in Eastern Orthodoxy, dissatisfied Sergius. In about 1354, he adopted a monastic rule that transformed his followers – against the will of some of them – into a fully communal, cenobitic organization, known to later generations as the Holy Trinity–St Sergius Monastery.

After that, his community continued to grow as more and more novices entered the brotherhood. Moreover, its leaders began to lay the foundations of liturgical magnificence and economic security. New recruits gave money or property to the monastery and pious laypeople donated land in return for prayers for their own souls or those of their loved ones. As Sergius, a remarkable blend of piety and practicality, doubtless realized, material comfort presented his community not only with opportunities for service but also temptations to the worldliness from which he had once fled.

St Sergius's powerful personality touched many of his contemporaries and influenced all spheres of national life. Metropolitan Alexis tried unsuccessfully to enlist him as his successor. He gave the ruler of Moscow, Dmitrii Donskoi, his blessing on the eve of the battle of Kulikovo Pole in 1380 and some years later attended the prince's funeral.[12] Such broad and profound influence proved, in the hands of his later disciples, to be a two-edged sword.[13]

Sergius's teaching and example inspired many of his followers to found communities of their own. Some chose locations near the centres of worldly power: the Andronikov, Simonov and Chudov (Miracle) Monasteries were all founded in Moscow and its environs in the 1360s and 1370s while Alexis was metropolitan. Others took the ancient admonition to flee to 'the desert' quite literally. Monasteries began to appear in remote areas of the Russian north. St Cyril, the second great leader of the monastic revival, left a community in Moscow to found a hermitage near Beloozero (White Lake) in 1393. Before long, like Sergius before him, he found himself abbot of a large and highly organized monastery. Moreover, he, too, had disciples such as St Savatii who, in the 1420s, founded the Solovetskii Monastery on an island in the White Sea, an inlet of the Arctic Ocean. In such locations, forsaken by all but God, the new monasteries gradually came to dominate the economic, social and cultural life of vast expanses of sparsely settled countryside.[14]

The monastic revival inspired the Russian Church to renew its missionary work among the non-Christian peoples of the area. Such efforts were, in a sense, a continuation of the gradual process of converting all of the peoples of the Russian lands – Slavic and non-Slavic alike – to Orthodoxy. Already in the thirteenth century, for example, missionaries from Novgorod had won many of the Finnish-speaking Karelians for the Eastern Church. In the last decades of the fourteenth century, one of St Sergius's contemporaries, St Stephen of Perm, gave the movement new life. A monk of unusual learning, Stephen turned his eyes towards the Komi, the Finno-Ugric nationality which inhabits the north-east corner of European Russia. After years of preparation, Stephen went into their territory in the late 1370s. In spite of opposition from the local shamans, his teaching and acts of charity won him many converts. To provide spiritual nourishment for his flock, he invented an alphabet for the Komi language and began the task of translating the Scriptures and devotional writings just as Cyril and Methodius had done for the Slavs centuries earlier. Thanks, in part, to his foresight, the Komi remained Orthodox, and have preserved their language and cultural traditions down to the present day.[15]

In the centuries following St Sergius's death in 1392, some of the new monasteries became extremely wealthy and influential. His own foundation, the Holy Trinity Monastery, led the way. By a variety of means – above all bequests and the purchase of land from impoverished nobles – the community gradually acquired huge estates scattered across central Russia.[16] By the end of the sixteenth century, it owned a total of 143,000 chetverts (roughly 240,000 hectares) of arable land in 27 different districts of Muscovy and, a century later, was by far the largest landowner in Russia other than the royal family.[17] Other communities enjoyed similar, although less spectacular, success. In much the same way, the St Cyril Monastery steadily swallowed up lands in the surrounding districts.[18] Founded in 1479, Joseph of Volokolamsk's monastery took advantage of bequests to achieve rapid growth in the sixteenth century.[19] In all cases, the tempo of acquisition was essentially the same – a steady pace through the fifteenth and most of the sixteenth centuries, culminating in unprecedentedly rapid and dramatic gains in the latter decades of the reign of Ivan IV late in the sixteenth. The fact that the monasteries came to control a disproportionately large share of society's primary economic resource eventually posed serious problems of both a moral and a political nature.

Land, by itself, had little value. The monasteries' prosperity depended on the peasants who farmed the estates which they acquired. The relationship between the monastic community and the peasant village shaped both partners. The wealthier monasteries had to create staffs of administrators, usually headed by a cellarer, to record and enforce the peasants' obligations. For their part, the peasants had to pay dues and perform services for their masters. Most often, they provided the monastery with a portion of their crops and livestock. By the sixteenth century, other forms of exploitation began to appear as well; peasants might be obligated to make payments in cash or work on the monastery demesne.[20] Their staffs of managers made the largest monastic estates the best-organized properties in Muscovy. Moreover, the size and variety of their holdings gave them the possibility of innovation in methods and flexibility in techniques of management. The wealthiest lay landlords were passive and disorganized by comparison.

Ownership of land gave the monasteries access to other natural resources as well. Like the rest of the population, monks and nuns depended on nearby forests for fuel and building material and caught fish in neighbouring waters. Some of the northern monasteries, particularly the Solovetskii with its island location, developed large-scale fisheries. In their inhospitable surroundings, the Solovetskii monks found an even more profitable venture – the production of salt. In their holdings on the desolate coast of the mainland, they set up simple work sites where, using wood floated down to the shore from the interior, they boiled down water from the sea and from brine springs until only the salt remained. After supplying local needs, the monastery's agents shipped the product to Moscow and other distant markets.[21]

The great monasteries of Muscovy also had vital military, social and political roles to play. To begin with, over the course of time, the government transformed them into fortresses, surrounding them with massive walls and imposing battlements. As a modern tourist can immediately see, even communities far from the frontiers of the realm – the Holy Trinity, for example – were heavily fortified. They were designed as places of refuge in case of invasion and garrison points for the government's troops. Moreover, in emergencies, they served as bank vaults where the ruling princes and their wealthiest subjects could keep their treasures secure.